Beleaguered Tower: The Dilemma of Political Catholicism in Wilhelmine Germany. Ronald J. Ross

Understanding World Politics. Kenneth W. Thompson.

Diplomacy and Revolution: The Soviet Mission to Switzerland, 1918. Alfred Erich Senn.

The New Corporatism: Social-Political Structures in the Iberian World. Frederick B. Pike and Thomas Stritch, eds.

America in Change: Reflections on the 60's and 70's. Ronald Weber, ed.

Social Change in the Soviet Union. Boris Meissner, ed.

Foreign Assistance: A View from the Private Sector. Kenneth W. Thompson.

Hispanismo, 1898-1936: Spanish Conservatives and Liberals and Their Relations with Spanish America. Fredrick B. Pike.

Democracy in Crisis: New Challenges to Constitutional Democracy in the Atlantic Area. E. A. Goerner, ed.

The Task of Universities in a Changing World. Stephen D. Kertesz, ed.

The Church and Social Change in Latin America. Henry A. Landsberger, ed.

Revolution and Church: The Early History of Christian Democracy, 1789-1901. Hans Maier.

The Overall Development of Chile. Mario Zañartu, S. J., and John J. Kennedy, eds.

The Catholic Church Today: Western Europe. M. A. Fitzsimons, ed.

Contemporary Catholicism in the United States. Philip Gleason, ed.

The Major Works of Peter Chaadaev. Raymond T. McNally.

A Russian European: Paul Miliukov in Russian Politics. Thomas Riha.

A Search for Stability: U. S. Diplomacy Toward Nicaragua, 1925-1933. William Kammań.

Freedom and Authority in the West. George N. Shuster, ed.

Theory and Practice: History of a Concept from Aristotle to Marx. Nicholas Lobkowicz.

Coexistence: Communism and Its Practice in Bologna, 1945-1965. Robert H. Evans.

INTERNATIONAL STUDIES OF THE
COMMITTEE ON INTERNATIONAL RELATIONS
UNIVERSITY OF NOTRE DAME

Marx and the Western World. Nicholas Lobkowicz, ed.

Argentina's Foreign Policy 1930-1962. Alberto A. Conil Paz and Gustavo E. Ferrari.

Italy after Fascism, A Political History, 1943-1965. Guiseppe Mammarella.

The Volunteer Army and Allied Intervention in South Russia, 1917-1921. George A. Brinkley.

Peru and the United States, 1900-1962. James C. Carey.

Empire by Treaty: Britain and the Middle East in the Twentieth Century. M. A. Fitzsimons.

The USSR and the UN's Economic and Social Activities. Harold Karan Jacobson.

Death in the Forest: The Story of the Katyn Forest Massacre. J. K. Zawodny.

Chile and the United States: 1880-1962. Fredrick B. Pike.

Bolshevism: An Introduction to Soviet Communism, 2nd ed. Waldemar Gurian.

East Central Europe and the World: Developments in the Post-Stalin Era. Stephen D. Kertesz, ed.

Soviet Policy Toward International Control of Atomic Energy. Joseph L. Nogee.

The Russian Revolution and Religion, 1917-1925. Edited and translated by Boleslaw Szcześniak.

Introduction to Modern Politics. Ferdinand Hermens.

Freedom and Reform in Latin America. Fredrick B. Pike, ed.

What America Stands For. Stephen D. Kertesz and M. A. Fitzsimons, eds.

Theoretical Aspects of International Relations. William T. R. Fox, ed.

Catholicism, Nationalism and Democracy in Argentina. John J. Kennedy.

Why Democracies Fail. Norman L. Stamps.

German Protestants Face the Social Question. William O. Shanahan.

The Catholic Church in World Affairs. Waldemar Gurian and M. A. Fitzsimons, eds.

Communal Families
in the Balkans:
The Zadruga

Communal Families in the Balkans:

CONTRIBUTORS

Leonard B. Schapiro • Stavro Skendi • Eugene A. Hammel

Olivera Burić • Daniel Chirot • Wayne Vucinich

Jozo Tomasevich • Ante Kadić • David B. Rheubottom

C. J. Grossmith • Vera St. Erlich • Emile Sicard

The Zadruga

Essays by Philip E. Mosely and Essays in His Honor

Edited by ROBERT F. BYRNES

Introduction by MARGARET MEAD

 UNIVERSITY OF NOTRE DAME PRESS
NOTRE DAME-LONDON

Copyright © 1976 by
University of Notre Dame Press
Notre Dame, Indiana 46556

Library of Congress Cataloging in Publication Data

Main entry under title:

Communal families in the Balkans.

(International studies of the Committee on International-
al Relations, University of Notre Dame)
"Most of these papers were presented originally in an
international conference in honor of Mosely held October
12-14, 1973 at Indiana University . . ."
Bibliography: p.
Includes index.
CONTENTS: Philip E. Mosely and his work: Schapiro,
L. B. Philip Edward Mosely, 1905-1972. Skendi, S.
Mosely on the zadruga, Mosely, P. E. The peasant family,
the zadruga, or communal joint-family in the Balkans and
its recent revolution. Mosely, P. E. Adaptation for
survival: the Varzic zadruga. Mosely, P. E. Distribu-
tion of the zadruga within southeastern Europe. Mosely,
P. E. The Russian family: old style and new. Bibliog-
raphy of books and articles, 1934-1971. [etc.]
1. Zadruga—Addresses, essays, lectures. I. Mosely,
Philip Edward, 1905-1972. II. Byrnes, Robert Francis.
III. Series: Notre Dame, Ind. University. Committee
on International Relations. International studies.
JC38.C64   321.1'2   74-27892
ISBN 0-268-00569-9

Manufactured in the United States of America

CONTENTS

PREFACE

Robert F. Byrnes

This book is designed to honor the work and character of a remarkable man, Philip E. Mosely, late Adlai E. Stevenson Professor of International Relations at Columbia University. It reprints his significant essays on the family and the zadruga, an institution in which he was especially interested in his early career as a scholar and to which he planned to return in retirement. It also includes original essays about him by close personal and professional friends and essays on the zadruga by scholars from France, the United Kingdom, the United States, and Yugoslavia.

Most of these papers were presented originally in an international conference in honor of Mosely held October 12-14, 1973 at Indiana University, eight members of whose faculty received much of their training in Russian and East European studies from Mosely at Columbia University. Thirty men and women from twenty-two universities in seven countries saluted Mosely by participating in this first international conference devoted to the zadruga. Some of the authors then revised their papers for publication on the basis of the lively discussions which took place. The essays by Mosely have been reproduced as they were published, except for elimination of some printing errors.

Few scholars of any country or time have attained Mosely's knowledge and understanding of the languages, peoples, and cultures of the Russian and Balkan peoples, and no American has taught or written with more penetrating insight. At the same time, he was recognized throughout the Western world as a particularly well-informed, penetrating, and lucid specialist on Soviet politics and Soviet foreign policy.

An outstanding scholar, a builder of imaginative research and instructional programs, a devoted public servant, Mosely above all was a dedicated and compelling teacher, not only in the lecture hall and seminar room but wherever he met with men and women interested in learning. Few have had his passionate interest in sharing knowledge.

Indeed, in spite of the acclaim his intellectual brilliance, his wide knowledge, and his professional achievements received, his friends everywhere remember and love Phil most because of the enthusiasm, fairness, and utter candor which marked everything he did. Few men have helped as many individuals as he did. He was, simply, a wonderful human being. Everyone who knew him admired and loved him. His appointment as Adlai E. Stevenson Professor of International Relations was particularly appropriate because he shared so many of the qualities for which Stevenson was so loved and respected.

I am grateful to Gordon Turner of the American Council of Learned Societies, Allen Kassof of the International Research and Exchanges Board, and George Wilson of the Office of Research and Advanced Studies of Indiana University for the generous support they and their offices provided for the conference on the zadruga and publication of this book. I deeply appreciate the care with which Theodore B. Ivanus, Ante Kadić, and Seid Karić all made certain that all citations in languages other than English were absolutely correct. Mrs. Stephen Lockwood was of enormous help in organizing and administering the conference and in typing the manuscript.

CONTRIBUTORS

OLIVERA BURIĆ, Senior Scientific Collaborator, Institute for Social Policy, Belgrade. Author of *Promene u porodičnom životu nastale pod uticajem ženine zaposlenosti* (1968).

ROBERT F. BYRNES, Distinguished Professor of History and Director of the Russian and East European Institute, Indiana University. Author of *Antisemitism in Modern France: The Prologue to the Dreyfus Affair* (1951) and *Pobedonostsev. His Life and Thought* (1969).

DANIEL CHIROT, Assistant Professor of Sociology, University of Washington at Seattle. Author of "The Growth of the Market and Servile Labor Systems in Agriculture," *Journal of Social History* (December 1974) and "A New Analysis of the Romanian Middle Ages 1300-1800 in Recent Romanian Scholarship," *Southeastern Europe* (Spring 1974).

CHRISTOPHER J. GROSSMITH, Department of Sociology, University of Exeter, England.

EUGENE A. HAMMEL, Professor of Anthropology, University of California, Berkeley. Author of *Wealth, Authority, and Prestige in the Ica Valley, Peru* (1962); *Ritual Relations and Alternative Social Structure in the Balkans* (1968), and *Power in Ica. The Social History of a Peruvian Valley* (1969).

ANTE KADIĆ, Professor of Slavic Languages and Literatures, Indiana University. Author of *From Croatian Renaissance to Yugoslav Socialism. Essays* (1969); *Contemporary Croatian Literature* (1960); and *Contemporary Serbian Literature* (1964).

MARGARET MEAD, Curator Emeritus, American Museum of Natural History. Author of *Coming of Age in Samoa* (1932); *Male and Female* (1949); *Soviet Attitudes toward Authority* (1951); and *The Golden Age of American Anthropology* (with Ruth Bunzel) (1960).

DAVID B. RHEUBOTTOM, Lecturer of Social Anthropology, University of Manchester, England. Co-author of *Decisions and Constraints: Analyses*

of the Developmental Cycle of Domestic Groups (with Anthony T.
'Carter, to be published in London School of Economics Monograph
Series).

LEONARD B. SCHAPIRO, Professor of Political Science, London School of
Economics and Political Science, University of London. Author of *The
Origin of the Communist Autocracy* (1955); *The Communist Party of
the Soviet Union* (1960); and *The Government and Politics of Soviet
Russia* (1965).

EMILE SICARD, Director, Institute of Applied Social Sciences and Vice
President of the University of Bordeaux II. Author of *La Zadruga
sud-slave dans l'évolution du groupe domestique* (1944) and *La Zadruga
dans la littérature serbe, 1850-1912* (1943).

STAVRO SKENDI, Professor Emeritus of History, Columbia University.
Author of *Albanian and South Slavic Epic Poetry* (1954) and *The
Albanian National Awakening, 1878-1912* (1967).

VERA ST. ERLICH, Professor Emeritus, University of Zagreb. Author of
Family in Transition—A Study of 300 Yugoslav Villages (1966).

JOZO TOMASEVICH, Professor Emeritus of Economics, San Francisco State
University. Author of *Financijska politika Jugoslavije, 1929-1934*
(1935); *International Agreements on Conservation of Marine Resources*
(1943); *Peasants, Politics and Economic Change in Yugoslavia* (1955);
and *War and Revolution in Yugoslavia, 1941-1945. Vol. I The Chetniks*
(1975).

WAYNE VUCINICH, Curator for Russian and East European Collections,
Hoover Institution on War, Revolution and Peace, and Professor of
History, Stanford University. Author of *Serbia Between East and West:
The Events of 1903-1908* (1954) and *The Ottoman Empire: Its Record
and Legacy* (1965).

INTRODUCTION:
PHILIP E. MOSELY'S CONTRIBUTION
TO THE COMPARATIVE STUDY
OF THE FAMILY

Margaret Mead

Philip Mosely's contribution to the comparative study of the family is almost a classic case of the benefits obtained when a scholar well trained in one field of study is persuaded to work in an adjacent field in which he has had no previous specific training. The human sciences have been plagued by a kind of overspecialization which results in fragmented and partial treatments of actuality. But it differs from overspecialization in the natural sciences. In the natural sciences, the units of research have at least been defined in systematic relationships to each other—atoms, molecules, and cells. This in turn has made possible the recombination of specialties and the development of new fields, such as biochemistry and biophysics. In the human sciences, however, the different specialities—history, anthropology, sociology, social psychology, and economics—have developed in parallel, too often dealing in an exclusive and myopic fashion with the same phenomena and analyzing at the same level of generalization. In most cases, practitioners of these several specializations do not even read the work of colleagues in their adjacent disciplines. History stands over and above the others in its particularity, its habit of specialization on periods or on areas of the world, and its refusal to generalize into neat cause and effect paradigms. Characteristically, of course, when a historian does take to generalization on a large scale, he produces horrendous and grandiose attempts to deal with the whole world in cycles and epochs that boggle the mind.

Mosely was trained as a historian, with a special emphasis upon diplomatic relations, in which he received splendid training at Harvard University from William L. Langer. After his return from his first Russian field trip, in which he lived among Russians in Moscow and studied documents in libraries, he supported himself while completing his thesis and preparing it for publication by serving as a research assistant and giving lectures at Leslie College for Teachers and a few public talks. After he found a teaching position at Union College, he applied for a Social Science Research Council fellowship to continue his study of international relations. His project was fascinating and important, and one for which he was uniquely qualified, a comprehensive treatment of Soviet-American relations between 1917 and 1921. However, the SSRC committee, in an action almost without precedent, gave him a fellowship but urged that he change his field of interest and study living peasant people in Southeastern Europe. Perhaps because Mosely already appreciated his remarkable ability to master languages, to acquire the techniques and the insights of other disciplines than history, and to understand the cultures of the Balkan peoples, or perhaps because of the pressures of the depression years and his urge to publish, he accepted this extraordinary opportunity. Whatever his motivations, instead of working with more documents, he went to the London School of Economics. There he studied population problems under Carl Saunders and anthropology under Bronislaw Malinowski. He then followed the SSRC instructions and proceeded to Romania to work with the teams which the extraordinarily innovative Professor Dimitrie Gusti had set up to work in Romanian villages.

Mosely knew that there were many techniques in the social sciences which he did not know, such as the genealogical method, the study of household budgets, and techniques for interviewing living subjects and establishing rapport with the leaders of communities whose language and culture he had first to learn. His very distinctive humility and recognition of what he did not know was countered by his assurance (the kind of necessary arrogance which helps make a first-rate scholar) that he could master what he did not know. He therefore set about these studies very systematically.

At that time, I had long discussions with him about field methods. I had done ethnographic fieldwork in six different cultures, and therefore had a great deal of firsthand experience upon which to draw. His seminar with Malinowski at the London School of Economics provided him with a general theoretical approach to anthropology, but his field experience of working in close association with those who were developing Gusti's team approach gave him a deeper understanding of those sciences which work with living human beings. This understanding not only made him a valuable lifelong collaborator with anthropologists but also provided the vivid sense of reality which infused his work on contemporary international relations. He prepared one of his best-known articles, "Some Soviet Techniques of Negotiation," in response to a request from Columbia University Research in Contemporary Cultures, a project inaugurated by Ruth Benedict for the anthropological study of cultures at a distance.[1] I am sure his mastery of the methodologies of other disciplines and his insights were such that a similar record of effective and understanding cooperation exists for his work in the fields of economics, political science and law, but I give the anthropological one as that with which I am most familiar.

Mosely's first collaboration in applied anthropology was a series of interviews with Gregory Bateson and myself in the spring and fall of 1941, on attitudes of German neighborhoods in Transylvania as they illuminated German attitudes toward *Lebenstelle*. In connection with these interviews, he wrote me on May 21, 1941, "I have never published anything substantial on my work in Transylvania. One reason is that no one on this side of the ocean has any idea of the existence of the neighborhood while quite a few scholars have heard of the zadruga. My approach to the nationality problem through the village unit is so unfamiliar that it seemed wisest to complete the book length study first and then base a number of subsidiary articles on that instead of the other way around. I am going back to my neighborhood study full blast in September. (I have refused requests for three articles in order not to get tangled up in lesser projects), and I am confident it will be ready sometime the following summer. However if you feel there is something in this approach to nationality relationships which should be made available right away, I could sit down with you and your neurologist friend [Richard M. Brickner] and under your general direction, or better, in partnership with you shape up an article or memorandum on the German-Rumanian social psychological strains in Southern Transylvania. Aside from one article on the psychology of a Rumanian repatriated linguist, two articles on Gusti's social work and sociology, and an article on the ethnic and economic features of the partition of Transylvania in 1940, and some comments on Transylvania in a general survey of the Balkan situation in 1938, I have not published anything on my Transylvania work."

I quote this letter in full as it illustrates so many aspects of Mosely's way of working, his willingness to put himself at the disposal of other people and their research interests, and his constantly expressed hope of finding time to complete and publish his own research in greater detail.

Other conferences followed. In the spring of 1942, he collaborated with a group of anthropologists in a report by the Council on Intercultural Studies to the Provost Marshall General's Office, which proposed interdisciplinary area studies as a wartime measure. This became important after the war and helped lead to the founding of institutes, such as the Russian Institute at Columbia University, of which Mosely was one of the inaugurators in 1946 and its director from 1951 to 1955.

In 1944 Mosely and I worked together in developing a table of the attitudes toward food, child care, and the position of the aged in Yugoslavia, as part of a report prepared by the Institute for Intercultural Studies for the Children's Bureau as a contribution to overseas relief plans (UNRRA). This chart, which we completed in one afternoon, specified the differences in attitudes for all of the major ethnic groups in Yugoslavia and reflected his encyclopedic knowledge of differentiated local customs.

In the autumn of 1943 Ruth Benedict, working for the Office of War Information, started preparing a series of memoranda on the cultures of various societies that were inaccessible to direct observation. This followed the precedent set by Geoffrey Gorer's memoranda on Japan and Burma ("Japanese Character Structure and Propaganda," New York: Institute for Intercultural Studies, 1942; and "Burmese Personality," prepared for the Office of War Information, distributed by the Institute for Intercultural Studies, 1943). Mosely provided Ruth Benedict with initial contacts and direction for a study on Romania, a piece of research she completed while he was in Moscow with Secretary of State Cordell Hull in the autumn of 1943. She assumed, it turned out incorrectly, that the village studies which Gusti, the great Romanian sociologist, had published dealt with typical villages. This was not the case. Several sessions of an informal group which met often during the war were devoted to discussing the Romanian material and to Mosely's wartime visit to the USSR.

In 1947 the Salzburg Seminar on American Civilization was established by Clemens Heller and a group of other Harvard students, with Mosely's patronage. I participated in the design of this complex cross-cultural project, which began a long association between Mosely and Clemens Heller. Later this led to Heller's coordination of the social sciences in Paris, which culminated in the establishment of the Maison des Sciences de l'Homme, with which Mosely was still concerned at the time of his death. In 1948 Ruth Benedict organized Columbia University Research in Contemporary Cultures, under a contract with the Office of Naval Research, 1947-1951; this included a Russian section. Mosely was an advisor and an active participant in this and in two successor research projects: the American Museum of Natural History Studies in Soviet Culture, contracted for by the Rand Corporation under a prime contract with the Air Force and Studies in Soviet Communication, conducted partly under the Center for International Studies at the Massachusetts Institute of Technology and partly under the Office of Naval Research in 1950-1952.

Mosely was responsible for McGraw-Hill's publishing my report on The Studies in Soviet Communication Project, *Soviet Attitudes toward Authority,* in 1951. In 1952 he became a member of the board of the Institute for Intercultural Studies, which is devoted to interdisciplinary research in contemporary cultures; he was elected Treasurer in 1960 and was subsequently elected president, an office he held at the time of his death. In 1961 and 1962, he arranged for my participation in the Second and Third "Dartmouth Conferences," unofficial American-Soviet conferences that played an important role in bringing Soviet and American intellectual leaders together for informal discussions of important international problems. In short, Mosely throughout the last thirty-five years of his life remained immensely engaged in assisting and promoting applied anthropology, a concern which deeply affected all his published work in all the areas on which he wrote.

We may now turn from the contribution which Mosely's field experience in Eastern Europe made to his work in the social sciences and international affairs and his cooperative work with anthropologists to his specific contributions in the field of family systems. Previous treatments of the zadruga and its recent evolution had hypothesized a specifically ethnic origin, possibly "a Dinaric race," for the zadruga form of household or had emphasized its functional character and economic and social conditions. Mosely was the first to make detailed studies of different kinds of zadrugas, in different areas, and among different ethnic groups in the same area, tracing the history of each as far back as possible. He concluded that zadrugas are not different in kind from smaller nuclear families, but are instead a form within which two or more biological families may join together in a communal arrangement, that furthermore small families may become zadrugas, and that zadrugas may split into small nuclear families. After an exhaustive survey of the areas within which zadrugas were still flourishing, areas in which they had almost disappeared, and areas where the form was new to the people when it was adopted, he concluded that an explication of the relevant socioeconomic conditions was more rewarding than a search for origins in any one ethnic group. He concluded specifically that the zadruga is a form specially suited to a pioneering situation—to clearing, occupying, and cultivating new land—and that conditions in which land is limited put a strain upon such communal arrangements.

This finding is especially interesting in the light of the pioneering role the kibbutz type of settlement has played in Israel and of the parallel pressures that occur in a kibbutz which has no land for generational increase. The zadruga was, in fact, a highly flexible form through which biological families were free to associate themselves or to separate, as occasion dictated.

However, the disinheritance of daughters, except where there were no male heirs, apparently was a custom essential for keeping the zadruga holdings intact and adjacent. New laws permitting women to inherit land, as well as the conditions of modernity, such as labor migration and industrialization, were conditions unfavorable to the zadruga.

However, I think we can see how Mosely cut through both the conventions of historical studies and the conventions of functional ones at a slightly different level. His historical training made him look for unique qualities in what he was studying. His anthropological background determined that he would look for patterns, not for statistical results, which he rejected in part because he found the statistics too inaccurate. But he also pierced through the kind of situation that arises when the name of an institution is transformed into a sociological category: this appears to have happened in the case of the zadruga. By using the term to cover an institution found in many parts of the area, but still preserving the name itself, students of the zadruga had been able to invest it with a quasi-mystical or "racial" quality. This "discovery" of a "racial" quality would not have been so likely had they used instead an abstract term, such as *joint family*. Such a general term concentrates on structural elements which do indeed occur in any part of the world, while the use of the term *zadruga* suggests that these Balkan joint families are peculiar to the Balkans. Moreover, using the local term for what is, in fact, living in zadruga, that is, in harmony with other biological families, gives the illusion that it was indeed a very distinct institution, rather than a particular variant of a shared family form. The meticulous bookkeeping and canons of division, which Mosely details in his accounts of the Varžić zadruga, were perfectly in keeping with the kinds of arrangements peasants made among themselves, as when a son or son-in-law took over the land of his father or father-in-law and agreed to provide for his livelihood. The zadruga was, it would seem, simply one kind of household, just as three-generation households and two-generation households have been two forms of households in the United States, with legal arrangements governing issues such as payment of taxes, sharing of costs, and permissible claims of dependency.

By emphasizing the fact that movement occurred in both directions—that is, that small families could become large families and live in zadruga, while large families could split up when they became too large—Mosely disposed of any one-way evolutionary argument which suggested that the joint family was the precursor of the small family. Granted that joint families with such extensive land and property-owning arrangements would not develop until land was cultivated and property accumulated, no further claim for one-way inevitable evolutionary development need be made. Under modern conditions of rapid change, in fact, we find very rapid transitions from one kind of household organization to another in many parts of the world. For example, the patriarchal isolated nuclear family of certain mountainous parts of Puerto Rico is replaced when several related women and their families move to a larger town. When families are in residence in a slum in San Juan, each man builds his own house and a patriarchal form again prevails. But after a move to a housing project, the father loses his predominant role again, as the women call upon the housing management for the tasks which the father had previously performed.[2]

Similarly, documentation of movement back and forth between biological family and living in zadruga helps to clear the vision of scholars who have been hypnotized by the use of a Balkan term for a Balkan institution. There is no doubt that the comparative science of culture has been enriched by the importation of local terminology for some hitherto unrecognized institutional form, such as taboo, mana, totem, and fetish. However, the local flavor contributed by the use of the local term sometimes obscures the more general and abstract nature of the institution. An area then begins to be characterized by the institution originally associated with it verbally or descriptively. This obscures the way in which the named institution relates to other institutions in the area. Discussions of the traditional Chinese family illustrate the way in which this may develop: many observers believe that the aspiration to verbal and architectural provisions for great extended families contradicts the actual existence of a large number of very small families. In short, the less a social form is confused by specific association with an area or a given language, the more useful it is as a tool for finding the same, or related social phenomena elsewhere. Mosely's specific studies therefore enabled him to see the way in which the institutions of joint families and single biological families fitted together as readily alternative forms.

I believe that a further set of conclusions could be drawn from his discovery that zadruga forms are exceedingly similar when used by different ethnic groups in the same or different communities. He concluded that social, economic and geographical conditions have evoked the similarity of form. Although he quoted obvious examples of diffusion, as when modernization occurred or changes took place in the laws of inheritance, he did not treat them explicitly as diffusion. He did not invoke the concept of diffusion, and he considered the question of origins rather immaterial. However, although the joint family is an obvious potentiality of human kinship systems, we must also take into account those elements, especially the constellation of recognizable component families in an egalitarian relationship to each other and the explicit recognition of lineages, which do make the Balkan joint family type distinctive. When the diffusion process is recognized, it is possible to suggest that the zadruga was an identified form, so that a country without the form could discuss importing it as an invention, as it might import parliamentary government, income taxes, or banks. Such institutions in their modern, widely diffused forms, often seem remarkably independent of the national culture within which they occur, however congruent they may have been with the particular culture within which they originated.

It would be interesting if future students of the zadruga would combine their various methods to study the limits of diffusion of the zadruga form, which showed very little variation within Southeastern Europe but which may contain features that would have limited its diffusion into other areas. The existence of the neighborhood form of organization stands somewhat opposed to the zadruga form, as a way in which single households can be combined on a geographical rather than a kinship principle. The two forms, seen abstractly, may combine, as in the Samoan Islands, where a family head who holds membership in a village council presides over very large households. Samoa has biological households as well as large extended families, but one striking characteristic differentiates the Samoan from the Balkan joint family and its assumption of equality among married males: the Samoan household is hierarchical, the head is titled, and only one title is held in a household.[3]

Where village membership and village responsibilities are emphasized far more than kin responsibilities, as in the mountain villages of Bali, each biological family—or in lieu of a husband and wife, a man and his mother or sister—constitutes a household which is a full social unit in the village structure.[4] The extent to which the emphasis on the single family household is compatible not only with the mobile anonymous conditions of modern industrialized life but also with other aspects of social organization, such as egalitarianism as opposed to hierarchy, might well be explored within traditional settings in the Balkans. The different ways the "head" of a zadruga is chosen and where and how these various degrees of egalitarianism within the zadruga fit in with other aspects or trends in the culture might provide clues to the extent to which the zadruga, although an identifiable and easily diffused form, was responding, at a microcultural level, to cultural-historical as well as to socioeconomic and geographical conditions.

In a sense, Mosely was making his very meticulous and detailed studies of individual zadrugas, and of groups in which zadrugas were and were not found, in order to make generalizations about the zadruga form as an institution, rather than to characterize Montenegrin, Serbian, Croatian or Bulgarian culture. When one seeks cross-cultural or areal generalizations, he places the emphasis inevitably on similarity, a type of similarity which also, under some conditions, leads to the invocation of race. When the same institution is studied to illuminate a national cultural style, then the similarities among different aspects of the culture are sought in the characteristics of several institutions within a society, institutions which may themselves differ markedly from one culture to another. Mosely was profoundly sensitive to national cultural differences and could characterize Polish or Czechoslovakian or Romanian culture with great precision. However, in his research on the zadruga, he was studying an institution. The Malinowskian emphasis on the functioning of institutions led inevitably to concentration on the similarities of structure and function, rather than on the kind of detail that reflects cultural differences. Tables and chairs are remarkably similar in form and function; the way in which different people sit on them, or at them, varies enormously.

The continuing use of the term zadruga thus permits a double reference, to a kind of household structure and to an area of the world where certain kinds of agriculture, herding, and religious practices prevailed. In 1953, when I reported on the tremendous changes which occurred among the Manus of the Territory of New Guinea, Mosely could comment, "It sounds like a zadruga fastened to a railroad station."[5] That comment is not the same as if he had said, "It sounds like a joint family attached to a railroad station," or if he had said, "It sounds like something that is happening with modernization in the Balkans." So the term zadruga subsumes a kind of historical, geographical specificity which is lost in the cross-culturally more useful term, joint family.

It is the very beautiful precision, historical perspective, and contemporary analysis which makes Mosely's work so rich and evocative and keeps before the student's eye the two aspects of cultural analysis—the *etic*, with its emphasis on cross-culturally viable units of comparison, and the *emic*, with its emphasis on those aspects which are specific to a particular culture. Mosely, in his treatment of zadruga, makes his greatest contribution by his definitive description of a family form within a cultural area.

The culture area concept was originally developed in anthropology as a museum device for grouping artifacts that were geographically related. Subsequently, such ideas as a culture center and marginal areas were elaborated, although Franz Boas always warned that no culture was marginal from its own point of view.[6] It has, however, been very fruitful to consider the way in which a geographical area does, through time, develop characteristics which provide a background for later differentiation, re-unification, acceptance or rejection of foreign traits. Bateson's more recent definition provides a more psychological treatment of the culture area concept as a way of holding history constant in an area of the world within which every constituent society may be assumed to have access to the same fundamental ideas, religious, social, economic, technical.[7] George Devereux's assumption that basic psychological emphases underlie contrastive or superficially different forms of social organization does this also.[8]

Mosely treated the whole of Europe as one large culture area and the Balkans as a subdivision of Europe—that is, as an area of historically interrelated cultures, within which there was a long history of mutual exposure to the same political institutions. I remember his commenting once when the question of learning fieldwork languages came up: "I am sure I could never learn Arabic." This struck me as a totally unintelligible statement from someone who had learned one European language and script after another, and who was able to give a lecture in one language when he had expected to give it in another or to shift from one script to a different one, if he felt someone was looking too closely over his shoulder. But when I exclaimed, he said: "But they are really all one language!" I realized then that he was treating all the European languages he had learned as though they were dialects. It may be that he had partly assimilated the Slavic attitude toward different Slavic languages that most Americans perceive as profoundly different from each other. Whatever the idiosyncratic origins of his attitude, it was also a basis from which he could see the different ethnic and national versions of the zadruga as part of a single culture area, within which changing economic and social relationships provided different contexts for local changes.

Mosely's studies of the zadrugas were after all within the tradition of all his published work, intensive, exhaustive general articles full of information which dealt with a subject in such a way that they provided a base for many subsequent detailed and related researches. They were pathbreaking in the field of Eastern European studies, like Franz Boas' famous study of Eskimo needle cases, in which Boas showed that artistic designs could develop from the realistic to the conventional and move also from the conventional to the realistic.[9] Unilinear theories of the evolution of art were dead. Later anthropological studies, such as Leach's *Political Systems of Highland Burma,* have made similar points, showing that two systems originally considered different, as many students had thought of the zadruga and nuclear families, were really alternative forms arising from a single cultural background when conditions were favorable.[10] But the impact of Mosely's work has been on the social histories of Southeastern Europe. His work on the zadruga was an areal study with areal consequences, and it has profoundly affected both our knowledge and our approaches.

NOTES

1. Margaret Mead and Rhoda Metraux, eds., *The Study of Culture at a Distance* (Chicago, 1953).

2. Helen Icken Safa, "From Shanty Town to Public Housing: A Comparison of Family Structure in Two Urban Neighborhoods in San Juan, Puerto Rico," *Caribbean Studies* IV, No. 1 (April 1964), 3-12; Safa, "The Female-Based Family in Public Housing," *Human Organization* XXIV, No. 2 (1965), 135-139; Hazel Dubois, *Community, Courtship and Marriage: Subcultural Variation in the Puerto Rican Family* (Ph.D. diss., Department of

Anthropology, Columbia University, 1965); Dubois, "Working Mothers and Absent Fathers: Family Organization in the Caribbean" (paper read at annual meeting of the American Anthropological Association, Detroit, Michigan, November, 1964).

3. Margaret Mead, *Social Organization of Manua,* "Bernice P. Bishop Museum Bulletin," No. 76. (Honolulu, 1930). Reprinted 1969.

4. American Museum of Natural History Expedition to Bali: 1936-1939.

5. Margaret Mead, *New Lives for Old: Cultural Transformation, Manus 1928-1953* (New York, 1956). Reprinted with a new preface (New York, 1966).

6. Leslie Spier, "The Sun Dance of the Plains Indians: Its Development and Diffusion," *Anthropological Papers of the American Museum of Natural History* XVI, Part 7 (New York, 1921); R. H. Lowie, "Age-Societies of the Plain's Indians," *American Museum Journal* XVII (1917), 495–496.

7. Gregory Bateson, "Cultural Determinants of Personality," in J. M. Hunt, ed., *Personality and Behavior Disorders* (New York, 1944), pp. 714-735.

8. George Devereux, *Reality and Dream: Psychotherapy of a Plains Indian,* 2nd ed. with preface by Margaret Mead (New York, 1969).

9. Franz Boas, "The Decorative Designs of Alaskan Needlecases: A Study in the History of Conventional Designs." Based on materials in the U. S. National Museum, *Proceedings of the U. S. National Museum* XXXIV, No. 1616 (1908), 321-344.

10. E. R. Leach, *Political Systems of Highland Burma* (New York, 1954). Reprinted 1965.

Part One:

Philip E. Mosely and His Work

A. Analyses of Mosely

Philip E. Mosely (1905–1972)

Philip E. Mosely in Albania in the
summer of 1938.

1: PHILIP E. MOSELY,
1905–1972
Leonard B. Schapiro

It is a great honor for me to pay tribute to Philip Mosely, whom I feel privileged to have known as a friend and whose work I hold in deep admiration and respect. I am bound to confess that I feel some embarrassment in addressing many who knew Mosely as a teacher and as a friend or as a colleague and who were more closely acquainted with him than I, an Englishman visiting the United States comparatively infrequently. However, it is perhaps fitting for an outsider to suggest what Philip Mosely's work meant to scholarship in the area of Russian and Soviet Studies and to convey to those who did not know him some impression of a most remarkable personality. His contributions to scholarship were manifold: by writing, by teaching, by promoting the work of others, by influencing opinion both in the non-Communist world and probably in the Soviet Union, and by organizing and encouraging the means which make research and study possible. I will try to tell something about each of these spheres of Mosely's activities. But first let me set out the essential facts of his life and career.

Philip Edward Mosely was born September 21, 1905, in Westfield, Massachusetts. The family into which he was born was neither wealthy nor influential. I mention this fact because Mosely himself used to stress it in order to illustrate, by his own example, and with pride in the virtues of his country, the way in which American society made it possible for a man without the advantages of privileged birth to reach a place of high honor in academic and public life. Mosely was educated at Harvard, where after a brilliant career he obtained his bachelor's and doctor's degrees. During his years as a Harvard student, he spent a considerable time doing research in the archives in the Soviet Union and developed the interest in Russia and its history that, together with his deep and enduring affection for Eastern and Central Europe, was to remain one of his main absorbing passions throughout his career as a scholar. After leaving Harvard, he taught, mainly international relations, at Princeton, at Union College, at Hunter College, and at Cornell, where he became an Associate Professor in 1940. During 1940 and 1941, while continuing his teaching at Cornell, he became closely associated with the work of the Council on Foreign Relations on peacemaking and the postwar settlement. He acted as Secretary of the Council's War and Peace Studies' Group, as well as Secretary of a study group concerned with exiled and allied governments. During this period, he produced many important memoranda for the Council and for the State Department. From 1942 until 1946 he was an officer of the State Department, where he served as Chief of the Division of Territorial Studies. He was a member of the United States delegation to the Moscow Conference between the Allied Powers which took place in 1943. During 1944 and 1945 he was a representative on the four-power European Advisory Commission which was established by the Moscow Conference to "study and make representations to the three governments upon European questions connected with the terminations of hostilities . . ." and which sat in London. He was a United States advisor at the Potsdam Conference in 1945 and at the Conference of Foreign Ministers in London and in Paris in 1945 and 1946. He was also the United States representative on the Commission for the investigation of the Yugoslav-Italian boundary in 1946. According to Mosely's own estimate, he spent some two thousand hours negotiating with the Russians during this period of five years.

After the war, in 1946, Mosely returned to academic life as Professor of International Relations at Columbia University, where he remained until 1955. Shortly after arriving at Columbia in 1946, together with Professor Geroid T. Robinson he founded the Russian Institute, which was to become one of the most influential centers of graduate study of Russia, not only in the United States but in the Western world. He served as its director from 1951 until 1955. During this period and in later years he also served on numerous university, academic, and public committees which influenced the development of the study of Soviet and pre-Soviet Russia in this country.

From 1955 until 1963, Dr. Mosely served the Council on Foreign Relations as its Director of Research, once again promoting the study of current international relations in one of the most important world centers in this field. In 1963, however, he returned to university life and what I believe was always his abiding interest, teaching. He was appointed the first Adlai E. Stevenson Professor of International Relations, and Director of the newly founded European Institute of Columbia University and became Associate Dean of the School of International Affairs.

During the postwar period, Mosely found time to travel again in Russia and in Eastern Europe. He visited the Soviet Union in 1956 and again in 1959. He had many formal and informal meetings with Soviet scholars and officials in connection with his manifold public and educational activities. At such meetings, Mosely's patient firmness and superb knowledge of Russia and the Russians came into their own. He was a brilliant linguist, with an outstanding gift for acquiring a new language in the shortest possible time. I can speak from personal experience of the excellence of his spoken Russian, French, and German. He taught himself Russian and Czech while still a boy. His Russian was perfected during the two years that he spent on research in the archives in the Soviet Union between 1930 and 1932. But he spoke a number of other languages with equal fluency, including Romanian, Serbo-Croatian, and Bulgarian, of which he acquired the knowledge during extended tours of Eastern and Central Europe in 1935 and 1936.

By the end of the 1960's, his health was declining: the disease, which was to claim him as a victim at the early age of sixty-six, already had him in its grip. He bore his illness with a courage which was both moving and inspiring to those who observed him. Up to the end, when his strength no longer permitted him to attend the university or the European Institute, he conducted seminars and received students and visitors at his apartment. He died on January 13, 1972, survived by his widow, Ruth, and by two married daughters.

Let me now try to give you, I fear, a very inadequate sketch of Mosely's work as a scholar, as a patron and promoter of scholarship, and as a teacher. Although he did not publish much in the field of pure history, this was his real and abiding interest. Indeed, it was because he was such a good historian that he was such a good interpreter of the present. We should probably all be living in a safer world if more politicians realized the connection between the accurate study of history and contemporary analysis. A few articles apart, the bulk of Mosely's work in the field of history which remains is his classic study, *Russian Diplomacy and the Opening of the Eastern Question in 1838 and 1839,* which was published by the Harvard University Press in 1934. This is a work of meticulous scholarship, based on extensive research in the diplomatic archives. It is still much used and read by students and historians concerned with this period and was therefore reprinted in 1969. Mosely intended to return to historical research after his retirement, which would have given him some respite from his continuous, indefatigable, unending labors in promoting the work of others.

But the dreams of the work which he was going to do during his retirement were not to be realized. And so, as far as his publications are concerned, the work for which he will be best remembered is his contribution to Western understanding of Soviet diplomatic practice, Soviet mentality, and the nature, development and prospects of the Soviet system of government and of Soviet foreign policy aims. His own experience of negotiations with the Soviet Union during and after the Second World War is embodied mainly in half a dozen long articles published between 1947 and 1955. These deal with different aspects of the hopes and failures of Allied attempts to build a new and better postwar world in cooperation with Stalin's Russia. I know from conversations with him that he attached great importance to these articles, to which he devoted scrupulous care to ensure their accuracy, regarding them, rightly, as source material on the history of interallied wartime relations. I should like to say a little more about these articles because together they form an important contribution to the understanding of Soviet foreign policy and to the history of relations between the Western powers and the Soviet Union.[1]

Two articles, both published in 1950, deal with Allied policy late in the war towards the future administration of vanquished Germany, in other words, the period when the foundations were laid for the conflicts between the West and the Soviet Union which were to acquire the general designation of the "Cold War." Two articles, one published in 1950 and the other in 1955, deal with the evolution of Soviet policy towards East Central Europe between 1945 and 1947. Two further articles, one published in 1947 ("Peace-making 1946") and the other (the classical and rightly famous "Some Soviet Techniques of Negotiation") in 1951, offer a distillation of Mosely's experience, observation, and wisdom on the difficult subject of diplomatic negotiations with the Russians.

The relatively harmonious relations between the Western Allies and Russia which existed during the war went sour once victory was in sight. This fact has affected the quality of the work of many of those who have written about negotiations for the postwar settlement. Some have thought it right to throw all the blame on Soviet craftiness; others, the more masochistic perhaps, have placed all responsibility for what happened on American "Imperialism." There is no trace of either kind of this nonsense in the balanced, fair and perceptive accounts of Phil Mosely. It is true that he writes as a partisan in the case of the postwar settlement in Germany, but as a partisan of the State Department's policy, in the formation of which he no doubt played the leading part as advisor (after 1944) to Mr. Winant, as against the War Department's policy or lack of policy. In the result (he contends), whatever opportunity there may have been to create a basis for postwar cooperation with the Soviet Union was lost. Such vital questions as access to Berlin or the administration of Germany as an economic unit were left to virtual improvisation by the military commanders on the spot. This situation above all played into the hands of the more determined Russians, who then, as now, were inclined to act first and argue afterwards. Even so, Mosely remained of the opinion that some chances may have been missed. "In hindsight," he wrote in 1959, "it is easy to say that the attempt (to lay a basis for some enduring measure of postwar cooperation) was hopeless and not worth making because the Soviet leadership would never abate its claim to reshape the world in its own image. . . ." But, he argues, the attempt should have been made and could have been made, had the Allies, particularly America, pursued a more integrated policy. In particular, he wrote, also in 1959, "much more should have been done to assure [Stalin] of assistance in rebuilding the Soviet economy: as it turned out, Stalin and the Soviet people soon felt that their vast sacrifices were forgotten by less war-damaged Allies as soon as the fighting was over."

The two articles on the German settlement leave little doubt of the imprint which Mosely's energy and sense left on the policy advocated by Mr. Winant, the Ambassador of the United States in London, and on the decisions of the European Advisory Commission: the failure lay, in Mosely's view, in the ultimate decisions in Washington. As one example of this, let me cite a memorandum by Mr. Winant in August 1944 urging the need for agreement in advance on reparations and on the need to consider giving economic aid to the Soviet Union. Since failure on both of these issues formed part of Mosely's later criticism of the wartime negotiations and since he had succeeded Mr. George Kennan as advisor to Mr. Winant in London in June 1944, there can be little doubt that the policy of this memorandum was Mosely's. It received little support from Washington.

As further evidence that Mosely never regarded the prospect of some kind of postwar cooperation with the Soviet Union as hopeless from the start, I should cite his strong resistance to the British proposal that Allied forces should remain after the end of hostilities on the lines to which they had advanced, far into the Soviet zone. Clearly this would have undermined any remaining Soviet confidence in the integrity of the Allies. Nor did he alter his views that this course would have been wrong when he wrote about the matter years later.

The settlements in Eastern Europe were more a crucial factor in inaugurating the so-called "Cold War" than the disputes over the administration of Germany and over reparations. In the case of Germany, Soviet policy in the period immediately after the war was in part improvised and in part dictated by the overwhelming conviction that the Soviet Union was entitled, because of the enormous sacrifices which it had made in the war, to recoup itself in the short run of German resources with little regard for the long run. In the case of Soviet policy towards what were to become the component parts of the Soviet Bloc, the Soviet government showed less improvisation and a good deal more regard for the long run and the implementation of a concrete plan: the creation of a strategic *cordon sanitaire* and the establishment, where possible, of governments friendly to the Soviet Union which, as Molotov repeatedly and frankly admitted, could not be secured by free elections.

Mosely's writings on this subject are among the very best; his great sympathy with and knowledge of the countries concerned and his understanding of Soviet aims and fears are blended in these articles with the fairness which characterized everything he ever wrote. What emerges from his writings on this difficult subject is a criticism of Allied policy for playing into Soviet hands. I do not think he would have contended that it was ever possible to reach agreement with the Soviet Union on setting up genuine democratic governments in the Bloc states. His main contention is that the Allies lost all possibility of forcing any kind of compromise or concessions by giving away position after position. Of course, the advantages were on the Russian side from the start, since the Soviet Union could exercise decisive influence through the local Communist parties and through organized terrorization of the populations. But Mosely blames President Roosevelt for pursuing, up to the Yalta Conference of February 1945, a policy of lack of interest in the future of East-Central Europe. In these circumstances, he says, "the pressure on Britain to accept Soviet-imposed decisions in the area of the Red Army's advance and thereby to gain some bargaining advantage for British interests elsewhere became almost irresistible." The result was the famous "spheres of influence" bargain negotiated by Churchill and Eden at Moscow in October 1944. And "when at Yalta the United States began shifting from passivity to active interest, its British partner was too far committed to its division-of-spheres policy to render strong support." Even so, for reasons which Mosely describes as "obscure," Roosevelt refused to accept the State Department's detailed plan for creating a four-power Emergency High Commission for Liberated Europe and did not put it forward, possibly for fear of jeopardizing Soviet participation in the war against Japan. As a result, all that emerged from Yalta was a high-minded Declaration for a Liberated Europe, one of the early exercises in hypocrisy with which the course of Western-Soviet relations has been studded.

Of particular interest is a paper which Mosely contributed in February 1950 to a symposium at the University of Notre Dame on "Soviet Policy and Nationality Conflicts in East-Central Europe." This shows the skillful way in which the Soviet Union manipulated the many conflicts on issues of nationalism in this area, with little regard for ideological principles, but always in the Soviet interest, or as Mosely says, "to enhance its own monolithic control and to strengthen its chosen instruments of local rule." This article includes a valuable analysis of the reasons for Soviet resistance to the tentative attempts by Yugoslavia to set up a Balkan Federation of Communist States, even though such a federation had been Comintern policy since 1924. "Stalin," Mosely observes shrewdly, "was not eager to see Tito's unexpected resistance to Soviet infiltration of his party, secret police and military apparatus extended to Bulgaria, and perhaps to Romania and Hungary, or even prospectively to Greece."

I have dwelt at some length on this group of articles because I think they best illustrate two abiding characteristics of all Mosely's writing on Soviet foreign policy: first, the acute and penetrating analysis, the ability to see a situation through Soviet eyes and against the Soviet ideological background— a rare quality, even today, let alone twenty or twenty-five years ago; secondly, the conviction that imagination, knowledge, and persistance could produce certain important accommodations with the Soviet Union. I do not mean by that the kind of euphoria common nowadays that the Soviet Union has shed its ideological background and become an ordinary, sensible, practical imperialistic great power like any other: Mosely was much too intelligent ever to fall for that. But I think he believed that in the course of time, circumstances, the gradual breaking down of suspicions, slow penetration of Western ideas, and many factors like that could lead to small but valuable accommodations. And, after that, I think he would have said, who knows? As Aristotle says, it is not on account of, but as a result of, the little things that the big things come into being. But, if one were embarking on this long-term course of very moderately optimistic gradualism, one had to know the rules of the game.

In 1951 in an article first published in a book, justly famous, frequently reprinted and translated, Mosely codified what he considered the basic principles for success in negotiating with the Russians.[2] Perhaps one's first reaction on re-reading this article twenty-two years later is the earnest hope that Western diplomats now find its many precepts obvious. I say "hope," because I am far from certain that this is so in respect of Mosely's wise observations: for example, that Soviet negotiators may distort the position of their Western counterparts for fear of being accused of having the wool pulled over their eyes by the capitalists; that very often Soviet negotiators have no instructions beyond drawing out the proceedings in order to discover as much as they can about the other side; that the speed with which a group of Western powers negotiating with Russians can reach agreement among themselves will be regarded on the Soviet side as evidence of a deep-laid conspiracy; that Soviet negotiators are often bound by detailed instructions to pile up grievances and to press each separate point, however trivial, to the bitter end as a test of the other side's nerves; that they are sometimes specifically charged to make accusations of bad faith and to persist in them throughout the negotiations; that it is unsafe for Western negotiators to rely on any agreement "in principle" with their Soviet opposite numbers, since it is more than likely that the Soviet government will continue to pursue its original aims "in practice" thereafter; and so on and so forth.

It is probably true that Mosely's analysis requires updating in some respects. I doubt if Soviet negotiators are as nervous today of falling foul of their masters as they were under Stalin. The Soviet Union has also developed new techniques: the mystery of preaching "peaceful coexistence" for a foreign audience and "intensification of the struggle with the West" for the home audience at one and the same time; the nuclear saber-rattling of Khrushchev with which the late President Kennedy was so masterly in dealing; or the suave arrogance of Brezhnev in claiming every right to do to others what others must on no account be allowed to do to him. Even so, the basic message of this superb analysis remains true and, to my knowledge, never equalled, as does also the conclusion its author drew from it: "The art of policy," he wrote in 1951, "will be to recognize, from a position of strength, future potentialities of negotiation, not with an expectation of bringing about a lasting or world-wide relaxation of Soviet ambitions, but as a means of alleviating individual sources of tension and thus of strengthening the Free World."

As I have said, the life of action and duty to which Mosely devoted himself precluded him from writing the great books which all who knew him felt he had it in him to write, and his untimely death deprived him of the well-earned retirement which he intended to spend writing. Even so, his output of lectures, articles, memoranda, introductions, and other shorter works adds up to a very impressive *oeuvre* of over two hundred items, as Chapter 7 of this volume, a bibliography of his books and articles, shows. The other themes range widely across areas and disciplines: sociology in Romania and Bulgaria, the zadruga, historiography in the countries of Eastern and Central Europe, Slavic studies in general, contemporary international relations, Soviet internal affairs, and Soviet foreign policy, to name only a few. Dr. Mosely also left behind a substantial amount of unpublished material, some of which relates to his study of the zadruga. He also left a considerable body of notes, correspondence, and photographs on Russia and on Eastern Europe, especially Romania, the product of many years of travel in the Balkans and of his contacts with scholars. I hope that this material will before long be put to good use by those competent to exploit it.

Space, and indeed such qualifications as I have, necessarily restrict me to a brief glance at Mosely's work in the field of Soviet domestic and foreign affairs. Unlike so many articles which are published on Soviet questions, his contributions can be re-read with pleasure and profit, let alone without embarrassment, years and decades after they were published. Not that he was always right, of course. He did not foresee, for example, in 1956 that the "Moscow-Peking Axis," as he called it, would be near breaking point two or three years later—but then who did? In the same year, when he revisited Moscow, he apparently failed to foresee that the cultural relations between Soviet and Western intellectuals then only beginning would before very long lead to a ferment inside some small sectors of Soviet society, or that some, if only a handful, of Soviet intellectuals would prove conclusively that generations of Soviet indoctrination had not destroyed their capacity for thinking as civilized human beings. But again, not many foresaw this development in 1956.

The permanent value of Mosely's analysis lies in its historical depth, in its imaginative perception of the Soviet situation, in its shrewdness and balance, and especially in its fairness. Above all, when he touched on the question of relations between the Soviet Union and the West he never shed his moderate optimism: one should not expect dramatic and uncharacteristic changes of policy or direction from the Soviet Union, but neither should one abandon all hope of slow, undramatic, piecemeal progress in reducing tension and eliminating possible areas of conflict.

These articles, which span some twenty years of Mosely's activity, reflect a consistency of outlook, as well as a fund of the kind of good sense very necessary, and rare, in analyzing Soviet foreign policy aims. In 1948, when this view was not so widespread as now, he warned that Soviet hostility to the Western world would continue because it was based not on certain territorial ambitions, which could be satisfied, but on ideology, on the Soviet leaders' belief in historical destiny and their place within it, which could not be appeased. In subsequent articles, especially after the advent of Khrushchev, he warned against overoptimistic hopes that Soviet foreign policy had changed in its essentials, and against the equally ill-founded belief that the Soviet dictatorship would disintegrate. At the same time he continued to believe that the "two-world system" of competitive coexistence, divided between the Soviet sphere and that of the Western powers, and held at arms' length by the nuclear balance of forces, remained the continuing hope for reduction of areas of tension through patient negotiations.

In the last important article which he published,[3] Mosely introduced a new note, a cautious hope that "competitive coexistence" might at long last give way to "détente," an attempt, as he put it, "to define some firm basis for a dangerously unstable international equilibrium." This cautious optimism derived from the small signs of movement in the direction of détente, in spite of the continuing Vietnam War: the "modest but useful agreements" which followed the Cuban missile crisis, the Soviet-sponsored Tashkent agreement between India and Pakistan, and the informal high-level United States-Soviet Union meetings in order to narrow the area of possible misunderstanding in the Middle East. He regretted that trade between the United States and the USSR, "one of the few instruments of peaceful influence available to American policy," as he described it, was not available to the United States because of the continuing Vietnam War and the consequent hostility of American public opinion to trading with the enemy.

However, together with his very restrained optimism, the article sounded certain notes of caution. As leader of the Western alliance, the United States could not, in his view, negotiate with the Soviet Union without the close participation of its allies, since to do so would violate "the entire *raison d'être* of the alliance from the point of view of its smaller alliance partners." On the other hand, participation of the smaller partners, he wrote, "sets narrow limits defined by established national interests and the sensitiveness of public and electoral opinions." Secondly, he warned that détente to be genuine must "reach inside the major powers to influence their thinking and feelings. Otherwise, the present hopes for a genuine détente will turn out in the end to have been merely a continuation of competitive coexistence under another name."

The issues examined in this last article are tantalizingly near those that confront the United States, the Western European powers, and the Soviet Union today. One can only speculate how Philip Mosely would have reacted to the situation were he still with us. As it is, we can but deplore the fact that when issues of such momentous importance for the future of the United States and of Western Europe are being debated and decided by the politicians, we are deprived of one of the all too few, wise, detached and unbiased voices in which high ethical principle, deep humanity, and genuine patriotism were always combined.

The sketch however inadequate which I have tried to give of Dr. Mosely's contribution to scholarship by his publications is based on the published record. The task becomes much more difficult when one attempts to summarize the varied and extensive public service of this utterly devoted man and his role as a teacher. Here, the answer lies not so much in the public record as in the recollection of colleagues, friends, associates, and students. I hope that a full and detailed account of Mosely's unique contribution to Russian and International Studies will be written before long. Meanwhile, I can only offer you a pale outline or summary of what I have been able to glean with the help of those to whom I have talked, from my own observations, and from the few short accounts that have appeared in print.

Like most busy and usefully occupied men, Mosely always seemed to have time to spare when it was a matter of public service, or helping someone who needed aid. His wisdom, his wide experience, his quick intelligence, his tact, and above all his unfailing good-humoured common sense naturally led to many demands on his time for advice, for service on committees, for participation in projects or conferences, as contributor, chairman, or editor of proceedings. He was, incidentally a superb editor. I wonder how many of the books, by authors now quite famous, which were published under the auspices of the Council on Foreign Relations during the years that Mosely was its Director of Research would have made much impact if they had not benefited from his rigorous and meticulous editing. Many authors were fortunate to secure Mosely's consent to write an introduction to their books, thereby guaranteeing to the reader that their books were at the least worth perusing. Innumerable works which have been published in the last quarter of a century have acknowledgments to Mosely in their prefaces. Besides all this,

Mosely's own zeal for improving the materials available for study, for promoting publications, and for helping the many scholars and others who were uprooted by the cataclysms of war, revolution, and tyranny added to the burden of his activity.

Yet another call on his time, which I think he welcomed, was presented by his extensive contacts with scholars from many parts of the world, Germany in particular, Eastern Europe of course, and last, but not least, the Soviet Union. I think Mosely particularly welcomed these contacts with Soviet scholars and even with Soviet officials. It responded to his sense of duty to maintain the bridges between East and West, however slender and however slight the prospects might be of genuine cultural contact in the case of many of the visitors. I think, also, that he derived great satisfaction, with his mastery of the language and his vast experience of Soviet negotiating techniques, from showing a really obstreperous Soviet visitor politely but firmly the limits beyond which he was not prepared to go. On the Soviet side, he was respected for his firmness and his integrity, and "Filipp Arturovich," as the Russians, both émigré and Soviet, usually called him, must have left his impact on many a Soviet intellectual. Mosely always maintained, and I am quite certain he was right, that you could win the respect of a Soviet official, or scholar-official, only if you stuck to your own principles. If one glossed over them or refrained from mentioning them for fear of causing offence, one earned nothing but contempt.

I have already referred to the importance of the Russian Institute of which Mosely was co-founder in 1946 and Director from 1951 until 1955. He helped to organize the Joint Committee on Slavic Studies. Publication of *The Current Digest of the Soviet Press* began while he was Chairman in 1949. He was the guiding spirit behind the Humanities Fund, the East European Fund, and the Chekhov Publishing Fund, all of which contributed much to Russian and East European life and scholarship in exile. He was chairman of large projects on the history of the Communist Party of the Soviet Union and on the history of Menshevism. He created and fostered the Archive of Russian and East European History at Columbia, a remarkable collection of materials, amassed as a result of his innumerable contacts, friendships, and unsparing efforts to trace, secure, and preserve manuscripts. These are dry facts. They tell us little of the many hundreds, more probably thousands, of people whom he helped, encouraged, and sustained.

And last, but by no means least, there was Philip Mosely the teacher. Many Americans who enjoyed the advantage of being his students are much better qualified to describe Mosely's qualities as a teacher than I am. I can only speak from what I have been told. He was not a great lecturer; perhaps he lacked the histrionic talents which this form of academic art requires. But he excelled in seminars, small groups, and tutorials, where his immense learning, his patience, and his clarity of mind could appear to full advantage. It was not only that, I believe. The predominant vice of the academic community is vanity, the kind of vanity which makes many university teachers prone to crush or to humiliate students, to advertise above all their own academic distinction, or at any rate renown, and to belittle everyone else's. Mosely was particularly free from this vice; indeed, no man could have done more to promote the academic work of others. He did his utmost to bring out the best in every student, to make a student feel that his contribution was important, and that he was an equal partner in the pursuit of truth. Formal academic instruction apart, Mosely always found the time to help and advise, whether a beginner or the author of a doctoral thesis, in matters large and small, academic or personal. He had the great gift of making himself accessible. He had none of the fears that a smaller man might have felt that he would demean himself by so doing. There was indeed true greatness in his modesty.

In 1855, when the Russian historian T. N. Granovsky died, the novelist Turgenev, a somewhat younger man (for whose character, as it happened, Granovsky had had little regard) wrote this about him:

All are at one in agreeing that Granovsky was an outstanding professor, that in spite of his somewhat hesitant manner of speech he possessed the secret of true eloquence. Still, there are some who, judging him by his published work, are somewhat incredulous, and see some hitherto uncomprehended mystery in the power and extent of his influence on people. The solution of the mystery is very simple: it is all to be found in Granovsky's personality.

In harmonious characters such as his was, even their faults are an essential part. Had Granovsky's personality been more colorful, or more assertive, his young students would not have turned to him with such trusting confidence. Granovsky was accessible at all times, he never sent anyone away. Steeped as he was in learning, having devoted himself to the task of enlightenment and education, he regarded himself, as it were, as part of the public domain, as the property of everyone in search of enlightenment or education. Everyone came to him without hesitation as to a spring by the wayside to drink the life-giving waters of learning which issued forth from him, and which were all the purer for the fact that he had added nothing of his own to what he taught. What was indeed his own and original about his teaching was precisely the absence of personal affectations and of clever talk for the sake of effect. He transmitted learning, which he deeply respected and in which he sincerely believed, in the form in which he received it. He did not distort it, he did not strive to bend it to his will, let alone to force it into a system. It was this same integrity in transmitting learning which explained the elegant beauty of his speech. For it was like the light which passes through the translucent crystal. The substance of the light is not changed, yet it has become alive with the play of many colours.

Such a man in an entirely different setting, and in a very different age, was Philip Edward Mosely. Those who did not know him can still find some reflection of his qualities in the work that has survived him. Those of us who were privileged to know him will never forget his quiet good-humoured gaiety, the wide range of his mind, his unfailing kindness and courtesy, the quick, impish wit, the shrewd judgment, the vast knowledge, the wise and balanced assessment of a situation which yet never lost sight of justice and truth. We can indeed count ourselves fortunate to have come under the influence of that most rare and precious of human creatures, a man of complete integrity.

NOTES

1. All of these articles were reprinted in Philip E. Mosely, *The Kremlin and World Politics: Studies in Soviet Policy and Action* (New York, 1960), pp. 131-245.

2. "Some Soviet Techniques of Negotiating," in Raymond Dennett and Joseph E. Johnson, eds., *Negotiating with the Russians* (Boston, 1951); reprinted in *The Kremlin and World Politics,* pp. 3-41.

3. "The United States and East-West Détente: The Range of Choice," *Journal of International Affairs* XXII (1968), 5-15.

2: MOSELY ON THE ZADRUGA

Stavro Skendi

In 1956, ten years after coming to the United States, I returned to Europe for the first time. I visited the Soviet Union, Austria, Yugoslavia, Germany, and France. I was surprised to learn that scholars in most of these countries did not know Mosely as an expert in Russian and Soviet studies, as he was widely known in this country, but that they highly appreciated his studies on the zadruga. Although Mosely's first published work was his dissertation, *Russian Diplomacy and the Opening of the Eastern Question in 1838 and 1839* (Cambridge, 1934), indicative of the three main interests he later developed, Russia, the Balkans, and Western Europe, his immediate subsequent publications dealt with the Balkans, particularly with the zadruga, and most European scholars knew and valued Mosely especially for this work.

But what is the zadruga? It is not easy to give an all-embracing definition. Let me revert to Mosely's own definition: "It can best be defined as an extended family consisting of two or more small biological families (father, mother, minor children), owning land, livestock and tools in common and sharing the same livelihood."[1] The peasants themselves called it *kuća* (household) or *velika kuća* (big household). At times, the term "undivided family" was also used. Zadruga was often used to refer to the communal family as a legal or property-owning entity. In this meaning, it was officially used in Civil Croatia after 1848 and in the Croatian-Slavonian Military Frontier (*Vojna Krajina*) after the organic law of August 7, 1807.

Scholars have frequently distinguished between the zadruga and the individual small-family, the so-called *inokoština*. The great authority of Vuk Karadžić contributed to this confusion in his *Srpski Rječnik* [Dictionary of the Serbian language], published first in 1818, by opposing the zadruga to the *inokoština*, and the influence of Jovan Cvijić, the prominent Serbian human geographer, also promoted this.[2] Mosely disagreed with these scholars. In the period he studied the zadruga in the field, as Valtazar Bogišić had done for Montenegro and Herzegovina,[3] he discovered that the peasants did not regard the zadruga and the *inokoština* as two separate institutions existing

14

side by side. In regions where the zadrugal spirit was strong among the peasants, any small family could, through biological expansion, become a zadruga—that is, was potentially a zadruga.

The general problems connected with the zadruga were discussed in Mosely's first study, entitled "The Peasant Family: The Zadruga, or Communal Joint-Family in the Balkans, and its Recent Evolution," published in 1940, in a collective volume on *The Cultural Approach to History*, edited by Caroline F. Ware. This discussed various important historical controversies. Was the zadruga a peculiarly Slavic institution, expressing some innate tendency of the Slavs toward family communism, or was it found also among non-Slavic peoples? Has it outlived its usefulness, and does it still survive? Parallels have been drawn between the zadruga and the Russian *mir*, which was a distributional land commune. Some scholars have held that the zadruga's origin was very old, probably of prehistoric times, while others have suggested that it was the product of the fiscal and legal systems of the Byzantine and Ottoman empires. While admitting the strengthening of the zadruga at the time of the last empires, Mosely refused to share the opinion of all these scholars. The hearth tax, the so-called *kapnikon*, which was levied on households, existed in Byzantium before the outset of the ninth century, but it was in the twenties of that century that Emperor Nicephorus expanded and strengthened it among the peasants in order to increase and secure state revenue.[4] This, however, does not account for the origin of the zadruga. The Ottomans levied a similar tax on the non-Moslems, a tax on the "fire," that is, on the household. Several documents (berats and firmans) issued to archbishops and bishops in the Balkans, expressly mention that "at the time of the collection of fiscal taxes, and even before, certain *zimmis* (infidels) gathered together in one house with their children, their close relatives and families," so that they could maintain that they were one family, for, according to the berat, the tax was collected for each separate "fire."[5] This explains still less the creation of the zadruga. It is a deception. The number of members alone does not constitute or define a zadruga; the relationship among the members to each other and the whole household is at its foundation.

In the second study, "Adaptation for Survival: The Varžić Zadruga," published in the *Slavonic and East European Review* in 1943, Mosely investigated thoroughly a zadruga in Slavonia. This was not one of the large zadrugas he knew, but was one composed of only twenty-six members, yet was so complex in structure and performance that it represented the zadrugas as a whole. From division of labor, hired labor, the home farm, and the land of the zadruga, he passed to the village land association, the drainage cooperative, livestock, livelihood of the zadruga, individual property, and the position of the head of the zadruga (the *starješina*). The reply of the *starješina* of a large household in Herzegovina to Mosely, when he was asked about his duties, was especially interesting. He said jokingly but "correctly" that he was the Minister of Foreign Affairs of the zadruga, for he was in charge of purchases and sales, and represented the zadruga before the authorities. Mosely paid attention next to the history of this zadruga, the growth of female inheritance, the division of zadrugal property, and the role of the zadruga in the village. Finally, he stressed the capacity of the zadruga not only to survive, but, despite the changes brought about by time, to modernize considerably its method of work and to broaden its economic basis. With the study of the Varžić zadruga, Mosely presented a complete picture of one of the most significant types of the Balkan communal family.

I consider "The Distribution of the Zadruga within Southeastern Europe," which he published in the *Joshua Starr Memorial Volume* of *Jewish Social Studies* in 1953, his most significant contribution. Other scholars, among them Jovan Cvijić, have mentioned regions in the Balkans which contained zadrugas, but none determined the zadrugal belts so minutely and precisely as Mosely. This certainly was not an easy task. He identified three principal zones, each containing various subdivisions. They pass through Albania, Montenegro, Serbia, Croatia, Slavonia, Bosnia-Herzegovina, Kosovo and Metohija, western and central Bulgaria, northern Greece and Macedonia, sometimes possessing exact and at other times fluid frontiers and overlappings. In Slovenia, he did not find any traces of zadrugal tradition. Under serfdom, and after its abolition, Slovene families followed a pattern of hereditary holdings. In general, where the zadruga had been closely associated with personal servitude of the peasants to the land-owning nobility, as in parts of pre-1848 Croatia-Slavonia, or until 1912 in the valleys of Macedonia, Mosely thought dissolution of the zadruga followed the overthrow of serfdom within a generation. Where the zadruga had been the foundation of the military colonies of the frontiersmen (*graničari*), as in the regimental villages of Croatia, Slavonia and the Banat, its disappearance was less sudden. Here, the change of attitude of the Austrian government toward the maintenance of the zadruga for military purposes (the Frontier after August 1881 was not administered militarily but was reunited with Civil Croatia) and the rise in economic well-being, limitation of family size, and the rise in social mobility together destroyed the basis for its continuance.

His broad interest in, and thorough investigation of, the zadruga led Mosely to conclude that one should give no importance to ethnic or nationality factors, in the modern context, and relatively little weight to religious differences but should devote primary attention to regional economic and social factors in attempting to account for differences in structure and viability of the zadruga.

One is inclined to ask why Mosely's studies on the zadruga were so highly appreciated. First, the Balkan peoples themselves manifested a deep interest in the zadruga. Schools of scholars, poets, and politicians regarded the zadruga as one of the poles of Balkan peasant life. Even in Romania, "which has almost completely no zadrugal tradition," as Mosely noted, some agitated in the interwar period to promote the zadruga as one means of fighting the subdivision of peasant-holdings and the growing proletarization of the village. Another reason Mosely was so valued was that most of the numerous studies on the zadruga contained much "romantic imagination and patriotic theorizing." Valtazar Bogišić has written that "thanks to certain constitutive elements of this family [that is, the zadruga], which have given rise to reflections by historians of law as well as by sociologists in general, no other social institution of the Slavs, with the exception of the Russian *mir*, has provided the writers of Western Europe with a more frequent subject of studies."[6] Mosely's studies were not founded on published works; they were based mainly on fieldwork, and they were realistic, not romantic. Thirdly, his studies were not limited to the peoples of Yugoslavia, as the case had been with most analyses before him, but covered the whole Balkan area.

It is regrettable that Mosely could not complete his study of the Balkan zadruga. Other studies and preoccupations took his time. They were all valuable, but his absence in the field today is deeply felt by American scholarship. If he had been able to complete his study on the zadruga, that work would have had an impact on scholars far beyond the frontiers of this country.

NOTES

1. "The Distribution of the Zadruga within Southeastern Europe," *The Joshua Starr Memorial Volume, Jewish Social Studies* V (1953), 220.

2. See the thorough study of the *inokoština* by Valtazar Bogišić, "D'une forme particulière de la famille rurale chez les Serbes et les Croates," *Revue de Droit Internationale et de Legislation Comparée* (Brussels), XVI (1884), 374-422; Jovan Cvijić, *La péninsule balkanique* (Paris, 1918), pp. 284-285.

3. Bogišić, p. 395.

4. George Ostrogorsky, *History of the Byzantine State* (New Brunswick, N.J., 1957), p. 167.

5. Berat of the Metropolitan of Tărnovo, Daniel, dated 1802, in Josef Kabrda, *Le système fiscal de l'Eglise Orthodoxe dans l'Empire Ottoman d'après les documents turcs* (Brno, 1969), p. 43; see also notes 1, 2, 3 on the same page. See also the berat of the Metropolitan of Chios, dated 1755, in Konstantine Amantos, "The Privileges of Islam in favor of Christians" (in Greek), *Hellēnika* VIII (1936), 152-153.

6. Bogišić, p. 379.

B. Mosely on the Family,
    Especially the Zadruga

3: THE PEASANT FAMILY: THE ZADRUGA, OR COMMUNAL JOINT-FAMILY IN THE BALKANS, AND ITS RECENT EVOLUTION

Philip E. Mosely

While historians have devoted much attention to the turbulent politics and intricate diplomacy of the Balkans, relatively little study has been made of the social development of the Balkan peoples. Yet during the last 50 to 150 years these peoples have undergone numerous and radical changes, including the destruction of serfdom and of a long-established caste system; the emergence of a preponderantly land-owning peasantry; an intense process of internal colonization; the growth of emigration to foreign countries; the development of modern systems of communication and transportation; the growing penetration of a money economy and the relative decline of a natural economy; the destruction of the old regional equilibrium between town and village; the development of national states, of national bureaucracies, and of national intelligentsias; the growth of professional life and of factory production; the extension of state services, of public education, of compulsory military service; the spread of literacy; the growing impact of statute law on customary law; and so forth.

The investigation of Balkan social development may be approached through several avenues. One of them is the study of an outstanding institution of peasant life in the Balkans, the "zudruga," or communal joint-family. Although no single definition embraces all varieties of the zadruga, it may be considered, tentatively, as a household composed of two or more biological or small-families, closely related by blood or adoption, owning its means of production communally, producing and consuming the means of its livelihood jointly, and regulating the control of its property, labor, and livelihood communally.

Reprinted from Caroline F. Ware, ed., *The Cultural Approach to History* (New York: Columbia University Press, 1940), pp. 95-108, by permission of Columbia University Press.

Studies of the zadruga have been chiefly historical and ethnographical in their approach. Historical literature has dealt mainly with the problem of the national or "racial" character and origin of the zadruga. At first historical controversy hinged largely on the question of whether the zadruga was a peculiarly Slav institution, expressive of some innate Slav tendency toward family communism, or whether it was found among non-Slav peoples. As a result of this discussion, traces of the zadruga have been found among widely scattered peoples, both Slav and non-Slav. A second aspect of the controversy has run parallel with the dispute over the origins of the Great Russian "mir," or distributional land commune. Some students of the zadruga have held that it was very old, probably of prehistoric origin, others that it arose as a product of the fiscal and legal systems of the Byzantine and Ottoman empires. The entire documentation on which the controversy is based consists of a few much-disputed statutes; probably the most that one can assert is that while Byzantine and Ottoman legislation seems to have favored the continued existence of the zadruga, it could hardly have penetrated so deeply into the life of the village as by itself to have created the zadrugal way of life.

The abundant ethnographical literature on the zadruga has, unfortunately, little value for the study of social history. The ethnographers have collected numerous examples of the zadruga, but without presenting a full analysis of the individual zadrugas with respect to their internal structures and their village and regional settings.[1] An undifferentiated approach to the study of the zadruga unconsciously assumes a uniform background for all Balkan zadrugas; in this part of the world, with its sharp regional variations, such an assumption is very misleading. There are, however, several valuable monographs which present full and detailed accounts of single zadrugas in Bosnia and Croatia.[2]

One purpose in making a fresh study of the zadruga is, by applying a uniform method of case-study investigation, to define the various regional types of zadruga found in the Balkans, to place the regional types in relation to their geographical and social environment, and to discover, as far as possible, the main lines in the evolution of the Balkan zadruga over the last hundred years or so.[3] This investigation was based on the method sampling, by picking typical villages or hamlets in each region, rather than by applying statistical methods over a broader area. The statistical material now available does not lend itself to refined treatment. In one village, for example, a family which had been divided into seven smaller families for nearly thirty years was listed in the official records as a joint-family, chiefly because the separate families had continued to inhabit a single courtyard.[4] In another village a former zadruga was listed as completely divided into individual small-families, although three of the small-families had, after the general division of the zadrugal property, recombined at once to form a new zadruga with twenty-three members.[5] In the beginning of the study it became obvious that the statistical method, if applied accurately and with significant results, would require several years of work in each separate region. It seemed preferable to leave the statistical approach to later workers in the field, and to devote the limited time available to a comparative study of regional types of zadruga and of regional patterns in its evolution.

Further stimulus to make this study, if such was needed, was supplied by the deep interest of the Balkan peoples themselves in the zadruga. Whole schools of scholars, poets, and politicians regard the zadruga as one of the poles of Balkan life, its peasant pole, in contrast with the čaršija or market place. For many decades economists and jurists as well as political leaders have debated whether or not the zadruga has outlived its usefulness and whether it should be encouraged or attacked. Of late the controversy has been especially sharp in Croatia.[6] Even in Rumania there has been a certain agitation in favor of promoting the zadruga as one possible means of combating the extreme subdivision of peasant holdings and the growing proletarianization of the village. Such a proposal seems highly utopian, but that it is being seriously discussed in a country which is almost entirely without a zadrugal tradition is in itself significant.

Before one or two of the conclusions reached in this new study of the zadruga can be presented, the procedure followed should be explained, at least in bare outline. With the assistance of local teachers, priests, or civic leaders, a "typical" village was chosen in each region to be studied, chiefly by eliminating those which showed deviations from the normal status of villages in the area. The next step was to go to the village and establish a friendly relationship with the leading villagers, usually with the elders of one or more zadrugas.

The following step, the first in the actual study, was to draw up a genealogy of the family; sometimes this reached back only 50 or 60 years, but not infrequently it covered a period of 100 or 150 years. The composition of the family now and in earlier periods could then be analyzed, together with the transmission of the leadership of the family from one head or elder to his successor. By inquiring about each woman who had married into or out of the zadruga, it was possible to ascertain the dowry received or given, or the bride-price paid or received, and to record significant changes in the sphere of marriage and dowry custom. A further step involved the recording of the division of labor within the zadruga among age groups, sex groups, and skill groups.

Another desirable step was to draw up a budget for the family; in some instances this was impossible, either because the peasant, who is very ready to narrate in great detail the history of his family, is reluctant to part with budgetary information, or because a high degree of natural economy resulted in wide yearly fluctuations in income and outlay. In these cases the study of the budget had to be replaced by two rough criteria of the balance between natural and money economy; one, the listing of labor services sold by the family through local wage labor or through migration in search of work, and of labor services bought by the family through the hiring of local laborers and artisans.

A further line of inquiry entailed listing all the landed property held or rented by the zadruga, its time and method of acquisition, together with an inventory of its livestock and equipment. It was also important to determine the boundaries of communal and individual property within the zadruga by listing and checking every possible kind of property and income. The analysis of the communal rights exercised by the zadruga in village or clan property, such as forests, pastures, and fisheries, and of the role of these rights in the zadrugal economy was very significant. A further line of inquiry dealt with the division of the zadruga, its causes, the methods by which it was carried out, and the problems of readjustment which it raised. General conversations with the individual members of the zadruga helped to draw out their attitudes toward the zadruga, the village, and the state, and to discover changes which had occurred within their memory. Other information was secured through direct observation of life in the zadruga and of the unspoken attitudes of its members, and through photographing the members of the zadruga, their possessions, and their activities.

One of the first surprises in studying the zadruga was to discover that it was not usually regarded by the peasants as an institution distinct from the individual, or small-family. In Croatia, to be sure, the term "zadruga" had long been popularized in the villages by the special legal status which it received in the codes of the former Military Border of Austria and in that of Civil Croatia; elsewhere the peasants do not use this term in describing what scholars call the zadruga—not even in pre-1912 Serbia, where the term is also used in the law code. Outside of Croatia, the zadruga is more commonly referred to as "a large household," or "a large house," "a lot of people," sometimes as "an undivided house." In Serbia proper "to live in zadruga" means "to live in concord" or "in harmony," not "to live in a zadruga." In brief, except in certain regions where the law codes have given a special status to the zadruga, and not always there, the peasants themselves make no distinction between the joint-family and the small or biological-family household, except to indicate the greater size of the former. Both the multiple family and the small-family are part of one social environment. When the social atmosphere, that is, the customary rules and attitudes, remains favorable to the communal family, the zadruga persists with much vitality; when new rules arise, hostile to the spirit of the zadruga, the communal joint-family disappears.

In regions where the zadruga spirit is strong among the peasants, any small-family may, through biological expansion, become a zadruga. In many parts of Bosnia and Herzegovina, the zadruga is strong today, even though its existence is ignored by the law. On the other hand, in the former Military Border of Croatia-Slavonia the separate zadrugal status of a substantial part of peasant land has been maintained by the law code, but the peasant family has been steadily approaching the non-zadrugal or small-family way of life. In that area, although a large part of peasant property is still zadrugal in legal status, the peasants usually treat it as individual, or Roman-law property. The important factor in the persistence or decline of the zadruga is the persistence or decline of traditional communal attitudes toward the family, toward ownership of land, and toward customs of dowry and inheritance, rather than the positive provisions of the written law.

One of the customary rules on which the zadrugal way of life rests is that, as long as there are male heirs to carry on the communal family, women inherit no share in the zadrugal land. In the zadruga of Simo Bašić, in the village of Dobrinje, in the district of Banjaluka, northern Bosnia, the custom is for the bride to bring to her husband's household a large hope chest or even two, filled with her own handiwork; this is called the "sprema" or "oprema." In return the bridegroom's family makes a compensating but less valuable payment called the "gage of friendship" or "ujme prijateljstva." The third transaction involved in the marriage is the "dar," or "gift," of the bride's father to the bride, made a year after the marriage, and consisting of livestock, usually a cow, or a cow and two sheep. The daughter, once married out of the zadruga, has no claim to a share of the inheritance in land, which passes to her brother. A daughter still unmarried at her father's death can claim from her brothers only the customary marriage outfit and the "gift." If a peasant family in this district has no son to carry on the household, one of the sons-in-law, usually the husband of the youngest daughter, becomes a member of his wife's household, in some cases even taking his wife's family name. By exclusion of women from the inheritance of real property and of agricultural equipment, the zadruga gives consistency to the large household. Wherever the zadruga is well preserved today, the rule of male inheritance is dominant. Significantly, in the same district, northern Bosnia, the custom of exclusive male inheritance also prevails among the small-families.[7] Both the joint-family and the small-family exist in the same social atmosphere, in this case, an atmosphere favorable to the persistence of the joint-family.

An entirely different picture is presented by the German village of Neudorf, or Novo Selo, near Vinkovci, Slavonia. This community, although settled by Swabian colonists in the eighteenth century, formed a part of Croatia-Slavonia. While all the land except the common lands was originally held by zadrugas, the communal families have divided rapidly during the last sixty years, until today it is rare to find one with as many as ten members. By a new law of the 1870's, exclusive male inheritance of land was abolished; according to the new rules of inheritance, zadrugal land could be divided among the daughters when there was no son, and in any division of a zadruga a woman member acquired the right to a share equal to one-half that of a man. A further factor which contributed to breaking down the zadruga was the adoption of "Zweikindersystem," or "two-child-family," instead of the larger families of earlier days; the restriction of births increased the number of families without sons, and hence the number of women who received land from their fathers as dowry or inheritance. For example, Jakob Jakober had no sons and four daughters; his thirty-two Joch of zadrugal land, or "Kommunionsland," were divided equally among his daughters and became their full individual property, or "Eigentum." In turn, a wife who had received land as dowry or heritage could now bequeath it as she wished to her own daughters and sons, or dispose of it in any way she might choose. By this process much former communal, or zadrugal, land has been transformed into full individual property.

In Neudorf there have been many conflicts over applying the rules for the division of the zadruga and its property. In the case of the zadruga of Georg Hupbauer, which divided in 1921 for the first time in about 130 years, much bitterness was aroused in some members of the zadruga because, contrary to the unwritten custom, but in accord with written law, the head of the household took a full share of the communal property for himself, in order to add it to the holding of his favorite son, Ludwig, with whom he then went to live. Another common complaint was that the head of the zadruga had bought private land, or "Eigentum," from the common earnings of the zadruga, and had then disposed of it as his individual property instead of treating it according to the rules customary for communal land.

One further trait which showed how far Neudorf had moved from the old communal-family way of life was the new custom of reserving a yearly support for life, or "Aussenhalt," for the former head of the zadruga, after its division. When Philipp Teiber divided his land among his three sons in 1888, he reserved ten Joch of land for his own support; as long as he lived his three sons worked this share of land, paid the taxes on it, and turned over the product to him. Another and now commoner type of "Aussenhalt" is illustrated in the case of Jakob's second son, Heinrich Teiber, who divided all his land among his three sons in 1926; by a written contract each son obligated himself to furnish the father with a fixed amount of wheat, corn, wine, firewood, eggs, poultry, and milk; Heinrich and his wife also had a separate room and kitchen, and kept house for themselves.[8] Nothing could be more remote than this from the life of a genuine zadruga, with its close family cooperation and common housekeeping. Although Neudorf still has a large part of its land in zadrugal status, the individualistic way of life has made such headway that the peasants try in every way to evade the restrictions inherent in the zadrugal property status, and as far as possible they treat all their property as full individual property of the Roman-law type.

A similar picture of the evolution away from the zadrugal way of life is to be found in Rokovci, a Croatian village in the same district, and, like Neudorf, a community of former "Grenzer," or soldiers of the Military Border. With the granting of rights of inheritance in zadrugal land to women, with the growth of the new custom of providing dowry in land for brides, and with the decline in the size of the family, there has been an increasing tendency to treat the zadrugal property as if it were individual property. Until about 1890 it was rare for women to receive dowry or inheritance in land; even after that time such dowry or inheritance might be sold and the proceeds given to the bride in cash, to avoid bringing into the zadruga the disturbing element of individual property in land. Today, however, as in Neudorf, every biological or small-family counts on receiving land from the bride's family as well as from the groom's. Even the practice of providing the older members of the divided household with a definite contractual support for life, here called the "uživanje," is almost as common in Rokovci as in Neudorf. Thus the evolution of the zadruga in a German and a Croatian village of the same region has been essentially identical, except that the Croatian village has still preserved one or two fair-sized zadrugas, one of twenty-three members.[9]

An interesting illustration of a similar change in the rules of inheritance is found in the hamlet, or "mahala," of the Stoynevi, in the village of Kopanitsa, Radomir district, western Bulgaria. Here until recently the custom prevailed of paying a bride-price to the bride's father, whose duty it was to give the bride an outfit of clothes, bedding, towels, and so forth, together with a chest to keep them in. The daughters had no claim to inherit any share of the land so long as there were any male heirs. About 1930, however, married daughters began demanding and receiving their legal share of the patrimony; according to the Bulgarian code of 1889, a daughter is entitled to a share equal to one-half that of a son. Once a sister has demanded and taken her legal share of the patrimony, her brothers are naturally forced, in compensation, to demand the shares to which their own wives are entitled by law; and thus in a few years the entire custom of land inheritance in Kopanitsa has been turned inside out. When a wife brings her own land or the expectation of inheriting land to her husband's household, her position within that household is naturally quite different from what it was when she brought merely her hands and her marriage outfit. When several wives bring different quantities of land, strong pressure arises for the division of the zadruga into its component small-families. Each small-family, instead of looking to the joint cultivation of the zadrugal property for its livelihood, turns to the creation of a new unit, based on the combination of the wife's and the husband's shares of their respective patrimonies. Inequalities of property among the wives accentuate still further the disintegrating tendencies within the zadruga and make its continued existence problematical.

There is one common method of compromise which aims to preserve the zadruga without depriving its individual wives of their dowry or heritage in land. It is illustrated in the case of the zadruga of Petar Pavlev, with twenty-four members, in the same Bulgarian hamlet. When in 1937 one of the wives, Zora, inherited twenty dekars of her father's land in the somewhat distant commune of Pernik, the zadruga undertook to work the land for her on shares. The zadruga provided the seed, and turned over something more than one-half the net product to Zora, who in turn used that separate income to pay school expenses for two sons and to buy extra things for her small-family.[10]

An even more systematic elaboration of the same type of compromise between the communal zadruga and individual inheritance is illustrated in the case of the Varžić zadruga, in the village of Zelčin, Valpovo district, Slavonia. Here, although nearly every wife has property of her own in land or livestock, it is not exploited by the zadruga itself, but by outsiders working on shares. Manda, Jozo's wife, has no land, but when she married in 1917 she received a cow, which she sold, and with the proceeds she bought two breed sows. These are kept by a neighbor in his own pen; when litters of sucklings are sold, she receives one-half the money, and with this non-zadrugal, or individual, income she buys additional sewing materials and dyestuffs toward preparing the marriage outfit, or "otpremnina," for her daughter, over and above the equal provision made by the zadruga for each of its marriageable girls. A more complicated case is presented by Kata, wife of Marko, in the same zadruga. After her wedding she received two sows, two cows, two calves, and three Joch, or "jutara," of land from her father. The land is worked on shares by a neighbor; Marko sold one cow and the calves and bought another Joch of land, which is also worked on shares by a fellow villager. From the income Marko's wife buys additional articles of clothing, and Marko provides himself with city-made shirts, cigarettes, and medical treatment. Usually when a girl marries out of the zadruga, dowry in land is provided by the girl's own mother out of her own dowry or heritage; in one case, however, the Varžić zadruga decided to buy a Joch of land with zadrugal money in order to provide a suitable dowry for one of its girls whose mother had married into the zadruga before the giving of land in dowry had become the rule.

It is interesting to note that this personal income, derived by individual couples within the Varžić zadruga from land and livestock received by the wives as dowry or heritage, merely supplements the identical allowances made by the zadruga itself to each of the six wives in it. Each wife receives 300 dinars in April, 300 in September, and 300 before Christmas to buy sewing materials for the needs of her small-family. In the autumn each wife shares in the sale of surplus chickens, which are disposed of to reduce the carry-over. In the spring each wife is assigned as many furrows of flax as she wishes to work; from the produce she makes linen for her family, and she may also sell the surplus flaxseed to add to her pocket money. As is plainly to be seen, this zadruga has worked out an elaborate compromise between the communal and the individual interests of its component small-families. The Varžić zadruga is, by the way, unusually prosperous and well organized. Its leaders are active in running the affairs of the village, the land community, the drainage cooperative, and the Croatian Peasants' party. They are quite aware that their zadruga of 26 members is an exception today and they strive deliberately to preserve it. For example, all its members but one, who provides his own tobacco out of his wife's separate property, have given up smoking and drinking. "If we should smoke and drink, we should have to lay out money for tobacco and wine, and then there would be quarrels about how much each consumed, and the zadruga would be in danger of breaking up," said Djuro, the co-elder of the household.[11] Their elaborate arrangement for harmonizing the continued existence of the zadruga with the development of female inheritance in land is thus only a part of the highly self-conscious and purposeful attitude of its members toward the zadruga as a whole.

The problem of the change in the customs of land inheritance deserves special emphasis because it has been, in many regions of the Balkans, a central factor affecting the continuance or dissolution of the zadruga. It also shows how the zadruga and the small-family exist in the same social environment and according to the same customary rules and are not two distinct institutions, each with its own rules, as ethnographers and legislators have often assumed. It is also interesting to note in passing the tremendous influence which this changeover in inheritance custom exerts on the very serious problem of checking the rapid subdivision of peasant holdings, and hence on the problem of maintaining the efficiency of peasant agriculture. The zadruga is likely to have its land in a few large fields, with all the advantages which that implies. The small-family, with its landholding formed by combining the heritages of both husband and wife, is likely to possess a rapidly increasing number of small, even tiny strips. To counteract the evil effect of excessive subdivision, consolidation, or "commassation," has been applied in some regions, notably in Slavonia and in a few villages of Bulgaria. But from the experience of the consolidations made in Slavonia during the twenty-five years before 1914 it is plain that, because of the decline of the zadruga and the consequent rapid partitioning of peasant holdings, consolidation loses its beneficial effect within two or three generations and has to be carried out all over again, with all the expense which it entails. The growth of the new custom of female inheritance in land, together with the decline of the zadruga, represents a broad, underlying cause of parcellation, which the purely technical procedure of consolidation is unable permanently to counteract.

The broader question of the break-up of the zadruga, aside from the development of female inheritance in land, would require extended treatment. In brief, it may be pointed out that any investigation of this problem should distinguish between two easily confused processes, the dissolution and disappearance of the zadruga and the normal process of subdivision. The very large zadruga is, and always was, the exception, although zadrugas of fifty, seventy, and even eighty-three members have been studied in the course of this survey. The zadruga of ten to twenty members is much more usual, however. A zadruga may increase to such size that the forces of disintegration outweigh the integrating tendencies. It may become difficult to control and coordinate the work of a large zadruga, the degree of blood relationship may have become rather remote, or a considerable part of the zadrugal land newly brought under cultivation may lie at some distance from the communal homestead. In these circumstances the overgrown zadruga is likely to split into several smaller ones, or into a number of small-families, out of which new zadrugas may in turn grow. In widely separated parts of the Balkans the peasants liken this process to the swarming of bees.

The dissolution of the zadruga is quite a different process. As shown above, it may in some regions grow out of a change in the customs of inheritance and dowry; in this case it is strongly influenced by the refusal or the failure of the written law to accept and sanction the customary law of the peasant family, even where the legislators may have attempted to protect the zadruga, as in Croatia. It may be due to an increase in the practice of working outside the household. When outside wages are an exception, they are readily turned into the common fund, but when working for hire becomes an essential element in the household economy, the zadruga is almost certain to dissolve into its component small-families. In general, proletarianization is far more likely to be fatal to the zadruga than prosperity, although cases are recorded in which growing prosperity has led to the break-up of the zadruga. As a special subtype of this category of social change, it is interesting to note the destructive effect exerted on the zadruga by large-scale emigration to and return from America, as illustrated in southern Albania, Dalmatia, and parts of Croatia. So long as the emigrant is absent from the village, his family remains under the protection of the zadruga. On his return he is eager to set up for himself, he has acquired new habits, and finds it difficult to readapt himself to the routine of the communal household. Other factors, such as increasing education, experience in the army, growing contact with the cities, give rise to new demands and to individual ambitions. Not infrequently the result is that the zadruga, like the native costume, is discarded merely because it is "old-fashioned." Besides the general causes at work to preserve or disrupt the zadruga, local factors may play a decisive part. For example, in some villages of Bosnia in 1918 the destruction of the seignorial control exerted by the Moslem landlords was accompanied by a rapid division of the zadrugas. In the upsurge of release, the peasants were eager to cast off all bonds, including those of the zadruga. In Montenegro and northern Albania the system of clan rights of usage relating to the forests, pastures, and fisheries is not on the whole favorable to the large household, while the control and protection exercised by the clans reduce the importance of similar services rendered elsewhere by the zadruga.

In retrospect, the zadruga with its large and coordinated supply of labor, has played an important part in bringing Balkan land under cultivation and in the settlement of the area. Under conditions of a predominantly natural economy, the zadruga, with its elaborate division of labor and its high degree of cooperative self-sufficiency, represented an ideal way of life for the peasants, because of its economic and protective strength and because of its power to provide local leaders and to preserve strong nuclei of national life at the peasant level. The zadruga played an important part in the wars of liberation of the Balkan peoples, for the large household could keep one or two fighters in the field and equipped, without its livelihood being disrupted. The zadruga has also left its mark on the political concepts of the Balkan peoples. One can hardly understand the long rivalry between the Obrenović and Karadjordjević families in nineteenth-century Serbia without remembering that for the Serbian peasant the king was a kind of zadruga elder on a national scale, and far removed from Hapsburg and Bourbon conceptions of monarchy. Today the zadruga contributes much to the vitality and beauty of village life in the Balkans. While there are strong tendencies running counter to its existence, the zadruga has shown in some regions a remarkable degree of adaptability to local conditions of life and work, and a notable capacity to absorb new agricultural techniques and to take the lead in the modern development of the village. Even when the zadruga disappears, it usually leaves a spirit of mutual help, which finds expression not only in the traditional cooperative labors of the peasantry but also in the modern cooperative organizations which are developing in the more progressive regions of the Balkans.

NOTES

1. The most important ethnographical studies are those of Valtazar Bogišić, *Pravni običaji u slovena; privatno pravo,* Zagreb, 1867, and *Zbornik sadašnjih pravnih običaja u južnih slovena; gradja u odgovorima iz različnih krajeva slovenskoga juga,* Zagreb, 1874; S. S. Bobchev, "Bulgarskata cheliadna zadruga v segashno i minalo vreme; istoriko-yuridicheski studii," *Sbornik za narodni umotvoreniya, nauka i knizhnina,* XII-XIII (Sofia, 1906-7), 1-207; Vasilj Popović, *Zadruga; istorijska rasprava,* Sarajevo, 1921; J . Cvijić, *La péninsule balkanique,* Paris, 1918; and numerous volumes of his *Naselja.*

2. Milan Karanović, "Nekolike velike porodične zadruge u Bosni i Hercegovini," *Glasnik zemaljskog muzeja u Bosni i Hercegovini* XLI (Sarajevo, 1929), 63-80; ibid., XLII (1930), 133-56: Držislav Švob and Franko Petrić, "Zadruga Domladovac," *Zbornik za narodni život i običaje južnih slavena,* XXVII (Zagreb, 1929), 92-110. The best juridical studies are those of V. Krišković, *Hrvatsko pravo kućnih zadruga; historijskodogmatski nacrt,* Zagreb, 1925; M. Utiešenović, *Die Hauskommunion der Südslaven,* Vienna, 1859, and same, *Die Militärgränze und die Verfassung,* Vienna, 1861. Several recent studies of social geography have thrown valuable light on the zadruga, especially those of G. Gunchev, "Vakarel, antropogeografski prouchevanya," *Godishnik na sofiskiya universitet,* XXIX (Sofia, 1933), 1-188; Herbert Wilhelmy, *Hochbulgarien. I. Die ländlichen Siedlungen und die bäuerliche Wirtschaft,* Kiel, 1935; Richard Busch-Zantner, *Agrarverfassung, Gesellschaft und Siedlung in Südosteuropa, unter besonderer Berücksichtigung der Türkenzeit,* Leipzig, 1938.

3. This investigation was made possible by a grant-in-aid of the Social Science Research Council in 1938.

4. Recorded Sept. 9,1938,village of Korovo, district of Peshtera, Bulgaria.

5. Recorded Aug. 20-21, 1938, village of Lazina, district of Karlovac, Croatia.

6. The zadruga has been championed by Milan Ivšić, *Les Problèmes agraires en Yougoslavie,* Paris, 1926; *Temelji seljačkoga zakonika,* Zagreb, 1933; *Seljačka politika,* Zagreb, 1937-38; and by Milovan Gavazzi, *Seljačka zadružna obitelj kao činjenica i kao problem,* Sarajevo, 1934. It has been attacked by Rudolf Bićanić, *Kako živi narod,* Zagreb, 1936.

7. Recorded Aug. 18-19, 1938.

8. Recorded Aug. 26, 1938.

9. Recorded Aug. 26, 1938.

10. Recorded Sept. 4, 1938.

11. Recorded Aug. 27-28, 1938.

4: ADAPTATION FOR SURVIVAL:
THE VARŽIĆ ZADRUGA

Philip E. Mosely

In Southeastern Europe the zadruga, or communal multiple family, has long
held a central place in peasant life and, especially during its decline in recent
decades, many controversies have been waged around it. While no single
definition embraces all varieties of zadrugas, for present purposes the zadruga
may be described as "a household composed of two or more biological or
small-families, closely related by blood or adoption, owning its means of
production communally, producing and consuming its means of livelihood
jointly, and regulating the control of its property, labor, and livelihood
communally."[1] The growth of an exchange-economy, the displacement of
peasant custom by the written law of the jurists and of the more
individualistic town, the spread of new rules of dowry and inheritance, have
contributed to break down the zadruga in many regions of the Balkans.
Naturally, the question has been asked whether the zadruga can survive. Can
it withstand the impact of growing individualism, of declining family-
solidarity, of increasing pressure on the land?

Many Balkan commentators on this problem are reluctant to see the
zadruga disappear. To many observers of village life, the zadruga, with its
relatively larger and more consolidated scale of landowning and its more
elaborate division of labor, possesses great advantages. Others look upon it as
an encouragement to slothfulness and the spirit of routine, as an impediment
to the development of individual initiative and of a progressive agriculture. In
general, the zadruga has shown a greater viability in the mountainous regions
of the Balkans than in the plains. It is all the more interesting to examine the
present structure and recent history of a zadruga located in the fertile plains
of Slavonia—a region surpassed only by the Banat, or Vojvodina, in the

Reprinted from *Slavonic and East European Review* XXI (American Series
II) (1943), 147-173, by permission of Cambridge University Press.

productivity of its agriculture and in its high standard of living. A study of the Varžić zadruga brings into higher relief the problem of the ability of the zadruga to survive, and even to progress, under the impact of changing custom and of an increasingly capitalistic and individualistic outlook on life.

The Varžić zadruga is located in the village of Zelčin, in the county of Valpovo, a part of the historic province of Slavonia. The surrounding district is one of plains, rich in black-soil, well-watered and sometimes inundated, and largely devoted to the production of cattle and swine, and, to some extent, of wheat and maize.[2] On one of the three streets of the village, radiating from a small irregular square near the church-yard, are the house, yard, and orchard of the Varžić zadruga. With twenty-six members, this household is the largest in the village.[3] It is made up of two brothers, Jozo (IV-9) and Djuro (IV-12), their wives, four married sons with their wives, and fourteen children. Except for the wives, who have married into the zadruga, the household consists of three generations of the descendants of Ivan Varžić (III-11), who died in 1915, and his wife Janja (III-12), who lived until 1927. Blood-ties are close, and they are further cemented by the close understanding of the co-elders of the household, Jozo and Djuro.

HEADSHIP OF THE ZADRUGA

Unlike most zadrugas, the Varžić household has a joint head, instead of a single one. Jozo and Djuro together serve as "house-head" (*kućni gospodar*). As Djuro put it, "My brother is older; I respect him. We are not set one above the other, but one brother beside the other." ("Brat moj je stariji; ja ga poštivam. Mi nismo jedan nad drugim, nego brat uz brata").[4] As Jozo is no longer so robust as formerly, much of his work is now supervisory. The affairs of the zadruga are decided by all the married men together, as "adult" and "married" are in effect synonymous to the peasant. "After supper we talk over what work we shall do on the morrow. As we all decide, with our sons, so we work. With us it is not as one person wishes, but however is better." ("Poslije večere me pripovijedamo, što da radimo sutra. Kako svi odredimo, sa sinovima tako i radimo. Kod nas nije tako kako voli jedan, već kako je bolje").

When there is a job to be done, the zadruga is well provided with hands to tackle it. At plowing or harvesting the entire zadruga turns to. On the day the household was visited, a heavy wagon-load of quick-lime ("kola sa krečom") had to be dumped into a slaking-pit; fourteen members of the family were on hand to assist.

DIVISION OF LABOR

In addition to the common tasks of the zadruga, special duties are assigned to each member. Three younger men, Šimo (V-13), Antun (V-17), and Marko (V-23), are "stablemen" (*kočijaš*) and look after the horses. Mikola (V-15) supervises the work of the swineherd (*svinjar*), whose duties are currently fulfilled by Žiga (V-19). "During vacation [from school] he is assisted by Pavao (VI-9) and Tomo (VI-11)" ("u ferije pomažu mu Pavao i Tomo"). Stjepan (VI-5) and Šimo (VI-6) are the cattleherders (*govedar*).

The work of the women is headed by Agica (IV-13), the wife of the younger co-elder, Djuro. Usually the women's work is managed by the wife of the head. As Manda (IV-11) is Jozo's second wife and entered the household after Agica had already been serving as the women's head, she has never held this function. In Zelčin the women's head is called simply "cook" (*kuvarica*), although in many parts of the Balkans she bears some more distinctive and impressive title. The cook is "always at home" ("uvijek kod kuće"), for she supervises the preparation of meals for the entire household as a unit. She is assisted by fourteen-year-old Anka (V-20), who is thus learning her household duties by apprenticeship, not to her mother, but to the head of the women's work.

The "cook" is also aided by an "orderly" (*reduša*). Each of the other five wives of the household serves in turn as *reduša*. The order of their service, determined by seniority of marriage, is: Manda (IV-11), Reza (V-14), Eva (V-16), Kata (V-18), and Kata (V-24). Although there are two "Kata's" no confusion arises, as each wife is commonly referred to by her husband's name in the possessive form; one Kata (V-18) is called "Tunova" and the other (V-24) "Markova."

Each of the five wives serves one week in turn as *reduša*, the term of her service running "from Sunday morning to Saturday evening" ("od nedelje u jutro do subote na veče"). She "fetches water and firewood, and washes the dishes" ("nosi vodu i drva, pere sudje"). When asked whether *reduša* came from *red*, meaning "order, making order," or from *red*, meaning "turn, shift," Djuro replied that it came from both meanings.

HIRED LABOR

Despite its abundance of hands, the Varžić zadruga hires a substantial amount of outside labor. About a kilometer distant from the village, in view across the meadows and a sluggish creek, is the dairy-farm (*salaš*), which is run by a hired-man (*sluga*), Mikola Barić, who hails from Kunišinci, a village about ten kilometers away. Jozo (IV-9) goes there every day to supervise the work. About twenty-five head of cattle are kept at the *salaš* from the first of December to the beginning of April. Mikola "works on halves" ("radi na polovicu"), that is, receives a part of the cheese produced for sale. In addition, he is provided with thirteen *metara* (about thirty-six bushels) of wheat a year, one thousand dinars ($20) in cash, and as much "wood as he uses" ("drva, koliko potroši"). When the cows are at the farm he has as much milk as he needs. The hired-man also has one yoke (1.42 acres) for maize, and a quarter-yoke for a vegetable garden.

Mikola Barić has worked for the Varžić household for the last four years, and in that time has acquired "a house, out-buildings, and two yoke of land" ("kuću, podkućicu, dva jutara zemlje") in his own village. The zadruga has loaned him money to buy land and pigs. When he works with the members of the household, he eats with them at their board. This is a typical case of a peasant poorly provided with land who hires out for a number of years in order to build up his own farm-unit.

Other zadrugas so well provided with hands as is the Varžić family would not be inclined to spend money on an outside worker, but would normally detail one married couple to run the outlying dairy-farm, perhaps each of the younger couples by turn. The Varžić zadruga is well-off, and its members are closely attached to the life of the household and of the village. They prefer to incur the additional expense of hiring an outside worker rather than have one of their small-families "exiled" to the isolated *salaš*.

At the peak of seasonal work the zadruga also engages laborers by the day. In 1938 "for the mowing we had hired-men, two days, with twenty workers a day, at twenty-five dinars ($0.50) a day, with plum-brandy and victuals" ("za kosidbu uzmemo nadničare, dva dana po dvadeset nadničara, po 25 dinara na dan, rakije, ranu"; properly "hranu"). For the potato-hoeing the zadruga engaged thirty laborers for three days, at fifteen dinars ($0.30) a day, with food and drink. The zadruga harvested its wheat without outside help, requiring six days to reap thirty yoke, with the use of a horse-drawn harvester and binder.

THE HOME-FARM OF THE ZADRUGA

The yard (*dvor*) of the Varžić household is separated from the village street (*ulica*) by a wall about eight feet high, which fills the gap between the "old house" (*stara kuća*), which is to one's left on entering, and the new "sleeping-rooms" (*kijeri*; properly, *kiljeri*), to the right. Entrance to the yard is through a large double-gate (*kapija*) and through two man-sized gates (*vrata*), one to the right of the wagon-gate, and one to the left of it leading directly to the porch of the old house. The latter, built sixty years ago, now serves mainly as a kitchen and a place for eating and gathering. Nearest to the street is the living and dining room (*kuća*), with wooden tables and benches, and a great hearth (*ognjište*) in one corner of it. Access to this room is through a smaller room, the "old house" properly speaking, with a large projecting hearth, used for baking in winter, which occupies most of the rear wall, opposite the outside door. The third section of the house is the kitchen (*kujna*), with a capacious Dutch-oven (*šporet*). Lengthwise of the "old house" runs a four-foot-wide porch (*trijem*), separated from the yard by a wooden wall (*zid*) forty inches high, which links up five pillars (*stup*) supporting the sloping, shingled roof.

Directly across the yard are the "sleeping-rooms" (*kijeri*), seven in all, built since 1925. Each room is of equal size, about twelve feet by fifteen, airy and clean, with a well-fitted door and window (*pendžer*) for each. A four-foot-wide porch also runs the length of the court-side of the *kijeri*. The first room is inhabited by Djuro, his wife and two unmarried children (IV-12, IV-13, V-27, V-28); the second, by Jozo, his wife and two of their grand-children (IV-9, IV-11, VI-5, VI-6); the third, by Simo, his wife and two younger children (V-13, V-14, VI-7, VI-8); the fourth, by Mikola, his wife and two children (V-15, V-16, VI-9, VI-10); the fifth, by Antun, his wife and two children (V-17, V-18, VI-11, VI-12); the sixth, by Marko, his wife and two children (V-23, V-24, VI-13, VI-14). The seventh room is now used as a supply-storeroom (*kućni kijer*), but will be available for the next son to marry, perhaps Žiga (V-19), who now sleeps in a hay-mow, while Anka (V-20) bunks down in the "old house." Built of plastered brick, the *kijeri*, with their red-tile roof, a gracefully proportioned porch, and well-made sills, doors, and windows, represent a very superior type of peasant housing.

In the courtyard, set back somewhat from the street and midway between the "old house" and the *kijeri*, is a brick barn (*ambar*; properly, *hambar*), in which are stored grains of all kinds, except corn on the cob. The adjoining woodshed (*šupa*), which is made of wood, contains a supply of stacked firewood ("drva složena u fatove"). To the right of the far end of the woodshed is a dug-well (*bunar*), with its picturesque sweep (*šipka*) balanced on a pillar (*stup*). Still farther back, close to the wattle-fence which separates the Varžic' yard from that of its neighbor, is a large hive-shaped stove (*pec*) used for baking bread out-of-doors in summer. Just back of the stove is a long chicken-coop (*kokošinjak*), slatted and set on stilts. Behind the coop, at the edge of the orchard, is an out-door wood-pile (*drvara*).

Behind the "old house," and extending twice its length, is a large pigfold (*tor za svinje*), which has a gate of its own giving onto the street. Beyond it is a large pigpen (*svinjac*), built of wood, and thatched. Beyond the pigpen are seventeen farrowing-pens (*kočani*) for breed-sows. Just beyond the "old house," separated from it by a wall of plastered brick, is a large corn-crib (*čardak*), slatted and raised on stilts. Farther on is a row of farm-buildings including a medium-sized wooden shed for storing implements (*veškujna*), an open wagon-shed (*kolnica*), a large hay-mow (*štagalj*), and finally the horse-barn (*štala za konje*). Beyond the horse-barn is a manure-pit (*djubrište*), and near it the out-door toilet. Off to the left is a wooden "cook-house" (*pecara*), for distilling plum-brandy (*rakija*) and making sausage (*kobasa*). Enclosed by the barns on one side and the farrowing-pens on the other, is a large cattle-yard, to which the livestock are brought on summer nights. Beyond the farm-buildings stretches a substantial orchard, with plum, apple, and pear-trees. In it are a lime-pit (*jama za kreč*) and another dug-well.

In addition, the zadruga owns another yard on the outskirts of the village, used only for housing some of its livestock. The dairy-farm, a kilometer away, has seven buildings, including a hut for the family of the hired-man, hay-mows, a horse-barn, and cattle-barns.

THE LAND OF THE ZADRUGA

The Varžić zadruga owns one hundred yoke (138.24 acres) of land. When it was formed in 1900, through the splitting up of an older zadruga, it came into possession of thirty yoke (42.68 acres) "from the father" (*od oca*). Since 1900 it has bought seventy yoke; sixty yoke, called "Močilno," in 1925 from a neighboring Magyar noble, Count Rudolf Norman, and ten yoke from a peasant. In 1900 the new zadruga, with ten members, had 4.27 acres per head; in 1938, with twenty-six members, it had 5.32 acres per head. The thirty yoke with which the zadruga started out were divided, and have remained divided, into sixteen parcels, at distances of from one minute to thirty-five minutes from the home-yard.[5] The possession of three-fifths of its land in one large unit of sixty yoke (85.36 acres) has great technical advantages. In Zelčin productive wealth is measured mainly by the number of cattle owned. As all the village livestock graze on the common lands during eight months of the year, the factor which decides the size of a herd is the capacity for winter-feeding during the remaining four months. For this the possession of large meadows is decisive. As no commassation has been carried out in Zelčin, the livestock are turned out to graze together on the stubble as well as in the communal pasture and forest.

THE ZELČIN LAND ASSOCIATION

The Varžić zadruga has no pasture of its own; for eight months in the year its livestock graze in the common lands owned by the Land Association. The creation of the Zelčin Land Association ("Zelčinska zemljišna zajednica") dates from the 1860's, when, after the emancipation of 1848, the lands of the peasants were separated from those of the noble, and the common pasture and woodland were placed under the control of the Association. Under serfdom each peasant household was supposed to be assigned eight yoke (11.38 acres), or one-fourth of a šešija (Ger. *Session*) of thirty-two yoke (45.52 acres).[6] For each šešija held the serfs (sing. *kmet*) rendered one hundred days of labor per year and one-tenth (*desetina*) of the crop. For pasturage, firewood, and building-material the serfs were allotted a portion of the forest jointly; "one-fourth of a šešija had one yoke of woodland" ("jedan fertalj šešije je imao jedno jutro šume").

In order to provide forage and fuel for the newly emancipated village, the Zelčin Association was assigned about one hundred and ninety yoke of pasture (*pašnjak*), and each household—there were then thirty-two or -three of them—received a share in the use of the common lands proportionate to the area of arable and meadow owned by it. Accordingly, the lands assigned to the peasants in the 1860's enjoy the additional right of using the communal pasture and forest. This "urbarial right" (*urbarsko pravo*) attaches to some twenty yoke out of the hundred owned by the Varžić zadruga. Its remaining eighty yoke, in theory, do not possess "urbarial right." In practice, however, each household sends all its livestock to the common pasture, and the use of the communal lands is, in fact, open on equal terms to all villagers; there is no attempt to enforce the rule as it was originally designed by the imperial bureaucracy, that the enjoyment of the common lands should be proportionate to the area of the individual holdings.

No tax is paid to the Association for the use of its land; for yearlings and older an annual tax of eleven dinars ($0.22) is collected by the communal administration (*općina*). Obviously, a family like the Varžić household, whose wealth is mainly in cattle, benefits greatly by the present arrangement. If the common lands were divided out among individual landholders on a basis of their urbarial-right land, the Varžić zadruga would come out at the small end of the partition.

The village feels a profound grievance against its former Magyar "spahi" (*spahija*). At the time of the separation (*segregacija*) of the peasants' land from the noble's demesne, the government had ordered the village to be provided with forest land equivalent to two yoke per household, or sixty-six yoke in all. According to the villagers, the landowner forced the peasants to plant fifty-six yoke of forest on the pasture assigned to the Association, thus giving them only ten instead of sixty-six yoke of his own woodland. The village feels to this day that the "Count" (*grof*) cheated it out of fifty-six yoke of pasture.

In 1910 the Association bought from the Counts Norman an additional twenty-five yoke of pasture. In 1938 it was negotiating for another two hundred and ten yoke, at a price of 480,000 dinars ($9600), together with a deed-tax (*pristojba*) of 14,000 dinars ($280). Part of the price was to be covered by selling off twenty-three yoke of its best stand of timber. Jozo (IV-9), who was in his twelfth year as President of the Land Association, was taking an active part in enlarging the property of the Association.

Today the main function of the Zelčin Land Association, aside from serving as titular owner of the common lands, is that of a cattle-breeding cooperative. The Association owns three bulls, which are kept in a pen (*bikara*) at the "village-house" (*seoska kuća*), owned by the Association. In 1937 a tax of one dinar per head of cattle was collected to buy oats for the bulls, as the local crop was poor. In addition, the Association owns five or six yoke of meadow, which are mowed by a peasant for one-third of the hay; the balance goes toward feeding the bulls, and, if that supply is inadequate, every household delivers hay to the bull-pen.

THE DRAINAGE-COOPERATIVE

An account of the landed property and usage-rights of the Varžić zadruga would be incomplete without some mention of its membership in the drainage-cooperative, an important undertaking in this low-lying and often marshy region. Eighty-two villages, including Zelčin, belong to the "Lower-Miholjac-Water-Cooperative ("Doljnjo-Miholjačka Vodna Zadruga"), which was founded around 1896 or 1898. The peasants feel a certain antagonism toward the Cooperative. They recall that it was founded by three "Counts" and a Hungarian Minister of Finance, Rudolf Norman, Janković, Pejačević, and Majlath, who first had their own lands drained, thus flooding the lands of the peasants and forcing them to join the Cooperative and to pay the greater part of the expense, as the peasants feel, for the benefit mainly of the "lord's land (*spahijska zemlja*).

In 1938 the President of the Cooperative was a deputy of the Croat Peasant Party, Martinović, but the complaints of the villagers still continued. They objected to paying twelve dinars ($0.24) a year per yoke to the Cooperative, and, in addition, to cleaning a fixed portion of the ditch and river system. The share of the Varžić zadruga consists of cleaning one kilometer of ditches and one of river, and requires about twenty-four days of labor a year. Criticism is directed principally to the cost of the central administration, which, it was claimed, amounted to 700,000 dinars ($1500), with "additional allowances for his wife, children, apartment, automobile, chauffeurs, janitors" ("doplata na ženu, na djecu, za stan, za auto, šofere, podvornike"). The annual meeting of the Cooperative is held in the late autumn at Doljnji Miholjac; at it accounts are rendered, and every third year a committee (*odbor*) of six members is elected.

LIVESTOCK

The main livelihood of the zadruga is derived from the raising of livestock. In 1938 it had four pair of horses and two foals, and eighty-two head of cattle (*marva*). The zadruga also had 111 head of swine, including seventy-eight shoats, twenty-two breed-sows, one boar, and ten hogs for fattening. The swine are sent throughout the year to root in the common oak-forest. The zadruga also had sixty geese, one hundred chickens, four dogs, and seven or eight cats.

All the livestock of the household is zadrugal (*zadružno*). However, this has not prevented the development of individual property of its separate members in both land and livestock.

LIVELIHOOD OF THE ZADRUGA

The Varžić zadruga is approximately eighty percent self-sufficient. It covers its own requirements in wheat, maize, oats, potatoes, cabbage, peppers, other vegetables, meat of all sorts, butter, cheese, milk, and plum-brandy It provides the greater part of its clothing and its wooden implements, and constructs its own buildings, hiring skilled workers only for brick-making and masonry-work. It buys shoes for Sunday-wear, sandals (*opanki*) for work, a few books, hats and furniture, and much of its clothing. The zadruga is as well provided as the average Vermont farmhouse with city-bought beds, wardrobe closets, bureaus, and wash-stands.

The zadruga's cash outlay is about as follows:

sugar, 50 kilograms at 16 dinars	800 dinars	$ 16.
coffee, 3 kilograms at 54 dinars	162	3.24
matches, 360 boxes at one-half dinar each	180	3.60
salt, 3 "metara" at 250 dinars	750	15.

allowance to wives, for clothing,		
900 dinars for each of six	5400	108.
sandals, three pair a year for each of ten		
men at fifty dinars each	1500	30.
shoes, for the women	500	10.
clothing, for men	2000	40.
school, five children at 30 dinars each	150	3.
kerosene	600	12.
farm equipment	500	10.
outside labor for repairs (1937)	250	5.
candles	220	4.40
village reading-room, 6 members at 1 dinar		
per week	330	6.60
newspaper, "Seljački Dom"	72	1.44

No written accounts are kept, and no formal account is rendered by the co-elders. Djuro estimated that annual expenditures for consumption amounted to 11,000 dinars; actually, the expenses listed above, omitting such items as may have been overlooked, totalled 13,414 dinars ($268.28).

The taxes of the zadruga, national and local (*državni i općinski porez*), amount to 20,500 dinars ($410). The expenditure in cash for hired labor totals 3350 dinars ($67). Thus, total cash outlay for the zadruga amounts to 37,264 dinars ($745.28). The per capita outlay, averaged for the twenty-six members of the zadruga, comes to $10.32 for consumption, $15.76 for taxes, $2.58 for labor, or a per capita total of $28.66. The measure of the well-being of the Varžić zadruga is not found in the small volume of its market transactions, but in its excellent conditions of living. Much poorer families usually satisfy a far larger proportion of their needs by purchase at the market or in the local shops.

The Varžić household tries deliberately to keep its cash expenditures at a low level. Coffee, for example, is mainly for entertaining guests; otherwise, milk is the usual beverage. It uses its home-grown honey, and buys little sugar. While the zadruga provides its own brandy, it discourages the use of tobacco; the only member who smokes is Marko (V-23) who has to buy his tobacco from the "individual property" (*osobac*) of his wife. As Djuro says, "We flee from every kind of purchase" ("bežimo od svake kupovine"). However, the household feels that it is prompt to contribute to any community purpose. In 1937 it provided a substantial amount of grain when a collection was made to purchase the *Collected Works* of Antun Radić for the reading room. It has also advanced money of its own to help the Association arrange for the purchase of a new pasture.

The cash income of the zadruga is derived from the sale of pigs, cattle, and wheat. In 1938 it sold thirty head of pigs, but no cattle, as the region was included in a foot-and-mouth-disease quarantine. In 1937 it sold twenty-three head of cattle, and thirty *metara* (one *metar* equals 2.838 bushels) of wheat. Sales and large purchases are usually made at Osijek, the largest nearby market and administrative center.

One item of expenditure, the "allowance for wives," requires special comment. Each of the six wives receives from the zadruga three hundred dinars ($6) in June (*lipanj*), the same in August (*kolovoz*), and again, before Christmas (*Božić*), or nine hundred dinars each year. Djuro remarked jokingly that each wife would spend nine thousand dinars if she could get it. Behind the jest is the real factor that the tendency toward increasing expenditures and the growing differences in taste and habits of life are disruptive factors in the zadrugal way of life. Because this growth of competitive spending is often felt first when young wives, coming from different backgrounds, enter the zadruga, the peasants traditionally blame the disintegration of the zadrugas on the women-folk.

In addition to their money-allowances, each wife receives in spring as many "furrows of flax" (*slogova konoplje*) as she wishes to work. After gathering the flax, she can sell the flaxseed, to buy additional thread or dyestuffs. Contrary to the practice of many zadrugas elsewhere, the women do not own and sell the eggs for their own use; the entire output of eggs is consumed within the household, as are the chickens at the home-farm. Of some three hundred chickens raised each summer at the outlying dairy-farm, fifty hens are kept over the winter; one-half of the remainder goes to the wife of the hired-man, and one-half is divided among the six wives, who sell them to buy extra sewing-materials. "From the [flax-] seed, from the chickens, they also buy" ("od semena, od pilića, još kupuju"). The wives also derive individual incomes from their "private property," which is kept strictly apart from the communal economy of the zadruga as a whole.

INDIVIDUAL PROPERTY

Side by side with the joint property of the zadruga, and separate from it, is the individual property of its members. Individual property, aside from clothing, musical instruments, and so forth, assigned to the individual by the zadruga, cannot arise within the zadruga, for its members have no individual inheritance of zadrugal property and they have no individual earnings, apart from the joint work of the household. However, during the last fifty years individual property has penetrated the Varžić zadruga very considerably, through the dowry (*miraz*) or the inheritance of the wives. The old custom of the village was, on her marriage, to provide each daughter with a "marriage-outfit" (*otpremnina*), consisting of one or two wooden chests filled with clothing for her, shirts for her husband, towels, and household linen; a cow or a sow might be added. The bride thereupon lost all claim to inherit the zadrugal property, which passed intact to her brothers. So long as a zadruga had any male member, no female member or ex-member could inherit its property. However, with the breaking up of many zadrugas and the increasing trend toward smaller families, women began to fall heir to the family property. In addition, since the 1890's the custom has been growing of providing some dowry in land for the daughters, sometimes in anticipation of their future inheritance, sometimes as an outright gift. The development of this new custom and its effects on the zadrugal way of life will be discussed below, in tracing the history of the Varžić zadruga. The development of individual property within the zadruga must be outlined first.

The oldest living wife, Agica (IV-13), received one yoke of land at Bosanjevci (four kilometers away) and four hundred florins (*forinti*) from her step-father (*očuh*). Djuro (IV-12) sold this parcel and bought 2400 "spans" (*hvati*; 2000 *hvati* equal one yoke) in Zelčin. This land is worked "on halves" (*na polovicu*) by a neighbor. In 1938 Agica's share amounted to seven *metara* (one *metar* equals 2.838 bushels) of oats, which she sold to buy additional clothing and embroidery materials for her daughter's "marriage-outfit."

Jozo's first wife, Eva (IV-10), received only her "marriage-outfit," as it was not yet customary in the 1890's to give land in dowry. After her father's death, the family lands passed to his brother, who is childless. In 1927, this uncle, Karlo Mikolin of Harkanovci (four kilometers away), made a gift of 10,000 dinars ($200) to the three sons of Jozo and Eva, Simo (V-13), Mikola (V-15), and Antun (V-17). With that sum they bought two yoke in Zelčin, which are worked on halves by Antun's father-in-law. In 1937 the two yoke gave a yield of twenty-six *metara* of wheat; the three brothers sold their thirteen *metara* at 155 dinars per *metar*, paid taxes amounting to 200 dinars, and divided the balance among themselves, each receiving 605 dinars ($12.10). This represents their "individual property" (*osobac, osobstvo*), which they may freely spend or save, apart from the zadrugal property and income. In August 1938 they had spent part of the 1937 return on their wives, and still had some of it in cash.

In addition to this gift of 1927, Karlo Mikolin has made his three grand-nephews eventual heirs to his entire property. He has "introduced Šimo, Mikola and Antun into zadruga" [with him] ("uveo je Šimu, Mikolu i Antuna u zadrugu"), in order to pass on his property to them, rather than to other relatives. Thus, these three members of the present zadruga have a prospect of inheriting within a few years a substantial property in their own right, apart from the dowry and inheritance of their wives. When these three brothers come into possession of their grand-uncle's land, it is quite possible that they will wish to work it themselves, instead of leasing it out "on halves." In that case, Šimo, Mikola and Antun might conceivably form a new zadruga of their own, separating their shares of the present zadrugal property from those of their half-brother Žiga (V-19) and of their two cousins, Marko (V-23) and Mato (V-27).

Jozo's second wife, Manda (IV-11), received one cow as her *osobac* at her marriage in 1917 or 1918. Manda sold the cow at once, and bought two breed-sows (*krmače*), which have never been kept at the zadruga, but are cared for by a neighbor "on halves." As each litter of shoats is sold, Manda receives one-half the sale-price, and buys additional materials for the "marriage-outfit" of her daughter, Anka (V-20), beyond the equal provision made by the zadruga for each wife's allowance. Manda still owns one of the two sows.

Reza (V-14), Šimo's wife, "brought her marriage-outfit" ("donela je otpremninu"), but no dowry, and hence has no *osobac*. However, her father, a widower with two married daughters, will leave to her half of his eight yoke. In return for looking after her father's household needs, by going daily to bake, cook, and clean for him, Reza will also inherit her father's house and buildings. However, the members of the zadruga feel that he should write out a will, in order to make sure of leaving this additional property to Reza. One can imagine that, if Reza inherits a substantial house and farm-yard, there will be a temptation for her and Šimo to break away from the zadruga and to claim their share of the zadrugal property, in order to set up their own household and farm. At present Reza's "individual property" is only an expectancy.

Eva (V-16), Mikola's wife, brought a marriage-outfit. At the time of her marriage her father was dead, and her zadruga was still headed by her grand-father. After the latter's death, her three uncles split the zadruga into in-dividual holdings, and gave Eva one and three-yoke as her "necessary part" (*nuzni dio*), that is, her legal share of the land. The land, which is in Bosanjevci, is worked by a neighbor "on halves." In 1937 it brought her no income, as the crop covered only the seed. In 1936, a good year, Eva received seven *metara* of wheat as her share; she sold the wheat at 150 dinars a *metar* and bought additional sewing and clothing materials.

Kata (V-18), Antun's wife, brought her "marriage-outfit," including bedding (*kreveti*) and "ducats" (*dukati*). When her father dies, he will leave his land to her, as her only brother has already separated out from his father, receiving his share of the property.

Kata (V-24), Marko's wife, brought a "marriage-outfit" and "furniture" (*namještaj ili mebli; mebli* is more common, but the peasants call it a *švabski* or "Swabian" [i.e., German] word, and try consciously to substitute the Croatian word, *namještaj*). A year after her marriage, Kata received two sows, two cows, two calves, and three yoke of land from her father as "dowry" (*miraz*). This gift was "of his own will" (*po svojoj volji*); it was not agreed upon before marriage.

Kata's three yoke are worked by a neighbor "on halves." In 1938 she received seven *metara* of wheat and twelve and one-half of oats, the wheat bringing 150 dinars a *metar,* the oats 110 dinars. Kata and Marko sold the wheat and oats. With the proceeds they buy "shirts, cigarettes; they arrange something better for themselves; the house [zadruga] provides only what is necessary" ("košulje, cigarete; popravi se nešto bolje, kuća daje samo nužno"). One of Kata's breed-sows died, after having produced one hundred shoats in six years; a single litter sometimes brought in over 1000 dinars ($20). The other sow was sold for 600 dinars ($12). "One cow died; one I sold" ("jedna krava je uginula; jednu sam prodao") for 1100 dinars; Marko sold the two calves for 1000 dinars. The "wedding-collection" (*za svatove*), contributed by the guests and amounting to 7000 dinars ($140), was in part lost; for 4000 dinars Marko bought one yoke in Zelčin, as his *osobac.* From it he received in 1937 eleven *metara* of wheat as his half, after paying the taxes and giving one *metar* to the man who reaped it for him. From this *osobac* Marko paid his own expenses when he had a long illness, although Djuro's (IV-12) operation for appendicitis was paid for by the zadruga.

Thus, apart from the zadrugal property, which is owned and used by the household as a unit, its various members have acquired, or have expectancies of acquiring, substantial amounts of individual property of the Roman-law type. The members are not permitted to spend any time working their own land or looking after their own cattle; all their time is devoted to the work of the zadruga, except for the sewing and embroidery of the women. As Djuro put it, "What she [a wife] has there [at her father's] we do not admit into our zadruga" ("što ona ima tamo, mi ne dademo u našu zadrugu"). The income from the *osobac* is never mingled with that of the zadruga. Yet, each individual small-family within the zadruga, especially each of the four younger couples, has its own income which it spends for its own pleasure beyond the uniform provision of necessities made by the zadruga for all its members, or else it saves it to increase its individual capital in the form of land or livestock. A point may come when the "individual property," added to the "ideal share" of the small-family in the zadrugal property, will promise an easier life. At that point, the urge to break up the zadruga and to separate out will become exceedingly strong. That this may well prove to be the case is suggested by one such break-up, which the zadruga underwent in 1900.

HISTORY OF THE ZADRUGA

The Varžić household first emerged as a self-directing economic unit as the result of the emancipation from serfdom in 1848. As Djuro says, "Jelačić freed Croatia from serfdom" ("Jelačić je oslobodio Hrvatsku od kmetstva"). The family-name, which it acquired somewhat prior to that, is pronounced indifferently as "Važić" or "Varžić." According to tradition, the "r" was added by the Magyar priest (*popa*), who kept the civil register of the village. There are numerous other Varžić families in Zelčin, but no attempt is made to keep track of blood-relationships beyond the lineage of Pavao (I-1). Three terms are used to refer to the zadruga. *Kuća* (house, household) is the everyday term. *Zadruga* is more often employed in referring to the communal family as a legal or property-owning entity. In this juridical sense it has been used officially in Civil Croatia since 1848 and in the nearby Border (Krajina) since the code of 1810. Finally, the members of the zadruga often refer to themselves as a *družina*, or "a lot of people", "a band."

When the zadruga emerged from serfdom, Pavao (I-1), the earliest ancestor of whom its members have any recollection, was its "househead" (*kućni gospodar*). His successors were Mikola (II-1), Ivan (II-4) and Djuro (II-6), in order of age and seniority alike. Djuro was succeeded by Šimo (III-15), then the oldest in the household, but not the eldest in seniority. In 1900 the zadruga, with Šimo as its head, numbered twenty members, including seven married men (*ljudi*), seven wives (*žene*), and six children (*dece*). It was at this time that the first and only partition of the zadruga took place.

It was Marko (III-1) who took the initiative of dividing. "Everyone was dividing up throughout Croatia; well, he too wanted to separate out" ("svi po Hrvatskoj su se delili, pa i on je volio da se odeli"). With four grown men in his own branch of the family, and only four others, one of them very elderly, in the rest of the zadruga, Marko felt that his smaller zadruga would be better off on its own land in its own house. "He thought it would be better so; he had three sons for the work" ("on je mislio da će biti bolje; on je imao tri sina za rad").

The decisive impetus to separate out came, however, from the fact that Marko had now acquired a substantial amount of individual property, thanks to the change in dowry and inheritance custom which had developed markedly in the 1890's. Marko's second wife, Eva (III-3), had received three yoke as *osobac* from her father, and was thus the first wife in the Varžić zadruga to have property of her own. "From his individual property her father bought her three yoke as a dowry" ("iz svoga osobstva njezin otac je kupio njoj tri jutra za miraz"). This small amount of individual property, nevertheless, would not have induced Marko to break away from the zadruga. At this very time a much larger individual holding happened to come his way.

Eva (III-3) was an only child; after her father's death, the property had passed, according to zadrugal custom, to his brother, with whom he lived "in zadruga." This uncle, Djuro Varžić, a distant relative of the present zadruga, being childless, now decided to transfer his eighteen yoke of land to Marko and Eva. He and Marko signed a contract (*ugovor*) at the village-office (*općina*), according to which Djuro transferred his land to Marko, who in turn pledged himself to furnish his uncle-in-law with "life-support" (*doranivanje*; properly, *dohranivanje*). Djuro was to live in his own house; Marko was to provide him annually with sixteen *metara* of wheat, one *metar* of pork, with salt, beans, and potatoes. Djuro was to keep his own cattle, and Marko was to provide their fodder. Marko was to distill plum-brandy for Djuro from the latter's plums. Markos' children "served" ("*doslužili*") Djuro by cutting wood and by sleeping at his house when he was ill. After Djuro's death, his widow continued to receive one-half of the contractual life-support.

Now in possession of twenty-one yoke of his own land, in comparison with about forty yoke for the zadruga as a whole, Marko (III-1) saw his advantage in claiming his share of the zadrugal property, and in setting up a new household with his three sons, two of whom were already married. Accordingly, in March (*ožujak*) 1900, the existing zadruga of twenty members was broken up into three smaller units. Marko (III-1) left the zadruga with his second wife (III-3), his three sons and two daughters-in-law (IV-1, IV-2, IV-3, IV-4, IV-5), forming a new household of seven members. On the same day Marko's half-brother Mišo (III-8) separated with his wife, Mara (III-10), and his daughter, Anka (IV-8), forming a small-family of three members. Unlike Marko, Mišo had received no *osobac* from either of his wives, except for a single cow given to Mara (III-10) on her marriage, for the custom of providing dowry or allowing inheritance in land by a woman who had married out of her own zadruga into that of her husband had not yet appeared in Zelčin in the 1880's. Ten members still remained in the zadruga, with Šimo as "house-head": Šimo (III-15), who died in the following year, his wife Janja (III-16), two of Marko's half-brothers, Mato (III-6), with his wife Jula (III-7), and Ivan (III-11; the progenitor of the entire zadruga of today) with his wife Janja (III-12), and the two sons and two daughters of Ivan and Janja: Jozo (IV-9), Djuro (IV-12), Kata (IV-14), and Vera (IV-15).

GROWTH OF FEMALE INHERITANCE OF LAND

Before tracing the procedure by which the division of the Varžić zadruga was carried out, it is necessary to discover how far back the origin of the new and disruptive custom of female inheritance of land can be traced. So long as the land belonged to a zadruga, a daughter who had married out of her own household had no further claim on its property, which passed to the surviving males, or, for lack of them, to a "son-in-law married into the house" (*domazet*). But, when zadrugas began to break up into numerous small-families, and when the small-families began to restrict their progeny to three, two or one child, the zadruga land began rather frequently to pass in the female line of descent.

The development of individual property through the dowry or the inheritance of the present wives of the Varžić zadruga has been traced. It is curious, but not surprising, to note that its members are inclined to assert the inheritance rights of its wives according to the written code, while stressing the older, zadrugal custom of no female inheritance in order to protect its own property. In a sense, it is trying to have the best of both systems of inheritance. Agica (IV-13), for example, received one yoke and 400 florins as a gift from her step-father, but she inherited nothing from her father. According to Djuro, Agica should have inherited four yoke, an ox, and other property, but her uncle, with the help of the Magyar priest and the "notary" [village official representing the Ministry of the Interior] (*notarius*), sold his own share and Agica's lawful share to his own son-in-law during the War of 1914-1918. To an outsider it seems quite possible that Agica's uncle was acting in harmony with the older, zadrugal concept, just as Karla Mikolin is now doing in taking his three grand-nephews "into zadruga" in order to bequeath to them his childless patrimony. This time the shoe is on the other foot, however, and the Varžić household is not so eager to see the customary, zadrugal rule prevail over the newer written law!

On the other hand, the zadruga is obviously reluctant to give its own daughters dowry or inheritance-rights in the lands of the zadruga. Kata (IV-14), the sister of Jozo and Djuro, received from the zadruga only her "marriage-outfit." In the case of Kata's younger sister, Vera (IV-15), the zadruga, from its joint property, bought her a yoke of land, as dowry, in addition to providing her with a "marriage-outfit," a heifer, and a sow. In this instance, the Varžić zadruga yielded to the newer custom, presumably because, with the growth of the new custom, the marriage which either Vera or the zadruga especially desired could not otherwise have been arranged.

In the preceding generations, down to the 1890's, no wife brought any land to the Varžić zadruga, and no daughter took with her to her husband's household any rights in the land of the zadruga. There is no need to list every such case of non-inheritance, from Eva (II-2) to Janja (III-12), who died in 1927. The first wife in the history of the zadruga to run counter to this rule was Eva (III-3), the second wife of Marko (III-1), who, as we have seen, took the initiative in partitioning the zadruga. Yet, curiously enough, when asked why zadrugas break up, Djuro, the present co-head, repeated without hesitation the answer, universal in Balkan villages, that it is because the women are allowed "to boss" (*gospodariti*). Only when asked if the female inheritance of land did not have something to do with Marko's decision to separate out, did he, after a moment's reflection, agree that this was, in fact, a cause of the break-up.

In addition to the influence of changing custom, successive legal enact-
ments concerning the zadruga are generally credited with having encouraged
the dissolution of the communal family. Prior to the emancipation of the
serfs in Civil Croatia, effected by the Imperial Decree of April 1, 1848, the
zadruga of a serf family, such as that of Pavao Varžić, was regulated, not
by the state, but by the serf-owner, who preferred the zadruga to the small-
family as a surer guarantee of getting in his dues in labor and in kind.
Within a generation after 1848 the pendulum was swinging violently the other
way. By the first general laws of Civil Croatia on the zadruga, in 1870 and
1874, division was permitted even at the request of a single member, and, for
the first time, women, even those who had married out of the zadruga, were
given a share in the inheritance.[7] According to the zadruga law of 1889,
which was in force in 1900, partition was made somewhat more difficult.
Even so, it provided that either the parties to the division might draw up
their own terms for separation, or, if they could not agree, the real estate
was to be divided according to descent by lineage, counting from those
"representatives of lineage" who were alive on January 1, 1837. Movable
property was to be divided into equal shares according to the number of souls,
with a half-share to each member under sixteen.[8] In actuality, the division
of the Varžić zadruga was carried out almost entirely on the basis of traditional peasant concepts of zadrugal justice, and was influenced hardly at
all by the written code of the law-schools and the courts.

DIVISION OF THE ZADRUGAL PROPERTY

The division of the property of the zadruga raised all kinds of problems
concerning the application of both customary and written law. Unlike many
less fortunate zadrugas, the Varžić household was able to effect its division
without recourse to lawyers or to the courts, except for the registration of
the new titles to the real estate in the "Register of Deeds" (*gruntovnica*).
In the elaborate settlement which was finally evolved from the clash of
interests and of legal concepts, different principles were applied in the distribution of each different type of property: the "patrimony," the "bought
land," the livestock, and the buildings.

In 1900 the "patrimony" (*dedovina*) consisted of approximately twenty-
six yoke. This was "old manorial land received from the measuring" [segre-
gation of peasant and noble land in the 1860's] ("staro spahijsko dobito od
mjere"). It was agreed that this land should be divided "by lineage" (*po
lozi*). The chief dispute arose over the question of who was entitled to
share in the division by lineage.

As Pavao (I-1) had had three sons, Mikola (II-1), Ivan (II-4), and Djuro (II-6), the patrimony was first divided into three "ideal shares." But Ivan's line had meanwhile disappeared from the zadruga. His son, Kuzman (III-13) had died about 1879; Kuzman's widow, Ceca (III-14), had "remarried out of the zadruga," thus forfeiting all rights in the Varžić zadruga and acquiring, according to zadrugal custom, the right of subsistence in the new household. Djurdja (IV-16), the daughter of Kuzman and Ceca, upon "marrying out" of the Varžić zadruga, had been provided by the zadruga with a "marriage-outfit," 300 florins, a cow, a sow, and two hives of bees (košnice pčela). This outfit, the zadruga reckoned, was equivalent in value to "a fourth" (jedan fertalj) of a šešija, or seven "old" yoke of land. In return, Djurdja had signed an agreement (namira), renouncing all further claim to the property of her father's zadruga, and her lineage was thus extinct or "married out."

Nevertheless, at the time of the division, Djurdja laid claim to her grandfather's third of the zadrugal "patrimony," with the intention of transferring her share to Marko (III-1). According to Djuro and Jozo, the present co-elders, Marko had been all the more eager to "divide out," as he was counting on receiving the "ideal share" attributed to Kuzman's lineage. Djurdja and Marko were unable to carry through their plan against the opposition of the rest of the zadruga and against the force of the zadrugal tradition, and Kuzman's third finally remained with the zadruga. This solution illustrates the strength of the tradition that the zadruga itself is the residual heir of any extinct lineage within it, and that a daughter, once married out of the zadruga, has no claim to zadrugal land so long as there is a male heir to carry on the household. In strict law, of the modern, written type, the claim could have been made that the equity in Kuzman's third should be divided equally between the lineage of Mikola (II-1) and that of Djuro (II-6), inasmuch as both lineages had contributed to extinguish Djurdja's potential claim. In this case the patrimony would have been divided by two lineages, instead of three, and the shares of Marko and Mišo in it would have been substantially larger than they actually turned out to be. However, so strong was the customary-law concept that neither party to the dispute seems to have raised this issue then or since.

In the division of the patrimony, the basis on which the residual zadruga, with Šimo (III-15) at its head, continually insisted, and to which Marko (III-1) finally agreed, was that Marko (III-1) should receive "one-fourth of one-third" (četvrtina od trećine); Mišo (III-8), the same, Šimo (III-15), one-third, as sole descendant of Djuro's lineage; Mato (III-6), one-fourth of one-third; and Ivan (III-11), one-fourth of one-third. Šimo, Mato, and Ivan at once lumped their "ideal shares" together to continue the zadruga, which, as shown above, also received the remaining one-third accruing to Kuzman's now extinct lineage. Thus, the residual zadruga, under Šimo, "got two-thirds and one-half of one-third"("su dobili dvije trećine i polovinu od trećine"), or ten-twelfths; Marko and Mišo each received one-twelfth of the patrimony. The fourteen fields of "grandfather's land" were now divided into twenty-six parcels, corresponding in value to the respective "ideal shares."[9]

In the division of the "bought land" (*kupovina*)—land which the zadruga had acquired between the "segregation" and 1900—a different principle was applied. This land was divided "according to souls of sixteen" and over ("po dušama od šesnaest godina"). The "bought land," consisting of three fields totalling fourteen and one-half yoke, was now divided into seven parcels, according to elaborate calculations based both on "souls" and on the yield of the various parcels.

In dividing out the livestock and food (*blago i rana*; properly, *hrana*), the zadruga likewise applied "division by souls," with one difference, that each "soul" over sixteen was assigned two shares, and each one under sixteen a single share. This is the only part of the procedure of division which was made in accordance with the provisions of the Law of May 9, 1889.[10] In this instance, it is safer to assume that the written law for once reflected one of the simpler and more widespread rules of customary law, rather than to suppose that the zadruga substituted written for customary law in this single exception. In accordance with the principle applied, Šimo's zadruga received three horses, eleven head of cattle, and twenty pigs, including eight breed-sows and twelve shoats; Marko received three horses, nine head of cattle, and eighteen pigs, including five sows and thirteen shoats; Mišo received one horse, two head of cattle, including a cow and a heifer, and four pigs, including one sow and three shoats. Foodstuffs on hand were divided similarly. Šimo's zadruga also received two wagons (*kola*) and one iron-tipped wooden plow, while Marko and Mišo shared a single wagon but received two iron-tipped plows.

In the division of the buildings of the zadruga, the principle of "division by lineage" was again applied.[11] Marko received the best hay-barn, one horse-barn, and "materials for a house" (*gradja za kuću*). With this material he built a wooden house, which his sons later replaced by one of plastered brick. Mišo was given one hay-barn, part of the pigsty (*svinjac*), and some materials to build a wooden house, in which he still lives. Šimo was assigned the "old house," which was valued at 700 florins, as much as all the other buildings together. Of the two members who remained "in zadruga" with Šimo, Ivan received a wheat-shed, a horse-barn, a hay-barn, and a wagon-shed; Mato, two horse-barns, a corn-crib, a pigpen fence (*plevnja*), and a bee-hive shed (*pčelinjak*).

ROLE OF THE ZADRUGA IN VILLAGE LIFE

This ingenious division of the zadrugal property illustrates the capacity of the zadruga-members for understanding and applying a system of traditional jurisprudence, based on customary law. Their ability to carry through this elaborate partition in a few days sheds light on the qualities of leadership which are developed in the management of a large cooperative household. These abilities are also prized by the village as a whole, and the co-elders of the Varžić zadruga play important roles in the organized life of the community. Jozo (IV-9) has been the "elder" (*starešina*) of the Zelčin Land Association for eleven years, and president of the Farmer's Union (*Gospodarska Sloga*) sponsored by the Croat Peasant Party. Djuro (IV-12) is president of the Peasant's Union (*Seljačka Sloga*), also promoted by the Peasant Party, and president of the School Board. Simo (V-13) is captain (*satnik*) of the Croatian Village Defense (*Hrvatska Seljačka Zaštita*), an unarmed semi-military body likewise organized under the auspices of the Maček Party; Marko (V-23) is a corporal (*rojnik*), and Antun (V-17) a member, in the same organization. The active leadership of a prosperous zadruga in village affairs is greatly facilitated by the division of labor within the large household; a well-managed zadruga can afford to devote a share of its time to public affairs, while the head of a small-family is hard pushed to get his own work done. In addition, a zadruga has considerable voting-power in village elections, if one adds to its own numbers a large share of its "in-laws" and god-parents.

While the Varžić zadruga has become the wealthiest family in the community, it has remained an integral part of the village; in every respect its members live and feel like the other villagers. Its peasant outlook has been preserved so completely that it has never considered educating any of its sons beyond the village-school, and thus fitting him to live outside the village as an artisan or tradesman, or, under favorable circumstances, as an official or a professional man. The thought of the zadruga-members is concentrated on preserving the zadrugal way of life. Both its mode of life and its handling of the vexatious problem of individual property illustrate this conscious striving to retain its unity and its identity. Its other main interest is in preserving and enlarging its economic basis.

One threat, analyzed above, to the continuation of the Varžić zadruga is the growth of individual property. Another weakness is sensed in a visible decline in the physical vigor of the stock. Jozo and Djuro are six feet tall, powerfully built. None of their sons is outstanding in physique. Marko (V-23) had had a long and expensive illness; Mato (V-27) was then undergoing medical treatment in a sanatorium. Djuro is a dynamic personality, a great power, naturally just, quick to sympathize with others or to show his own feeling. When he came to speak of his son who had died in 1935 at the age of nineteen, and displayed an elaborate stone bought for his grave, he turned aside to weep for a moment.

Djuro is a man of definite views, which he upholds vigorously yet courteously. For example, he is opposed to commassation, or consolidation of holdings, because, as a result of the working of the new customs of dowry and female inheritance, the consolidated holdings are soon cut up again into many small strips, and the whole expensive procedure of commassation has to be applied over again. He was bitter against the Stojadinović regime, mainly because he felt that the Croat regions were not treated fairly in the distribution of the tax-burden and of governmental benefits. He was well-stocked with arguments, drawn from the newspapers and pamphlets of the Croat Peasant Party, of which he was one of the local leaders. However, he seemed to have no dislike of Serbs as such. His hatred for the Hungarian landlord ran deep, from his description of the life of the peasants under serfdom, to the difficulties involved in arranging to buy additional pasture from the descendants of the former serf-owner.

* * *

The Varžić zadruga represents one of the most complex and significant types of the Balkan communal family. In a region in which production for the market is unusually well-developed, in which individualistic laws and tastes have penetrated rather deeply, it has not only survived the first shock of the new custom of dowry and female inheritance of land, but has modernized considerably its method of work and broadened its economic basis. The Varžić zadruga has deliberately been stemming the tide which, for fifty years, has been running in favor of the small-family. In accomplishing this primary aim of self-preservation, it has also thrown up vigorous and popular personalities to lead in the political and social development of the village.

According to the predictions of economic liberalism, the Varžić zadruga should have disappeared some forty-odd years ago. Yet, through a profound instinct to preserve the traditional values of the close-knit communal family, it has achieved stability and prosperity. Whether the younger generation will have the same desire and the same ability remains an open question. The accumulation of individual property outside the zadrugal pattern, the growing demand for luxury, the pressure to conform to the recent changes of custom, the ravages of war, these factors may, singly or in combination, result in the destruction of the Varžić zadruga. While it lasts, it is an example of social and economic efficiency to the neighboring small-families and small-zadrugas. The zadruga can be destroyed from within by a single strong will, once the present co-elders have passed from the scene. In the meantime it is an outstanding instance of the power of a multiple communal household to survive and flourish through conscious adaptation to the new conditions of a changing social environment.

NOTES

1. For a general discussion of the problem of the zadruga, see P. E. Mosely, "The peasant family: the zadruga, or communal joint-family in the Balkans, and its recent evolution," *The Cultural Approach to History,* edited by Caroline F. Ware (New York, 1940), pp. 95-108.

2. Data collected on August 27 and 28, 1938. The present tense refers everywhere to the year 1938. The field-trip was made possible by a grant-in-aid of the Social Science Research Council.

3. For the genealogical structure of the household, see Appendix I. Each member is identified in the accompanying table by generation (Roman numeral) and by placing within the generation (Arabic numeral).

4. Deviations from literary Croatian express the actual words of the informants; a few unusual accentuations are indicated by the acute accent.

5. For a description of the parcels, see Appendix II.

6. In the nearby Military Border (*Krajina*) the standard holding for "border-peasants" (*graničari,* Ger. *Grenzer*) was a *Viertelsession* of eight and one-half "new" yoke; Hermann Haller, "Neu-Passau und Neu-Banovci, zwei Schwabensiedlungen in Syrmien" (*Auslandsdeutsche Volksforschung,* I [1937], 49).

7. V. Krišković, *Hrvatsko pravo kućnih zadruga; historijskodogmatski nacrt* (Zagreb, 1925) pp. 31-34.

8. Ibid., pp. 96, 100.

9. For the detailed listing of the fields included under *djedovina* and *kupovina* and their division in 1900, consult Appendix II.

10. Cf. Krišković, op. cit., p. 96; Articles 23 and 33 of the Law.

11. This runs directly counter to Krišković's assertion (op. cit., p. 90) that wooden buildings are usually treated in the partition of a zadruga, as movable property. If this were the case, they would have been divided according to "souls" with a double share going to each "soul" of sixteen or over, and Marko and Mišo would have received one-half, instead of two-twelfths, of the buildings by value. The discrepancy in Krišković's statement of the law is all the more striking in that Marko and Mišo actually treated their shares in the buildings as movable property by dismantling them and setting them up in new locations.

VARŽIĆ FAMILY TREE

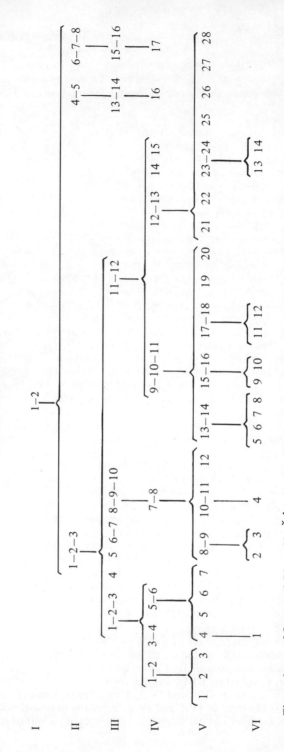

The *zadruga* of Jozo and Djuro Varžić includes: IV, 9, 11, 12, 13; V, 13, 14, 15, 16, 17, 18, 19, 20, 23, 24, 27, 28; VI, 5, 6, 7, 8, 9, 10, 11, 12, 13, 14; a total of 26.

The *zadruga* of Mišo Varžić includes: III, 8; IV, 8, V, 8, 9, 11, 12; VI, 2, 3, 4; a total of 9.

The household of Stjepan Varžić includes: IV, 2, 3, 4, 6, V, 4; VI, 1: a total of 6.

FAMILY-TREE OF THE VARŽIĆ ZADRUGA

Symbols: *living in 1938; d. dead; ae. aged; b. born; m. married (out of zadruga).

    I- 1: Pavao
    I- 2: Stana, his wife, name doubtful
   II- 1: Mikola, son of I-1 and I-2
   II- 2: Eva Sratić, first wife of II-1
   II- 3: Janja Varžić, second wife of II-1
   II- 4: Ivan, son of I-1 and I-2
   II- 5: Manda Mihaljević, wife of II-4
   II- 6: Djuro, son of I-1 and I-2
   II- 7: Jula Matoković, first wife of II-6
   II- 8: second wife of II-6, name forgotten
  III- 1: Marko, son of II-1 and II-2, b. 1848, d. 1926
  III- 2: Reza Pavošević, first wife of III-1
  III- 3: Eva Važić, second wife of III-1, b. 1855, d. 1928
  III- 4: Kata, daughter of II-1 and II-2, m.
  III- 5: Djurdja, daughter of II-1 and II-2, m.
  III- 6: Mato, son of II-1 and II-3
  III- 7: Jula Djurković, wife of III-6
 *III- 8: Mišo, son of II-1 and II-3, b. 1858
  III- 9: Eva Krstić, first wife of III-8
  III-10: Mara Pavlić, second wife of III-8
  III-11: Ivan: son of II-1 and II-3, b. 1860, d. 1915
  III-12: Janja Balikić, wife of III-11, b. 1860, d. 1927
  III-13: Kuzman, son of II-4 and II-5, b. 1850, d. 1879
  III-14: Ceca Zetović, wife of III-13, remarried out of zadruga
  III-15: Šimo, son of II-6 and II-7, d. 1901
  III-16: Janja Pavošević, wife of III-15
   IV- 1: Mikola, son of III-1 and III-2, b. 1865, d. 1934
  *IV- 2: Ceca Šimošić, widow of IV-1
  *IV- 3: Stjepan, son of III-1 and III-3, b. 1873
  *IV- 4: Manda Šimošić, wife of IV-3, b. 1873
   IV- 5: Tomo, son of III-1 and III-3, b. 1888, d. 1928
  *IV- 6: Janja Pavošević, widow of IV-5, b. 1895
   IV- 7: Jozo Horvat, husband of IV-8, b. 1883, d. 1925
  *IV- 8: Anka, daughter of III-8 and III-10, widow of IV-7, b. 1885
  *IV- 9: Jozo, son of III-11 and III-12, b. 1884
   IV-10: Eva Mikolin, first wife of IV-9, b. 1884, d. 1917
  *IV-11: Manda Madjarić, second wife of IV-9, b. 1893
  *IV-12: Djuro, son of III-11 and III-12, b. 1889
  *IV-13: Agica Bošnjak, wife of IV-12, b. 1893
  *IV-14: Kata, daughter of III-11 and III-12, b. 1893, m.
  *IV-15: Vera, daughter of III-11 and III-12, b. 1895, m.
  *IV-16: Djurdja, daughter of III-13 and III-14, m.
   IV-17: Jula, daughter of III-15 and III-16
    V-1, V-2, V-3, sons of IV-1 and IV-2, d. in infancy, names forgotten
   *V- 4: Kata, daughter of IV-5 and IV-6, m., living in household of Stjepan
          Varžić (IV-3) as her husband, Marko Magić, is out of his head

  V- 5: Milan, son of IV-5 and IV-6, b. 1913, d. 1929
*V- 6: Agica, daughter of IV-5 and IV-6, b. 1918, m.
*V- 7: Manda, daughter of IV-5 and IV-6, b. 1921, m.
*V- 8: Franjo Horvat, son of IV-7 and IV-8, b. 1903
*V- 9: Manda Alšić, wife of V-8
  V-10: Jozo Horvat, son of IV-7 and IV-8, d. ae. 23
*V-11: Manda Magić, widow of V-10
*V-12: Mikola Horvat, son of IV-7 and IV-8, b. 1922
*V-13: Šimo, son of IV-9 and IV-10, b. 1903
*V-14: Reza Berečić, wife of V-13, b. 1903
*V-15: Mikola, son of IV-9 and IV-10, b. 1905
*V-16: Eva Strugačević, wife of V-15, b. 1907
*V-17: Antun, son of IV-9 and IV-10, b. 1910
*V-18: Kata Pavošević, wife of V-17, b. 1910
*V-19: Žiga, son of IV-9 and IV-11, b. 1922
*V-20: Anka, daughter of IV-9 and IV-11, b. 1924
  V-21: Stjepan, son of IV-12 and IV-13, d., ae. 1 yr.
  V-22: Stjepan, son of IV-12 and IV-13, d., ae. 2 mos.
*V-23: Marko, son of IV-12 and IV-13, b. 1913
*V-24: Kata Magić, wife of V-23, b. 1913
  V-25: Ivan, son of IV-12 and IV-13, b. 1916, d. 1935
*V-26: Janja, daughter of IV-12 and IV-13, b. 1918, m.
*V-27: Mato, son of IV-12 and IV-13, b. 1924
*V-28: Manda, daughter of IV-12 and IV-13, b. 1930
*VI- 1: child of V-4, name not recorded, living in house of IV-3
*VI- 2: Mara Horvat, daughter of V-8 and V-9, b. 1925
*VI- 3: Jozo Horvat, son of V-8 and V-9, b. 1929
*VI- 4: Djuro Horvat, son of V-10 and V-11, b. 1925
*VI- 5: Stjepan, son of V-13 and V-14, b. 1921
*VI- 6: Šimo, son of V-13 and V-14, b. 1923
*VI- 7: Eva, daughter of V-13 and V-14, b. 1928
*VI- 8: Mladen, son of V-13 and V-14, b. 1932
*VI- 9: Pavao, son of V-15 and V-16, b. 1926
*VI-10: Mara, daughter of V-15 and V-16, b. 1929
*VI-11: Tomo, son of V-17 and V-18, b. 1928
*VI-12: Pero, son of V-17 and V-18, b. 1932
*VI-13: Fabijan, son of V-23 and V-24, b. 1932
*VI-14: Janja, daughter of V-23 and V-24, b. 1934

APPENDIX II

The "patrimony" (djedovina) was divided as follows in 1900:

No.	Name of parcel	Minutes from house	Total area in "spans"	Marko's share	Mišo's share	Zadruga's share
1.	Markov laz	1	4,207	1,200	—	3,007
2.	Staro selo	3	ca. 5,000	—	1,300	3,700
3.	Ruščansko	5	ca. 4,030	1,200	1,200	1,630

4.	Gaj–1st	15	ca. 4,000	—	—	4,000
5.	Gaj–2nd	15	ca. 2,000	—	—	2,000
6.	Zelčinice	20	ca. 4,540	1,200	1,200	2,140
7.	Gorača	15	ca. 5,000	1,200	—	3,800
8.	Selišče–1st	14	4,300	1,200	—	3,100
9.	Selišče–2nd	14	2,200	—	—	2,200
10.	Duže	15	4,038	1,200	—	2,838
11.	Gajić	25	4,000	—	1,300	2,700
12.	Vraničevo	30	4,000	1,200	—	2,800
13.	Plana	35	4,000	1,200	—	2,800
14.	Ležaj	20	500	500	—	—

The "bought land" (*kupovina*) was divided as follows:

15.	Velika Bara	20	16,000	—	—	16,000
16.	Zelčinice	30	3,000	1,200	200	1,600
17.	Mlaka	15	10,000	3,333	1,666	5,000

5: THE DISTRIBUTION OF THE ZADRUGA WITHIN SOUTHEASTERN EUROPE

Philip E. Mosely

The zadruga, or communal multiple family, has long been recognized as one of the basic forms of social organization within the societies of Southeastern Europe, but it has usually been an object of romantic musings and patriotic theorizings rather than of precise investigation. The scarcity of detailed descriptions of its structure and functioning has been paralleled by the absence of exact records concerning its incidence and the factors which have made for its preservation or its disappearance.[1]

The difficulty of utilizing official statistics even to identify the location of larger than average households was brought home to me during my field-studies in several Bulgarian counties. In passing I should note that in pre-war Bulgaria statistics were, so far as I could observe, gathered and processed with greater care than in nearby countries. However, in one Bulgarian village in Kyustendil county, I discovered on the spot that several medium-sized communal families, averaging fifteen or sixteen members each, had been recorded in the census on the basis of the component small or biological families, with five or six members apiece. In another village, in the Rhodope Mountains, the official statistics recorded the presence of several large communal families, averaging some twenty-seven members each. Investigation in the village showed that these supposedly communal families had, in fact, broken up almost thirty years earlier, as a by-product of their transfer from Ottoman to Bulgarian rule, in 1912. However, several smaller households, which had formerly constituted a large zadruga, had continued to live in the same large stone houses grouped, in each case, to form a large enclosed barnyard.

The village, inhabited by Bulgarian-speaking Moslem Pomaks, lacked convenient sites for building additional homes. Its stone houses could not be readily dismantled and divided, as frequently occurs in regions of wooden

Reprinted from *The Joshua Starr Memorial Volume, Jewish Social Studies* V (1953), 219-230.

construction, and the spacious enclosed farmyards were adequate for the needs of several smaller families. Hence the heirs of the former large zadrugas had remained in the old communal houses, and were still recorded by the census-taker as constituting single large households, even though each small household now had its own land, livestock and equipment.

In this brief study, I shall not rely on statistics, but shall attempt to summarize my own impressions, based on direct observation and on a few reliable studies. The conditions described here relate to the period just prior to World War II, and thus sum up a long period of slow or rapid changes. The political and social changes which have affected the Balkan villages during and since World War II have doubtless been drastic in their impact. Probably the Pomak villagers who received me so hospitably in 1938 are among the Bulgarian Moslem groups which have been uprooted since 1949. Many of them were expelled across the frontier into Turkey, whose language they do not speak, and others are reported to have been taken from their villages and families for conscripted labor in mines and on construction projects.

But first, a brief reminder of what the zadruga is: it can best be defined as an extended family consisting of two or more small or biological families (father, mother, minor children) owning land, livestock, and tools in common and sharing the same livelihood. In a society of zadrugal tradition, a family may grow for several generations without undergoing a division of the household or of its property. I had occasion before the war to study zadrugas of fifty, sixty-four, seventy-five and eighty-three members, although family communities of eight to twenty members were encountered far more frequently. One special feature of the zadrugal tradition, one which distinguishes it clearly from the patriarchal family, is that each male member of it possesses a recognized, if latent, right to a share of the communal property and is free, if he chooses, to leave the zadruga, to take his share of its property, as defined by customary or written law, and to found either a small family or, in cooperation with one or more members of the former large household, a new and smaller zadruga.

In contrast to patriarchal custom, zadrugal custom rests on the equality of married males within it, and basic decisions are made by them jointly. The zadruga head, designated by seniority of age or descent, by rotation or by election, serves as the executive agent of the community. In one large household in Herzegovina, the "elder" or "starješina" described himself to me, both humorously and correctly, as the zadruga's "minister of foreign affairs," for it was he who carried on buying and selling and argued with the tax-collector.

Even in regions where the zadruga has been declining steadily, the peasants are well aware of its great role in the past. When conditions within Turkey or near the Ottoman frontier made life and property insecure, a zadruga possessing from ten to fifteen "guns" was a real strongpoint. Each male over fourteen was considered a full-fledged member of the community only if he had a gun, which the zadruga provided. In long periods of guerilla warfare, from the Karadjordje uprising of 1804 until 1945, the zadruga, unlike the small family, could maintain several fighters in the field, while the old men, women and boys carried on the work of the household.

Probably the greatest single importance of the zadruga was that the organization of labor into substantial units facilitated the conquest of the Balkan forests by the herdsman and the plowman. It is often forgotten that the larger part of the Balkans was the scene of an intensive pioneering effort throughout the nineteenth century. Pre-1912 Serbia, long famous for its dense forests, from which its central region took the name "Šumadija," may have contained around 300,000 inhabitants in 1815. Today it has few trees and contains around 3,500,000 inhabitants. The conquest of the forest and the soil was accomplished through human and animal labor, usually organized in zadrugas. Similar though less striking changes have occurred in many other parts of Southeastern Europe, and there too the zadruga was often the basic social instrument for the task of pioneering.

Within Southeastern Europe it is possible, even on the basis of the incomplete data available, to trace crudely certain areas of high and low incidence of the zadruga. At the same time it is possible, though more difficult, to outline hypotheses which may help to explain these differences in its incidence. This article represents a first attempt to identify the regional distribution of the zadruga and to suggest tentatively some explanations for these social phenomena.

As a result of my field-studies I believe I have identified three principal belts of zadruga society, each containing numerous sub-regions. One belt consists of the tribal society of pre-1912 Montenegro and of Northern Albania. Until recent decades, this tribal region probably represented the most ancient social system still extant in Europe. Here the zadruga, formerly a strong element within the tribal system, had largely disappeared by 1938.

A second and larger belt extended south, east and north from the tribal regions, throughout the mountain systems of Bosnia, Herzegovina, western Croatia, northern and central Macedonia and central Albania (east of Tirana and Berat). In this non-tribal zone the raising of cattle and sheep, together with the late persistence of insecurity of life and property, and the continuance of a largely natural economy, gave the zadruga a strong lease on life into the twentieth century. In the absence of peasant servitude to the landlords the strong family household was the center of personal security, economic effort and social satisfaction. Isolated areas of conditions similarly favorable to the zadrugal way of life can also be identified in the mountains of western Bulgaria, in northern Greece and in southwestern Albania (Kurvelesh).

A third belt can be traced, again, to the north, east and south of the second, extending out irregularly across the plains and rolling valleys of Croatia, Slavonia, pre-1912 Serbia, western and central Bulgaria, southern Macedonia and southern Albania. Here the zadrugal tradition had, in earlier times, possessed varying degrees of strength, but by the late 1930's its influence and its memory were fading steadily. Where the zadruga had been closely associated with personal servitude of the peasants to the landowning nobility, as in parts of pre-1848 Croatia-Slavonia, or until 1912 in the valleys of Macedonia, the overthrow of serfdom was usually followed within a generation by the dissolution of the zadruga. Where the zadruga had been the foundation of military colonies of the "foot-Cossacks" of *Grenzer,* as in the regimental villages of Croatia, Slavonia and Vojvodina (Banat), its disappearance was less explosive. Here the rise in economic well-being, the limitation of family size, the rise in social mobility, destroyed the basis for its continuance.

Beyond this third belt the zadrugal tradition is unknown, or has been long overlaid by other social traditions. To the northwest of the Balkan peninsula, Slovene society shows no trace of a zadruga system. Under serfdom, and after its abolition, Slovene peasant families followed a pattern of hereditary holdings, maintained more or less intact as family and productive units through transmission to a single son, the eldest or the youngest, more often the latter. Other male heirs were assisted by the family to learn a trade or to become petty officials; or, at worst they became urban laborers or migrated. Once established in new occupations and usually in new locations, they had no right to share in the family capital.

A not dissimilar custom prevailed on the coasts of Dalmatia and Albania. Here the inherited Venetian system of the colonate denied the peasants the right to subdivide their landholdings, and thus encouraged the surplus sons to look to the sea and later to migration overseas for the livelihood which was denied them on the small parcels of cultivable land. The opportunity for a zadruga to pioneer into the uplands and forests was denied here by the narrow fields and the sun-baked karst.

Similarly, the Mediterranean system of agriculture, coupled with fishing, sea-faring and emigration, has been typical of most of Greece and of eastern Bulgaria. The openings to traders and artisans within the Ottoman Empire, the nearness of large consuming centers like Istanbul, Salonika and Athens, the lack of elasticity in the supply of land, the long-established and precise bounds of individual ownership, made the small family on its barely adequate plot, supplemented by outside earnings, the dominant social form. In the following survey of factors which appear to have influenced the distribution of the zadruga I shall not refer to the Mediterranean zone except in respect to regions where its influence has impinged on areas of zadrugal custom.

In outlining briefly the three principal zones within which the zadrugal way of life has played an important role, I lumped together the tribal zone of "old" Montenegro (pre-1912) and of Alpine Albania, as an area in which the zadruga has declined rapidly during the present century. As a matter of fact, the causes for this decline are, I believe, somewhat different in the two tribal regions. In Montenegro a variety of factors has been at work to undermine both the tribe and the zadruga; in tribal Albania the tribe has remained strong while the zadruga has undergone a steady decline.

So long as Montenegro remained an independent state (until 1918), the absolutism of the ruler, scarcely modified by a pseudo-constitution, was balanced uneasily on a seething caldron of tribal loyalties, rivalries and conflicts. As long as the ruler was himself viewed by other Montenegrins as the leader of one tribe, or an alliance of tribes, who had been clever and ruthless enough to raise himself above the others, the tribal way of life remained rather stable.

However, when Montenegro was absorbed into a centralized bureaucratic state after 1918, the political, military and economic functions of the tribes began to wither away rapidly. Along with other rights, the tribes were deprived of the right to assign the use of their lands, and the cultivable land rapidly passed into individual ownership in law and fact, as it had been tending to do in practice. The forest and pasture remained, theoretically, at the disposal of the tribes, as before; but in practice representatives of the central government took over effective control of their use. Blood-feuds, the tribal way of maintaining justice, gave way to courts and gendarmes. In many regions the tribal assemblies ceased to meet, for lack of real business to transact; elsewhere, they were forbidden by the central government because they were regarded as the focus of Montenegrin separatism. Former leading tribal families retained some personal and political influence, especially by attaching themselves to Pašić's Serbian Radical Party. Tribal attachments remained strong, especially when Montenegrins met in Belgrade or in Detroit.

As long as cultivable land was regarded as a free good which belonged to the tribe and could, when not in use by one tribesman, be plowed by another, the zadruga offered an effective way of bringing the stubborn soil into use. As the scarce land remained in constant use by one family and then passed into its legal possession, there was no pioneering function left to the zadruga. The assured possession of a definite piece of land by a small family was now more important than the maintenance of a larger and more mobile unit of collective labor power, such as the zadruga had provided.

In Montenegro it became clear to me that the zadruga thrives or persists when there is a surplus of cultivable or usable land, even if the available soil is submarginal from a strictly economic point of view, for the joint family is an efficient social instrument for the heavy work of bringing land into use. When the physically usable land has all been taken up, the zadruga has rough going. For one reason, a greater number of persons cannot get a sufficient livelihood from an unchanged and inflexible quantity of land. In addition, since each zadruga has a fixed quantity of land available at any given time, and since, over a period of time, zadrugas increase inequally in size of membership, a zadruga which grows in numbers but can neither buy nor pioneer additional land will find its expected margin of livelihood shrinking away. Under these conditions the urge to break up the zadruga is likely to take an acute form, while the socially approved method of breaking it up is continuously present in the latent right of each male zadruga-member to claim his share of the common property. Zadrugal land, particularly the inherited land or patrimony, is usually divided on the basis of genealogical descent; thus each of three brothers would receive one-third of the land when the zadruga separated into three small-families. But if, in the next generation, one brother had one son, the second had two and the third had three sons, these sons would receive, respectively, one-third, one-sixth and one-ninth of the land. Thus, the "ideal" or latent shares of the partners in a zadruga vary greatly and these "ideal" shares determine the actual sharing of the land when the zadruga splits up into its component small-families.

When hunger presses in upon a zadruga in which several brothers or cousins have varying numbers of dependents, the urge to separate out overcomes family pride. In studying the break-up of one Montenegrin zadruga I found this motive well expressed. "I had two children; my brother had five. Why should I work to feed his when there was not enough to feed all? I could live better on my own share of the land, and my children would have more land after me."

Since by the beginning of this century increasing numbers of Montenegrins could not gain a livelihood in the barren mountains, they began to migrate in search of work. Many kept their families and their plots of land in the villages, and used their outside earnings to buy additional land, thus driving the price of scarce land to uneconomic levels. Fortunately they paid very little in taxes; otherwise, many more families would have been driven off the land because of its rising price. Migration, and differential incomes gained through it, led to competition in the way of life, to the increasing centering of life on the small family. As one Montenegrin described it, "I went to Argentina and sent money home. When I returned after five years, the house (the zadruga) had used up my money. So I separated out with my wife and children; when I again sent money from Argentina, it was all for them."

In the mountains of northern Albania tribal loyalty and custom had remained strong up to the end of World War II, and they are reported to be a dominant factor even today. Still, the tribal way was changing. The opportunities for raids, for subsidy from the Ottoman government, were gone. The tribal Albanians, while possessed of proportionately more usable land than the Montenegrins, were increasingly hard-pressed. The opportunity for the zadrugal type of pioneering was diminishing. Still, it is not easy to build a hypothesis which will explain the decline of the zadruga in this region. Outward migration was slight. Usually only persons condemned to exile for crimes against the tribe, such as shooting a woman or child, left the tribe, never to return.

Perhaps the relatively slower decline of the zadruga in tribal Albania should be explained by the relatively slow increase of pressure or population on a somewhat more elastic supply of land (given a stable and inelastic system of cultivation), and by a self-sealing impermeability to outside economic and cultural influences, such as those which, in Montenegro, worked solely in favor of the individual family and against the zadruga. It is perhaps a tenable assumption that the zadruga was always a less necessary and a less stable form of organization in the tribal areas. Personal security, political influence, access to usable land, social satisfactions through joint enterprises in war and in jollification were centered primarily on the tribal unit rather than on the zadruga. This overshadowing of the zadruga by the tribe stands out in contrast to the strong zadrugal tradition which has played a dominant role in the second of the three zones.

Although the second zone consists of many local regions, it shares certain basic conditions, whether one studies the Skopska Crna Gora of northern Macedonia, the Shëngjergj region east of Tirana, or the Banja Luka region of northern Bosnia. Its regions are relatively remote in social distance, if not always in geographical space, from modern lines of communication, and from towns. They show a high degree of self-sufficiency in their economic life, often providing all their foodstuffs except coffee and sugar, chiefly valued for their ceremonial values in tendering hospitality, and making at home most of their clothing and part of their footwear. Seasonal transhumation with herds and flocks has survived in some parts, and some groups of Aromunian herdsmen have no permanent homesites, although they follow permanent routes with their flocks and herds.

In this zone security against Turkish tax-collectors and gendarmes, as well as against marauders, was greater for larger units. As numbers grew, life itself depended on a continuous pioneering of new land, until in many regions the tops of the mountains are fully cultivated, leaving the mountainsides to forest and grazing. At the same time these regions had escaped the grip of the Turkish landlord, the *spahi*, together with his constant interference in their lives. The Turkish authorities, and to a considerable extent the new governments which succeeded them, had to be satisfied with a more or less nominal tribute. It is unnecessary, in my opinion, to explain the strength of the zadruga in these regions of diverse languages, dialects and religions by reference back to a "Dinaric" race, as some writers have maintained. When large numbers of people of the second belt settled in the plains regions beyond it, they soon adjusted their way of life to the conditions imposed or offered by the new environment.

One striking feature of the second belt, with its strong zadrugal conditions, was that each small family was, potentially, a zadruga. If a small family prospered, escaped the natural and political catastrophes which threatened it periodically, and developed its livelihood parallel with the growth of its numbers, it was bound to be a zadruga within two generations. Many efforts have been made to distinguish between the small family, or *inokoština*, and the communal zadruga, as if they were two separate institutions existing side-by-side. This misplaced assumption ignores the fact that customs, particularly of ownership, inheritance and dowry, are uniform within a peasant community which operates without a caste system. If the customs favor the persistence of a social organization like the zadruga, then the whole customary basis is zadrugal, and each small family may, under favorable conditions, develop into a zadruga. If the customs change so that each marriage carries with it a regrouping of property based on the wife's receiving a dowry or inheritance in land, then the basis of life ceases to be zadrugal in character, and within a short time the small family will be the only viable form of family organization.[2]

From an investigation of zadrugas in about twenty regions of the second belt I came to the conclusion that in this zone the basic shift from a zadrugal to a small-family basis of peasant society was not due primarily to political and economic causes. Actually, the change from Ottoman rule to local national rule was primarily a psychological change, expressed in the development of national pride. In the mountain regions the direct effect on the villages was slight. The major shift from zadrugal to individual land-owning was also not prepared or accompanied by any significant changes in the instruments or organization of labor. Changes in the legal system, especially in giving to women rights of dower and inheritance in land, made themselves felt, in practice, only with a lag in time; and by 1938 these changes had not been felt in many parts of the second belt. Where they were felt, this has occurred, it seemed to me, only after a psychological revolution had already begun in the minds of the peasants.

I was driven to conclude that in this second belt the breakdown of the zadruga was being brought about primarily by a psychological change, by the sudden realization that the zadruga was not "modern," and that it was "modern" to live in single households. The phenomenon of psychological revolutions occurring in an economically stable or even stagnant environment is one which needs much further study. In any case, by 1938 the second zone displayed, in most of its regions, a definite tendency toward the disintegration of the zadrugal tradition. Although large numbers of zadrugas persisted, many larger ones had already broken up into smaller ones, and only a relatively few zadrugas, among the small number of case-studies which could be made, showed a tendency to grow in numbers and in strength.

Geographically and socially the second zone tends to merge through valleys and across foothills into the third zone, in which the disintegration of the zadruga began several generations ago. In this wide belt, the zadrugal tradition of inheritance of land solely through the male line had crumbled away by 1938, and the spread of the new custom of the transmission of land through the female line was an almost insuperable obstacle to the development of new zadrugas. This process of disintegration was well under way in the plains of Croatia-Slavonia by the 1870's, in pre-1912 Serbia by the 1880's and 1890's, and in the Bulgarian valleys by around 1900. Here, unlike the situation in the mountainous belt, economic changes accompanied the psychological revolution. The growth of transportation, of more constant exchanges between village and town, the increasing use of manufactured goods in place of homemade wares, the appearance of differentials in consumption, the greater frequentation of towns, and the impact of townsmen-made laws favoring individual ownership, had their composite effects. While many medium-sized zadrugas, of ten to twenty members, persisted for several decades and some persisted in 1938, the pioneer values of the zadrugas had faded to a tradition of pride, rather than representing any longer a social necessity.

As these three basic belts of zadrugal tradition began to emerge from my field-studies, I was particularly struck by the absence of ethnic or national differentiations in the structure and functioning of the many and varied types of zadrugas which I had identified. In central Bosnia, for example, I studied Croatian, Serbian and Moslem-Slav zadrugas within a single valley, and except for differences in proper names, forms of greeting and religious customs, I found no essential difference among the three groups, which have been so sharply distinguished by their religious and national sentiments and loyalties. This would suggest that in Bosnia the zadrugal way of life is much older than the religious and national differentiations which developed later. Similarly, in the region of Korçë (Koritsa) in Albania, I studied Albanian-Moslem, Albanian-Orthodox, Bulgarian and Aromunian (Kutso-Vlah) villages within a single small region, only to find no significant differences in the structure and functioning of the zadruga or in the process of its decline. Here a common ethnic unity could not be assumed, but nevertheless the uniformity of social functioning was striking.

In the region of the former Military Border of Slavonia, I found Croat, Serb and German villages in a rather late stage of disintegration of the zadruga, again with no recognizable differences of significance. Here, however, it had to be assumed that the zadrugal organization had not been native to the German colonists, but had first been imposed upon, later fully assimilated by, them. The one region in which a national difference might be imputed was in Southern Albania, in the valley south of Gjirokastër (Argyrokastron). Here the communal family structure was in a more advanced stage of destruction within a Greek village which I studied than it was in a neighboring one inhabited by Moslem Albanians.

I concluded, however, that this represented a difference in stage of development rather than a national divergence. The Greek village had many of its people in America, and in 1938 it lived more from remittances than from cultivation of the land. American-style clothes, the use of English among the villagers in discussing topics unfamiliar to the village way of life, and a highly individualized attitude toward the family and its livelihood had completely overlaid the earlier tradition in a little more than one generation. While the nearby Albanian village had also witnessed a substantial migration to and return from America, it had not undergone any significant restructuring through the inflow of capital and income, and the returning migrant had been reintegrated into the village pattern, which was still largely shaped by the small zadruga.

Differences in religion were, I found, of some significance. Although new acts of polygamy had been forbidden in Yugoslavia and Albania by 1938, this custom had some effect on the structure of the zadruga. In several Moslem zadrugas I found that the father or the elder brother had two wives. In these communities the second wife was acquired only after the younger males had each been provided with his wife. In two cases the first wife of the elder had selected the second wife and governed the latter's life in detail. In effect the first wife had "retired" in full honor as the head of the female side of the household, while the new and younger wife had to carry many extra burdens, including fulfillment of the commands of the senior wife.

In two other case-studies of Moslem zadrugas, I found that the household of the second wife of the zadruga elder was established in another locality, and that members of the zadruga spent part of the year in one household and part in the other. In winter most of the flocks and herds were taken to the second household, in the coastal plain, to graze. In summer they were brought back to the hills and were managed from the first household.

In a Moslem zadruga I also found one example of the levirate, under which the surviving brother had married the widow of his heirless brother. In Christian zadrugas, on the other hand, the widow would not be allowed to remarry within the zadruga, although she would customarily continue to live and work within it, especially if she had children, sharing in its livelihood but not in its property. Otherwise, she could return to her parents' home or remarry.

In all case-studies but one I found that marriage within the zadruga was unknown and was considered as out of the question even if the degree of consanguinity was so remote as to make intra-zadruga marriage possible under the rules of the church. The one exception to this which I came upon had occurred in a Croatian zadruga near Karlovci. This household had grown so large, with seventy-five members, that while its members could recite their genealogies for four generations back to the oldest living members, they would not trace their lines back to a common progenitor. This zadruga, in fact, broke up shortly after a marriage had taken place within its membership, in 1929. But in 1938 I could not discover any connection between the marriage and the break-up of the community. Probably both the intra-zadrugal marriage and the dissolution of the zadruga were signs rather than causes of a psychological withdrawal of loyalty from the family community. Unlike the ethnic factor, however, the religious factor is associated with significant differences among zadrugas located within the same region.

The predominant association of zadruga types is with specific regions. Since the identification of these regional types has been planned as the subject of a collection of case-studies, I can only offer the conclusion here, without the evidence. Regional variations can be identified in all aspects of zadruga life. In fact, they are so numerous that even the generalized definition of the zadruga given earlier cannot accommodate all zadruga types which have been recorded. One striking aspect of the zadruga is its high degree of adaptation to regional variations in economic and social conditions and needs. In that sense it must be regarded as a social instrument which was both highly stable and highly flexible under conditions of a local, self-sufficient and insulated economy, and of a stable, preliterate and isolated culture. In a realistic study of the zadruga it is necessary, I have found, to give no weight to ethnic or nationality factors in their modern context, and relatively minor weight to religious differences, and to devote primary attention to regional economic and social factors in attempting to account for differences in the social and psychological structure and the viability of the zadruga.

NOTES

1. The author was enabled to make case-studies of the zadruga in some forty-five localities within Yugoslavia, Albania and Bulgaria in 1936, thanks to a post-doctoral fellowship of the Social Science Research Council, and in 1938, thanks to a grant-in-aid of the Council. For a general report of the methods used, see his "The peasant family: the zadruga, or communal joint-family in the Balkans, and its recent evolution," in *The Cultural Approach to History*, edited by Caroline F. Ware (New York, 1940), pp. 95-108.

2. For a study of rapid change from zadrugal to small-family custom in the third zone, see P. E. Mosely, "Adaptation for Survival: The Varžić Zadruga," *Slavonic and East European Review*, Vol. XXI (American Series, Vol. II), March 1943, pp. 147-173.

6: THE RUSSIAN FAMILY:
OLD STYLE AND NEW

Philip E. Mosely

Despite Lenin's generally conservative views on questions of individual morals and personal taste, the dominant attitude of the new Bolshevik rulers toward the family was one of hostility. For almost two decades after the October Revolution the expressed purpose of the new leadership was to undermine and eventually to destroy the family. To the Bolshevik shapers of the new regime, the family appeared as the final refuge of the original sin, the urge to acquire and own private property, as the center of loyalties which resisted the demands of the totalitarian party for complete subordination of the self to the collective, and as the channel through which pre-Bolshevik and therefore anti-Bolshevik values were transmitted to the new generation. Admittedly, the family, unlike the banks, could not be dissolved by decree, but new legislation, new educational pressures, and the forces of party discipline were mobilized to reshape the family to the demands of a hostile and demanding regime.

Since about 1935 the Soviet regime has come to terms with the Russian family. It has endeavored, with considerable success, to harness its great strength to serve the needs of the regime, to stabilize and strengthen Soviet society. In the course of adapting its attitudes and policies to the requirements of operating a monolithic collective society, the Soviet leadership has swung full-circle in such matters as freedom of divorce, freedom of abortion, and responsibility of the parents for the upbringing and conduct of the children.

The Bolshevik revolutionaries were in revolt against the family institutions of the society within which they had grown up. In this, as in so many other aspects of their thinking, they represented a totalitarian-minded trend within a numerous, variegated, and amorphous intelligentsia. The picture

Reprinted from Ruth Nanda Anshen, (ed.), *The Family: Its Function and Destiny*, rev. ed. (New York, 1959), pp. 104–122. Copyright © 1959 by Harper & Row, Publishers, Inc.

which the Bolsheviks painted of the pre-revolutionary family was a simplified and distorted focusing of stereotyped images which the radical intelligentsia had formed of the existing types of Russian families.

SOME STEREOTYPES OF THE PRE-REVOLUTIONARY FAMILY

In the eyes of the intelligentsia, the family of the nobility, particularly the landed gentry, had grave vices. Within this class the element of hereditary social prestige, noble descent, and inherited property, especially in the form of landed estates, played an important part in the selection of a marriage partner. While many of the gentry families reflected a genuine warmth and intimacy of family life and of moral equality among the members of the family, the pattern of loveless marriages, contracted under family pressure or for social ambition, and followed by emotional and ethical estrangement between husband and wife, was sufficiently fixed as a stereotype so that the intelligentsia rejected it as unacceptable. After the revolution, the elimination of most forms of inherited wealth, aside from small remnants of jewelry, furniture, clothing, and books, sufficed to destroy the gentry as a class; its surviving members strove as individuals to fuse with the intelligentsia, to which many of them had, in fact, attached themselves spiritually and socially before the revolution.

Several of Chekhov's plays, such as *The Cherry Orchard* and *Three Sisters,* expressed a clear presentiment of the crumbling of the gentry way of life and the family pattern upon which it rested. In the decades before the revolution the traditional motives for subordinating the individual to the extended family and its demands were rapidly losing their force, and new values, based on the contribution of the individual to the needs of a rapidly changing society, were taking their place. With this change, marriage and the formation of the small independent family were becoming acts of individual choice, not a response to the expectations of the extended family.

The merchant class in Russian society was viewed with even less sympathy than the gentry by the liberal and revolutionary intelligentsia. It was generally depicted, as in the plays of Ostrovsky, as a milieu of extreme conservatism in politics and religion and of overbearing paternal authority. For many of the new educated groups, seeking new paths for Russia, the break with the older ideals of orthodoxy, nationalism, and autocracy was intimately intertwined with a rejection of the domination of the property-holding and property-accumulating father image, personified most vividly in the literary figure of a tyrannical merchant paterfamilias.

Within the peasantry of the pre-revolutionary period, two main types of family structure and psychology can be distinguished. The well-to-do peasant family, which owned or held under collective tenure sufficient land to meet its full needs and perhaps to accumulate some modest property, was a strongly paternalistic structure. For it, questions of making influential alliances with other "strong" families and accumulating property through dowry or inheritance were more important than personal preferences when it came time to marry, and the families of married sons usually remained in the household and under the control of the father. The subordination of both wives and grown-up sons even to despotic decisions of the father found legal support both in village custom and written law until the bonds of the commune and the extended family were loosened by the growth of a money economy and the partial agrarian reforms instigated by Stolypin.

On the other hand, the legally absolute power of the father, it must not be forgotten, was tempered by a widely ramified pattern of kinship, in-law and godparent relationships. In all family decisions, such as marriage or inheritance, blood kin, in-laws, and godparents had a firm right to be heard as the voice of village custom and conscience. Even when new legislative decrees, between 1907 and 1914, opened the way for individual peasants to break away from the control of the land-repartitional commune and for the adult sons to escape from the control of the father through claiming their shares of the land upon marriage, actual custom was usually slow in changing. The areas where the patriarchal family predominated were relatively slow to respond to the revolutionary stimuli of 1917; in the second revolution, the collectivization of the villages in 1929-1933, they resisted the pressures of the regime longest.

Within the numerous land-poor peasantry, a different type of family structure prevailed. For a large part of the peasantry, caught between overcrowding on the land and the widening gap between low productivity and the growing numbers of mouths to feed, the concept of "peasant dignity," of a stable family living a largely self-sufficient life under the old patriarchal customs, was only a mirage. In this segment of society, the inability of the father to inherit, acquire, or utilize under communal tenure sufficient land to maintain his family forced him to seek work elsewhere, leaving the wife and small children in the village. Many peasant fathers went tramping across Russia in search of seasonal work on the estates of the gentry, in lumber camps, or on construction jobs, or they sought unskilled jobs in the new factories to earn the money to pay their taxes, leaving their "hungry allotments" to be cultivated by their wives, aged parents, and children.

This type of family placed great responsibilities on the wife and mother. Even when land-poor peasants gave up their village allotments and moved their families to growing mill towns, mining settlements, or cities, the precariousness of the father's employment, together with the frequent need for the mother to seek some form of outside earnings, while also running the household and bringing up the children, made the mother-centered family a common phenomenon among the newly recruited urban working class. Family distress, both in the villages and in the growing urban slums, was undermining the patriarchal structure of the peasant family. Gorky's *Mother* springs to mind as a mirror of the predicament of a poor peasant family painfully undergoing the transition from village poverty to urban slums.

THE INTELLIGENTSIA IDEAL OF THE FAMILY

The main impetus to reshape all aspects of Russian life, including the family, came from the intelligentsia. In its development as a non-class or extraclass layer of society, from the 1840's and especially from the 1860's on, the intelligentsia also turned away more and more from the established political, social, and religious order. Relying upon its new functions in a modernizing society and upon the education which equipped it to perform these new roles, rejecting both property and custom as a basis for defining the status of the individual within a caste society, the intelligentsia also rejected the authoritarian and property basis of the husband-wife and father-child relationships.

The concept that woman has equal rights to seek emotional and ethical satisfaction in love and marriage and equal freedom to choose her marriage partner was foreshadowed in Tatiana's famous love letter in Pushkin's *Eugene Onegin*. The image of woman as an ethically equal partner was reenforced by the example of the wives of the Decembrists, who followed their husbands into exile in Siberia after the abortive revolution of December 1825. When the first waves of terrorism swept over Soviet society, one bitter complaint of Russian women was that the Soviet secret police, far from allowing them to express their devotion to their exiled husbands, frequently sentenced wives and children to separate and remote places of forced residence, thus destroying the families. Alternatively, as a special favor, the police urged the wives to secure a divorce as quickly as possible and to change their names, in order to escape persecution.

The family ideal, approved and in large part practiced by the pre-revolutionary intelligentsia, required a marriage to be a complete union of ideals and emotions, centered outward on service to "the people." It was presumed to be based upon a free and equal choice of both partners, uninfluenced by considerations of social class or property. Being based on equal and free decision, marriage should, in this view, be terminable by mutual consent, provided one partner or both, after long and patient effort and sacrifice, came to the conclusion that a divorce was necessary to his or her self-fulfillment in life.

Officially, until 1917 divorce was not possible under the canon law of the Orthodox Church; in practice, annulments could be obtained by people of wealth or high social standing, rarely so by people of other social groups. Freedom of choice in marrying, freedom of divorce, and freedom to choose whether and how many children to bear, as well as freedom of both husband and wife to take an equal part in working for the improvement of society, were central to the lofty family ideal of the intelligentsia. It was an ideal which assumed a high standard of enlightenment, self-discipline, and social responsibility in the individuals who undertook to practice it, and it was this ideal which the revolutionary wing of the intelligentsia set up as the new norm for the entire people of Russia.

THE REVOLUTION AND THE FAMILY

Lenin's decrees of November 1917, on peace, on the division of the lands of the nobility, church, and state among the "toiling peasantry," on workers' control of the factories, and on the right of national self-determination, proclaimed the revolutionary purposes of the new regime. Other less noticed decrees were designed to revolutionize the traditional structure and role of the family. Complete freedom of divorce by either marriage partner was enacted, making both marriage and divorce a purely individual act; more than casual cohabitation was recognized as equivalent to a registered marriage. From then until 1935, either partner in marriage could terminate it by signing the necessary form at a ZAGS office (Registry of Acts of Civil Status), without previous notification to husband or wife and without any hearing or review. The state intervened only to obligate the economically stronger ex-partner to provide alimony for the needs of minor children or of an ex-wife or ex-husband who was physically incapable of self-support. Freedom of abortion was also decreed, as an expression of the right of each woman, married or not, to decide whether she wished to bear children. When its economic conditions permitted it, the state medical service provided abortions free of charge.

In theory, the new Soviet state and the new ruling party aspired to take over the complete training of children from the earliest feasible age. Bolshevik enthusiasts drew up elaborate plans for the collective rearing of children from the nursery up. The new rulers saw clearly that the new revolutionary order, which aimed to effect a complete transformation of Russian society, could not risk leaving the early education of children in the hands of people who, in their overwhelming majority, were not in sympathy with it. In practice, however, the new regime took responsibility only for the upbringing of the several hundred thousands of homeless waifs, a by-product of the years of civil war, famine, and social breakdown. Most Soviet children continued to be brought up by their parents, though the Young Pioneer and Young Communist organizations soon set about taking over from the family the function of political indoctrination.

Like Lenin's slogan of the early fading away of the state after a comparatively brief period of dictatorship of the proletariat, the early postrevolutionary ideas concerning the family owed a great deal to Rousseau and Bakunin, and something to Friedrich Engels. The revolution summoned the people to break the mold of the past, emancipate the individual, and give full scope to all his capabilities, including his naturally "good" social instincts. All that was necessary was to destroy the bad institutions of the past, including the family, for the people then to create good customs in place of repressive institutions.

The chaos and strain of revolution and civil war, economic and social disruption, even famine, did far more than the new Soviet decrees to disrupt inherited patterns, to destroy property as a basis of the family, especially in the cities, and to make clear the primacy of the collectivist demands of the party and state over the inner-directed aspirations of the traditional family.

THE SECOND REVOLUTION AND THE FAMILY

After the "breathing spell" of the New Economic Policy, 1921-1927, with its partial return to capitalist practices in agriculture and retail trade, a new and even more drastic wave of revolutionary reconstruction was inaugurated with the launching of the first of the five year plans of industriali zation and the forcible collectivization of agriculture. During the first Five Year Plan, 1928-1932, a militant minority of the Communists and Young Communists, reviving the slogans of War Communism, also strove to complete the revolution by eliminating the family from Soviet life. Both in the cities and the new collective farms the various functions of the family were to be taken over by the collective. The preparation of meals was to be carried on by collective dining rooms. At this time many apartment houses were built without individual kitchens, to be ready for the Utopia of woman's emancipation from cooking and washing. Nurseries, kindergartens, and schools would carry out the upbringing of children in the new spirit of collectivism. Marriage would express only the emotional preferences, lasting or transitory, of two free partners; it must not deflect them away from their enthusiastic and separate participation in meeting the goals of the party or into seeking "petty-bourgeois self-satisfaction" within the family. The inability of the regime to provide anything approaching a minimum supply of "communal" restaurants, laundries, and nurseries was the main cause for the failure, and the virtual abandonment by 1933, of this ambition to eliminate the main housekeeping and child-rearing functions of the individual family.

The forced industrialization of the Five Year Plan, accompanied by rapid inflation of the cost of living and by severe scarcities of food, clothing, and housing, pressed more and more women into factory or office employment in order to keep the family going, and special programs were inaugurated to attract and train them. One curious experiment, designed to utilize the still slender stock of machinery on a more intensive scale, was the introduction of the "continuous" five-day work week. Under this arrangement, which lasted from early 1930 to late 1932, most factories, offices, and government stores were to operate on two shifts every day while each day one-fifth of the employees would have their rest-day. The abandonment of the seven-day week meant that people in the cities quickly lost the use of the names of the days of the week; Sunday, no longer easily identified by name, lost its religious significance. Since husband and wife could have the same rest-day only by bureaucratic accident, it normally became impossible to carry on any family activities jointly even on those days. The populace was firmly convinced that this tinkering with the calendar, reminiscent of similar experiments during the more exalted period of the French Revolution, was deliberately designed to weaken the family, and the need for enabling the family to have a common day of rest was cited as one of the reasons for restoring the seven-day week.

A similarly drastic transformation of the village family was sought, as a social by-product, through the collectivization of agriculture. The traditional peasant family, with its strong paternal authority and its fierce attachment to the household ownership or use of land, implements, and livestock, was to give way to the collective farm, within which each member, including women and adolescents, was to receive separate payment for work performed, based on a proportionate share in the total production of the collective. "Brigadiers," in charge of labor gangs, took the place of the heads of the household as organizers of farm work. Since each member over 14 now received his individual annual compensation, the father's control over income and expenditures by women and unmarried sons was to be eliminated. The provision of the "labor book" for each member symbolized the atomization of the traditional household and the establishment of an income nexus between each of its members and the collective.

In the first wave of forced collectivization, 1929-1932, the Bolshevik leadership proclaimed the ideal of the "commune," regarding the "artel" or collective as a temporary compromise. In the commune, which was established in substantial numbers, all productive property, down to the last bit of garden plot, piglet, chicken, or hoe, was turned over to the collective. Completely equal sharing of the product was at first praised as a direct step to communism, only to be abandoned and denounced as "equalization" of return for different values of labor. The communes also set about building collective kitchens, dining rooms, laundries, and nurseries, as in the urban projects, and for the same dual purpose of freeing the women for work on the collective and reducing the role of the family to a minimum.

Both the resistance of the peasants and the economic costs of achieving the ideal of the commune led the government to disband this type of collective and to denounce it as a "leftist" deviation. By 1933 the government had lowered its sights to press for the artel, in which the individual household has continued to have its own garden plot and small livestock and its own housekeeping functions. Even though the major resources and activities of production passed to the control of the artel, the common property and labor of the individual *kolkhoz* household has remained absolutely essential to the survival of its members. Since 1933 the balance of functions and benefits between household and collective has been readjusted frequently, and it is clear that the Bolshevik party regards the peasant family with deep suspicion as the root of the peasants' attachment to private property and private gain. In his final pronouncement, in October 1952, Stalin again set the goal of transforming the collectives into state farms, in which the peasants would become paid workers, minus their individual garden plots and livestock, and hence deprived of their individual source of foodstuffs and outside petty income.

EFFECTS OF SOCIAL DISRUPTION

As one by-product of the strains and stresses of forced industrialization and collectivization, hundreds of thousands of Soviet families were uprooted and in many cases dispersed beyond recall. The "liquidation of the kulaks as a class" removed at least one million of the more prosperous or hardworking peasant families from their villages. Husbands and fathers were scattered across the vast reaches of the Soviet Union to provide forced labor, while women and children were often removed forcibly to other areas, rather than being left in their familiar villages. Other millions of peasants moved either voluntarily or under contract to the growing cities, where they again found conditions very unfavorable for normal family life. Between 1930 and 1939, a large part of the intelligentsia, which had managed during the 1920's to settle more or less comfortably into the new Soviet routines, was uprooted in the recurrent waves of undiscriminating terror from above. Sentencing of the breadwinner to forced labor or to compulsory places of residence was usually followed by the confiscation of the family's apartment and the exile, often to different localities, of the mother and minor children. Those "elements" which the regime regarded as "harmful" were, so both the victims and the populace felt, being ground into human dust, which, if it survived the uprooting, could be remolded more easily into the desired patterns of conformity.

The early 1930's, made especially poignant by the extensive famine of 1932-1933, also saw additional hundreds of thousands of families disrupted and scattered by famine, and hundreds of thousands of homeless waifs again reappeared in the ways and byways of Russia. Again, the Soviet government undertook a major effort to provide a collectivist upbringing for them, through nurseries and youth hostels. Another large-scale disruption occurred during World War II. Several millions of people were evacuated from the Western areas threatened with Nazi occupation and resettled east of the Volga. Several additional millions of people were evacuated or fled westward in the course of the war. After the war several millions were resettled in the liberated areas. All these vast movements, in addition to the normal but accelerated movement of people to the growing cities, and to the outlying regions, have tended in one direction—to break down older regional and traditional attachments, to weaken or eliminate the awareness of extended blood ties, and to make the individual small family, consisting of husband, wife, and minor children, the typical subunit of a mobile, industrialized society.

The feeling of family or "clan" solidarity extending far beyond the individual household, which had traditionally been strong in all levels of its relatively static society, has further been undermined by the tumultuous development of social mobility, especially among the urban population. It had long been customary to maintain and identify an elaborate pattern of blood, in-law, and godparentage relationships, and the Russian language has a very complex vocabulary of these terms. "Mother's brother," "father's brother," "wife's father," "husband's father," "wife's brother's son," "god-father's son"—these are but a sample of the precise terms of relationship which were in daily use in a static and patriarchal society. The breakdown in the use of these terms, which began in the nobility and intelligentsia before the revolution, has been followed by their disuse and "social forgetting" in the post-revolutionary society. Similarly, the former loyalty to the extended family, with its sharing of prestige or shame, its duty of mutual help, its decision-sharing, and its constant visiting back and forth, has disappeared from urban life. Other ties, more precariously based on common functional status and political and cultural compatibility, have taken its place.

THE EFFECTS OF SOCIAL MOBILITY

Presumably, growing urbanization and the spread of geographical mobility would in any case have eroded the functions of the extended family and made the small family the most important social group mediating between the individual and the large-scale institutions of state, party, and economy. In the development of Soviet society the opening of many new ladders of individual upward mobility, and the structure of these ladders, has hastened this change and has forced it on at an often painful speed. Both industrialization and collectivization, as well as the tremendous swelling of the apparatuses of government and party, police, and army, have led to the rapid expansion of the "Soviet intelligentsia," until today it numbers perhaps some 25 millions. The upward mobility of these millions is based on two factors: education, especially technical education, and an active, demonstrated, constantly reviewed political loyalty to the Communist Party and its purposes.

If one brother rises steadily on these two stilts or ladders, while his siblings remain on an uneducated and a politically indifferent or hostile level, the mobile brother soon finds it unpleasant, disadvantageous, and even somewhat dangerous to maintain close ties of communication and mutual help with his "backward" kin. The tremendous expansion of educationally and politically mobile careers has helped to harness the forces of both idealism and self-interest to the purposes of the Soviet regime. It has also eliminated, in practice, the former loyalties to the extended family and has made the ambitious, mobile small family a valuable instrument for transmitting the demands of the leadership to its individual members. The upward mobility of the small family, and the ever present threat of its extreme and sudden downward mobility, has made it a subordinate partner rather than a rival of the party-state.

The family is often regarded as a channel for the transmission of traditional, unchanging, or slowly changing values and hence as a force of resistance to rapid and drastic changes imposed from above by a minority leadership. This was largely true of the first two decades or less of Bolshevik rule and helps to explain the determination of the ruling party to undermine and even to destroy the family. The fierce pressures of the regime were directed to destroying the family's traditional role as the transmitter of values and attitudes to the next generation and to monopolizing this function for the party and its instrumentalities. In this aim it had achieved substantial success by the mid-1930's, a success far greater in urban than rural areas and among the more mobile than the more static groups. The new and vastly expanded Soviet intelligentsia had every incentive to follow the new pattern of values laid down for it by the leadership. That part of the pre-

Soviet intelligentsia which survived into the mid-1930's and beyond did so to a very great extent through "forgetting" its earlier ethical and intellectual values and actively propagating the new values demanded by the regime. "Why make life difficult or perhaps impossible for our children by telling them about past times or other ways of life? They must live and work under this regime. We must help them to do so." The role of the immigrant family in America provides many examples of a similar effort to help the younger generation to adapt to its new environment and to avoid conflict between old and new values by tacitly surrendering the opportunity to transmit the older ones. Perhaps we have assumed too readily an automatic effort by the adult generation to transmit to its children the values with which its members were brought up. We may have underestimated its active role in absorbing, at least partially, and transmitting or not resisting new values which are pressed upon it by a larger environment, acting upon it through permissive or repressive means.[1]

SINCE THE MID-1930's

In the mid-1930's, half-way through the second Five Year Plan, the Soviet leadership turned to consolidating the enhanced political and economic power which it had conquered in a bitter revolution from above. In agriculture it now rejected the commune, with its complete sharing of work and rewards; it accepted the individual garden plot and livestock of the *kolkhoz* members as a permanent compromise with the peasant's attachment to private property and enforced a rigid system of differential rewards for work performed. Within industry it also set its sights substantially below the Utopian promises of 1929-1931, strengthed the role of management, and enforced a system of piecework differentials more rigorous than any trade union could tolerate under capitalism.

A temporary relaxation of terror, 1934-1936, promised a more secure future for the new Soviet intelligentsia, which also benefited from the abandonment, in 1936, of the system of disabilities based on ancestry. Previously, in order to give preference in education and party membership to the children of workers and peasants, rigid quotas had been enforced against persons of nonworker and nonpeasant descent. The return to a strict system of examinations in the educational system also marked the reconciliation of the regime with the rapidly expanding Soviet intelligentsia, which was now hailed by Stalin as the mainstay of the regime.

The same tendency to arrive at workable compromises between the Utopian aims of the period of upheaval and the persistent institutions of everyday life had widespread repercussions on the party's policy toward the family.

Instead of praising a cavalier attitude toward family obligations as a sign of "advanced" or "revolutionary" emancipation from "bourgeois prejudices," the party cells were instructed to watch over the family life of their members and to expel those guilty of loose living, of overfrequent marriage and divorce, or of neglecting their wives and children. After an unusually long and full public discussion, the government, in 1935, abolished freedom of abortion, except on rigidly defined medical grounds, even though the balance of expressed views favored its continuance. The abuse of alimony by some unmarried mothers was reversed by forbidding the search for paternity, thus placing on the woman the social and economic consequences of extramarital liaisons; the state also increased somewhat the assistance available to unmarried mothers. The previous right of an unmarried mother to exact alimony from several putative fathers was abolished, and proof of sexual relations with several men relieved all of them of any obligation.

Permanence of the marriage tie was now to be regarded as a good thing in itself and, for the first time since the revolution, the state asserted an interest in divorce. By new decrees the other partner was to receive prior notice of the wife's or husband's intention to request a divorce, and provision was made to look into the family situation and to urge a reconciliation, although a firm insistence by either partner continued to be an adequate ground for granting a divorce. The courts were instructed to be more stringent in enforcing alimony settlements, especially for the support of minor children. Somewhat ironically, while three divorces were permitted to any individual, each successive divorce was taxed by a higher fee, thus making a second or third divorce dependent on a higher income.

Contrary to the earlier ideal of bringing each individual into direct relation to the state and party, new legislation strengthened both the authority and the responsibility of the parents. Whereas the revolutionary ideal had emphasized the emancipation of youth from parental control or "tyranny" and had praised the rejection by "progressive" youth of the notions of their "backward" parents, the new spirit, after 1935, tended to restore the parents' authority, short of physical punishment, as it did that of the teachers. By successive decrees the parents were made materially and criminally responsible to the courts for "hooligan" acts or damage caused to persons or property by children who ran wild. With one hand, the regime urged all women to seek work, by ridicule and rewards; with the other, it punished the parents for failing to educate and control their children properly.

The concept of joint family liability for the acts of each of its members was carried to an extreme with the enactment of a decree punishing desertion or escape from the Soviet Union. If one member of a family "deserted" his country, all members of his family were subject to detention

at forced labor for up to five years, whether or not they had any fore-
knowledge of his intention. In enacting this rule of "mutual liability," the
Soviet regime was turning back to the customs of pre-Petrine Russia to find
a weapon against real or suspected treason. On the other hand, the new pro-
family policy found expression in special awards to mothers of large families
and in supplemental family allowances beyond five children, as well as in a
special graduated tax imposed on bachelors and on couples with three or
fewer children (this tax was abolished in 1957).

THE RUSSIAN FAMILY TODAY

It is difficult to form a clear picture of the present trends in the village
families of Russia today. The great disparity in numbers between men and
women, due to the uneven impact of collectivization, war, and economic
incentives, has given rise to many social problems. The consolidation of
kolkhoz and party controls has eliminated the economic role of the extended
kinship family in the work and life of the village. New channels of social
mobility have been drawing the more ambitious and perhaps the more able
away from the village ever since forced collectivization was launched in 1929.
The father has long since relinquished his patriarchal role as the conserver
and transmitter of property or use-rights in land, and the mother-sustained
family has become even more widely typical.

In the families of the urban intelligentsia and among the skilled workers,
the family is strongly oriented toward advancing the children beyond the
level attained by the parents. Focusing the ambition of the children on
reaching a higher educational and career level diminishes the authority of the
parents but may create a strong basis for understanding and gratitude in
later life. The great value attached to improving the opportunities for their
children means that more must be done for each child, despite the restoration
in 1956 of free secondary and higher education and the provision of a large
number of complete scholarships for the most talented. This strong urge
toward fewer but better equipped children, together with the dismally low
level of urban housing, probably accounts for the restoration, in 1957, of
almost complete freedom of abortion, as a convenient though economically
and psychically wasteful method of favoring the small family.

In one respect the economic and social pressure for mothers to seek employment has tended to modify this pattern, by bringing the grandmother
or *babushka* into a very important role. Many Soviet families look to the
grandmother to carry the main burden of shopping, cooking, and bringing up
the small children. In the first two decades of the regime, this often meant
that a child's earliest impressions were derived not from his overworked

and harassed parents but from a loving grandmother, frequently a deeply religious peasant woman, a carrier of the older patriarchal values. Since the war and especially since the Soviet Union has now entered its fifth decade, the numbers and the role of the grandmothers, at least in the cities, appear to have diminished considerably, and along with it their role as the transmitter of pre-Bolshevik concepts. The old *babushka* who kept both her beloved ikon and its Soviet equivalent, the lithograph of Lenin or Stalin, side by side in her corner of the single bedroom is probably rare today.

So far as casual observation goes, the traditionally relaxed and affectionate treatment of children within the Russian intelligentsia family goes on unchanged. Swaddling, with its alternating cycle of complete binding and unbinding of the infant in its first year, though criticized, seems to be as widespread as ever among the Great Russian population. The concept that the family represents an escape from the ever pressing demands of the regime for hard work and political conformity certainly makes a stable and happy family an essential environment of psychical "unbinding," which alternates with and relieves the "binding" demanded of its subjects in their actions and attitudes outside the family. The strongly puritanical strain in the Russian intelligentsia, reinforced by the demands of the party for purposeful effort and by the austere standards of living, keeps to a minimum the element of sexual curiosity and secondary stimulation. Even the literary expression of lyrical sentiments, permitted within narrow limits as a compensation for the extreme sufferings of the people in World War II, is still taboo today, despite the pleadings of writers and critics for greater leeway.

All in all, the ideals of the ruling party and of the new Soviet intelligentsia appear to run parallel and to reinforce each other. Both ideals treat love in monogamous marriage, with several minor children, who should be carefully trained and equipped to better themselves in life, as the appropriate norm. The two ideals diverge to the extent that the family aspires to have more and better housing, more free time together, more comforts, more privacy from the eyes of the party and police. On the whole, the party leadership has given more satisfaction to these desires since Stalin's death, and this new attitude is widely appreciated within Soviet society. The compromise has proved a workable one.

The most important and lasting changes which have reshaped the Russian family (no attempt has been made in this brief treatment to trace the changes among the numerous non-Russian peoples of the Soviet Union) over the last 40 years have been due to basic changes in the environment, rather than to the stated aims of the ruling Communist Party toward the family. Most of the changes can be traced to the explosive spread of industrialization and urbanization, to the dramatic increase in social mobility, to the expanding functions of a numerous managerial and white-collar class, and to the displacement of inherited property by educational status as a determinant of location and income within a fluid society. Certain specific sources of change, such as the transfer of millions of "socially harmful elements" to forced labor, or the only less forcible resettlement of further millions of people, have been due to the Bolsheviks' arrogation to themselves of the right to dispose of the lives of their subjects in order to strengthen their power and achieve their goals. Over the past four decades, the doctrinaire purposes of the ruling Communist Party—no less doctrinaire for having swung round 180 degrees on more than one occasion—appear to have had a relatively modest effect on the evolution of the Russian family and on its often painful adaptation to a radically changing political and economic environment.

NOTES

1. Similar findings, based upon interviews with a large sample of ex-Soviet people, have been reported in an excellent study by Kent Geiger, "Changing Political Attitudes in Totalitarian Society: A Case Study of the Role of the Family," *World Politics*, January, 1956, pp. 187-205, especially pp. 204-205.

C. The Published Work
of Philip E. Mosely

7: BIBLIOGRAPHY OF BOOKS
AND ARTICLES, 1934–1971

Russian Diplomacy and the Opening of the Eastern Question in 1838 and 1839 (Cambridge, Massachusetts: Harvard University Press, 1934), 178 pp.

Translator and editor, *The Great Russian Revolution,* by Victor Chernov (New Haven: Yale University Press, 1936), 466 pp.

"A Pan-Slavist Memorandum of Ljudevit Gaj in 1838," *American Historical Review* XL (1935), 704–716.

"Russia's Asiatic Policy in 1838," in Donald C. McKay, ed., *Essays in the History of Modern Europe* (New York: Harper and Brothers, 1936), pp. 48–62.

"The Sociological School of Dimitrie Gusti," *Sociological Review* (London), XXVIII (1936), 149–165.

"Russian Policy in Asia, 1838–39," *Slavonic Review* XIV (1936), 670–681.

"Lumea Psihologica a unui 'american' din Sant," *Sociologie romaneasca* I, No. 7–9 (1936), 75–78.

"Cercetari rurale in Bulgaria," ibid., No. 11 (1936), 31–33.

"Englisch-russische Flottenrivalität," *Jahrbücher für Geschichte Osteuropas* I (1936), 549–568.

"Is Europe Heading for War?" *Phi Kappa Phi Journal* XVII, No. 2 (1937), 55–64.

"The Post-War Historiography of Modern Bulgaria," *Journal of Modern History* IX, No. 3 (1937), 348–366.

"A New Rumanian Journal of Rural Sociology," *Rural Sociology* II, No. 4 (1937), 457–465.

"Recent Soviet Trials and Policies," *Yale Review* XXVII, No. 4 (1938), 745–766. Reprinted in *The Kremlin and World Politics: Studies in Soviet Policy and Action* (New York: Vintage Books, Inc., 1960), pp. 67–90.

"Freedom of Artistic Expression and Scientific Inquiry in Russia," *Annals of the American Academy of Political and Social Science,* CC (1938), 254–274. Reprinted in *The Kremlin and World Politics: Studies in Soviet Policy and Action* (New York: Vintage Books, Inc., 1960), pp. 91–128.

"Hitler and Southeastern Europe," *Yale Review* XXVII, No. 2 (1938), 249–272.

"War," in *Tentative Formulation of Some Contemporary Social Problems for Teachers of Social Studies*. (New York: Mimeographed by the General Education Board, 1939), 38 pp.

"Whither Russia? The Historical Background," *Areopagus* VIII, No. 2 (1939), 4-5.

"Russian Policy in 1911-12," *Journal of Modern History* XII (1940), 69-86.

"Is Bessarabia Next?" *Foreign Affairs* XVIII, No. 3 (1940), 557-562.

"Iceland and Greenland: An American Problem," *Foreign Affairs* XVIII (1940), 742-746.

"Transylvania Partitioned," *Foreign Affairs* XIX, No. 1 (1940), 237-244.

With C. E. Whipple, "The War Rolls Toward the Near East," *Yale Review* XXX, No. 2 (1940), 273-290.

"Nicolae Iorga," *American Historical Review* XLVI, No. 2 (1941), 506-507.

Editor, *Supranational Organization and Cooperation of the Democracies: An Outline of Suggestions for Research*. (New York: Social Science Research Council, 1941), 36 pp.

"The Peasant Family: The Zadruga, or Communal Joint-Family in the Balkans, and Its Recent Evolution," in Caroline F. Ware, ed., *The Cultural Approach to History* (New York: Columbia University Press, 1940), pp. 95-108.

"Intervention and Nonintervention in Spain, 1838-39," *Journal of Modern History* XIII, No. 2 (1941), 195-217.

"Repatriation of Greeks, Turks, and Bulgars after the Graeco-Turkish War, 1919-23," University of Pennsylvania Bicentennial Conference *Studies in Political Science and Sociology* (Philadelphia, 1941), pp. 171-180.

"The United States as Viewed by Other Nations," *Annals of the American Academy of Political and Social Science* CCXVIII (1941), 110-121.

"The United States and the Balance of Power," *The Impact of War on America* (Ithaca, 1942), pp. 97-122.

"The Small Nations and European Reconstruction," *Christianity and Crisis* II, No. 9 (1942), 2-5.

"Adaptation for Survival: the Varžić Zadruga," *Slavonic and East European Review* XXI (American Series II) (1943), 147-173.

"Soviet Policy in the United Nations," *Proceedings of the Academy of Political Science* XXII, No. 2 (1947), 28-37.

"Peace-Making, 1946," *International Organization* I, No. 1 (1947), 22-32. Reprinted as "Peacemaking, 1946," in *The Kremlin and World Politics: Studies in Soviet Policy and Action* (New York: Vintage Books, Inc., 1960), pp. 246-262.

"U. S. Policy and the U.S.S.R.," *Survey Graphic* XXXVI, No. 12 (1947), 674-677.

"Council on Foreign Ministers," *1947 Britannica Book of the Year* (Chicago: Encyclopaedia Britannica, Inc., 1947), pp. 241-243.

"Paris Peace Conference," *1947 Britannica Book of the Year* (Chicago: Encyclopaedia Britannica, 1947), pp. 582-585.

With Sidney B. Fay and Quincy Wright, "Containment or General Settlement with Russia?" *University of Chicago Round Table*, No. 512, January 11, 1948.

With others, *You and the Russians* (New York: Columbia Broadcasting System, 1948), 9 pp.

"Czechoslovakia, Poland, Yugoslavia: Observations and Reflections," *Political Science Quarterly* LXIII, No. 1 (1948), 1-15.

With others, "The Meaning of Czechoslovakia," *University of Chicago Round Table*, No. 519, February 29, 1948.

"The 'Books for Europe' Program," *Items of the Social Science Research Council* II (1948), 3-5.

Face to Face with Russia (New York: Foreign Policy Association, 1948), 63 pp.

"Soviet Policy in a Two-World System," *International Journal* III, No. 3 (1948), 191-200. Reprinted in *The Kremlin and World Politics: Studies in Soviet Policy and Action* (New York: Vintage Books, Inc., 1960), pp. 291-303.

"Across the Green Table from Stalin," *Current History* XV, No. 85 (1948), 129-133, 167.

"Aspects of the Russian Expansion," *American Slavic and East European Review* VII, No. 3 (1948), 197-213. Reprinted in *The Kremlin and World Politics: Studies in Soviet Policy and Action* (New York: Vintage Books, Inc., 1960), pp. 42-66.

"The Berlin Deadlock," *American Perspective* II, No. 7 (1948), 331-339.

"Foreign Ministers' Conferences," *1948 Britannica Book of the Year* (Chicago: Encyclopaedia Britannica, 1948), pp. 322-323.

"Peace Treaties," *1948 Britannica Book of the Year* (Chicago: Encyclopaedia Britannica, 1948), pp. 574-576.

"European Recovery Program," *1948 Britannica Book of the Year* (Chicago: Encyclopaedia Britannica, 1948), pp. 287-288.

Editor, *Annals of the American Academy of Political and Social Science* CCLXIII (1949), *The Soviet Union since World War II*, 211 pp.

"Soviet Relations since the War," ibid., pp. 202-211. Reprinted in Hans J. Morgenthau and Kenneth W. Thompson, eds., *Principles and Problems of International Politics: Selected Readings* (New York, 1950), pp. 381-393; in Herman Ausubel, ed., *The Making of Modern Europe* (New York, 1951), II, 1131-1146; in Robert A. Goldwin and Marvin Zetterbaum, eds., *Readings in Russian Foreign Policy* (Chicago: American Foundation for Political Education, 1953), III, 151-162; and in *The Kremlin and World Politics: Studies in Soviet Policy and Action* (New York: Vintage Books, Inc., 1960), pp. 304-322.

"Eastern Europe," *How Can We the People Achieve a Just Peace?* Selected speeches, Second Annual Session, Mount Holyoke College Institute on the United Nations (South Hadley, Mass., 1949), pp. 68-70.

With George Shuster and Quincy Wright, "United Nations: Success or Failure?" *University of Chicago Round Table*, No. 605, October 23, 1949, pp. 1-10.

With Aleš Bebler and Alan Simpson, "Can Yugoslavia Survive?" *University of Chicago Round Table*, No. 610, November 27, 1949, pp. 1-12.

"Slavic Studies," *Items of the Social Science Research Council* IV, No. 1 (1950), 9-10.

"Dismemberment of Germany; the Allied Negotiations from Yalta to Potsdam," *Foreign Affairs* XXVIII, No. 3 (1950), 487-498. Reprinted in *The Kremlin and World Politics: Studies in Soviet Policy and Action* (New York: Vintage Books, Inc., 1960), pp. 131-154.

With Walter Johnson and Malcolm P. Sharp, "Who Killed the Peace?" *University of Chicago Round Table*, No. 625, March 12, 1950, pp. 1-13.

"Soviet Research in the Social Field," *Proceedings of the American Philosophical Society* XCIV, No. 2 (1950), 105-110. Reprinted as "Social Science in the Science of Politics," in Alex Inkeles and Kent Geiger, eds., *Soviet Society, a Book of Readings* (Boston: Houghton Mifflin, 1961), pp. 478-484.

"Slavic Studies," *Items of the Social Science Research Council* IV, No. 2 (1950), 21.

"The Occupation of Germany: New Light on How the Zones Were Drawn," *Foreign Affairs* XXVIII, No. 4 (1950), 580-604. Reprinted in *The Kremlin and World Politics: Studies in Soviet Policy and Action* (New York: Vintage Books, Inc., 1960), pp. 155-188.

"The Treaty with Austria," *International Organization* IV, No. 2 (1950), 219-235. Reprinted in *The Kremlin and World Politics: Studies in Soviet Policy and Action* (New York: Vintage Books, Inc., 1960), pp. 263-288.

"The Problem of Asia," *University of Chicago Round Table*, No. 644, July 30, 1950, pp. 1-11.

"Slavic Studies," IX-e Congrès International des Sciences Historiques, *Rapports* I (Paris, 1950), 607-620.

"Council on Foreign Ministers," *1950 Britannica Book of the Year* (Chicago: Encyclopaedia Britannica, 1950), pp. 208-209.

"European Recovery Program," *1950 Britannica Book of the Year* (Chicago: Encyclopaedia Britannica, 1950), pp. 261-263.

"Organization for European Economic Cooperation," *1950 Britannica Book of the Year* (Chicago: Encyclopaedia Britannica, 1950), pp. 524-526.

"The Rise of Soviet Power," *U. S. Naval War College, Information Service for Officers* III, No. 4 (1950), 13-42. (Classified.)

With others, "The State of American Foreign Policy," *University of Chicago Round Table*, No. 668, January 14, 1951, pp. 1-10.

"Soviet Policy and the Revolutions in Asia," *Annals of the American Academy of Political and Social Sciences* CCLXXVI (1951), 91-98.

"Soviet Exploitation of National Conflicts in Eastern Europe," in Waldemar Gurian, (ed.), *The Soviet Union: Background, Ideology, Reality* (Notre Dame, Ind.: University of Notre Dame Press, 1951), pp. 67–84. Reprinted as "Soviet Policy and National Conflicts in East Central Europe," in *The Kremlin and World Politics: Studies in Soviet Policy and Action* (New York: Vintage Books, Inc., 1960), pp. 221–245.

"European Recovery Program," *1951 Britannica Book of the Year* (Chicago: Encyclopaedia Britannica, Inc., 1951), pp. 262–265.

"The Failure of the Old Imperialism," *Bulletin of the Institute of Social Sciences* I, No. 3 (1951), 25, 34.

With others, "Is There an Entering Wedge for Peace?" *University of Chicago Round Table*, No. 710, November 4, 1951, pp. 1–10.

"The Zagreb Congress," *The Nation* CLXXIII, No. 19 (1951), 391–392.

"The World Impact of the Russian Revolution," in A. William Loos, ed., *Religious Faith and World Culture* (New York: Prentice-Hall, Inc.,1951), pp. 143–156. Reprinted in *The Kremlin and World Politics: Studies in Soviet Policy and Action* (New York: Vintage Books, Inc., 1960), pp. 221–245.

"Some Soviet Techniques of Negotiation," in Raymond Dennett and Joseph E. Johnson, eds., *Negotiating with the Russians* (Boston: The World Peace Foundation, 1951), pp. 271–303. Reprinted in condensed form in *Problems of Communism* I, No. 2 (1952), 27–32; in *Soviet Conduct in World Affairs: A Selection of Readings,* compiled by Alexander Dallin (New York: Columbia University Press, 1960), pp. 196–227; in condensed form as "Problems of Negotiating with the Soviets," in Alvin Rubinstein, ed., *Foreign Policy of the Soviet Union* (New York, 1960), pp. 412–415; in *The Kremlin and World Politics: Studies in Soviet Policy and Action* (New York: Vintage Books, Inc.,1960), pp. 3–41; in condensed form as "Negotiating with the Russians," in Alfred J. Rieber and Robert C. Nelson, eds., *The U.S.S.R. and Communism, Source Readings and Interpretations* (Chicago: Scott, Foresman and Company, 1964), pp. 266–276; as "Some Soviet Techniques of Negotiation," *Hearings* before the Subcommittee on National Security and International Operations, Ninety-first Congress, First Session, Washington (1969), pp. 16–32.

"Negotiating with the Russians," *Foreign Policy Bulletin* XXXI, No. 10 (1952), 1–2.

"Should U. S. Negotiate with Russia about Germany?" *Foreign Policy Bulletin* XXXI, No. 17 (1952), 5–6.

With others, "What is the American Tradition in Foreign Policy, Ideals or Power?" *University of Chicago Round Table*, No. 734, April 20, 1952.

"Soviet Policy and the Korean War," *Journal of International Affairs* VI, No. 2 (1952), 107–114. Reprinted in *The Kremlin and World Politics: Studies in Soviet Policy and Action* (New York: Vintage Books, Inc., 1960), pp. 323–335.

"Drahomanov and the European Conscience," *Annals of the Ukrainian Academy of Arts and Sciences in the U. S.* II, No. 1 (1952), 1-5.

With others, "The Mediation of Labor and International Disputes," *University of Chicago Round Table,* No. 757, September 28, 1952, pp. 1-10.

"Trieste: Apple of Discord," *Foreign Policy Bulletin* XXXII, No. 6 (1952), 3, 8.

"The Nineteenth Party Congress," *Foreign Affairs* XXXI, No. 2 (1953), 238-256. Reprinted in *The Kremlin and World Politics: Studies in Soviet Policy and Action* (New York: Vintage Books, Inc., 1960), pp. 336-360; as "Economic Aspects of the Nineteenth Party Congress," *Problems of Communism* II, No. 2 (1953), 8-10.

"Columbia's New Treasure-House of Russian History," *Columbia Library Columns* II, No. 2 (1953), 17-24.

"The Distribution of the Zadruga within Southeastern Europe," *The Joshua Starr Memorial Volume, Jewish Social Studies* V (1953), 219-230.

"The New Look in Soviet Foreign Policy," *Foreign Policy Bulletin* XXXIII, No. 2 (1953), 5-7.

"The Kremlin's Foreign Policy since Stalin," *Foreign Affairs* XXXII, No. 1 (1953), 20-33. Reprinted in part in *Discussions of Foreign Affairs* II, No. 3 (1953), 6-7; in *The Kremlin and World Politics: Studies in Soviet Policy and Action* (New York: Vintage Books, Inc., 1960), pp. 363-381.

With others, "Meaning of Democracy," *University of Chicago Round Table* No. 807, September 27, 1953, pp. 1-11.

"The Break in the Iron Curtain," *Institute of Social Studies Bulletin* II, No. 4 (1953), 37-39.

"The Historical Development of Russia," *Naval War College Review* VI, No. 6 (1954), 1-22. (Classified.)

"Soviet Policy in the Two-World Conflict: Some Prospects," *Journal of International Affairs* VIII, No. 1 (1954), 107-113; translated and reprinted as "Sowjetpolitik im Zeitalter," *Ost-Probleme* VI, No. 28 (1954), 1102-1105; in *The Kremlin and World Politics: Studies in Soviet Policy and Action* (New York: Vintage Books, Inc., 1960), pp. 382-390.

With others, "Indochina and the Geneva Conference," *University of Chicago Round Table,* No. 838, May 2, 1954, pp. 1-13.

"Soviet Hopes for Success are Concentrated on the East" (delivered in Russian, translated into English), *Proceedings of the Conference of the Institute for the Study of the History and Culture of the U.S.S.R., March 20-22, 1953* (Munich, 1954), pp. 120-122.

"Opening Statement," *Academic Freedom Under the Soviet Regime; A Symposium of Refugee Scholars and Scientists Who have Escaped from the U.S.S.R., on the Subject, "Academic Freedom in the Soviet Union as a Threat to the Theory and Practice of Bolshevik Doctrine,"* (Munich: The

Institute for the Study of the History and Culture of the U.S.S.R., 1954), pp. vii–viii.

"Introductory Remarks," *Three Columbia Bicentennial Lectures* (Florian Znaniecki, Waclaw Lednicki, Oscar Halecki) (New York: The Polish Institute of Arts and Sciences in America, 1954), pp. 5-6.

"Comments on Ideology and Reality in the Soviet System," *Proceedings of the American Philosophical Society* IC, No. 1 (1955), 31-33.

"The Russian Institute of Columbia University," *Proceedings of the American Philosophical Society* IC, No. 1 (1955), 36-38.

"Waldemar Gurian and Russian Studies in America," *Review of Politics* XVII, No. 1 (1955), 44-46.

"Foreword," *Two Studies in Soviet Control: Communism and the Russian Peasant*, by Herbert S. Dinerstein, and *Moscow in Crisis*, by Leon Goure and Herbert S. Dinerstein (Glencoe, Ill.: The Free Press, 1955), pp. vii-xi.

"Can Moscow Match Us Industrially?" *Harvard Business Review* XXXIII, No. 2 (1955), 101-108. Reprinted in *The Kremlin and World Politics: Studies in Soviet Policy and Action* (New York: Vintage Books, Inc., 1960), pp. 406-424.

"How 'New' is the Kremlin's New Line?" *Foreign Affairs* XXXIII, No. 3 (1955), 376-386. Reprinted in *The Kremlin and World Politics: Studies in Soviet Policy and Action* (New York: Vintage Books, Inc., 1960), pp. 391-405.

With others, "Russia's Foreign Policy," *University of Chicago Round Table*, No. 885, March 27, 1955, pp. 1-6.

Russia After Stalin (New York: Foreign Policy Association, 1955), 55 pp.

"Will Tito Turn East?" *Foreign Policy Bulletin* XXXV (1955), 157-159.

"Hopes and Failures: American Policy Toward East Central Europe, 1941–1947," *Review of Politics* XVII, No. 4 (1955), 461-485. Reprinted with slight revision in Stephen D. Kertesz, ed., *The Fate of East Central Europe; Hope and Failures of American Foreign Policy* (Notre Dame, Ind.: University of Notre Dame Press, 1956), 51-74; in *The Kremlin and World Politics: Studies in Soviet Policy and Action* (New York: Vintage Books, Inc., 1960), pp. 189-220.

"Review" (of Part VI, "Russia and the Community of Nations: Messianic Views and Theory of Action,") in Ernest J. Simmons, ed., *Continuity and Change in Russian and Soviet Thought* (Cambridge, Mass.: Harvard University Press, 1955), pp. 550-554.

Editor, "The Soviet Union and the United States: Problems and Prospects," *Annals of the American Academy of Political and Social Science* CCCIII (1956); "Russia Since Stalin: Old Trends and New Problems," 192-198. Reprinted as "Die Sowjetunion und die Vereinigten Staaten von Nord-Amerika: Probleme und Aussichten," *Europa Archiv*, May 5, 1956, pp. 8797-8802; in *The Kremlin and World Politics: Studies in Soviet Policy and Action* (New York: Vintage Books, Inc., 1960), pp. 425-455.

"Soviet Foreign Policy: New Goals or New Manners?" *Foreign Affairs* XXXIV, No. 4 (1956), 541-553. Reprinted in *The Kremlin and World Politics: Studies in Soviet Policy and Action* (New York: Vintage Books, Inc., 1960), pp. 438-455.

"Concluding Remarks," *Report on the Soviet Union in 1956,* A Symposium of the Institute for the Study of the U.S.S.R., April 28-29, 1956 (Munich, 1956), pp. 203-207.

"Russia Revisited: Moscow Dialogues, 1956," *Foreign Affairs* XXXV, No. 1 (1956), 72-83. Reprinted in *The Kremlin and World Politics: Studies in Soviet Policy and Action* (New York: Vintage Books, Inc., 1960), pp. 456-471.

"Foreword," *Bolshevism in Turkestan, 1917-1927,* by Alexander G. Park (New York: Columbia University Press, 1957), pp. ix-x.

"The Moscow-Peking Axis in World Politics," in Howard L. Boorman, Alexander Eckstein, Philip E. Mosely, and Benjamin Schwartz, eds., *Moscow-Peking Axis: Strengths and Strains* (New York: Harper and Brothers, 1957), pp. 198-227. Reprinted in *The Kremlin and World Politics: Studies in Soviet Policy and Action* (New York: Vintage Books, Inc., 1960), pp. 472-503.

Introduction, "Professor Michael Karpovich," in Hugh McLean, Martin E. Malia and George Fischer, eds., *Russian Thought and Politics* (Gravenhage: Mouton & Co., 1957), pp. 1-13.

"Collectivization of Agriculture in Soviet Strategy," in Irwin T. Sanders, ed., *Collectivization of Agriculture in Eastern Europe* (Lexington: University of Kentucky Press, 1958), pp. 49-66.

"Columbia's Dynamic Archive of Russian History and Culture," *Columbia Library Columns* VII, No. 2 (1958), 32-36.

"Khrushchev's New Economic Gambit," *Foreign Affairs* XXXVI, No. 4 (1958), 557-568.

"The Bases of American Foreign Policy," *The Listener* LX, No. 1531 (1958), 147, 165. Reprinted as "The Bases of U. S. Foreign Policy," *The New Leader* XLI, No. 33 (1958), 3-5.

"Russia and the West: Notes of Discord and Hope," *Worldview* I, No. 10 (1958), 6-8.

"The Russian Family: Old Style and New," in Ruth Nanda Anshen, ed., *The Family: Its Function and Destiny* (New York: Harper & Brothers, 1959), revised edition, pp. 104-122.

"The Growth of Russian Studies," in Harold Fisher, ed., *American Research on Russia* (Bloomington, Ind.: Indiana University Press, 1959), pp. 1-22.

"The New Challenge of the Kremlin," in Stephen D. Kertesz and M. A. Fitzsimons, eds., *Diplomacy in a Changing World* (Notre Dame, Ind.: University of Notre Dame Press, 1959), pp. 117-132. Reprinted in *The Kremlin and World Politics: Studies in Soviet Policy and Action* (New York: Vintage Books, Inc., 1960), pp. 538-557.

"Introduction," in Peter S. H. Tang, *Russian and Soviet Policy in Manchuria and Outer Mongolia, 1911–1931* (Durham, N.C.: Duke University Press, 1959), pp. vii-viii.

The Kremlin and World Politics: Studies in Soviet Policy and Action (New York: Vintage Books, Inc., 1960), 557 pp. Reprinted in Japanese (Tokyo: C. E. Tuttle Co., 1962), 345 pp.

"The Invitation to Learning Reader on War and Peace," (New York: Carnegie Endowment for International Peace, 1960), pp. 31–39, as broadcast on the Columbia Broadcasting System Radio Network.

"Memorial: Michael Vetukhiv, Founding President of the Academy," *Annals of the Ukrainian Academy of Arts and Sciences in the United States* VIII, No. 1–2 (1960), 5–14.

"How the Kremlin Keeps Ivan in Line," *New York Times Magazine,* February 10, 1961, pp. 16, 67–68.

"Soviet Myths and Realities," *Foreign Affairs* XXXIX, No. 3 (1961), 341–354. Reprinted in *Congressional Record–Senate* (Mr. Proxmire) CVII, No. 65 (April 18, 1961), 5696–5699; in abridged form in *Der Spiegel,* Hamburg, May 17, 1961, p. 76; in abridged form, *Current,* No. 13 (1961), pp. 47–51; in *Documentation Française,* No. 1098 (1961), pp. 1–7; in Shukan (weekly) *Toyo Keizai* (Sekai-Shuko) Tokyo, July 29, 1969, pp. 36–42; as "Somjetsamveldet I Dag," *Syn og Segn* 7, (1961), 308–321; in *The Soviet Union, 1922-1962. A Foreign Affairs Reader* (New York: Praeger Publishers, Inc., 1962), pp. 428–440.

"Research on Foreign Policy," *Research for Public Policy* (Washington, D.C.: Brookings Institute, 1961), pp. 43–72.

"Is it 'Peaceful' or 'Coexistence'?" *New York Times Magazine,* May 7, 1961, pp. 19, 122–124. Reprinted as "The Meaning of 'Peaceful Coexistence,'" in Alfred J. Rieber and Robert C. Nelson, eds., *The USSR and Communism: Source Readings and Interpretations* (Chicago: Scott, Foresman and Co., 1961), pp. 312–315.

"American Policy: Dangers and Prospects," in Stephen D. Kertesz, ed., *American Diplomacy in a New Era* (Notre Dame, Ind.: University of Notre Dame Press, 1961), pp. 551–568.

"Regional Alliances Best Hope of Free World," *Nation's Business* IL, No. 10 (1961), 61–64.

"Is Khrushchev Another Hitler: A Size-up by International Experts," *U.S. News and World Report* LI, No. 18 (1961), 44–45.

"Khrushchev's Party Congress," *Foreign Affairs* XL, No. 2 (1962), 183–195. Reprinted as "Bundeszentrale für Heimatdienst," in *Das Parlament,* Bonn, Germany; in Samuel Hendel, ed., *The Soviet Crucible,* 2nd ed. (New York: D. Van Nostrand Co., 1963), pp. 458–462.

"Communism: Its Implications for Higher Education," in George S. Pathemos, ed., *Higher Education in a World of Conflict* (Athens, Ga.: University of Georgia Press, 1962), pp. 135–169.

"The Soviet Challenge: Today and Tomorrow," Wingspread, Institute for World Affairs Education of the University of Wisconsin–Milwaukee, with the Johnson Foundation (Racine, Wis.: Johnson Foundation, 1962).

"Foreword," in Kurt London, ed., *Unity and Contradiction: Major Aspects of Sino-Soviet Relations* (New York: Praeger Publishers, Inc., 1962), pp. ix-x.

"The Meanings of Coexistence," *Foreign Affairs* XLI, No. 1 (1962), 36-46. Reprinted in *The Soviet Union, 1922-1962: A Foreign Affairs Reader* (New York: Praeger Publishers, Inc., 1962), pp. 478-488; in Norman A. Graebner, ed., *The Cold War: Ideological Conflict or Power Struggle* (Boston: D. C. Heath & Co., 1963), pp. 87-94; as "The Policy of 'Peaceful Coexistence', " in Randolph L. Braham, ed., *Soviet Politics and Government: A Reader* (New York: Alfred A. Knopf, Inc., 1965), pp. 480-491.

"Soviet Foreign Policy Since the Twenty-Second Party Congress," *Modern Age* VI, No. 4 (1962), 343-352. Reprinted in David S. Collier and Kurt Glaser, eds., *Berlin and the Future of Eastern Europe* (Chicago: Henry Regnery Company with the Foundation for Foreign Affairs, Inc., 1963), pp. 60-73; as "The Limits of Liberalization," *Current,* No. 36 (1963), pp. 56-58.

Editor, *The Soviet Union, 1922-1962: A Foreign Affairs Reader* (New York: Praeger Publishers, Inc., 1962), 488 pp.

"Is It Peaceful? Is It Coexistence?" *The New York Times Magazine,* September 1, 1963, pp. 7, 18-19.

"The Chinese-Soviet Rift: Origins and Portents," *Foreign Affairs,* XLII, No. 1 (1963), 11-24. Reprinted in George P. Jan, ed., *Government of Communist China* (San Francisco: Chandler Publishing Co., 1966), pp. 574-586.

"The New Western Europe and the World Strategy of Democracy," *Modern Age* VII, No. 4 (1963), 343-354. Reprinted in David S. Collier and Kurt Glaser, eds., *Western Integration and the Future of Eastern Europe* (Chicago: Henry Regnery Company with the Foundation for Foreign Affairs, Inc., 1964), pp. 1-16.

"Khrushchev's Foreign Policy: Coexistence or Conflict?" Focus on the Soviet Challenge. Seventh Annual Institute on United States Foreign Policy, No. 4. Global Focus Series, published by the Institute for World Affairs Education, The University of Wisconsin–Milwaukee, July, 1963, pp. 47-61, 63-64, 68, and 78-79.

"Khrushchev at 70–Who is Next?" *The New York Times Magazine,* April 12, 1964, pp. 14, 96-97, 99-100. Reprinted in abridged form as "After Khrushchev–Who?" *Sunday Chronicle* (London), May 21, 1964.

"Recent Developments in the Soviet Bloc," *Hearings* before the Subcommittee on Europe of the Committee on Foreign Affairs, House of Representatives, Eighty-eighth Congress, Second Session, Washington, D.C. (1964), pp. 320-323.

"Foreword," in John A. Armstrong, ed., *Soviet Partisans in World War II* (Madison: University of Wisconsin Press, 1964), pp. v-viii.

"Changing Challenge of Communism: Some Implications for United States Policy," *Proceedings of the Academy of Political Science* XXVII, No. 4 (1964), 99-119.

"Soviet Policy in the Developing Countries," *Foreign Affairs* XLIII, No. 1 (1964), 87-98.

"The Soviet Citizen Views the World," *The Review of Politics* XXVIII, No. 4 (1964), 451-472.

"The Changing Soviet Challenge," *Wingspread* (Racine, Wis.: The Johnson Foundation, 1964), pp. 1-15.

"East-West Trade," *Hearings*. A Compilation of Views of Businessmen, Bankers, and Academic Experts, Committee on Foreign Relations, United States Senate, November, 1964.

"Present Trends in U. S.–Soviet Relations," *Journal of the School of International Studies* (New Delhi) VI, No. 2 (1964), 117-132.

With others, "The Future of Eastern Europe," *East Europe* XIII, No. 5 (1964), 11-15, passim.

"Heiwa-Kyōzon Jidai no Kiki" [Crisis in the Period of Peaceful Coexistence], *Yomiuri Shinbun* (Tokyo), August 23, 1964, p. 17.

"Introduction: Power and Ideology in the Communist States," in Adam Bromke, ed., *The Communist States at the Crossroads Between Moscow and Peking* (New York: Praeger Publishers, Inc., 1965), pp. 3-20. Japanese translation (Tokyo: Jiji Press, through Charles E. Tuttle Co., Inc., 1965), pp. 3-20.

"Some Vignettes of Soviet Life," *Survey,* No. 55 (1965), pp. 52-63.

"Foreword," in Scipio (pseud.), *Emergent Africa* (Boston: Houghton Mifflin Company, 1965), pp. 5-6.

"Requirements for a European Deterrent in the 1970s," in Karl H. Cerny and Henry W. Briefs, eds., *NATO in Quest of Cohesion* (New York: Praeger Publishers, Inc., for the Hoover Institution on War, Revolution, and Peace, 1965), pp. 257-269.

"Negotiating With the Communists," transcribed from the television series "What Everyone Should Know about Communism," produced by Ellis Mott, prepared by Edward H. Weiss Company for The Purex Corporation, as a public service, 1965.

"Eastern Europe and United States Policy," *Intercom* VII, No. 4 (1965), 15-18.

"The Soviet Union and the United Nations," *International Organization* XIX, No. 3 (1965), 666-667. Reprinted in Norman J. Padelford and Leland M. Goodrich, eds., *The United Nations in the Balance* (New York: Praeger Publishers, Inc., 1965), pp. 302-313.

"Ideological Diversities and Crises within the Communist Area," *Modern Age* IX, No. 4 (1965), 343-353.

"New Trends and New Needs in the Study of Contemporary Western Europe," *American Council of Learned Societies Newsletter* XVI, No. 6 (1965), 1-14. Reprinted in abridged version in the *Report on the Eastern Regional Conference on European and Atlantic Area Studies,* Airlie House, Warrenton, Va., May 5-6, 1967, pp. 31-35.

"The Communist Bloc in the 1960s," in Robert A. Goldwin, ed., *Beyond the Cold War: Essays on American Foreign Policy in a Changing Environment* (Chicago: Rand McNally and Co., 1965), pp. 96-114.

"Ideological Diversities and Crises Within the Communist Area," in David S. Collier and Kurt Glaser, eds., *Western Policy and Eastern Europe* (Chicago: Henry Regnery Company, with the Foundation for Foreign Affairs, Inc., 1966), pp. 44-59. Reprinted as "Ideologische Differenzierungen und Krisen im kommunistischen Herrschaftsbereich," *Die Politik des Westens und Osteuropa* (Cologne: Verlag Wissenschaft und Politik, 1966), pp. 67-83; first published in *Modern Age* IX, No. 4 (1965), 343-353.

Translator and editor, *The Great Russian Revolution,* by Victor Chernov (New York: Russell & Russell, 1966), 447 pp. First published by Yale University Press, 1936.

"Communist Policy and the Third World," *Review of Politics* XXVIII, No. 2 (1966), 210-237.

"The Soviet Union Since Khrushchev," *Headline Series,* No. 175 (New York: Foreign Policy Association, 1966), 78 pp. Abridged, "La Politique étrangère de l'URSS après Khrouchtchev," *Politique Étrangère* XXXI, No. 1 (1966), 5-18.

"Comments in Retrospect," in Martin F. Herz, ed., *Beginnings of the Cold War* (Bloomington, Ind.: Indiana University Press, 1966), pp. 193-194. Abridged from *The Kremlin and World Politics: Studies in Soviet Policy and Action* (New York: Vintage Books, Inc., 1960), pp. 155-156.

"Soviet Foreign Policy since Khrushchev," in Rodger Swearingen, ed., *Soviet and Chinese Communist Power in the World Today* (New York: Basic Books, Inc., 1966), pp. 27-55.

"Eastern Europe in World Power Politics," *Modern Age* XI, No. 2 (1967), 119-130. Reprinted as "Osteuropa im Kräftespiel der Weltmächte," in Alfred Domes, ed., *Osteuropa und die Hoffnung auf Freiheit* (Cologne: Verlag Wissenschaft und Politik, 1967), pp. 76-92.

"International Affairs," in Warren Weaver, ed., *U. S. Philanthropic Foundations. Their History, Structure, Management, and Record* (New York: Harper & Row, 1967), pp. 375-395.

"The Kremlin and the Third World," *Foreign Affairs* XLVI, No. 1 (1967), 64-77.

"Scope, Magnitude, and Implications of the United States Antiballistic Missile Program," *Hearings* before the Subcommittee on Military Applications of the Joint Committee on Atomic Energy, Congress of the United

States, Ninetieth Congress, First Session, Washington, (November 6 and 7, 1967), pp. 52-63, 88, 96.

"Challenges and Handicaps to United States Policy," in *The United States and Eastern Europe,* a report of the Pacific Northwest Assembly at the University of Oregon, Eugene, February 20-March 3, 1968, pp. 15-19.

"Eastern Europe in World Power Politics," in David S. Collier and Kurt Glaser, eds., *Elements of Change in Eastern Europe: Prospects for Freedom* (Chicago: Henry Regnery Co., 1968).

Russian Diplomacy and the Opening of the Eastern Question in 1838 and 1839 (New York: Russell & Russell, 1969), 178 pp. First published by Harvard University Press, 1934.

"Soviet Search for Security," in J. C. Hurewitz, ed., *Soviet-American Rivalry in the Middle East, Proceedings of the Academy of Political Science* XXIX, No. 3 (1969), 216-227.

"The United States and East-West Detente: The Range of Choice," *Journal of International Affairs* XXII, No. 1 (1968), 5-15. Reprinted as "Die Vereinigten Staaten und die Ost-West Entspannung," *Entspannung Sicherheit Frieden* (Cologne: Verlag Wissenschaft und Politik, 1968), pp. 53-65.

"Foreword," *New Trends in Kremlin Policy,* Special Report Series Number Eleven, August 1970 (Washington, D.C.: Georgetown University, The Center for Strategic and International Studies, 1970), pp. v-viii.

"The Universities and Public Policy—Challenges and Limits," in Stephen D. Kertesz, ed., *The Task of Universities in a Changing World* (Notre Dame, Ind.: University of Notre Dame Press, 1971), pp. 34-51.

Part Two:
Historical and Sociological
Studies of the Zadruga

8: SOME MEDIEVAL EVIDENCE
ON THE SERBIAN ZADRUGA:
A PRELIMINARY ANALYSIS OF
THE CHRYSOBULLS OF DEČANI

Eugene A. Hammel

Scholarly efforts to understand the zadruga take two general forms. One explains the zadruga by pointing to particular social conditions that bring it into existence and influence its variations. This stresses the similarity between the south Slavic zadruga and similar examples of domiciliary organization in a wide variety of cultures, including non-Slavic ones. The second explains it by stressing the persistence of ideology, customary practice, and the ancient ethnic roots of this social form, considered as unique and different from other kinds of household structure, similar perhaps only to the Russian *mir*. Of course, these styles of explanation are but the two common threads of most efforts to understand any social institution: the functional, stressing comparison and efficient causality, and the historical or genetic, stressing singularity. They are most effective when they are together the warp and weft of a single explanatory fabric.

I have earlier placed much emphasis on the functional mode of explanation, following in large measure the example set by Philip E. Mosely, but using some of the same historical sources cited as evidence for the ancient and traditional lineage of the zadruga.[1] I am not, of course, alone in this endeavor; the example was set by Stojan Novaković almost a hundred years ago.[2] Any functional explanation of the zadruga or of its variations ought to be valid in any time and place. Thus, if we feel that taxation practices play a role in its formation, taxation ought to be examined in the medieval

The author is indebted to the Center for Slavic and East European Studies, Committee on Research, and the Computer Center at Berkeley for support. He is also grateful to Djordje Soć for his help in coding the manuscript and to Ruth Deuel for the computer programming that led to these results.

as well as in the modern evidence. If population pressure, or a pioneering ecology, or the need for defense stimulate it, we ought to find such factors operating in the same direction in the fourteenth century as well as in the eighteenth or nineteenth. However, basic to any such endeavor is the first step, finding out what domiciliary organization really is, on the ground, and in real communities, rather than just in the exhortations of codes, testaments, or other expressions of what ought to be.

It is surprising how rare such basic ethnographic information is, how difficult of interpretation, and how often unreliable. Most Serbo-Croatian primary literature, although it may refer to the size of households, generally ignores their structure and frequently mentions only the very large households. Novaković complained about this defect long ago, noting that some households are large simply because of high fertility, not because of complex family organization.[3] Here and there one finds nuggets of good data and solid pieces of interpretation, not the least of which are Mosely's papers on the subject.[4] However, for detail and temporal span, the best descriptions are those furnished by Halpern for the period from the middle of the last century into this one.[5] Oddly enough, when one considers how much basic ethnography has been published in Serbia, the next best data come from the dusty parchments of the Middle Ages, and it is to these that I now turn.

THE MEDIEVAL DOCUMENTS

Two kinds of medieval documents contain explicit data on household organization in Serbia. (I ignore here the very rare references in codes and proclamations, rare perhaps because the zadruga was so common that no one needed to mention it. I explicitly avoid the Austrian legal evidence for the Croatian-Slavonian Military Frontier, which I consider part of a different, though related, phenomenon.) These two kinds of documents are the chrysobulls of the medieval Serbian Empire and the defters of the Ottoman. The chrysobulls are the establishing or confirmatory charters of monasteries, naming the properties of these in complete detail, often including listings of the serfs or other persons attached to the lands of the monastery. The defters are Ottoman tax rolls written on a variety of occasions, such as the accession of a new sultan, a change in taxation practices, or in some historical periods regularly, much as the Internal Revenue Service comes around with its annual scything. These documents apparently abound, but they are not always useful for our purposes. Most of them are still in their original, untranscribed form, either in the MS style of medieval Serbian or in the pre-Atatürk orthography of Ottoman Turkish. Some of the Serbian documents have been transcribed into a standard linear orthography, using the fonts for Old Church Slavic; some of the Ottoman ones have been translated into modern Serbian, Turkish, or Hungarian.

You can appreciate that the corpus of data with which I can deal is so limited because I have few of the skills necessary to deal with these materials. Like many of my ethnographic predecessors, I find myself in a strange land, of a strange tongue, and hampered also because all of my informants are dead. I would shrink from the task and leave it to the historians and palaeographers who have the necessary competence, but they have left the field largely untilled since Novaković's initial plowing (perhaps with the exception of Jireček), contenting themselves with picking along his furrows. No one, to my knowledge, has ever returned to the original evidence in detail. All I can offer in my defense is curiosity and a middling knowledge of modern Serbian. Fortunately, knowledge of the modern language and some study of Old Church Slavonic help one proceed through the restricted syntax of tax rolls written in medieval Serbian. This is a bit like reading Vulgar Latin from a knowledge of modern Spanish and memories of *amo, amas, amat.*

These impediments of ignorance and incapacity aside, the documents would give any investigator serious difficulty. In order to be useful for analysis, a document should distinguish the boundaries of households within its listings without ambiguity. One must be able to tell where one household stops and another begins. Further, the relationships of the individuals to one another within a household must be explicit. Finally, all the members of a household should be included in the listing.

I know of only one document that approaches these requirements, the chrysobull of Chilandar, written probably in 1357, granting certain villages in the Strumica region to the monastery of Chilandar on Mt. Athos.[6] This document is unique in its specificity. It clearly marks the boundaries of households by a variety of syntactical devices, listing the land, stock, and other chattels of families, and giving the names of male and female, adult and immature family members by their relationship to the head of the household or to others included in the unit. No other document deigns to mention women, except for some who are widowed heads of households, and even the Chilandar MS may underreport girls by as much as 30 percent. Moreover, for all its virtues, the Chilandar MS lists only 137 households, a paltry sample for such an important task. The chrysobull of Sveti Stefan, written between 1313 and 1318, lists about 500 households that are clearly distinguishable one from the other, but it is not specific about the number of persons in households and the relationships between them.[7] A typical entry, for example, would read: "Jovan with his brothers." One cannot distinguish households of two brothers from those of three, four, five, or more. A better list is the Ottoman defter of the county of Belgrade in 1528 which includes about

2,000 well-defined households with clearly stated membership.[8] A second document dealing with the same set of villages, dated a few years later, enables one even to estimate the proportion of listed males who are married, thus permitting a more accurate interpretation of household structure.

THE CHRYSOBULLS OF DEČANI

The Goliath of these documents, however, consists of a pair of chrysobulls naming the properties of the monastery of Dečani in the region of Metohija. Each list covers more than fifty of the same villages. Each contains about 2,000 households and more than 5,000 persons. I will use these documents, particularly the first one, to exemplify the process of analysis and the limits placed on our knowledge by the nature of the evidence, and to draw some preliminary conclusions.

In 1880, Miloš S. Milojević presented to the Serbian Scholarly Society the original MSS and his linear transcriptions thereof, of the two chrysobulls of Dečani. At the behest of the Society, Stojan Novaković and the Archimandrite N. Dučić checked the transcription and arranged publication in the same year. The editors made few comments on the two MSS (Milojević had made none whatever), except to note that the chrysobull consisted of two examples, not much different from each other and that the first was signed by King Stefan Dečanski and the second by him and by his son. In other words, the two MSS were taken as two copies of the same document, verified in one case by a single royal signature and in the second by two. Eleven years later, in his pathbreaking work, *Selo* [The village], Novaković still referred at one point to "the two texts" of the MS, but at other points marvelled at the important differences between them, which he attributed to the geographical mobility of the population and the eagerness with which persons attached themselves to the monastery and settled in its villages. He suggested 1330 as the date of one document and 1336 as the date of the other. In other words, his later work provides a second interpretation, that one document is clearly later than the other, by a defined amount of time, and that it is not a literal copy but must have been based on a second census that reflected changes in population. The establishment of these points is critical to interpretation of the documents. Clearly, if we have two independent censuses of about 2,000 households each, six years apart in the fourteenth century, with substantial overlap between them, so that some villages, households, and persons are represented in both, we will have found a gold mine for historical demographic research. Unfortunately, all that glitters is not gold.

DATING

The first problem concerns the dating of the two MSS. To avoid confusion at this point, I will refer to the two MSS as MS-a and MS-b. MS-a is signed by Stefan Uroš III, later called Stefan Dečanski, "by the grace of God king of all Serbian and littoral lands." In the lines preceding the signature, the MS notes its signing at the royal house at Porodimlja and refers to the recent victory over and death of the Bulgarian king Mihail Šišmanić at Velbuzhd (Kyustendil) on July 28, 1330. MS-b is a reasonably faithful copy of MS-a up to the signature, which reads "Stefan Uroš III by the grace of God king of all Serbian and littoral lands," differing from the signature in MS-a only in the use of the word "third" rather than the letter *gamma* which was employed in MS-a to denote "third." The second signature in MS-b is "Stefan faithful in Christ the Lord, king of all Serbian and littoral lands and of the Greek and Bulgarian regions." A brief text in Greek follows, then more in the medieval Serbian which contains a reference to the "holy" or "saintly" Stefan Uroš, and to the monastery of Dečani. Some gaps in the MS follow; then some portions that seem unrelated to Dečani at all, from my reading; and finally a signature of Stefan Lazarević, who became king and later Despot of Serbia after the defeat of Kosovo in 1389. That signature is dated June 9, 1397.

Now, some background. Stefan Dušan, the son of Stefan Uroš III (Dečanski), assumed the status of co-king at the age of thirteen in 1321, so that he could have been co-signer of such a document at any time after 1321. Inscriptions in the monastery establish its beginning date of construction as 1327 and that of completion as 1335. One inscription in the monastery, dated 1348, refers to the son of Stefan Dušan, Uroš IV. Stefan Uroš III (Dečanski) died in 1331 (according to some accounts by the hand of his son, Dušan), and Dušan (Stefan Uroš IV, known as Stefan Dušan Silni) became sole king. In 1346, he was proclaimed Emperor. These facts combine to suggest the following argument.

MS-a cannot date before 1330, because of the date mentioned within it (the battle of Velbuzhd), and it cannot date after 1331, because its signer died in that year. 1330 is the most likely date for MS-a. Since MS-b is a fairly faithful copy of MS-a, including the original date and signature, it is most likely later than MS-a, signed in addition by Dušan, but the example preserved is an even later copy of the original, made as late as 1397 or later. If the signatures of Stefan Dečanski and his son were personally made or witnessed, then MS-b could be not later than 1331, because Stefan Dečanski died in that year. However, it is more likely that MS-b is a confirmatory copy, signed by Dušan on or after his accession to the full and sole kingship.

Dušan's signature, however, is that of king, not of emperor. Thus, it must date before 1346, the date of his proclamation of imperium, even though the references to Greek and Bulgarian lands in the signature suggest that the process of expansion was already under way. A date between 1335 and 1346 seems fairly certain. Novaković also advances the argument that Uroš IV was mentioned in an inscription of 1348, and that one might expect that he would have been mentioned in any other text signed by Dušan. Thus, if he were not mentioned, the text might date before his birth in 1337. Novaković thus settles on 1336 for the date of MS-b. I think we can say with fair certainty, on the basis of these arguments, that MS-b is later than MS-a by at least five and no more than sixteen years, perhaps no more than six.

There is, however, some disturbing internal evidence. If one compares villages, families, and persons between the two MSS, one senses that MS-a may be later than MS-b. For example, MS-a has ten instances in which a man is identified by his own Christian name plus the notation, "*otac mu bil___*" ("his father was ___"). There are no such instances in MS-b. Two of the ten persons so identified in MS-a are absent or fragmentarily present in MS-b. Of the remaining eight, all are identified in MS-b by the phrase "*otac im___*" or "*otac mu___*," both of which could be read as "his father (or their father) is ___." If these differences in tense are interpreted literally, MS-b must be older than MS-a. The differences may only be stylistic. However, one may ask why a scribe would bother to make stylistic differences with that degree of consistency when only copying a document.

On the other hand, the evidence of the number of families in villages contradicts this. Whenever the number is different for a given village in the two documents, it is almost always larger in MS-b than in MS-a, suggesting growth and fission of households, with MS-b later than MS-a. This internal evidence is equivocal, but intriguing. We can make no final judgment now, but must await careful comparisons between pairs of households in the two lists. Because the relative temporal position of the two MSS is not yet perfectly certain, and the span between them also somewhat doubtful, I will refrain from further comparison and restrict what follows to a discussion of MS-a.

THE CHRYSOBULL OF 1330

This document consists in its transcription of sixty-eight pages. It has some gaps, principally in the initial, declamatory passages and the beginning of the census listing, but is otherwise apparently complete. It lists fifty-three villages, with a set of artisans (*sokalnici*) and a set of cooks (*madjupci*) distributed through these villages. A typical village listing begins with a description of the village boundaries, but the bulk of the listing, and thus of the entire MS, consists of a listing of persons, by name, juxtaposed or linked by coordinating conjunctions. The relationships between these persons are specified by kinship terms and by the use of various linking devices, such as pronouns in the dative case, names of other persons in the dative case, preposition plus pronoun or name in the accusative, patronymics, and the like. The listing of persons is also broken by punctuation marks, represented in the transcription by periods. Individuals are sometimes identified by occupation, such as priest, and sometimes by ethnicity or social status. Serbians are never mentioned as such, but two Greeks and a Bulgarian are so identified. Vlachs, shepherds of medieval Serbia, are also identified when they occur in the midst of a listing, and several villages are listed as Vlach villages. Similarly, there is one Albanian village.

The names of persons and places, often archaic, fall strangely on the ear and are sometimes cause for mirth. One of the Albanians was named *Svinoglav* (Pighead), another *Progon Mira* (Persecution of Peace). One unhappy chap was listed as *Nikola, do dna lud*, or "Nicholas, crazy to the very bottom." Another was *Golo Zlo* (Naked Evil). Forty-one years before the battle of the Marica, fifty-nine before Kosovo, one serf was named *Aladin*. One village was named Govnečije, which I leave to the etymologists to explain away.

An example of such listings follows: it is from the village of Istinići, on page 5 of Milojević's transcription. My own transcription is into the modern Serbo-Croatian alphabet, as nearly as I can arrange it.

> Selo Istinići. a u njih Jegoš a sin mu Miloš. a ded im Dragić. Mavren a sin mu Rajko i Ratko i Bogoje i Dobroslav. Priboje a sin mu Radovin. i Rajko i Djurdje. Radoslav a sin mu Denko. (Village Istinići and in them Jegoš and his son Miloš. and their grandfather Dragić. Mavren and his son Rajko and Ratko and Bogoje and Dobroslav. Priboje and his son Radovin. and Rajko and Djurdje. Radoslav and his son Denko.)

Several problems of interpretation immediately arise. Although some kinds of grouping of persons are clearly involved, one cannot easily determine what kinds of groups they are, or what their boundaries are in the listing. Ellipses and other problems of identification of the relationships between persons occur. Before we can count or classify anything, we must make some preliminary assumptions.

What Kinds of Groups Were They?

No matter what the precise boundaries of the groupings in the listing may be, they demarcate sets of individuals related by kinship. No explicit statement indicates that these were residential groups, although everything we know about Balkan ethnography would suggest that these were just the groups of kinsmen who would live with or close to one another. You will note that all the persons given in the example above are males; indeed, only one woman is mentioned in the entire list of more than 5,000 persons. From what we know of Byzantine, medieval, and Ottoman taxation practices, we would conclude that the persons listed were what Serbian sources call *poreske glave*, or taxable heads. They could have been listed in sets of kinsmen simply as a device in tax accounting. However, since we possess Ottoman tax lists in which kinsmen are scattered helter-skelter in a list, the order in this one suggests that the sets of kinsmen possessed something in common besides consanguinity, probably a common domicile.

The document also has a certain patterning evident in the way it lists persons. After the first male, whom I have taken to be the head of the group, his sons generally follow, if he has any. After his sons come his brothers, if he has any, then his brothers' sons, if they exist. Some miscellaneous uncles or in-laws may occur, but the person mentioned last, if at all, is usually the grandfather of the house (*ded*). The Serbian scholars who have dealt with these kinds of lists have always assumed the included groups are households, zadrugas. No one can prove that they were zadrugas, rather than a looser territorial aggregate, such as a set of agnates living close to one another, or simply an extended kin network. But if we admit what careful ethnography seems to make clear, namely that the zadruga has a flexible spatial definition varying from the *vajat* (sleeping hut) to co-owned but differently located farms, it seems most reasonable to take these groups as zadrugas.

What Are the Boundaries?

There are two ways to define the boundaries of the groups in the listing. One is to consider as co-members of the same group all individuals linked by coordinating conjunctions. In the example above, by this definition, Jegoš, Miloš and Dragić would all have been members of the same zadruga. Another way is to utilize the punctuation marks in the MS as the boundaries of households. By this definition, in our earlier example, Jegoš and Miloš would have been in one household and Dragić in another. Novaković uses the first of these definitions. This makes the zadrugas appear larger than if the other definition is used. For the purpose of this study, I use the second, more conservative definition, but without claiming that it is the only or even the best way to define the internal boundaries. I will not consider other possibilities of establishing sub-groups within the zadrugas on syntactic grounds, such as differentiating the two Serbian coordinating conjunctions, *i* and *a*.

Specification of Kin Relationships

Many of the kinship relationships specified in the MS are straightforward, but others require interpretation. The first is the problem of group nouns, such as (and I will use the modern Serbian equivalents here and throughout) *deca* and *braća* (children, brothers). We do not know whether the scribe used such group nouns, rather than listing specific individuals, because he was lazy, or because the status of those persons or of their fathers made it unnecessary to list them individually under existing tax regulations. Different censuses, as already noted, have different procedures in this regard. In the Dečani chrysobull, the group nouns are used relatively rarely, almost always constituting the only specification following the name of the head. For example, in fifty instances a man is listed *sa decom* (with children) only; two in which he is listed *sa decom* and with his own father; one in which he is listed *sa decom* and with a brother who is himself given as *sa decom*; six in which a man is listed *sa braćom* (with brothers) and *sa decom*; one in which he is listed *sa decom* but having another adult male of unstated kin relationship in the house; and two with a brother in addition to the head, one of these brothers having a set of children given as *deca*. The first difficulty with such specifications is that we cannot count how many people are involved. The second is that we may not want to count them in the same way we count other individuals listed. Intuitively, it seems likely that a census which named so many persons individually, those listed by group nouns only were old enough to notice (that is, more than infants), but not old enough to tax or to require to labor for the monastery.

The second major problem is that of ellipsis. You will note in the example above from Istinići that Mavren could be interpreted as living with one son and three unrelated males, since these three are not listed as kinsmen at all. However, it seems more reasonable to assume ellipsis and interpret all of them as sons. Throughout the analysis of the document, I have assumed that any person listed without a specification of relationship had the same relationship to the head of the group as the person before him in the list. If no person in the list had any relationship given, I assumed them to be brothers to one another. Thus, in Istinići, I judged that Rajko and Djurdje were brothers; it makes very little ethnographic sense to assume anything else. In this instance, if we shift to Novaković's definition of the household boundaries, ignoring the punctuation, Rajko and Djurdje immediately become sons of Priboje and thus brothers between themselves and to Radovin.

However, I have not always taken the kinship terms in the MS literally. If a listing gave "brothers" and "sons" interspersed, I have considered some of those sons to be brother's sons. For example, in the village of Prapraćane there occurs: "Bogoje a sin mu Dragin a brat mu Toloje a sin mu Branislav" (Bogoje and his son Dragin and his brother Toloje and his son Branislav). Dragin should certainly be interpreted as the son of Bogoje. It makes no sense to interpret Toloje as the brother of Dragin, for that would make him simply another son of Bogoje, and he could have been so listed more easily. Thus, we consider Toloje the brother of Bogoje. The more difficult point of interpretation is Branislav. Is he the son of Bogoje or of Toloje? If he were the son of Bogoje, he could as easily have been listed right after Dragin. If he were the son of Toloje, he might have been listed as *bratanac*; that kinship term, meaning brother's son, does occur in the MS, but it is rare and never occurs just after "brother." Therefore, I assume that Branislav is Toloje's son and Bogoje's nephew. Wherever the kinship terms "son" or "children" occur immediately after the kinship term "brother," I have assumed that nephews of the head were intended. All the internal evidence in the MS supports such an interpretation, the scribe sometimes seeking with patronymic, or dative, or accusative reference to establish that a son of the head listed *after* a brother was properly identified as son of the head.

Finally, the word *ded* causes a problem. This can be taken to mean grandfather, old man, or household head. Since not all households contain a *ded* but must surely have had a head, we must choose between grandfather and old man. Where a household listing gave clear evidence of two generations without the *ded*, for example, a head, his son, and his "grandfather," I took the "grandfather" to mean the grandfather of the *son,* thus the father of the *head.* This interpretation is borne out by the frequent use of the phrase "their grandfather" in such situations, indicating that the meaning was more that of "old man," rather than everyone's grandfather in the literal sense or the grandfather of the head. We adopt this usage frequently in English, as when parents speak of their own parents as "Grandpa and Grandma," using their children's terms. Further, if there were no clear indication of two generations in the household, as when a set of brothers was listed with "their grandfather," I took the "grandfather" to be their father. That this usage is not inconsistent with the first is supported by the strong likelihood that such brothers may have had small children who were simply not listed in the document, even as *deca.*

The rigorous application of these rules resulted in some anomalies, but I re-examined them and adjusted the analysis to conform to the text. The rules, of course, are not immutable. The original data were coded for computer manipulation in as literal a transcription of the original MS as possible, short of putting medieval Serbian text into the machine. They can be changed quite simply if found to be inadequate, and I have no doubt that some of them will be altered as the analysis proceeds into its final stage.

ANALYSIS

I want to stress that the statistical analysis which follows is preliminary. It was conducted on 2,003 of the 2,069 non-fragmentary households in the manuscript not subject to serious questions of interpretation. Although the questions of interpretation for the remaining sixty-six households have been settled, time has not permitted a complete re-analysis of the data for the 2,069 households. With respect to these 2,069, we may observe that they contained 5,211 persons individually listed, 75 given as *deca*, and 12 given as *braća*. Since the most conservative estimate of the number of persons listed by a group noun is two, we may surmise that there were at least 150 "children" and twenty-four "brothers." If we exclude all these, the mean number of presumably adult males per household was 2.5; if we include these, the number of presumably adult and semi-adult persons was 2.6 per household.

Unless otherwise indicated, all data given below pertain to the sample of 2,003 households. They can be classified in a variety of ways. We must first decide whether we wish to regard all of them as necessarily complex households if they contain more than one person, that is, whether we wish to assume that all individually listed males were married. Novaković at least implicitly accepted all the males listed as married and heads of their own conjugal family units, combined into larger zadrugas. However, we have evidence from at least one Ottoman list that unmarried adult males were placed on the tax polls. This same list suggests that about twenty-five percent of the males listed but who were not themselves heads of households or in the senior generation were not married. Ancillary evidence from other medieval documents also suggests that males were placed on tax rolls and labor rolls before marriage.

I believe that we must assume that some men listed in MS-a were not married and that the Ottoman list cited gives us as good an estimate as any of the proportion thereof, indeed the only estimate. I will therefore take .25 as the probability that a listed male who was not a household head and not in a generation senior to any listed male (exclusive of those given as *deca* and *braća*) was not married. These procedures are the same as those employed in an earlier analysis of the census of Belgrade county in 1528, and they permit us to reduce the list of households to a statistical tabulation of coresident heads of conjugal family units.[9]

Some examples will illustrate. Of a hundred households consisting of a man listed with his son, we would assume that seventy-five consisted of a man with a married son and twenty-five of a man with an unmarried son. Only the former would constitute multiple-family households, or zadrugas, for the purposes of this analysis. Of a hundred households consisting of a man with two sons, we would expect about fifty-six of these to consist of a man with two married sons, thirty-eight of a man with one married son, and about six of a man with no married sons. These last would not qualify as multiple family households. All of these expectations are based of course on simple probability theory and on the assumption that the marital status of one son is statistically independent from that of another. Ethnographically, we know that such statuses are often dependent and that factors such as age might affect the actual composition of families. Nevertheless, as an approximation, this procedure is an improvement over the even less tenable assumption that all listed males were married.

Proceeding in this way, we come to an interesting result. About forty-one percent of the households in the Dečani list of 1330 are "nuclear" (or, more strictly, non-multiple), consisting of a man alone, or a man "with children," or a man with a son or sons probably unmarried; some may contain an unmarried brother. Even if we accept Novaković's implicit position that all listed males were married, the proportion of nuclear families would be at least thirty-one percent. On the other hand, if the estimate of the proportion of listed males who were unmarried is too low, the proportion of nuclear families would be even higher. By way of comparison, we may note that the census of Belgrade county in 1528 also yielded a nuclear proportion of forty-one percent, that of Sveti Stefan in 1313-1318 of about seventy-four percent, and that of Chilandar in 1327 of about eighty-two percent.

Eighteen percent of the households at Dečani in 1330 consisted of a father and married sons, the father being head. An additional eleven percent consisted of father and married sons, one of the sons being head. Only six percent of the households consisted of a grandfather, his sons, one of whom was head, and some number of married grandsons, and only one household had three-generational depth in which the grandson was head. Similarly, less than one percent of the households were three-generational, with the grandfather retaining the headship. Much more common were fraternal joint families, or what Laslett and I have come to call multiple lateral family households with secondary units lateral.[10] Seventeen percent were of this type, with none of the brothers having any married sons of their own. An additional seven percent were of this same type, but with some of the brothers having married sons of their own.

DISCUSSION

First, a word of caution. The proportions given are rough, and they depend on the assumptions noted. Any attempt to interpret them, to draw some sense of process out of these synchronic statistics, must be considered tentative. We know nothing directly about marital status, because women and small children are not listed individually. We know nothing about ages. But let us see what we can discern, even if only dimly.

Although it is clear ethnographically that not everyone would have begun his married life as head of a nuclear family, and even more likely that most people would have begun it within a zadruga, it is probable that every male lived some portion of his life as head of a nuclear family. Very few would have been members of a zadruga from the cradle to the grave, or else it would have been very unlikely that as many as forty-one percent of the households were nuclear at one point in time. Let us assume that every male did live at some point as head of a nuclear family. Let us further take this point as the arbitrary starting point of the cycle of familial development for *types* of families, even though we know that it is not the initial point for *individual* families.

How old is a man who is head of a nuclear family? Even if he married while still resident in a zadruga, he ought to be no older on the average than twice the mean age at marriage, plus perhaps a bit for the time required to bear a son. This is because if he married at age A, had a son after the lapse of period P, and the son married at his own age A, the father would be aged 2A + P at the point the son by his own marriage changed the nuclear family into a multiple family household, if he remained in it. If age at marriage for males was as low as twenty, men in nuclear families would be no older than perhaps forty-five.

How young is a man who is head of a nuclear family? All the ethnographic evidence, and this historical evidence as well, suggests that men did not remain in multiple family households very long after their own sons reached maturity or even approached it. I think it is fair to guess that a man might have moved out of the original zadruga by the time some of his sons had reached fifteen. That kind of estimation puts the age of heads of nuclear families in the range 35-45, with the lower boundary probably generously high.

Take, then, such a man. He and his peers comprise forty-one percent of the population of household heads. What is most likely to happen to them next? Some will die, but the data provide us no direct evidence on that. From the data, the next most likely event is that one of their sons will marry, so that some of the household heads will have a married son or several such. Eighteen percent of the households fall in this category. What is the next most likely thing to happen to these men? Two events stand out: one, that the headship will descend to a son, and the other that the father will disappear, with one of the surviving sons assuming the headship of his brothers. Of course, if the father had had only one son, in this last instance the son would be head of a nuclear family (or solitary household, if he were unmarried).

Some of the fathers would disappear by death, their age at this point being generally over forty-five. Such deaths would contribute substantially to the proportion of seventeen percent of households occupied by a set of brothers who as yet had no married sons of their own. In some instances, however, the brothers may have already split in such a way that the father remained with one of them, who assumed headship, caring for the old man, while the others may have remained in a group. These would contribute to the number of households consisting of a single son who was head, with his retired father.

Even more important as contributors to this type of family would be sons with no surviving brothers who assumed headship. Together such one-son families comprise seventy-two percent of those consisting of a retired father with married sons. The statistics provide some support for the notion that sons in small sibling sets tended to stay together with their father, while fission was more likely in larger sibling sets, perhaps with one son going off with the father. A rough count shows the average number of sons living with fathers to be 1.9, while the average number of brothers living together without a father is 2.6.[11]

Thus, we see that after a family reached the stage at which the father had one or more married sons, the next most likely developments were that he would die, leaving the sons as a set of coresident brothers, or that he would remain with one son (perhaps his only son) in what amounted to a stem family household. The first of these developments was more likely than the second. More rarely, the father would remain in a household with several sons, relinquishing the headship to one of them before they had their own adult children, and even less often would he retain the headship if a son had his own adult son. At the next stage of household development, the most frequent pattern is that of a set of brothers with adult sons of their own, but they constitute only seven percent of the households, suggesting that fission into nuclear families was already very well advanced by that time, i.e. by the time these brothers were themselves about age forty-five or more. The rarest of all the forms belongs to the next stage, in which the household contains a retired grandfather, a retired father, and an adult grandson who is the head.[12]

CONCLUSIONS

What have we learned from this cursory examination of the medieval record? As with other medieval lists, this one supports the notion that the Serbian zadruga was fundamentally a kinship-based residential organization not altogether different from that of most peasant societies, except for the longer span of its cycle and lack of exclusivity in rights to coreside. Although it had clear legal functions and was certainly recognized as a variety of household in customary law, it was not a corporation based primarily in the law but rather acknowledged by it. If it had been a corporation based in the law, as it evidently was at some periods in the Military Frontier, we would not have seen the strong evidence for fission and the quite regular character of the developmental cycle known from so many other patrifocal or virifocal peasant societies. Further analysis of this document and its successor should tell us much about ethnic variation, variation between status groups, and change over time. It is already evident that a certain amount of household development can be seen between the first and second documents, that the household organization of the Vlachs, Albanians, and Serbian serfs differed in some aspects, and that the artisans and cooks scattered through the villages of Dečani were more frequently found in nuclear households than their peasant or pastoral brethren.

The evidence from this and other medieval documents, as well as that from the ethnographic record of the past hundred years, can be properly interpreted only in comparative perspective. The two questions that have guided most discussion on the zadruga—is it an ancient, ethnically peculiar institution, or is it an institution produced by economic and ecological pressures—do not have mutually exclusive answers. In the first place, the zadruga seems a rare institution, cast in concrete by law codes or foisted on the peasants by systematizing scholars. What we see in the evidence is households and families, and larger residential groupings, such as wards and villages. These are the precipitates in observable form of culturally and psychologically determined rules of decision-making, influenced by economic, ecological, and political considerations. It is precisely because the zadruga is not an institution but the precipitate of individually made decisions (except where it is *made* into an institution) that household form is so flexible. That many of the decision-making rules and external factors resulting in multiple-family household organization are particularly common in the history of the South Slavs is clear. However, we should always realize that much of what is common to them, particularly in the kinship system, is part of the ancient Indo-European heritage, attested still in kinship terminologies. We should also be aware that multiple-family organization is not uncommon under particular economic and ecological circumstances in societies with agnatic kinship systems, even beyond the Indo-European group. Finally, we should remember that some aspects of kinship ideology and terminology are mirrored in social systems whose principles of organization are diametrically opposed to the agnation so typical of Indo-European ones, with an almost uncanny precision.[13]

For all of these reasons, we must conclude that the existence of the zadruga is not at all unusual, but to be expected under certain conditions. Further, we conclude that continuing debate on whether it exists or not, or whether it is an institution peculiar to this or that people or not, is a waste of time. All the analytical comments that can be made about the "institution" of the zadruga have been made repeatedly over the last hundred years. It is time to concentrate on the subtle interplay of factors that create variation in household form, on social life as a dynamic process, and to abandon what Leach in another context has referred to as butterfly collecting.[14] It is, indeed, time to return to the example set by Mosely.

NOTES

1. Eugene A. Hammel, "The Zadruga as Process," in Peter Laslett, ed., *Household and Family in Past Time* (Cambridge, 1972), pp. 335-373.

2. Stojan Novaković, *Selo* [The village] (Belgrade, 1965). This was originally published in Belgrade in 1891. Further in this tradition, see V. Krišković, *Hrvatsko pravo kućnih zadruga—historijsko dogmatski nacrt* [Croatian law of family zadrugas. A historical-dogmatic (axiomatic) sketch] (Zagreb, 1925), Ognjeslav M. Utiešcnović, *Die Hauskommunionen der Südslaven* (Vienna, 1859). For a general review in English of the medieval landscape and later developments, including the relationship of the zadruga to economic and demographic conditions, see Jozo Tomasevich, *Peasants, Politics and Economic Change in Yugoslavia* (Stanford, 1955).

3. Novaković, p. 161.

4. Philip E. Mosely, "The Peasant Family: The Zadruga, or Communal Joint-Family in the Balkans and its Recent Evolution," in Caroline F. Ware, ed., *The Cultural Approach to History* (New York, 1940), pp. 95-108; "Adaptation for Survival: The Varžić Zadruga," *Slavonic and East European Review* II (American Series), (1943), 147-153; "The Distribution of the Zadruga within Southeastern Europe," *The Joshua Starr Memorial Volume, Jewish Social Studies* V (1953), 219-230.

5. Joel Halpern (with David Anderson), "The Zadruga: A Century of Change," *Anthropologica* XII (1970), 83-97; Halpern, "Serbia: The Census of 1863," in Peter Laslett, ed., *Household and Family in Past Time* (Cambridge, 1972), pp. 401-427, Joel Halpern and Barbara Halpern, *A Serbian Village in Historical Perspective* (New York, 1972).

6. Eugene A. Hammel, "Household Structure in 14th Century Macedonia," based on the transcription by Lj. Stojanović, *Stari srpski hrisovulji, akti, biografije, letopisi, tipici, pomenici, zapisi, i dr.* [Old Serbian chrysobulls, acts, chronicles, monastery rulebooks, commemorations, inscriptions, etc.], *Spomenik III* (Belgrade, 1890).

7. Lj. Kovačević, *Svetostefanska hrisovulja* [The chrysobull of Sveti Stefan], *Spomenik IV* (Belgrade, 1890).

8. Eugene A. Hammel, "The Zadruga as Process," based on Hazim Šabanović, *Katastarski popisi Beograda i okoline 1476-1566, Turski izvori za istoriju Beograda, Knjiga I, Sveska I, Gradja za istoriju Beograda* [Cadastral censuses of Belgrade and vicinity 1476-1566, Turkish sources for the history of Belgrade, book 1, volume 1, materials for the history of Belgrade] (Belgrade, 1964), 31-242.

9. Hammel, "The Zadruga as Process," p. 350 ff.

10. Hammel and Peter Laslett, "Comparing Household Structure over Time and Between Cultures," *Comparative Studies in Society and History* XVI (1974), 73-109.

11. However, this difference could stem partly or entirely from the fact that fathers might die before all their sons were mature enough to be listed. Thus, households with a father might seem to have smaller sibling sets in the filial generation, while by the time the father had died, more of his sons would be listable, so that in the absence of their father, the sons, as brothers, would appear more numerous.

12. I have omitted from discussion and from the statistics the eight households of the 2003 that included afinallv related males: six with a daughter's or sister's husband (*zet*), one with wife's brother (*šurak*), and one with both *zet* and *šurak*. The patrilocality and virilocality of the residence rules are quite clear.

13. See F. Lounsbury, "The Formal Analysis of Crow and Omaha-type Kinship Terminologies," in Ward Goodenough, ed. *Explorations in Cultural Anthropology* (New York, 1964), pp. 351-394.

14. Edmund Leach, "Rethinking Anthropology," in *Rethinking Anthropology* (London, 1961).

9: THE ZADRUGA AND THE CONTEMPORARY FAMILY IN YUGOSLAVIA

Olivera Burić

The South Slav zadruga has been the subject of extensive study by both Yugoslav and foreign authors.[1] The majority of these works have been of a monographic character, and therefore constitute a valuable source of material for theorists endeavoring to explain the growth, persistence, and disappearance of this form of social organization. They describe the zadruga principally from ethnographic and folkloristic points of view, but they also contain much material dealing with its legal and economic characteristics. Some scholars have even tried to approach this traditional Yugoslav family organization from a political perspective. However, no one has yet provided a broad and unified overview in terms of contemporary social science; and sociology, in conjunction with related disciplines, should now enter this field of investigation to provide an integrated picture of the zadruga. I will therefore focus on the question of continuity from the traditional zadruga to the contemporary Yugoslav family and even to some important societal values.

Contemporary Yugoslav students of the family have generally ignored the continuing influence of the zadruga on modern life. Rather, they have tended to view the Yugoslav family in terms of the permutation and disappearance of traditional elements and have stressed the introduction and routinization of innovation. This positive orientation towards change and the rejection of tradition as a symbol of backwardness and conservatism are understandable because of the recent history of Yugoslavia.

On the other hand, both foreigners and some Yugoslav ethnologists writing of the zadruga have often expressed great admiration for the human qualities of this mode of family organization and its system of values which stress mutual aid, cooperation, familial collectivism, egalitarianism, and a democratic spirit. They have enthusiastically noted that the zadruga provides

The English version of this paper was translated from the Serbo-Croatian and edited by Professor Andrei Simić, Department of Sociology and Anthropology, University of Southern California.

a social setting in which children, the elderly, and the infirm are uniformly protected, and resources are equitably distributed according to need. In effect, they portray the zadruga in glowing terms for affording its members a high level of personal security and satisfaction. However, some of these accounts tend toward romantic idealism and reflect a desire to slow the course of history and to preserve an archaic, "utopian" social form. Others appeal to political ideology, seeing the zadruga as a sure defense against the spread of socialism and communism.[2] Regardless of their validity, all of these points of view have stimulated discussion and remind us that the realities of social process must not be lost from sight, and that each step in the development of the forces of production requires corresponding and appropriate forms of social relationships and organization.

In this respect, some Yugoslav scholars have been critical of foreign investigators who have sought to elucidate the origins of the zadruga in terms of ethical principles and ideas,[3] and to explain its disappearance as a result of psychological factors.[4] Similarly, some have also criticized the suggestion that the changes within the Yugoslav social system were stimulated by the zadruga tradition. While these are certainly untenable hypotheses, one must also reject the views of those extreme critics who in their criticism of conservative interpretations reject many elements of lasting value from the traditional past. Undoubtedly, many such legacies have made a positive contribution to modern South Slav society, though identifying and describing them would require long and exhaustive research.

Therefore, I will limit myself to analysis of elements which clearly form a bridge between the zadruga and the contemporary Yugoslav family. Specifically, this paper will address the following points:

1. the remnants of the family zadruga structure;
2. the nature of kinship ties;
3. the survival of the zadruga system of values: collectivism, solidarity, egalitarianism, and democratic perspectives.

Finally, in addition to specifying the degree of continuity exhibited by the zadruga and the contemporary Yugoslav family, I intend to delineate those characteristics which stamp the zadruga as a unique manifestation among all other types of family organization, be they of the contemporary nuclear variety, or of various traditional extended configurations.

CHANGES IN THE STRUCTURE OF THE ZADRUGA

For almost a century, scholars have noted the erosion of one of the principal attributes of the South Slav corporate family, the size of households. Moreover, they have recognized both a decrease in the number of constituent members of individual zadrugas, and in the number of families which joined such unions. This process is still occurring today, as Yugoslav census materials testify. However, these demographic data indicate only numbers of households and their size, not the number of constituent families of which they are comprised. These statistics categorize households according to size on a scale of one to eight, with the latter including all those of eight or more members. To place this in proper perspective, one must keep in mind that the zadruga need not consist of a specific number of members, but may vary in size from as few as five to as many as one hundred.[5] Therefore, we can assume statistical categories of five, six, and seven, and especially eight or more include at least some cases of extended families which in structure and organization correspond more or less to what is commonly termed the zadruga. In this respect, the censuses of 1948, 1953, 1961, and 1971 provide a clear picture of the range of family size in Yugoslavia.

TABLE 1

YUGOSLAV HOUSEHOLDS ACCORDING TO NUMBER OF MEMBERS[6]

(in %)

Year	Total Households	Number of Household Members							8 and over
		1	2	3	4	5	6	7	
1948	100%	12.9	14.1	15.5	15.9	13.6	10.3	6.9	11.0
1953	100%	12.2	14.4	16.4	16.8	13.6	10.0	6.6	9.9
1961	100%	13.5	15.4	17.2	14.7	13.6	9.2	5.4	6.9
1971	100%	12.9	16.3	19.0	21.3	12.9	8.0	4.3	5.3
% of change, 1948–1971		+2.2	+4.5	+5.2	−0.5	−2.3	−2.6	−5.7

These figures indicate that the percentage of households of eight or more members declined by over half over a period of twenty-three years, while the number of middle-range households (with five, six, and seven members) decreased at a somewhat lower rate. In the same period, the greatest increase occurred in households with four members, households we can safely assume to be composed for the most part of single nuclear families consisting of a married couple and two children. A somewhat smaller increase occurred in the percentage of households with two or three members, while the so-called "bachelor" or "single" households remained at approximately the same level for over two decades. The decrease in the number of large Yugoslav households can be taken as an indirect indicator of the dying of the last family zadrugas. However, it is interesting to note that the process of decline in the size of households has not occurred at the same rate in all regions and among all national groups.

The reduction in the size of residence groups has proceeded at a slower rate in those regions where households have always been smaller, in Slovenia, Vojvodina, and Croatia, and more rapidly in those where they have been traditionally larger, in Serbia, Bosnia-Herzegovina, and Macedonia, areas where the zadruga has been important. However, there are exceptions to this pattern. In some regions also typified by large extended corporate families but where the pace of economic and industrial development has been slow, the decline in the size of households has been small. For example, the average number of household members in Montenegro has decreased the least, by only 0.17 persons, while in Kosovo the number has even risen. (See Table 2.)

We can also view changes in the structure of Yugoslav households from another perspective, the nature of kinship ties of constituent family members. The 1953 census represents the only attempt made statistically to elucidate this characteristic. These data are all the more significant when one considers that the geographic entities considered approximate the ethno-cultural divisions within the Yugoslav population. (See Tables 3 and 4.)

These figures clearly demonstrate the relationship between the family structure of households, on one hand, and the level of economic development and the cultural characteristics of a region, on the other. For example, Slovenia, whose economy is approximately at a Central European level, has the highest percentage of households composed of single individuals, and Vojvodina, a rich agricultural region with a long history of extensive contact with Central Europe, evidences the most frequent occurence of the nuclear family. In sharp contrast, Kosovo, economically the least-developed area of Yugoslavia, with a strong Middle Eastern tradition, shows the highest incidence of extended families, households in which live a variety of kin, in addition to the nuclear family. However, in 1953 a significant percentage of all Yugoslav families were of the extended type. Moreover, if households consisting of single persons and non-kin are excluded from consideration, the figure then rises from 30 percent to approximately 35 percent.

As previously mentioned, the number of Yugoslav families composed of one member has remained at the level of approximately thirteen percent for the past twenty-three years (see Table 1). Presuming that all those who live alone are unmarried, we may ask whether this population group has exhibited internal changes through time, in terms of other characteristics. In this respect, a comparison of statistics spanning a ten-year period reveals the following picture. (See Table 5.)

While the number of individuals living outside marital unions has remained quite constant, significant changes have taken place in the composition of this population segment. During the last decade, a marked increase has occurred in the number of men and women who either do not marry or who postpone marriage. The frequency with which women escape unsuccessful marriages

TABLE 2

AVERAGE NUMBER OF HOUSEHOLD MEMBERS BY REPUBLIC AND AUTONOMOUS REGION IN YUGOSLAVIA[7]

Year	Yugoslavia	Bosnia Herzegovina	Montenegro	Croatia	Macedonia	Slovenia	Serbia			
							Total	Proper	Vojvodina	Kosovo
1921	5.10									
1931	5.14									
1948	4.37	5.15	4.51	3.94	5.28	3.78	4.39	4.54	3.61	6.36
1953	4.29	5.04	4.55	3.81	5.30	3.66	4.32	4.44	3.50	6.42
1961	3.99	4.64	4.43	3.56	5.02	3.47	3.96	3.97	3.31	6.32
1971	3.82	4.41	4.34	3.43	4.68	3.35	3.76	3.63	3.18	6.61
Change 1921-1971	-1.28	-0.74	-0.17	-0.51	-0.60	-0.43	-0.53	-0.91	-0.43	+0.25

TABLE 3

YUGOSLAV HOUSEHOLDS ACCORDING TO FAMILY COMPOSITION IN 1953[8]

Structure of Households	Yugoslavia	Bosnia Herzegovina	Montenegro	Croatia	Macedonia	Slovenia	Serbia			
							Total	Proper	Vojvodina	Kosovo
Total Households (%)	100	100	100	100	100	100	100	100	100	100
Single	12.2	8.8	15.0	14.0	7.0	17.3	11.6	11.7	13.0	5.5
Nuclear	53.9	59.8	59.1	53.8	53.0	57.6	51.2	47.3	60.6	43.3
Extended	29.6	27.1	24.9	27.8	38.5	19.9	33.3	37.5	20.5	47.2
Nuclear or Extended with Non-kin	3.2	4.0	1.0	3.0	1.0	4.2	3.2	2.6	4.3	4.0
Non-kin only	1.0	0.3	--	1.4	0.5	1.0	1.0	0.9	1.6	--
Unknown	0.1	--	--	--	--	--	--	--	--	--

TABLE 4

YUGOSLAV FAMILY STRUCTURE IN 1953

(Based on Table 3)

Structure of Families	Yugoslavia	Bosnia Herzegovina	Montenegro	Croatia	Macedonia	Slovenia	Serbia			
							Total	Proper	Vojvodina	Kosovo
Total Families (%)	100	100	100	100	100	100	100	100	100	100
Nuclear	62.2	65.8	69.6	63.4	57.4	70.5	58.3	54.1	17.1	45.8
Extended Families	34.2	29.8	29.1	33.0	41.7	24.3	38.0	42.9	23.9	50.0
With Non-kin	3.6	4.4	1.3	3.6	0.7	5.2	3.7	3.0	5.0	4.2

TABLE 5

YUGOSLAV POPULATION 15 YEARS OR OLDER ACCORDING TO MARITAL STATUS[9]

(in %)

Marital Status	1961 Total		1961 Males		1961 Females		1971 Total		1971 Males		1971 Females	
Married	65.7		67.9		63.7		65.4		67.0		64.0	
Unmarried	34.3	100%	31.9	100%	36.1	100%	34.4	100%	32.8	100%	35.8	100%
Never Married		69.5		85.8		56.5		71.3		87.2		56.7
Widowed		26.3		11.5		38.3		23.5		9.5		35.5
Divorced		4.2		2.7		5.2		5.2		3.4		6.8
Unknown		– –		0.2		0.2		0.2		0.2		0.2

and obtain divorces has also risen noticeably.[10] This phenomenon is a sign of pronounced change in the position of women in society; women no longer regard marriage as their only alternative, as was the case in the context of the traditional family. This lack of options for women was particularly characteristic of the zadruga, where marriage was the universal expectation. In contrast, in contemporary Yugoslavia women are less and less obliged to tolerate unhappy and unsuccessful marriages, and are assured of a more independent position in society than in the past. This is reflected in the higher percentage of women employed in 1971, in contrast to the situation thirty years earlier.

TABLE 6

PERCENTAGE OF WOMEN EMPLOYED IN THE YUGOSLAV WORK FORCE[11]

1940	1961	1971
18.0	26.5	32.6

In contemporary Yugoslavia, with the exception of the very highest levels of skills and education, where men still experience greater mobility, women advance more rapidly in terms of training and qualifications than men.[12]

TABLE 7

INDEX OF GROWTH OF THE YUGOSLAV WORK FORCE[13]

	1961	1971
Growth of the Female Work Force	100	140.5
Growth of the Male Work Force	100	114.2

Factors associated with rapid modernization in Yugoslavia have also contributed significantly to the disintegration of the zadruga form of familial organization. The foremost of these is industrialization, which has radically reduced the percentage of agriculturalists in the total population.

An accelerated rate of urbanization, increased spatial and vertical mobility, and the development of extensive communication networks have been closely associated with the Yugoslav industrialization process. Of the total population of 20,522,972 (according to the 1971 census), 8,235,985 had moved from their place of origin. About 6,000,000 peasants have migrated to cities, and approximately one-third of the present urban population is of immediate

TABLE 8[14]

YUGOSLAV AGRICULTURAL POPULATION (%)

Yugoslav Agricultural Population (%)

	1948	1953	1961	1971
Total	67.2	60.9	47.0	38.2
Men	65.9	58.9	46.7	36.8
Women	51.9	62.8	52.2	39.6

rural origin. One effect of these changes has been the disappearance of village endogamy, and the opening of rural communities to influences from the outside world. Not only has the number of exogamous marriages as a whole increased, but those of an interethnic character have also grown. During the period from 1950 to 1964, the percentage of interethnic marriages rose from 9.1 percent to 12.4 percent. However, regional differences occur here too, as in other phases of the modernization process. For example, the most ethnically endogamous Slavic-speaking group are the Slovenes, while the Montenegrins most frequently marry members of other ethnic groups. Of the non-Slavic nationalities, the Albanians are the most closed, and the Hungarians the most open with regard to interethnic marriage.[15]

As the statistics show, the size of Yugoslav households has steadily declined. However, we should remember that a broad range of household size characterizes the zadruga. Some relatively small families may be of the zadruga type while other quite large households may be of the nuclear variety. Thus, it is difficult to ascertain with assurance whether the increase in household size in Kosovo is due to a proliferation of the zadruga or simply to a rise in the birth rate. In fact, a number of factors must be considered in attempting to project the number of zadrugas in a population, while using household size as an indicator. In this regard, Bogišić observed in the last century that there was no significant difference between extended and nuclear village families, and that these types of families simply represented different stages in the fission and fusion process which characterized the zadruga: "It is a great error . . . to attribute the qualities of corporacy and economic collectivity, which are characteristics of our rural family, exclusively to households comprised of a number of families, and to deny these to . . ." families of *"inokosna"* structure, that is, rural families of a temporary nuclear type.[16]

A number of more recent investigators have voiced similar opinions regarding the zadruga. For instance, Joel Halpern holds that the extended family is not actually disappearing, but that the reformulation of an existing process is taking place.[17] According to him, the South Slav family has changed from a lateral to a lineal type of extension. This suggests that the presence of the nuclear family in its narrowest sense is not a reliable indicator of the existence or absence of the zadruga. Current research dealing with this problem suggests that identification of the zadruga depends not only on data regarding family size, but also on the nature of internal organization, the quality of interpersonal relationships, and the salient characteristics of a household's ties to the external environment. The existence or absence of zadrugas can be ascertained only through such a broad approach.

In spite of the many pressures that have contributed to the decline of the zadruga, households of an unaltered traditional type still exist in some parts of Yugoslavia. A number of such zadrugas have been located and studied by, among others, the French ethnologist Émile Sicard, and the American scholars Philip E. Mosely and Joel Halpern. A large number of eminent native ethnographers have also dedicated themselves to study of the zadruga.[18] In 1968, a Yugoslav journalist, Milan Kovačević, filmed a television documentary about the Medići zadruga near the Bosnian town of Jajce, which consists of about sixty members. This same zadruga has also been the subject of ethnological studies by Miličević[19] and Gubić.[20] These materials provide one of the richest sources of data concerning the contemporary zadruga.

In contrast to most Yugoslav scholars who have written monographs regarding specific zadrugas, Blaga Petrovska[21] conducted a broad survey encompassing all of Yugoslav Macedonia. During 1968 and 1969, working with the cooperation of local authorities, the priesthood, and the peasantry, she succeeded in locating twenty-seven family zadrugas. These had the following internal composition: three households contained three separate families; fourteen consisted of four each; and ten were composed of six or more. The generational structure of these zadrugas was of two types: twenty-three contained three generations, while four consisted of four. However, Petrovska was unable to find any households as large as those which had existed before the Second World War, with as many as forty or more members. The average size of these contemporary Macedonian zadrugas was seventeen; twenty households had between twelve and eighteen members, five had eighteen to twenty, and two had between twenty-one and twenty-five members. Of these zadrugas, twenty were of the so-called "paternal" type (očinske), consisting of a father and his married sons, while seven were of the "fraternal" type (bratske), made up of a wide variety of patrilateral male kin with their wives and children. Investigation of the occupational structure of these zadrugas reveals that only forty-eight percent of the able-bodied males were employed exclusively in agriculture. However, with the exception of four cases, in each household at least one adult male worked solely in agriculture. In all cases, regardless of the occupational structure, the constituent members contributed their earnings to a common fund.

The significance of Petrovska's study is that it provides conclusive evidence of the tenacious survival of this traditional form of family organization. Moreover, such data also make a valuable contribution to the study of archaic South Slav civilization. However, the question whether the values associated with the zadruga, and which distinguish it from other forms of social organization, have disappeared from Yugoslav society as a whole is of even greater interest.

THE CONTEMPORARY YUGOSLAV FAMILY AND KINSHIP

Research regarding the contemporary Yugoslav family, both in its rural and urban variants, points to the stubborn maintenance of close ties both within the family and within the extended kinship group as a whole. These bonds apparently have not significantly slackened during any phase of the industrialization and urbanization process. In this respect, Yugoslavia may differ from most other developing nations, where evidence suggests that family and kinship ties are frequently severed during the primary phase of modernization, resulting in the isolation and alienation of the family group. In contrast, except for a few areas under strong Central European cultural influence, such a phase of familial alienation from the broader kinship network has not occurred in Yugoslavia. Indeed, the contrary has been the rule, even during periods when society as a whole was emphatically rejecting other remnants of the past. Moreover, the maintenance of kinship ties has played a vital role in the modernization of Yugoslav family life and society.

Before the Second World War, Sicard prophetically noted that "the zadruga will disappear but its spirit will remain. . . . A spirit of mutual aid in the form of the *moba*, because its primary aim is not living together, but rather taking from the soil all it can yield. Therefore, family quarrels are forgotten . . . the spirit of the zadruga does not die after its division; the *moba* remains, that is to say, the custom of mutual aid which constitutes one of the oldest traditions of the South Slavs."[22] Similarly, a number of contemporary authors have cited the tenacity of elements associated with the zadruga. For example, Konstantinović-Čulinović has observed that while "zadrugas were formally disappearing . . . their division was frequently incomplete, and people continued to share their basic property: wells, carts, mills, plows, communal graves. . . ."[23] She further notes that old family zadrugas still survive in the Croatian area of Zagorje into the 1970's, and that "in the collective conscience of the inhabitants . . . the old values of social behavior live on."[24] In a similar vein, the Halperns comment that "the successive division of zadrugas has taken place within increasingly smaller groups . . . however, mutual help continues when the group divides, labor is exchanged, equipment is borrowed freely, and money is loaned without interest."[25] Simić, in his study of rural-urban migration in Serbia, writes, "though households are smaller, the developmental cycle of the family shorter, and contemporary village life more individualistic than in the past, elements of corporacy and associated values linger on. Although communal patterns of production and consumption no longer bind together large groups of agnatically related kin . . .. there remain strong feelings of collective responsibility and representation, as well as a firm moral imperative regarding kinship relationships."[26] In summary, Hammel observes that, "the ideology of kinship is much the same as it always was."[27]

The values associated with mutual aid and kinship corporacy persevere today in village and city alike, and are particularly notable in the context of relationships linking rural and urban kin. They may be expressed in the form of material aid, such as the help urban families extend to their peasant relatives by participating in seasonal agricultural labor, or by the substantial contributions of food villagers make to their city kin. In the city, apartments are always open to country relatives who arrive for medical treatment, to negotiate business, to educate their children, or to seek employment. Hammel has noted that "about a fifth of a sample of 500 Belgrade workers said that a kinsman had helped them to find a job."[28] In effect, relatives are willing to perform all kinds of services, and to intervene in times of need. During their formative years, children are offered the protection of a web of kinship ties. Relatives are always ready to rush to the aid and defense of a child, whatever the problem. Moreover, such help is offered not only during crises, but also at times of rejoicing, occasions that must be shared with kin no matter how far distant. In the case of weddings and other rites de passage, relatives sometimes even come from abroad to participate.

Weddings provide an excellent example of kinship solidarity. In both the village and city, festivities frequently assume gigantic proportions. Even today, they have not lost their traditional character, and changes have been principally in form rather than in content. For instance, automobiles have replaced horses, and electric household appliances have been substituted for native handiwork as gifts. A common Sunday sight in Serbian villages, provincial towns, and even Belgrade, is a long column of automobiles festooned with flowers and embroidered towels, decorated as once were horse-drawn carts and fiacres. At the head of the parade flutters an enormous national flag. Behind the car bearing the white-clad bride and groom follow the wedding sponsors and attendants, the closest kin, and other relatives, in the order of their places in the family hierarchy. To the accompaniment of piercing horns, the wedding party sets off from the houses of the bride and groom to the opština (the District or Commune Hall) (and in some cases also to the church), where the ceremony is performed. Following the nuptial rites, a reception is held, and traditional wedding customs are performed. The magnitude of such rituals is such that the aid of kinfolk in their organization and realization is essential. Moreover, kin will also extend substantial assistance to the newlyweds in establishing their new household.

Contemporary Yugoslav scholars often ignore or treat in a cursory manner the strong ties which link both close and distant kin into a network of reciprocity. This phenomenon has been taken as common knowledge, as belonging to the natural order of events. Such manifestations have been all too pervasive and obvious to arouse interest. However, this has not held true in the case of foreign investigators, and the works of Sanders,[29] Halpern,[30] Hammel,[31] and Simić[32] have revealed the depth and tenacity of kinship relationships among contemporary South Slavs.

Recent Yugoslav economic research suggests the importance of kinship for the standard of living. Investigators encounter great difficulty in ascertaining the nature of family budgets. For example, income derived from the receipt of agricultural products, or from services rendered by village or urban kin to their city or country counterparts, has generally been ignored, although this represents a significant contribution to a family's standard of living. Similarly, otherwise unemployed housewives make substantial contributions to the household budget through temporary work on the holdings of their rural kin. One investigation pointed out that about half the families studied spent their annual vacations in the countryside, where they participated in the principal agricultural tasks.[33] In many instances, the rural relatives help provide the annual vacation. Frequently, during the summer months, relatives care for or entertain children. In other cases, an entire family will move in with kin who have a house on the seashore or in the mountains. The constellation of the traditional zadruga is sometimes approximated in this recreational framework. On the other hand, such an annual vacation may at times represent a burden rather than a true rest, though even in this negative guise the respite from the routine of modern urban life has positive aspects.

Undoubtedly, kinship reciprocity has exerted a positive influence on Yugoslav social development. However, strong attachments to one's kin, and a set of values stressing the obligatory rendering of assistance at all costs, have also produced a number of negative phenomena, which are usually termed "familiarizm" in a pejorative sense.

COLLECTIVISM AND SOLIDARITY

The South Slavs esteem highly the idea of collectivism. However, opinion is divided concerning its exact nature and form in the Balkans. During the last century, this problem attracted the attention of Bogišić, who made the following observations:

It had been fallaciously believed that the individual is totally absorbed by our village family. It appears that the Great Russian peasant family integrates the individual in a very different manner from that of the South Slavs. However, even in this case, as elsewhere . . . individual rights are not lost, but retained. It is erroneous to confuse the collective character of the peasant family with the communism of the first Christians. . . . [34]

There is no justification for regarding collectivism and individualism as antipodes, either in earlier times or today. Moreover, the present greater refinement of ideas regarding the concept of collectivism adds weight to this contention. The transformation of attitudes regarding collectivism has gone hand in hand with the metamorphosis of the Yugoslav family. Collectivism has less and less signified communal living and the common holding of economic assets, but has become associated with a more generalized participation in kinship reciprocity. Familial collectivism today above all else revolves around sentiments of common membership in a particular lineage. For some, these feelings encompass only close relatives, while for others, they include quite distant kin. Although some stress on patrilineality still perseveres, especially in the village, matrilateral ties have grown in importance, particularly in the city. [35] This appears for the most part in terms of informal mechanisms. Married daughters first turn to their own mothers for aid, and such older women frequently act as foci of kinship solidarity. Thus, women often sustain the ties between village and city. Today husbands often become more attached to their wives' families than to their own. A current bit of folk humor wryly comments on this circumstance: "Where are you from?" "From where my wife is from!!"

Sentiments of common membership and kinship solidarity are supported by a concomitant system of values. To help a relative in need is a moral imperative that one seldom dares transgress. In contemporary Yugoslavia, though many young people are achieving high levels of educational and social mobility, they rarely forget those family members who have aided them. Such obligations are regarded as part of the "natural order," and people uncritically strive to fulfill them. As in the normal course of events in other societies, most parents attempt to rear their children to the best of their ability. In return, Yugoslav children also consider it their duty to care for their parents in old age and infirmity, wherever they live and whether or not social services and help are available.

The high level of collectivism and solidarity typical of the South Slav kinship group does not mean that internal conflict or dissent do not occur. The current dramatic changes the contemporary Yugoslav family is experiencing frequently bring such conflicts to a head with serious consequences. However, I believe that the values and moral attitudes associated with familial collectivism and solidarity have not yet been seriously eroded. Moreover, these ideas today reach beyond the family and have taken on a broader and more universal character. This has been a complex process, and it is difficult to trace the exact links to traditional forms of South Slav social organization. Even so, it appears likely that basic attitudes and values associated with collectivism in both its familial and social contexts can be attributed, at least in part, to the zadruga, which nurtured such concepts for centuries.

Moreover, the zadruga once played a role transcending the narrow boundaries of the kinship group. In this respect, it made a major contribution to the centuries-long struggle of the South Slavs against foreign domination. For example, the Austro-Hungarians offered special privileges to Slav zadrugas settled in the Croatian-Slavonian Military Frontier because they represented a bulwark against Turkish aggression. Similarly, Svetozar Marković describes the role of the Serbian zadruga under Turkish rule as a strong impediment against the military domination of the Ottoman Empire and as a protector of national identity.[36]

In contemporary Yugoslavia, the inculcation of values associated with collectivism has facilitated the unification of different social and ethnic segments and regions into programs of common action. Such participation has frequently been accomplished through considerable personal sacrifice in order to promulgate the well-being of the community as a whole. Such activities range from village collective labor parties (*mobe*) to voluntary youth brigades carrying out projects in underdeveloped regions of the country. This all adds weight to the evidence suggesting the presence of a deeply ingrained collective spirit pervading the South Slav mentality.

EGALITARIANISM AND DEMOCRACY

Closely allied to sentiments of collectivism and solidarity are those of egalitarianism, equal participation in the decision-making process. In contemporary Yugoslavia, this egalitarianism is reflected in political life by a democratic system of participatory decision-making. Many scholars consider this same quality of egalitarianism the quality which distinguishes the zadruga from other traditional forms of the extended family. In this regard, Mandić holds that the zadruga differs from other forms of extended familial organization because of the presence of the element of democracy:

> The organization of the zadruga is democratic, while the structure of the Russian fraternal family is autocratic. In the former case, the household head may be deposed and elected at will, while in the latter, the *bol'shak* is a lifelong chief with unlimited authority.[37]

Ilić also notes these same democratic tendencies in the zadruga:

Whenever the household doubts the rectitude of the headman, they have the right to replace him, and in extreme cases, to ostracize him . . . The headman's power is not absolute. In most cases, it is limited by the will of the other household members, i.e., by the Household Council. [38]

Sicard's opinion regarding the participatory nature of decision-making within the traditional South Slav corporate family is in a similar vein:

The power of the headman does not resemble that of the *paterfamilias*. In administration, he seeks the counsel of others, and the disposition of holdings is resolved at a community meeting by a vote that must be unanimous. . . . In contrast to the power to command endowed in the *paterfamilias*, the members of the zadruga delegate to the headman only the right to advise. [39]

Mosely provides a concise definition of the character of democracy in the zadruga, pointing out at the same time its limitations: "Decisions regarding all affairs in the zadruga are made by all married men together." [40]

The most systematic analysis of the salient differences between the patriarchal family and the zadruga was made by Bogišić in the nineteenth century. Considering a single element of organization, the control of property, he noted the essential characteristics which distinguished what he termed the "urban" or "Roman" (patriarchal) family on the one hand from the "village family zadruga" on the other:

IN THE URBAN FAMILY	IN THE ZADRUGA
a. As in the Roman family, the father has the absolute right to dispose of all property without consultation with, or permission from, other family members.	The elder or headman (*starešina*) cannot dispose of zadruga property without the consent of other adult members.
b. During his lifetime and upon his death, the father has the right freely to dispose of property except where national laws retain something in benefit of the children.	As is the case during his lifetime, the headman cannot freely dispose of zadruga property in legacy.
c. Even when infirm, the father has the right to direct the household; this cannot be denied him without his assent; when he is replaced, a deputy functions in his name.	The headman, young or old, can always be replaced when the zadruga members deem it necessary and beneficial.

d. While the father may dispose of household property on his own authority, it is natural that he should divide it during his lifetime among his children, though no one has the right to force him to do so.

According to customary law, any adult male member of the zadruga may demand his share of the communal property at any time.

e. As a rule, inheritance is divided at the time of the father's death, since upon the death of the headman the family in effect also ceases to exist.

Upon the death of the zadruga headman, another takes his place, but this is all that need occur, since the division of property does not depend upon anyone's death; the functioning of the family continues as in the past.[41]

Rights in property constitute one of the most crucial areas of social life. Therefore, the associated decision-making process should provide a reliable indicator of the level of democracy present in both the family and in society as a whole. In this respect, the zadruga was synonymous with a democratic form of organization that did not recognize the prerogative of the powerful. This is reflected in a still-current folk saying from Slavonia: "Svaka sila za vremena, samo Božja vikom traje, a zadružna redom ide" [Every power is temporary, only God's lasts forever, and in the zadruga it passes from one to the next].

Within the institution of zadruga, one can discern various patterns of participatory democracy. For example, Ilić believes that the power of the headman was more circumscribed among the Serbs and Croats than among the Montenegrins. He observes that the headman in Montenegro was not always obliged to render accounts to the household community. For instance, in the case of disposal of property, in Montenegro only the elder members of the zadruga needed to agree, while in Serbia the Household Council had to concur, and in Croatia the decision was rendered by a majority.[42] Citing similar variations, Konstantinović-Čulinović believes that the Croatian Zagorje was the area characterized by the highest level of democracy, and contrasted most sharply with the Dinaric region of western Yugoslavia, where headmen held the absolute right of decision. Another element which manifested considerable variation was that of female position in the power structure of the zadruga. In Zagorje, women frequently acted as household heads,[43] and in Montenegro elderly women sometimes joined the household Council or acted as principal advisors.[44] Similarly, in Bosnia and Herzegovina women were traditionally granted suffrage. On the other hand, in Serbia, probably as the result of strong Middle Eastern influence, democracy applied only to males, and women were not allowed to join the Household Council or to become zadruga heads.

The presence of democratic forms did not signify the lack of an internal hierarchy within the zadruga. Every member was expected to show obedience to the elected headman. This was especially true for minors and women, and in many regions equal participation in decision-making was apparently limited to adult male members. However, regardless of their limitations, these specific democratic elements distinguish the zadruga from other forms of extended family organization and constitute its uniqueness.

The democratic process was embodied in a family group which was also the primary unit of production in the society. In fact, at one time the zadruga constituted the only significant economic entity among the South Slavs. During centuries of harsh foreign occupation, the Slavic population of the Balkans was forced to withdraw to the countryside, where the totality of life centered in village communities. In contrast, the relatively small urban centers were settled by foreign immigrants: Greeks, Turks, Tsintsars (a merchant class reputed to be of Thracian origin), Gypsies, and others. Thus, for centuries the South Slavs possessed no level of social organization outside the family and the village. At this time, the basic producers were agriculturalist zadruga-members, who participated in this early form of democratic process. However, the zadruga was not merely a productive unit, that is, simply an integrated collective of producers of society's basic needs, but also a procreative entity.

Individual zadrugas were composed of nuclear families which were clearly differentiated in terms of separate sets of conjugal relations. The nuclear family was not the owner of property, and it carried out many of its functions in the context of the zadruga, but it still retained a clear-cut sphere of prerogatives in marital and family life. Within this framework, sharp distinctions based on the ascribed characteristics of sex and age blocked the democratic process. Thus, judging from the evidence, the contemporary South Slav family could not possibly have inherited a tradition of egalitarianism and democratic decision-making from the tradition of the nuclear family within the zadruga. Moreover, the submissive role of women which typified heterosexual relationships within the component nuclear families of the zadruga was subsequently strengthened by marriage codes based on Roman law. Today, though the Yugoslav socialist revolution has accorded women full legal rights, women are still struggling for equality with men within the family.

The traditional values of egalitarianism and democracy embodied in the zadruga have found expression in the Yugoslav family of today. However, it is difficult to trace specific causal links to the zadruga, especially because the contemporary basis of social relationships is so totally different from that which prevailed in the past. Nevertheless, the values associated with collectivism and corporate solidarity and those related to democracy and egalitarianism all have deep roots in Yugoslavia. Their current evolution has simply transcended their previous familial boundaries, giving them a more universal and humane character reflected in a mentality antagonistic to absolute power, social injustice, and what we regard today as "unjustified social distinctions, alienated power, power of the bureaucracy, and power of the technocracy." This offers at least one explanation of widespread Yugoslav popular acceptance of any program oriented toward leveling social differences, or abolishing centers of alienated power. It also helps explain the enthusiastic popular acceptance of ideas promulgating participatory democracy in all areas of life.

CONCLUSIONS

The most significant recent change in the structure of the Yugoslav household has been a reduction in its size. Over the last fifty years, the average number of members in a family has declined from 5.1 to 3.8. However, while the great corporate households consisting of scores of members have all but disappeared from the Yugoslav countryside, many modes of behavior and values associated with the zadruga have survived both in the contemporary family and in society as a whole.

While modernization has transformed the economic basis of Yugoslav society, familial and kinship relationships are still characterized by a high level of solidarity, and economic and ritual reciprocity. A strong egalitarian and democratic element expressed in the participatory nature of the decision-making process typified the traditional zadruga, and has found continuity in a more humane and universalistic form in society as a whole.

NOTES

1. Ljubomir Andrijević, *Bibliografija o porodičnoj zadruzi kod naših naroda* [Bibliography concerning the family zadruga among our people], *Glasnik Etnografskog Muzeja,* No. 36 (Belgrade, 1973). This work contains about eight hundred entries.

2. Živoin Petrich, "Opposition between Communism and Bourgeois Democracy as Typified in the Serbian Zadruga Family," *Illinois Law Review* XVI (1922), 423-435.

3. Oleg Mandić, "Radovi E. Sicarda o zadruzi kod Južnih Slovena" [The works of E. Sicard concerning the South Slav zadruga], *Historijski Zbornik* III (1950), p. 376.

4. Milenko Filipović, "A Review of Philip E. Mosely, 'The Distribution of the Zadruga within Southeastern Europe,' " *Radovi Vojvodjanskih Muzeja,* No. 3 (1954), p. 357.

5. Valtazar Bogišić, *O obliku zvanom inokoština u seoskoj porodici Srba i Hrvata* [Regarding the form called *Inokoština* among Serbian and Croatian village families] (Belgrade, 1884), p. 40; Vasilj Popović, "Zadruga" (The zadruga), *Glasnik Zemaljskih Muzeja Bosne i Hercegovine* XXXIII (1921).

6. *Statistički Godišnjak Jugoslavije: 1973* [The statistical yearbook of Yugoslavia: 1973] (Belgrade, 1973), p. 88. Numbers in this and the following tables have been rounded off.

7. Ibid., pp. 82, 348.

8. Dušan Breznik, *Društvene statistike* [Social statistics] (Belgrade, 1960), p. 114; Dušan Breznik, *Recherches sur la Structure Familiale des Ménages en Yugoslavie,* International Population Conference, New York, 1961 (London, 1963), pp. 187-198; *Statistički Bilten* [Statistical Bulletin], No. 30 (1954).

9. *Statistički Godišnjak Jugoslavije: 1973,* p. 84.

10. The number of widowers and widows is understandably decreasing, since the survivors of marriages in which the husband or wife died during the war are now dying out.

11. Olivera Burić, *Položaj žene u sistemu društvene moći Jugoslavije* [The position of women in the system of social power in Yugoslavia], *Sociologija* XIV (1972), 62.

12. Ibid., p. 63.

13. Ibid., p. 62.

14. *Statistički Godišnjak Jugoslavije: 1973,* p. 88.

15. Ruža Petrović, *Etnički mešoviti brakovi u Jugoslaviji* [Ethnically mixed marriages in Yugoslavia], *Sociologija* VIII (1966), 89-104.

16. Bogišić, p. 50.

17. Joel M. Halpern and Barbara K. Halpern, *A Serbian Village in Historical Perspective* (New York, 1972).

18. Among others, refer to the work of Milenko Filipović, Spiro Kulišić, Milenko Barjaktarević, Andrija Stojanović, Nikola Pavković, Blaga Petrovska, Mark Krasnići, and Vesna Konstantinović-Čulinović.

19. Josip Miličević, *Porodična zadruga "Medići"* [The "Medići" family zadruga]. Proceedings of the Fifteenth Congress of Yugoslav Folklorists, Jajce, 1968 (Jajce, 1969), pp. 65-70.

20. Ljubomir Gubić, "Porodična zadruga 'Medići' " [The "Medići" family zadruga], *Zbornik Krajiških Muzeja* (1969), pp. 173-184.

21. Blaga Petrovska, "Semejni Zadrugi vo Makedonija" [Family zadrugas in Macedonia], *Sociologija Sela* (in press).

22. Emile Sicard, "Osnovni elementi jugoslovenske porodične zadruge" [Basic elements of the Yugoslav family zadruga] , *Arhiv za Pravne i Društvene Nauke* IL (1936), 575.

23. Vesna Konstantinović-Čulinović, "Posljednje porodrične zajednice u Hrvatskom Zagorju" [The last family communities in the Croatian Zagorje], *Zbornik za Narodni Život i Običaje* VL (1971), 447.

24. Ibid., p. 447.

25. Halpern, p. 43.

26. Andrei Simić, *The Peasant Urbanites* (New York, 1973), p. 51.

27. Eugene A. Hammel, "Economic Change, Social Mobility and Kinship in Serbia," *Southwestern Journal of Anthropology* XXV (1969), 195.

28. Ibid., p. 194.

29. See among others, *Balkan Village* (Lexington, 1949).

30. See among others, *A Serbian Village* (New York, 1958).

31. See among others, *Ritual Relations and Alternative Social Structures in the Balkans* (Englewood Cliffs, N.J., 1968); *The Pink Yo-Yo: Occupational Mobility in Belgrade, ca. 1915-1965* (Berkeley, 1969); "The Balkan Peasant: A View from Serbia," in P. K. Block, ed., *Peasants in the Modern World* (Albuquerque, 1969), pp. 75-98.

32. See among others, "Kinship Reciprocity and Rural-Urban Integration in Serbia," *Urban Anthropology* II (1973), 205-213.

33. Olivera Burić, *Promene u porodičnom životu nastale pod uticajem ženine zaposlenosti* [Changes in family life brought about by the wife's employment] (Belgrade, 1968), pp. 91-92.

34. Bogišić, pp. 200-201.

35. Hammel, "Economic Change, Social Mobility, and Kinship in Serbia," p. 195.

36. Svetozar Marković, "Porodična zadruga i njen ekonomski značaj" [The family zadruga and its economic significance], Chapter 2 in *Srbija na istoku* [Serbia in the East] (Novi Sad, 1872), pp. 133-143.

37. Mandić, p. 379.

38. Ananije Ilić, "Sistem prava u kućnoj zadruzi u Crnoj Gori" [The system of law in the Montenegrin zadruga household], *Sloga* (1936), p. 88.

39. Sicard, pp. 572-573.

40. Philip E. Mosely, "Adaptation for Survival: The Varžić Zadruga," *The Slavonic and East European Review* XXI (American Series II) (1943), 148.

41. Valtazar Bogišić, *O obliku zvanom inokoština u seoskoj porodici Srba i Hrvata* [Regarding the form called *Inokoština* among Serbian and Croatian village families] (Belgrade, 1927), p. 171.

42. Ilić, p. 85.

43. Konstantinović-Čulinović, p. 448.

44. Ilić, p. 84.

10: THE ROMANIAN COMMUNAL VILLAGE:

AN ALTERNATIVE TO THE ZADRUGA

Daniel Chirot

Romania is outside the Southeastern European zadrugal zone. To be sure, traces have been found of extended family structure. In the Banat, for example, Romanian-speaking zadrugas apparently existed, but this area had a substantial Serbian population.[1]

In some Transylvanian Romanian villages, extended families occupied particular wards of the village. These families were called *vecinătăţile* (the neighborhoods, from the Romanian word *vecin*, neighbor), and they had certain limited economic, political, and social functions. They were primarily active at burials, when they defrayed funeral costs and helped the bereaved family. They organized some types of work, particularly those relating to cleaning their section of the village, collecting wastes for fertilizer, and maintaining streets. The village authorities used the "neighborhoods" to disseminate important news through the "father of the neighborhood." Members were supposed to meet at least once a year in a neighborhood "council." In many ways, this Romanian institution was quite similar to the *Nachbarschaft* (from the German *Nachbar*, neighbor) which performed similar functions in some Transylvanian Saxon villages. Both types of "neighborhoods" were headed by a similar type of "father" (*tata de vecini* in Romanian, *Nachbarvater* in German), who was elected by the "council."[2] But this sort of limited familial institution is far from the zadruga, which was characterized by joint control and utilization of the resources of the household.[3] To mistake any trace of extended family structure for signs of previous zadrugal organizations would undoubtedly lead to the hypothesis that zadrugas existed throughout the world.

Philip Mosely's work can serve as proof of the absence of a true zadruga in Romania. He was thoroughly familiar with Romanian village life in the 1930's and with the studies of the Gusti school of rural sociology, since he worked with the school. Further, his field notes from Romania (which I

139

examined at the Columbia School of International Affairs in March 1973) include charts, genealogies, and whatever bibliographic references he could find on Romanian family structure. This material is organized in such a way as to suggest that he was seeking evidence of zadrugal organizations in Romania. In particular, the detailed notes on certain Saxon villages show that he once planned an article on the *Nachbarschaft*. Along with these notes, I found a copy of Henri Stahl's 1936 article on the *vecinătate*. However, in his subsequent work, Mosely did not include Romania within his three zadrugal zones.[4] He evidently came to the same conclusion as Stahl, who wrote that aside from a few examples of zadrugal organizations found among Romanians in border regions where they were mixed with Serbs or Bulgarians, Romanians never had such an institution.[5]

We must pose two questions about this absence of the zadruga in Romania. First, why did traditional Romanian villages have no early zadrugal tradition? In view of the Gusti school studies of the very archaic traditional villages in the Romanian Carpathians in the 1920's and 1930's,[6] one would suppose that any traces of zadrugas would have been uncovered. The question can only be answered in a very tentative way, because of the scarcity of evidence about Romanian village life in the early middle ages. Let us put it aside for the time being and return after having dealt with the more fruitful second question.

Why did no Romanian zadrugal tradition develop? This second question is useless if one accepts the naive assumption that all family forms are descendant simply from age-old tradition, from ancient racial memory, or from mystically carried value systems. A more realistic approach, such as the one offered by Philip Mosely, suggests that the question is not superfluous because many of the conditions which nurtured and even seem to have extended the scope of zadrugal organizations in Albania, Yugoslavia, and Bulgaria also existed in Wallachia and Moldavia in the period from the sixteenth to nineteenth centuries. (Unless otherwise specified, Romania here will refer to Wallachia and Moldavia. Transylvania, the Banat, and the Dobruja have all had rather different social, political, and economic histories, and they must be treated apart from the two native principalities which arose in the thirteenth and fourteenth centuries.) In 1953, Mosely wrote: "It is unnecessary, in my opinion, to explain the strength of the zadruga in these regions of diverse languages, dialects and religions by reference back to a 'Dinaric' race, as some writers have maintained."[7] Rather, the zadruga was a functional adaptation to certain material and political conditions.

In Mosely's view, the most important factor was the need to mobilize labor to conquer the Balkan forests. Thus, the massive growth of the Šumadija in Serbia in the nineteenth century was the product of large-scale clearing of forests and their transformation into usable pasture and plowland.

The completion of this colonization effort and the subsequent crowding of the land have been important in weakening the zadruga.[8] The very same conditions existed in Romania. As late as the nineteenth century, the bulk of the Romanian population lived in the Carpathian mountains and in the sub-Carpathian depressions. Since then, a population explosion produced by the clearing of new plains lands by settlers from the hill and mountain areas has occurred. From 1831 to 1962, the population of Wallachia as a whole went up 300 percent, and the population of the plains rose 600 percent.[9] (This is not counting the city of Bucharest, whose inclusion in the statistics of the Wallachian plain would make that area's growth even more spectacular.) In the middle ages, much of the now denuded plain was covered with wild forests, and the now treeless Wallachian plains county of Teleorman is named after a Cuman word meaning "wild forest."[10] The eastern Wallachian plain had a steppe, the Bărăgan, which was equally intractable and which remained virtually empty until the second half of the nineteenth century.[11]

A second reason for the existence of the zadruga was the ". . . persistence of insecurity of life and property."[12] Romania was subjected to the same insecurities as the rest of the Balkans. Until the nineteenth century, the Turks, the Tatars, and before them other Asiatic people were a perpetual threat to the security of rural folk. As late as the 1830's, Romania had its own *haiduci* (Bulgarian, *haidutsi*, Serbian, *hajduk*).[13] Romania in the 1930's was not so insecure as Albania at that time, but a century earlier this particular factor cited by Mosely was as important in Romania as in Bulgaria, Yugoslavia, or Albania.

A third reason given by Mosely was the existence of a heavily pastoral economy until quite recently in some of the zadrugal areas.[14] The reliance on pasture land rather than agricultural land was presumably a strong deterrent to the division of land into small private plots and a stimulus to holding communal land. The Romanians of the middle ages were also largely pastoralists, and agriculture did not replace animal raising as the main basis of the economy until the nineteenth century.[15]

My purpose, however, is not to contradict Mosely's arguments, because they seem to me quite valid. The need for common pasture land rather than small individual plots, the insecurity of life, and finally, in the period that saw the change from a pastoral to an agricultural economy, the need for an easily mobilizable labor force were important in maintaining communal forms of village life in Romania, just as in other parts of Southeastern Europe they maintained the zadruga. But in Romania, the village as a whole was communal, not the extended family. Within the village, families were considerably smaller than in the zadrugal areas. The tradition was that sons, except for the youngest, left their father's home at marriage. The youngest son stayed to support his parents in old age, and he received for this the paternal home as his inheritance.[16] In other words, the Romanian communal village must be seen as a functional alternative to the zadruga and by its existence precluded the development of zadrugas.

This leads directly to a major paradox. In the sixteenth century, Romanian villages were free and communal. Except for house and garden plots, village lands were owned jointly by the entire community and could be used at will by villagers according to their need.[17] But from the sixteenth to the nineteenth centuries, the communal village dissolved. Some villages became serf villages. In others, villagers became individual proprietors.[18] In the process of dissolution, communal villages split up into extended families which might have turned into zadrugas. But this was a very transitory stage on the road to individualization of property. Permanent zadrugal institutions were not formed. A brief look at the process which governed the division of communal lands will illustrate the point.

When a communal village was divided, land was allocated to the several large ancestral families who made up the village. The forefathers of these extended families were assumed to have been the sons or brothers of the village founder. Thus, a village would be said to "walk on X number of old men." The land would be divided into X number of equal strips. Each extended family then divided its own lands and gave them to the individual nuclear families. This was done in the same way so that as many equal strips were created as there were nuclear families. Division was not always equal, for certain richer or more powerful families could impose an unequal division. Also, extended families with few descendants could hand out larger individual strips than those with more descendants, so that an individual's placement within the village genealogy was crucial. But whether equal or unequal, the division followed the system of "old men." At least in theory, only the descendants of the original "old men" had rights to the land. The procedure suggests strongly that powerful extended families existed. Further, because of the need for cooperation among villagers, it is hard to understand why families should proceed to divide lands into nuclear family holdings. Yet, the documents are clear. This type of division was increasingly common from the sixteenth until the nineteenth century. By the early twentieth century, only a few isolated villages (notably in the Vrancea in the Moldavian Carpathians, the region of Nerej) were still communal, and individual property rather than extended family property was the general rule.[19]

Two facts highlight the paradoxical nature of this development. First, villages divided in this way formed a very distinctive physical pattern. Each extended family or "old man" received a large strip going from one end of the village territory to the other. Succeeding divisions were then made in the same way, in strips running the length of the territory. This resulted in a peculiar territorial layout, as successive divisions narrowed the width of strips without affecting their length. Ultimately, this produced strips that ran for kilometers but which were so narrow that, as peasant lore had it, "A man sleeping crosswise on his land would have his boots stolen by one neighbor and his hat by the other."[20] (In a few of the uncollectivized highlands of Romania, one can still see this sort of pattern; in the 1930's, it was very common.) But only free villages divided their lands in this way. Old serf villages had a much more chaotic pattern of land holdings resembling a "puzzle." Evidently, serf villages divided their lands only later, and then in a seemingly random way that did not follow the traditional rules of division by "old men."[21]

To add to the peculiarity, in the Vrancea, which had never had a formal division of lands, another type of land tenure pattern was emerging in the twentieth century. As the Vrancea was becoming more crowded and peasants were beginning to claim private fields from communal lands, property was beginning to take on the aspect of the "puzzle" village. Chaotically arranged plots rather than long strips gave the Vrancea the appearance of a former serf area. But the Vrancea had always been free.[22]

The second paradoxical fact is that the original division in the free villages into strips by "old men" was generally based on fraudulent genealogies. At the time of division, mythical ancestors would be invented, and villagers would be placed in the invented, non-traditional village genealogy. Many documents relating to land division prove this. Also, outsiders were often allowed to take possession of village lands by the process of fraudulent fraternization, by which an outsider could become a "blood brother" of a village resident and thus gain rights over the patrimony of an "old man."[23]

These two sets of facts, that serf villages on the one hand, and the Vrancea, on the other, did not divide their lands into "old men," and that many of the genealogies used to divide lands in free villages were pure invention help explain why no zadrugal institutions developed after the dissolution of communal villages. But first, a brief history of Romania's changing polity and economy over six centuries is necessary. Otherwise, the whole situation seems too irrational and confused for explanation.

THE STAGES OF THE POLITICAL ECONOMY,
1300-1900

The evolution of Romania can be divided into five fairly distinct stages: a tributary-trade state from about 1300 to 1500 (or rather, two of them, one in Wallachia and the other in Moldavia); a period of decline of this state from 1500 to 1600; a period of "fiscal serfdom" from about 1600 to 1750; the period of the rise of "cereal serfdom" from 1750 to 1864; and finally, the period of "neoserfdom" from 1864 to 1917.

The Tributary-Trade State (1300-1500)

When Wallachia became an independent state in the latter part of the thirteenth century, and when Moldavia followed in the mid-fourteenth, free communal villages which were lightly taxed by the state characterized their political economy.[24] The state was led by a prince, the *voievod,* and a court nobility, the *boieri.* The state imposed a tribute on the villages, but this was neither heavy nor even the state's main source of revenue. The state also taxed the active east-west trade route that ran through Romania, and it participated in this trade. Thus, there was a disjuncture of sorts between the state and village society, as the villages were left very much to themselves.[25]

The Wallachian state was born after the Cuman state was destroyed by the Mongols. The Cumans had ruled Wallachia as a tributary-trade state, leaving the villages independent but imposing a tribute. Also, trade, mines, and fisheries were operated by the state or taxed. In the villages, native chiefs, *cneji,* were responsible for the collection of tribute. The system was probably the same one which had operated under preceeding nomad conquerors: Huns, Avars, Bulgars, Magyars, and Pechenegs.[26] The disorder which followed the Mongol sweep through this area allowed the *cneji,* led by warlords of village confederations, the *voievozi,* to reconquer the land and to establish a succession state to the long series of foreign states which had dominated Wallachia. The *cneji* formed the basis of the new court nobility that established itself in the fourteenth century.[27]

Moldavia's origins were somewhat different. The Mongols ruled that province much longer, until the mid-fourteenth century. In the 1350's, a Romanian *voievod* from Maramuresh (northern Transylvania) reconquered the land and established a native state. It too was a succession state organized along the same lines as Wallachia.[28] (Transylvania was also organized in the same way, but the imposition of permanent Magyar rule changed the social structure. The local *cneji* first served as intermediaries between the Magyars and the Romanian population, but they were gradually either absorbed into the Magyar nobility or fell back into the ranks of the peasantry.)[29]

Trade was of vital importance to both states; it was their basic resource. There were three important routes. The Black Sea-Lvov-Baltic route ran through Moldavia. A Black Sea-Danube-Adriatic route to Ragusa and Venice ran through Wallachia, as did a route going from the Black Sea north across Wallachia and the Carpathian passes to the German trading cities of Transylvania (chiefly Braşov and Sibiu), and from there into Central Europe and into Germany.[30]

In large part, the Mongol conquest stimulated the great expansion of international trade which characterized this period.[31] The Black Sea Genoese colonies, the two new Romanian states, and the newly created German trading cities of Transylvania all lived from the revival of the northern silk route and were important entrepôts in the trade carried on between the West and the East. Evidence from the Brașov trade registers in 1503 (at a time when the trade routes were probably already in serious decline) shows how important this international trade was for the Wallachian state. Of all the goods arriving in Brașov from Wallachia, its immediate neighbor to the south, eighty percent (by value) were Oriental goods that were Wallachian re-exports. Almost all of these Oriental goods in 1503 were carried by agents of important nobles, the *voievod,* or the state.[32] Thus, the state and the nobility did not have to tax the villages heavily. In fact, the dues the villages owed were largely limited to meeting the immediate food needs of the nobles, the monasteries, and the princely court.[33]

The Collapse of the Tributary-Trade State (1500-1600)

Starting in the second half of the fifteenth century, but greatly accelerating in the sixteenth, four factors changed the respective position of the court, the lords, and the villagers.

First, the Ottoman Empire imposed a growing tribute on the Wallachian and then on the Moldavian states. In the mid-fifteenth century, the tribute imposed on Wallachia was 10,000 gold coins. In 1521, it rose to 24,000, in 1558 to 50,000, in 1567 to 65,000, in 1582 to 95,000, in 1585 to 125,000, and in 1592 to the enormous and intolerable sum of 155,000 gold coins.[34] Whereas in the fifteenth century, the Romanian states could pay this tribute relatively easily from the profits and taxes from the international trade routes running through their territory, by the late sixteenth century this would have been impossible.

Secondly, international trade declined very seriously. By 1550, the Brașov trade registers show that the trade between Brașov and Wallachia had fallen by fifty percent since the beginning of the century.[35] This was no doubt due to the Portuguese circumnavigation of Africa and the consequent shift in trade routes, as well as to the disruptions caused by the Turkish conquest of Constantinople and of the Genoese Black Sea colonies.[36] Therefore, as the Romanian states' need for revenue to pay the Ottoman tribute rose, their most important source of revenue declined.

Third, the commercial economy penetrated the villages.[37] The villagers were largely pastoralists, and their main product was sheep. Constantinople relied heavily on Romania for its meat.[38] At the same time, the court, the nobles, and the monasteries began to shift their attention to the villages to provide an important source of revenue to replace that lost to the decline of the old trade routes. A three-way struggle developed between the villagers, the nobles, and the princes. The villagers wished to retain their independence, and the princes and nobles (lay and ecclesiastic) vied for this new source of revenue. The Turks intervened repeatedly in favor of the nobles against the princes to weaken native political institutions.[39]

Fourth, a severe population decline occurred. In 1400, Wallachia had a population of about 500,000 people. By 1600, this had fallen to between 150,000 and 180,000. This was due to the misfortunes of perpetual warfare, and to the pillaging and mass requisitioning of men, food, and animals, but also to the steeply rising taxes in the sixteenth century, which forced men to flee the country.[40]

One of the chief ways of subjecting villages was to take advantage of insolvency caused by high taxes. Insolvent villages had two choices: to sell themselves to a protecting lord, or to flee. Once in command, lords were still faced with the problem of raising revenues from the villagers. Flight was so common, and the taxable base of the population had fallen so low that the *Voievod* Michael the Brave in the 1590's prohibited flight from villages owned by lords. In other words, serfdom was decreed.[41]

The Failure of Fiscal Serfdom (1600-1750)

The serfdom decreed by Michael failed. It proved too difficult to prevent the flight of pastoral villagers, and lords found it more efficient to sell villages their freedom in return for cash.[42] By the early eighteenth century, serfdom had become quite rare. Still, collecting taxes and maintaining an adequate fiscal base constituted a problem. In order to repopulate the land, the Turks therefore ordered the Romanian governments to abolish serfdom so that conditions in the villages would be more favorable. This was done in Wallachia in 1746 and in Moldavia in 1749.[43]

This abolition, however, was purely theoretical, largely because Romanian serfdom was not a classical form of serfdom in which serfs worked a lord's demesne. There was no lordly demesne, and animals were still far more important than crops in so far as the exchange economy was concerned.[44] Instead, Romania had a fiscal serfdom in which lords took a portion of the serfs' product. The reforms of the 1740's did not end this: villagers were now theoretically allowed to move more or less at will. However, movement was hedged with so many substantive restrictions that it is not clear how free the villagers actually were. Lords were recognized as "owners" of villages they had previously controlled, and they maintained their right to collect dues for use of village lands. The tithe and corvée obligations were kept, and the latter was generally paid in kind and/or cash instead of in work.[45] In retrospect, the abolition of serfdom had few effects. Lords kept the rights they had had before, and they and the state both still faced the problem of runaways whenever the taxes and dues were too high. This limitation, added to the basically pastoral nature of the economy, kept dues fairly low. In the mid-eighteenth century, the corvée load amounted to six days a year; in Russia at that time the *barshchina* averaged about two to three days per week.[46]

The Rise of Cereal Serfdom (1750-1864)

Beginning in the second half of the eighteenth century, but accelerating very rapidly after 1829, Romania began to produce cereal crops for export, first to Constantinople, and after the Treaty of Adrianople in 1829, to Western Europe via the newly opened Black Sea. The lords used their titular ownership of the villages to impose dues on cereals. In the nineteenth century, huge new areas of the plains were turned to cereal production. From the early 1830's to the mid-1840's, Wallachian wheat production rose about 160 percent.[47] The villagers were changed from pastoralists to cultivating peasants, and the role of animal production in the Romanian economy, particularly in the export sector, fell dramatically.[48]

This change was accompanied by a bitter struggle between the peasants and the lords. The former claimed ownership of the lands they cultivated; the latter claimed ownership of all village lands. In 1864, the question was decided. In a reform which again "ended serfdom," lords received one third of the land in the villages they controlled, and peasants two thirds. By this time, serfdom had been reinstituted in the form of very high labor dues the peasants paid the lords for the right to cultivate land. Though payment of labor dues were made largely in cash and kind rather than actual labor, the measure of payment was still the labor day, and these stood at about fifty-six per year, more than nine times higher than a century before. In the reform, lords received the best third of the lands, and peasants were left with too little. Further, they still had to pay dues on the portion of the land which they now theoretically owned.[50]

Neoserfdom (1864-1917)

Unable to live on their lands, the peasants had to lease lands from the lords at high rents. A sharecropping system developed which made the peasants virtual serfs bound to the land by heavy debts in a system Romanian agrarian historians have called "neoserfdom."[51] As the population rose, the problem worsened, for a real land shortage developed. This, of course, strengthened the landlords. By 1900, about one half of one percent of all landowners (several thousand families) owned slightly over half the land; the small peasants who owned ten hectares or less formed ninety-seven percent of the landowning population but owned forty-two percent of the land.[52] Romania had become a major wheat exporter, but at a severe social cost.[53]

The system ended only after World War I, when a reform was decreed to avoid a Bolshevik Revolution.[54]

This brief outline allows us to trace the evolution of the communal village within the context of the economic and political forces which were shaping Romania from the sixteenth to the late nineteenth centuries.

THE EVOLUTION OF THE COMMUNAL VILLAGE

By the greatest of chances, we have evidence concerning the social organization of the traditional communal villages in the middle ages. A few survived into the twentieth century in the Vrancea, and ample documentation exists for this area from the eighteenth and nineteenth centuries. Henri Stahl was therefore able to reconstruct the traditional pattern that probably had existed until the sixteenth century throughout most of the country.[55]

The communal villages could exist as independent entities only in a largely pastoral economy with very rudimentary cultivation techniques and a low population density. Forest and pasture lands were available for any who needed them. Small clearings were made in the forests by burning the trees and underbrush, and these clearings were cultivated for a few years. They were then abandoned as yields declined. The clearings belonged to individuals as long as they were cultivated; then they reverted to the collectivity. Only house plots and gardens near the houses were permanently alienated from the collective patrimony. The villages were probably organized into confederations in which land disputes between villages were settled. These confederations antedated the formation of the Romanian states, because there is documentary evidence that in the very early days of the states village boundaries had already been drawn up "from the earliest times."[56] From these confederations emerged the *voievozi* who led the reconquest of the land from the Tartars. In the early days of the Romanian states, the confederations remained largely independent from the states, except for the tribute they paid. The relationship between the state and the villages may be deduced from examination of the relationship which existed between the Vrancea and the Moldavian state in about 1700. Dimitrie Cantemir, exiled former Prince of Moldavia living at the court of Peter the Great in Russia wrote, in his *Description of Moldavia*:

The second lesser republic in Moldavia is Vrancea in the country of Putna near the boundary of Wallachia, surrounded on all sides by very wild mountains. It numbers twelve villages and two thousand farms, and is ignorant of cultivation, being content like Câmpulung with the grazing of sheep. Similarly, the inhabitants pay a definite fixed tribute yearly to the prince, are ruled by their own laws, and utterly reject the prince's orders and his judges alike.[57]

The chief link between the Vrancea and the Moldavian state was a court official, the "Vornic of the Vrancea," who was the region's tax collector.[58] As Stahl has shown through numerous citations of old documents, this was the probable organization of rural Romania in the early days of the native states.[59]

The Disagregation of the Communal Village

Increasing commercialization of village products and the pressures of the nobles on the villages in the late fifteenth and in the sixteenth centuries jeopardized the communal villages in two ways. First, commercialization of village products made some families richer than others. These families then expended their use of communal property and created relative shortages for the others. This initiated a struggle between rich and poor villagers.[60] Second, outsiders, chiefly nobles and merchants (and as seen above these were not two distinct groups), tried to insert themselves into village life. In order to do this, they had to be part of the village community. The easiest way to do this was to bribe a villager into becoming a "blood brother." Thus, outsiders could gain rights over jointly held property and begin to exploit village lands with their greater wealth and power. This created the same relative shortage that occurred when richer villagers did the same thing.[61] In order to protect themselves, villagers had to break the communal solidarity of the village. If lands were divided among the families, the treachery of one greedy villager could not jeopardize the lands of the others. The key reason for the division of communal lands was protection from exploitation by rich natives or outsiders.[62]

The very same process was observed in the Vrancea in the late nineteenth and early twentieth century. Lumber companies bought out a few villagers and proceeded to strip the Vrancean forests, thus impoverishing the entire area and destroying the basis of its mixed forest-pastoral economy. Though this had not yet led to a firm division of lands by the 1930's, Stahl noted that the communal system was in a state of advanced disintegration.[63]

It was to the advantage of lords seizing villages to prevent the division of lands. For the villagers, the opposite was true. Once the process of division had begun, it continued within extended families to prevent a whole extended family from falling under an outsider's domination through the betrayal of one family member.

A substantial number of villages fell under lordly domination during the sixteenth century because of their inability to pay taxes. Such villages had no division of land; the new possessor would maintain communal forms simply by replacing the village council and establishing himself as the main arbiter of land usage. Communal villages were easier to administer because the whole village could be made collectively responsible for dues. This same process took place in Russia in the eighteenth century for very similar reasons, but there the *mir* was a new invention, or the recreation of a long dead form of organization.[64]

This explains why serf villages had the same land usage pattern as undivided communal villages. The daily organization of economic life remained quite similar. Only free villages, or villages which had repurchased their freedom from lords, had the freedom to divide their lands.[65]

Of course, many villages were mixed, part free and part serf, partly divided and partly jointly owned. There were also frequent instances of divided villages, in which some families had fallen into serfdom while others had avoided this.[66] But the general pattern elaborated here spread throughout Romania and produced either serfdom or the breakup of communal villages, except in the few remote areas that escaped the process until very recent times.

Land Clearing and the Spread of Cereal Cultivation

In the original communal villages, landclearing was a relatively small-scale and simple operation, and the isolated clearings made in the forest were not large. As cereal cultivation spread in the eighteenth and nineteenth centuries, the same process continued, but on a much larger scale. Clearings now grew into each other and were cultivated permanently instead of being abandoned. (This was one of the main problems of late nineteenth century Romanian cereal agriculture; primitive slash-burn techniques were applied to large-scale permanent cultivation, and the yields were consequently very low.)[67] This produced the chaotic "puzzle" field system of the serf villages of the plains. It was quite a different matter in the free villages that had had a formal division of their lands. But in the Vrancea, which was only moving toward a final division of lands in the 1930's, clearings were still growing into each other, so that the land tenure pattern resembled that which existed in the serf villages.

When the land was divided into private holdings by the law of 1864, officials were astonished to note that communal forms of organization still survived in many villages. [68] The law of 1864 put an end to these survivals in the former serf villages, as the lords changed their form of exploitation from the old pattern of imposing dues on villages to using peasant labor through various sharecropping arrangements.

The Distribution of Free and Serf Villages

By the late sixteenth century, about one third of all Romanian villages were entirely serf, and so many parts of others were serf that at least half the population was serf. [69] But review of available records from that period, particularly at the distribution of villages owned by the biggest landlord, the *Voievod* Michael the Brave, shows a distinctive pattern. Virtually all of Michael's villages were in the plains, which were more open to Turkish and Tartar raids than the hills and mountains. [70] They were more accessible to the tax collector. They were also more lightly peopled than the hills and mountains, and they contained many more abandoned villages. Imposing serfdom on plains villages was easier because village organization was much weaker than in the more hilly areas, and the villagers remaining tended to be in desperate straits. It was also much more important to impose serfdom on these plains areas which were so underpopulated.

The available statistics on the distribution of free and serf villages in the eighteenth century suggest that sixty to eighty percent of the plains villages were serf by the early 1700's, and from fifty to sixty percent of the hill and mountain villages were still free. [71] (The use of "free" and "serf" may seem confusing after the formal abolition of serfdom in the 1740's. These terms refer to whether or not villagers had to pay dues to lords who owned the villages. As shown above, the formal abolition of serfdom made little difference in the life of the countryside.) By 1864, less than ten percent of the plains villages were free, while in the hills and mountains thirty to fifty percent of the villages were still free. Thus, the entire period from the sixteenth to the late nineteenth century was one of gradual seizure of free villages. [72] At times the process was slow, as in the seventeenth century. During the late eighteenth and nineteenth centuries, the growing demand for wheat hastened the process. Villages that had not yet divided their lands were seized whole; in others, single families had to be bought out. The process was easiest in depopulated or as yet unpopulated areas in the plains. There, a lord could claim a village, entice colonizers from free but relatively crowded hill and mountain districts by offering them favorable conditions, and establish a village on traditional communal lines. The only distinction between these villages and the free communal villages was that the lord had replaced the village council as boss of the village. Then, as the land was progressively cleared, the lord would raise the dues and gradually reduce the villagers to serfdom.[73] Almost all of Romania's wheat was grown in the plains, where there were the fewest free villages.[74] The major landclearing operations of the nineteenth century also took place there. Landclearing could therefore proceed under a communal sort of organization, but for the ultimate benefit of the lord. Once the population density was sufficiently high, communal forms could be abolished and replaced by a sharecropping system.

This explains the seeming paradoxes which opened this discussion. It explains how communal forms could decline when landclearing operations were going on; the serf villages of the plains carried out most of the clearing, and they continued to be organized on communal lines. Meanwhile free villages were dividing up their lands. This also explains why free villages were characterized by "long strips" and serf villages by a "puzzle" structure. Finally, this process explains the urgency which led so many free villages to invent genealogies for themselves in order to divide up their lands and escape serfdom.

All this is too simplified. There were some free villages in the plains, and some serf in the hills. Often, free villages divided up their lands bit by bit instead of all at once.[75] Lands closest to the village would be divided, and more distant forest and pasture would remain jointly owned. Lords could seize villages at various stages of disintegration. They could force villages into a communal sort of organization. When villages redivided their lands after repurchasing their freedom, they might then be seized anew on grounds of tax delinquency. A powerful noble might also simply seize villages by outright force, for in this struggle lords were not always so bound by legalities as to respect formal village actions. All sorts of variations existed, so that at any one time between 1600 and 1900 many different forms of land tenure systems and forms of social organization coexisted in Romania. But the schematic outline given here explains the main trends during the entire period.

REASONS FOR THE ABSENCE OF A
ROMANIAN ZADRUGA

The first question posed about the original absence of the zadruga in Romania must now be dealt with, however sketchily the answer may be phrased.

Romanian communal villages were apparently territorially rather than family based units from a very early period. The thorough mixture of Latin and Slavic terms in the Romanian agricultural language,[76] as well as in the general language, suggests that the old Dacoroman population was quite thoroughly mixed with Slavic elements from the sixth to the twelfth centuries.[77] This precludes the possibility of a homogeneous ethnic foundation of the villages, and thus, the possibility of single family villages. From at least the early middle ages, villages were probably composed of mixed ethnic elements. Traditional Romanian villages have long had a strongly endogamous marriage tradition, while most south Slav communities were strongly exogamous. This also argues for the traditional existence of multi-family villages in Romania.[78] The fact that many Romanian villages claimed a single ancestor is not proof to the contrary; Stahl has shown that this was a myth created at the time of the division of lands in order to legitimize the newly invented genealogies used as the basis of that division.[79] The Vrancea had no mythology about ancestral founders of the villages, just as there were no long genealogies, even in the 1930's, because there was never a formal division of the land into private plots.[80]

The communal village provides an alternative solution to the problems of land clearing, of a pastoral economy, and of insecurity in a sparsely populated area. There was no reason for zadrugal organizations.

The answer to the second basic question can also be given. The communal village disintegrated because of the seizure of villages by lords. Where possible, lords maintained communal forms because they made control of the villages easier. In the plains, these forms made the land clearing operations of the eighteenth and nineteenth centuries easier. Where they could, lords prevented the fracturing of villages into extended families. Where lords failed to do this and land was divided into extended families' plots, the same forces that had brought about the original division continued to fracture the extended families and dissolved their jointly owned plots into individual plots. There was no opportunity for a zadrugal type of organization to develop.

Had sixteenth century Romania been organized along zadrugal lines, it is quite conceivable that lords would have tried to maintain this form of organization for the same reasons which prompted them to maintain communal organization. But, of course, this was not the case.

This does not close the issue. Recognizing that the communal villages and the zadrugas served similar functions leaves open the question of what consequences these two forms of organization had in the long run.[81] Many have argued that the existence of the zadruga in Yugoslavia has left strong marks on contemporary society. Many of these claims have been extrava-

gant.[82] But even Mosely felt that the zadruga encouraged social cooperation.[83] The existence of the zadruga may, in part, explain the relative success
of the Serbian and Bulgarian peasant cooperative movements in the 1920's
and 1930's.[84] The Romanian cooperative movement of that time was a total
failure.[85] On the other hand, the destruction of native aristocracies in
Bulgaria and Serbia under Turkish rule may explain this difference. In
Romania, as in parts of Albania and Bosnia, the existence of a native
aristocracy which survived the end of Turkish rule had many observable
nefarious consequences.[86] No one can be certain what parts of Romanian
national culture can be attributed to the lack of zadrugal institutions, and it is
impossible to compare Romania to Bulgaria and Yugoslavia on this basis. The
frequent misuse of research in this kind of cross-cultural exploration and the
problems associated with making firm conclusions suggest that the question
will never be answered.

One clear and surprising difference exists between the tradition left by the
communal village and that left by the zadruga. Whereas the zadruga has been
a source of nationalistic pride and research for some time, the Romanian
communal village has hardly been studied until relatively recent times, when
Stahl rediscovered it. Romanians have not developed a nationalistic mystique
about it and few are interested in studying it.

Even as skilled a social scientist as Philip Mosely was led to a dead end in
so far as Romania was concerned. The attention he paid to the *vecinătate* and
the *Nachbarschaft,* and his lack of notes on Nerej and the Vrancea region (he
knew the village and visited it with Stahl, who was a friend of his) suggest
that he failed to note the similarity between the communal village and the
zadruga, and that he focused instead too closely on a formal description of
family institutions.

In general, overly strict attention to forms of social institutions confuses
comparative research. It is tempting to try to establish a single evolutionary
scale on which to place various related institutions in order to identify the
sources and the relationships. Social forms can take so many different aspects
that attention to the functions of institutions can often illuminate social
history better than a comparison of forms. The zadruga and the communal
village were not related in any linear sequence. Yet, comparisons between the
two highlight their similarities and the common role they played in the social
history of Southeast Europe.

NOTES

1. Henri H. Stahl, *Contribuţii la studiul satelor devălmase romînesti*
[Contributions to the study of communal Romanian villages] (Bucharest,
1959), II, 109-110.

2. Henri H. Stahl, "Vecinătățile din Drăguș" [The neighborhoods of Drăguș], *Sociologie Românească* [Romanian Sociology] I (1936), 18-31.

3. Joel M. Halpern and Barbara K. Halpern, *A Serbian Village in Historical Perspective* (New York, 1972), p. 17.

4. Philip E. Mosely, "The Distribution of the Zadruga Within Southeastern Europe," *The Joshua Starr Memorial Volume, Jewish Social Studies* V (1953), 219-230.

5. Stahl, *Contribuții*, II, 110.

6. Henri H. Stahl, *Nerej, un village d'une région archaïque* (Bucharest, 1940), three volumes.

7. Mosely, "The Distribution of the Zadruga," p. 226.

8. Ibid., p. 3.

9. Constanța Rusenescu and Dragoș Bugă, "Territorial Distribution and Growth of the Population Between the Carpathians and the Danube, in the 19th and 20th Centuries," *Revue Roumaine de géologie, géophysique et géographie, série de géographie* X (1966), 77-80.

10. Nicolae Dunăre, "Interdependența Ocupațiilor Tradiționale la Români. Factor de Stabilitate și Continuitate" [The interdependence of traditional occupations among the Romanians. A factor of stability and continuity], *Apulum* VII (1968), map on page 544 showing extent of forests in the middle ages; also, *Judetele României Socialiste* [The counties of Socialist Romania](Bucharest, 1969), p. 472, for origin of word Teleorman.

11. Rusenescu and Bugă, "Territorial Distribution," pp. 76, 78.

12. Mosely, "The Distribution of the Zadruga," p. 221.

13. Marcel Emerit, *Les Paysans Roumains depuis le traité d'Andrinople jusqu'à la libération des terres (1829-1864)* (Paris, 1937), p. 51.

14. Mosely, "The Distribution of the Zadruga," p. 221.

15. Emerit, *Les Paysans Roumains*, pp. 216-217, 229-236.

16. Henri H. Stahl, *Les Anciennes Communautés Villageoises Roumaines* (Bucharest and Paris, 1969), pp. 56-57. This is a one-volume summary of the three-volume *Contribuții* (1958, 1959, 1965). An English translation is forthcoming, translated by Daniel Chirot (Westport, Conn.: Redgrave Information Resources, 1975).

17. Ibid., pp. 50-56, 241-244.

18. Ibid., pp. 247-248.

19. Ibid., pp. 77-85.

20. Ibid., p. 94.

21. Ibid., p. 119.

22. Stahl, *Nerej*, I, 264-265.

23. Stahl, *Les Anciennes Communautés*, pp. 85-91. Stahl cites a particularly amusing case of a division made in 1846, in which some lawyers were declared to form one of the major lineages, and two priests were declared to be another one of the lineages; also, ibid, 212-215, and Gheorghe Cront, *Instituții Medievale Românești* [Medieval Romanian institutions](Bucharest, 1969), pp. 231-233.

24. Andrei Oțetea and others, *Istoria Romîniei* [Romanian history] (Bucharest, 1962), II, 172.

25. Henri H. Stahl, *Studii de Sociologie Istorică* [Studies in social history] (Bucharest, 1972), pp. 5-62.

26. Nicolae Iorga, *L'Histoire du commerce de l'Orient au Moyen Âge* (Paris, 1924); Constantin C. Giurescu, "Le commerce sur le territoire de la

Moldavie pendant la domination Tartare (1241-1352)," *Nouvelles Études d'Histoire* III (1965), 56-70; Constantin C. Giurescu, *Istoria Pescuitului și a Pisciculturii în Romania* [History of fishing and of fish breeding in Romania] (Bucharest, 1964), I, 55-62; Stahl, *Les Anciennes Communautés*, pp. 42-45.

27. Ioan Bogdan, *Scrieri Alese* [Collected writings] (Bucharest, 1968), pp. 165-186; Henri H. Stahl, *Controverse de istorie socială românească* [Controversies of Romanian social history] (Bucharest, 1969), pp. 258-275.

28. Stahl, *Controverse*, pp. 274-275; Oțetea, *Istoria Romîniei* II, 165-171.

29. Maria Holban, "Mărturii asupra rolului cnezilor de pe marile domenii din Banat în a doua jumătate a secolului al XIV-lea" [The evidence on the role of the *Cneji* on the large estates of the Banat in the second half of the fourteenth century], *Studii și Materiale de Istorie Medie* [Studies and materials for medieval history] II (1957), 407-417.

30. Petre P. Panaitescu, *Interpretări Românești* [Romanian interpretations] (Bucharest, 1947), pp. 136-137; Radu Manolescu, *Comertul Tării Romînești si Moldovei cu Brașovûl (Secolele XIV-XVI)* [Wallachian and Moldavian trade with Brașov in the fourteenth to sixteenth centuries] (Bucharest, 1965), pp. 15-35.

31. Iorga, *L'Histoire du Commerce*, pp. 87-110; Giurescu, "Le commerce sur le territoire de la Moldavie," p. 66.

32. Manolescu, *Comerțul*, pp. 177, 180. In pages 187-253, Manolescu gives a very detailed accounting of those who were involved in the trade, in what periods, and under what circumstances.

33. Stahl, *Les Anciennes Communautés*, pp. 169-176.

34. Damaschin Mioc, "Cuantumul birului pe gospodăria tărănească în Țara Românească în secolul al XVI-lea" [The size of the capitation tax in the peasant household in Wallachia in the sixteenth century], *Studii și Materiale de Istorie Medie* V (1962), 160.

35. Manolescu, *Comerțul*, p. 177.

36. Ibid, p. 174; Albert H. Lybyer, "The Ottoman Turks and the Routes of Oriental Trade," *English Historical Review* CXX (1915), 588.

37. G. Zane, "Originea și desvoltarea economiei de schimb" [The origins and development of the exchange economy], *Enciclopedia Romậniei* [Romanian encyclopedia] III (1938), 248.

38. Lia Lehr, "Comerțuc Țării Romînești și Moldovei în a doua jumătate a secolului XVI și primá jumătate a secolului XVII" [Wallachian and Moldavian commerce in the second half of the sixteenth and first half of the seventeenth centuries], *Studii și Materiale de Istorie Medie* IV (1960), 245.

39. D. Ciurea, "Quelques considérations sur la noblesse féodale chez les Roumains," *Nouvelles Études d'Histoire* IV (1970), 87-88; Stahl, *Les Anciennes Communautés*, pp. 190-205.

40. Ștefan Ștefanescu, "La situation démographique de la Valachi aux XIVe, XVe eť XVIé siècles d'après les conjonctures socio-politiques," *Nouvelles Études d'Histoire* IV (1970), 47-61.

41. Stahl, *Les Anciennes Communautés*, pp. 188-189.

42. Constantin Giurescu, *Studii de Istorie Socială* [Studies in Social History] (Bucharest, 1943), pp. 204-205.

43. Șerban Papacostea, "Contribuție la problema relatiilor agrare în Țara Romînească în prima jumătate á veacului al XVIII-lea" [Contribution to the

problem of agrarian relations in Wallachia in the first half of the eighteenth century], *Studii şi Materiale de Istorie Medie* III, 304; Andrei Oţetea, "Consideraţii asupra trecerii de la feudalism la capitalism în Moldova şi Ţara Românească" [Considerations on the passage from feudalism to capitalism in Moldavia and Wallachia], *Studii şi Materiale de Istorie Medie* IV, 335-336.

44. Ilie Corfus, *Agricultura Ţării Româneşti în prima jumătate a secolului al XIX-lea* [Agriculture in Wallachia in the first half of the nineteenth century] (Bucharest, 1969), p. 25. A French language translation of this work was also published in 1969 by the Romanian Academy, but it omitted many of the footnotes from the original work.

45. V. Mihordea, *Maîtres du sol et paysans dans les principautés roumaines au XVIIIe siècle* (Bucharest, 1971), pp. 202-237.

46. Jerome Blum, *Lord and Peasant in Russia from the Ninth to the Nineteenth Century* (New York, 1964), p. 445.

47. Corfus, *Agricultura*, charts on pp. 302-379.

48. Emerit, *Les Paysans Roumains*, pp. 229-236.

49. This is the number that is usually accepted. It was first calculated by Nicolae Balcescu in his *Question économique des Principautés danubiennes,* (Paris, 1850). In fact, since the lords wanted direct work less than increased dues, a translation of corvée obligations into actual work days is difficult. Corfus (*Agricultura*) has shown that the amount of payment demanded for each day of corvée rose, so that Balcescu's calculation is roughly correct in terms of the price asked in the eighteenth century. Legally, the number of days of corvée did not increase in the first half of the nineteenth century; the real dues increased tremendously. (Corfus, pp. 77-107.)

50. Emerit, *Les Paysans Roumains*, pp. 506-525; Constantin Garoflid, "Regimul agar în România" [The agrarian regime of Romania], *Enciclopedia României* I (1938), 578-579.

51. Constantin Dobrogeanu-Gherea, *Neoiobăgia* [Neoserfdom] (Bucharest, 1908), Chapter IV. This chapter is reprinted in *C. Dobrogeanu-Gherea: Scrieri Social-Politice* [Socio-political writings] (Bucharest, 1968), pp. 233-250. A useful English summary of this theory is in David Mitrany, *Marx Against the Peasants* (Chapel Hill, 1951), pp. 27, 45, 166-167.

52. C. Jormescu and I. Popa-Burca, *Harta Agronomică a Romaniei* [Agrarian map of Romania] (Bucharest, 1907), table 11, section III.

53. The best brief summary of the consequences of the changes from 1864 to 1917 is Henry Roberts, *Rumania: The Political Problems of an Agrarian State* (New Haven, 1951), Chapter I.

54. David Mitrany, *The Land and the Peasant in Rumania: The War and the Agrarian Reform 1917-1921* (London 1930).

55. Stahl, *Nerej*, I, 3-32, 225-279.

56. Stahl, *Les Anciennes Communautés*, pp. 28-32.

57. Section reproduced in Doreen Warriner, ed., *Contrasts in Emerging Societies* (Bloomington, 1965), p. 129.

58. Stahl, *Nerej*, I, 227.

59. Stahl, *Les Anciennes Communautés*, pp. 163-189.

60. Ibid., pp. 84-85.

61. Ibid., p. 126.

62. Ibid., pp. 76-79.

63. Stahl, *Nerej*, I, 360-378.

64. Blum, *Lord and Peasant*, pp. 510-514.

65. Stahl, *Les Anciennes Communautés*, pp. 128-134.

66. Ibid., pp. 213-219.

67. Ibid., pp. 118-119. An agricultural census of 1905 conducted by the Ministry of Agriculture, Industry, Commerce, and Domains showed that even then most of the tools on the large estates belonged to small peasants who were continuing to cultivate with very backward techniques. See *Statistica Maşinilor şi Instrumentelor Agricole, 1905* [Statistics of agricultural machines and tools] (Bucharest, 1907). Ninety-six percent of all plows were then owned by peasants, even though they only owned forty-five percent of the land. For the record of agricultural yields, see *Anuarul Statistic al Romăniei, 1909* [Romanian yearbook of statistics, 1909] (Bucharest, 1909), pp. 146-147.

68. Stahl, *Les Anciennes Communautés*, pp. 111-112.

69. See my calculations in Daniel Chirot, *The Origins and Development of an Agrarian Crisis: The Social History of Wallachia, 1250-1917* (Ph. D. Diss., Columbia University, 1973), pp. 65-66.

70. Ion Donat, "Satele lui Mihai Viteazul" [The villages of Michael the Brave], *Studii şi Materiale de Istorie Medie* IV (1960), 465-506.

71. Stahl, *Contribuţii*, I, 32-48.

72. Ibid.

73. Stahl, *Les Anciennes Communautés*, pp. 237-240.

74. Corfus, *Agricultura*, charts on pp. 302-379.

75. A typical case is described by C. Stănica in "Hotarul satului Orodel-Dolj" [The boundary of the village Orodel in the County of Dolj], *Sociologie Romănească*, II (1937), pp. 28-31.

76. Dunăre, "Interdependenta," pp. 530-540.

77. Al Rosetti, *Istoria Limbii Romăne* [The history of the Romanian language] (Bucharest, 1968), pp. 285-301.

78. Constantin Daicoviciu, Emil Petrovici, and Gheorghe Stefan, *La formation du peuple roumain et de sa langue* (Bucharest, 1963), p. 51. Most Romanian historians accept the thorough mixture of Slavs and Dacoromans within the village community. Thus, it seems improbable that villages, even at this early stage, were composed of single extended families that would grow until they split to form new villages. The fact that Romanian villages were traditionally endogamous, while south Slav villages were exogamous, is cited by Nicholas Georgescu-Roegen, "The Institutional Aspects of Peasant Communities: An Analytical View," in Clifton R. Wharton, ed., *Subsistence Agriculture and Economic Development* (Chicago, 1969), p. 80.

79. Stahl, *Les Anciennes Communautés*, pp. 49-50.

80. Stahl, *Nerej*, I, 131-132.

81. For a discussion of functionally equivalent institutions and comparative functional analysis, see Robert K. Merton, *On Theoretical Sociology* (New York, 1967), pp. 73-138.

82. Robert Lee Wolff, *The Balkans in Our Times* (New York, 1967), p. 171.

83. Philip E. Mosely, "The Peasant Family: The Zadruga, or Communal Joint-Family in the Balkans, and its Recent Evolution," in Caroline F. Ware, ed., *The Cultural Approach to History* (New York, 1940), p. 108.

84. Mitrany, *Marx Against the Peasant,* pp. 113-114.

85. Gr. Mladenatz, "Posibilitățile și dificultățile cooperației în satul Românesc" [The possibilities and difficulties of cooperation in the Romanian village], *Sociologie Românească* II (1937), 108-111.

86. Wolff, *The Balkans,* pp. 66-67.

Part Three:

The Zadruga, Past and Present:

Some Illustrations

11: A ZADRUGA IN BILEĆA RUDINE

Wayne Vucinich

The zadruga existed in Serbian society since medieval times and has long fascinated the scholarly world. Indeed, few subjects in the historiography of Yugoslav peoples have received as much attention as the zadruga. However, scholars have not given adequate attention to regional differences in the zadruga, mainly because of the lack of documentation. The medieval sources, including Czar Dušan's Code, give us hardly more than an inkling about the zadruga family. After the Ottoman conquest in the 1460's of eastern Herzegovina, where Bileća Rudine is located, specific data on the zadruga are equally wanting. As a result of numerous armed encounters between the Ottoman rulers and their Christian subjects, nearly all church and monastery records perished. Family records are nonexistent, for illiteracy was almost total. The only records of consequence are those in the Dubrovnik and Istanbul archives. However important these records may be for understanding the social and economic status of the zadruga, they are not likely to provide information on the structure and organization of a zadruga family.

Because patriarchal society survived in eastern Herzegovina until recently, field investigation of the surviving traditional institutions still yields abundant data. A scholar may also rely on a few legal documents and widely scattered fragmentary materials published in numerous journals and collective works. The only significant studies of the social life in eastern Herzegovina are Jevto Dedijer's *Bilećske Rudine* and *Herzegovina,* published in 1903 and 1909 respectively, under the auspices of the Serbian Royal Academy of Sciences. Both works were based largely on field study by Dedijer.

What follows is a personal account of my own zadruga in the village of Orah, commune of Zarječje, in the region of Bileća Rudine in eastern Herzegovina. It is based largely on my own boyhood experience and observations, supplemented by transmitted family traditions and observations based on long interest in social life in the locality. Like the other essays in this section, it will describe a zadruga and the changes it underwent in a different area and under different conditions than that described in Professor Mosely's classic study "Adaptation for Survival: The Varžić Zadruga."

THE MEDIEVAL AND OTTOMAN LEGACIES

Despite frequent social dislocation and shifts of population away from and into Bileća Rudine, the medieval institution of the zadruga survived in the region until after the Second World War, little changed in structure or in social and economic functions. Economic and social conditions favored large families. Both the medieval Serbian and the Ottoman governments encouraged zadruga life. The feudal landlords preferred the zadruga, for it was a surer source of revenue, easier to control, and a more reliable source of labor power than small individual families. For the peasants, zadruga provided some economic security and protection from unfriendly neighbors and marauders. It provided working hands to care for the animals and to work in the field. A larger zadruga family could pay the hearth tax more easily than a small nuclear family.

Until very recently, the inhabitants of Bileća Rudine engaged primarily in pastoral activities. The physical arrangement of rural communities remained almost unchanged from medieval times. The lands of each village (*udut, atar*) were delimited by stone markers (*medje*) and divided into private arable and grazing lands and the grazing and forest commons (*mera*). Until 1918, most of the land belonged to the feudatories (*vlastela, spahije*, agas, begs) and were cultivated by the peasant tenants (*meropah, čivčija, kmet*), who owned small plots of land (*milać, baština, očevina*). The size of the plot was about the same in medieval and in the Ottoman periods; in the latter period, it amounted to about half-*dunum* (*dunum, dulum*), that is, about 500 square meters.

Customary law regulated the use of the common pastures and forests in the village. Pasture lands were also traditionally provided in the distant mountains (*planina*), to which the peasants drove their own and their feudatory's livestock for summer grazing. Some of the mountain pastures belonged to the state, some to the feudatories. In 1858 and 1869 the Ottoman government issued special regulations governing the use of pastures and forests that did not belong to anyone (*mubah*) or the use of which was permitted to all. These laws confirmed much of the existing practice. The second of the laws, with minor changes, remained in force until the end of the First World War.

In the medieval as well as the Ottoman period, the peasant paid taxes to the landlord and the state, in kind and in money, and rendered a certain number of unpaid days of labor to the landlord. Both in medieval and in Ottoman days, the peasants were subjected to a variety of additional dues and imposts. On special occasions the peasant brought his Ottoman landlord a shoulder of lamb and honey, and at Easter time colored eggs. These contributions were no doubt symbols of the peasant's fealty or servility to the landlord. Under the Turks, the peasant paid a poll tax (*cizye*) in lieu of military service, but he was not attached to land as he was under the medieval

Serbian feudal system. Another difference between the medieval and the Ottoman feudal systems was that the Christian peasant (*dimmi, zimni*) under Ottoman rule was accorded the privileges of the scripturian but was excluded from the Islamic state and legal system. Thus, he lived in isolation within his own religious community (*millet*), withdrawn into his own social institutions. Such a climate favored the zadruga, which throve especially during Ottoman rule.

After the second half of the sixteenth century, the Ottoman feudal system began to break down. The abuses of peasants by legal landlords (*spahije, timarci*) and landlord usurpers (aga, *çiftlik-sâhibi*) increased. The harsh conditions of life led to ever more frequent major peasant insurrections. Many state lands passed into private hands, as *timars* (held on condition of military service) became converted into unconditional ownerships.

Social unrest, droughts, and epidemics precipitated emigration from Bileća Rudine. New settlers in turn occupied the deserted villages. These shifts of populations often caused family dislocation, but the traditional cultural and social institutions in Bileća Rudine, such as the zadruga, remained unchanged, because they were common to the emigrating and immigrating families. The migrations of population were particularly frequent in the eighteenth century and up to the middle of the nineteenth century, when they stopped and the population of individual villages gradually expanded. During this time, at the end of the eighteenth century, my family settled in Bileća Rudine.

The first half of the nineteenth century was a time of frequent unrest in Bosnia and Herzegovina. The Ottoman rulers endeavored to establish order and to check dissolution of the empire. They had hoped to strengthen the central power, to modernize and improve administration, and to stabilize the agrarian situation and tenant-landlord relations. In 1847, Táhir Pasha, vizier of Bosnia and Herzegovina, abolished the peasant's compulsory unpaid labor (*kuluk, angarija, beglučiti*) for the landlord, and established one-third of the grain harvest as the tenant's tax obligation (*hak*) in Bosnia. The landlord was obliged to provide his tenants a home and farming tools. Táhir also undertook to improve the system of tax collection. However, these measures could not be implemented, and the agrarian crisis continued.

The Safer Decree of 1859 guaranteed to the peasants in Bosnia and Herzegovina the rights of tenantry on the land they tilled (which amounted to a hereditary lease), so long as they fulfilled their obligations and services to the landlord and the state. The abolition of obligatory unpaid labor was confirmed. The size of the *hak* the tenant paid to the landlord remained one-third, except in Herzegovina (including Bileća Rudine), where the peasant's tax was less than one-third of the harvested grain. Some concessions to the peasant were made in regard to secondary levies, and the landlords were obliged to build homes for their tenants. After 1859, the landlord could no longer demand from his tenants free billeting and food when on visit, and the tenant could bring charges against his landlord before appropriate authorities if the landlord abused him. The Safer Decree allowed the peasant to leave the land on prior notice. The aga could not remove the peasant from the land except as provided by the Decree. He had no judicial authority over the peasant, and he could not control the peasant's life and property. If the tenant, the head of the zadruga or a nuclear family, died, his heir was obliged to enter into a new agreement with the landlord.

The basic provisions of the Safer Decree in 1859 remained in force until 1918. The burdens imposed on peasants were neither particularly high nor onerous. However, the peasant continued to resent until 1878 the abuses which accompanied the collection of taxes and the ever-present threat to his personal security and property. He also complained that the landlord frequently failed to meet his various obligations to the peasant. Perhaps the most important aspect of the Safer Decree was that it enabled the peasant to buy the land from the aga. Yet, until 1876 the non-Moslems could not obtain a deed (*tapu, tapija*) on land that belonged to a Moslem although a few did manage to enlarge their landed properties. In that year, a law gave the tenant priority in the purchase of the land he cultivated. The law was important since the urge for land was the life ambition of every peasant family. The most characteristic feature of peasant psychology is the attachment to every clod of soil, regardless of practical considerations. Each generation managed to expand slightly the family landed properties through purchase from the feudal landlord or in some other way.

MY FAMILY IN OTTOMAN DAYS

My family's history is obscure. According to legend, the family came from the Montenegrin tribe of Piperi, though the toponymic and ethnographic data suggest that it may have descended from the tribe of Drobnjaci. The legend tells how one Gajun Vucinich murdered a Turk, sometime late in the eighteenth century, and escaped to avoid Turkish reprisal. He first settled near Trebinje, later moved with his family to Bileća Rudine, and put down on the landed estate (agaluk) of a feudal landlord in the village of Mosko. After a short stay Gajun asked his landlord for permission to settle on the latter's land in the village of Orah, and the request was granted.

According to the legend, Gajun raised a family which included three sons and four daughters. After marriage, the sons, with their spouses and children, continued to live together, while the daughters married and left the family. Gajun died about 1815. His surviving sons lived together until about 1830; Todor, the eldest of them, was the head of the house. When the zadruga broke up, Todor remained in the family house in Orah, while his two brothers established homes on the aga's estate in the adjoining village of Panik. This is all that we know about the family's origin, and only a part of the information may coincide with facts. Moreover, nearly every family in Bileća Rudine has a similar family legend.

My great-grandfather Todor died in 1863 and was survived by four sons and three daughters. The four sons with their spouses and children continued to live together in a zadruga, while the daughters married and left home. The eldest of the four sons, my grandfather Jeremije (1822-1890), was the head of the house; he started a *čitulja*, the record of births, marriages, and deaths in the family. Even this sole document on the history of our family is incomplete, since no one in the house was literate and the priest failed to record the changes which occurred in the family.

Like every zadruga, my grandfather's zadruga family made a strenuous effort not only to preserve its inherited patrimony intact, by preventing the loss of land through inheritance on the female line or through sale, but to expand it. Only in dire necessity would a zadruga family sell parts of its patrimony, which belonged to the living and the yet-to-be-born in the family.

Incidentally, until the demise of the Ottoman Empire, the only wealth a Christian peasant could acquire was in the form of livestock, because the Ottoman taxation system favored animal breeding. Because of this and favorable geography, my grandfather's zadruga came into possession of a large herd of light stock and a few head of heavy stock, milk cows and draft animals. Under peaceful and orderly conditions, my grandfather's zadruga was able to eke out a living. But the almost constant strife instigated by unbearable social conditions and fanned by nationalistic agitators precluded normal existence. Yet in these difficult days the zadruga was far more able to provide security and livelihood than an individual family could.

In the early 1870's, the economic situation in Bileća Rudine improved and was probably better than at any time before. Nonetheless, social unrest and national ferment were still present. When the Serbian peasants in nearby Nevesinje rose in June 1875, the insurrection soon engulfed Bileća Rudine. World attention was focussed on that Balkan insurrection, and despite the efforts by European diplomacy to restore peace, war broke out in 1876 between Montenegro and Serbia, on the one hand, and the Ottoman Empire on the other hand. Finally, in 1877, the Balkan question led to war between Russia and the Ottoman Empire.

Grandfather Jeremije from the start participated in the insurrection and then in the war that followed was an officer-commander of one of the armed bands that cooperated with the Montenegrins. He brought the family unprecedented laurels, became the most distinguished member of the entire clan, and was decorated for bravery by Prince Nikola of Montenegro. Two of his sons, my Uncles Ivan and Rade, as teenagers took part in the well-known battle of Vučji Dô. For Uncle Ivan's efforts, in the late 1930's, many years after his patriotic deeds, the Yugoslav government awarded him a modest pension.

MY ZADRUGA FAMILY
UNDER AUSTRO-HUNGARIAN OCCUPATION

The war between the Ottoman Empire and the three Slavic states was finally ended by the Treaty of Berlin in 1878. Under the treaty most of Bileća Rudine, including the village of Orah, came under Austro-Hungarian occupation, while some of the region was transferred to Montenegro. From this time the two separated parts of what had once been a single Bileća Rudine ethnographic region developed differently. Like her predecessors, and for much the same reasons, Austria-Hungary favored the zadruga family. The changes which occurred in zadruga life under Austro-Hungarian rule came as a result of increased exposure to urban influence and more rapid development of money economy.

In 1885 my grandfather's zadruga split up. Three brothers and their families moved out, while the fourth, my grandfather Jeremije, the eldest of the brothers, his wife Marija (1848-1895), five of his sons and five daughters, remained in the zadruga home, which was eventually rebuilt and enlarged. Before death overtook him, Jeremije had married off two of his five daughters and one son, Ivan. Until he died in 1890, grandfather Jeremije was the head (*domaćin*) of the zadruga.

Uncle Ivan succeeded his father as head of the house and remained so until the end of the First World War in 1918. He married my Aunt Andja in 1896 and had ten children. Four children died in infancy, one was killed in the Second World War, and five survived him when he died in 1943. By 1905, my remaining three aunts and one uncle, Rade, were also married. Between 1905 and 1910 my father, Spiro, and uncles Djoko and Todor emigrated to the United States. The three brothers who went to America retained full rights as members of the zadruga; they occasionally sent money to the brothers left at home, which enabled them to purchase more land and to build a water cistern and several outbuildings. Each brother, like many an emigrant, hoped to return home after saving some money. My father was the only one who married. He had five children, two of whom died in infancy. My father and mother died in Butte, Montana, in the 1918 flu epidemic, leaving behind three children. One of my uncles, Todor, also died in America, while the third one, Djoko, returned to Bileća Rudine.

My father's zadruga was in the economic sense one of the more stable in the village. In other words, it was a family in "good standing" (*dobro stojeća kuća*), as the locals would put it, because it had a few head of stock more than its neighbors, a few more *dunums* of land, and someone in the United States who sent occasional checks.

Austria-Hungary retained the Ottoman system of land tenure, but security of person and property were assured and the peasant's tax to the aga was established at one-fourth of the harvested "white" (*bijelo*)–rye, wheat, barley, and maize–and one-fifth of the harvested "green" (*zeleno*)–potatoes and cabbage. The peasant also provided the landlord one-third of the hay he mowed. The head of the family could, if it served his purpose, make an agreement (*ćesim*) with the landlord to pay him annually a fixed amount of money (usually between twenty and thirty forints) instead of taxes in kind. The peasant was not obliged to pay either *hak* to his aga or the tithe (*desetina*) to the state from what he produced on his *milać*, which included a vegetable garden.

In addition to law and order and the improved system for the assessment of the *hak* introduced by Austria-Hungary, several other measures affected agrarian relations in a positive way. A special order issued in 1895 provided for settlement of agrarian disputes. The tenant's rights to the land he worked were entered into the land registers. Of special importance was abolition of the tithe in 1905 and introduction of the flat rate (*paušal*) taxes. No longer was it necessary to register the harvest in order to assess the tithe, and the peasant paid a fixed tax in money based on an average of the tithes he had paid during the preceding ten years. Freed from the pesky assessor (*procjenitelj*), the peasant family could now dispose of its harvest as it wished. The system lightened the peasant's tax burden and encouraged him to increase production.

Because of inability to adjust to Christian rule, some of the former Ottoman feudal landlords after 1878 sold land to their tenants and either moved to larger towns or emigrated to Turkey. For this and other reasons, the opportunity for Christian peasants to acquire land from the Muslims increased. Since the Austro-Hungarian government made purchase of land easier, our zadruga was able in a modest way to expand the family patrimony.

However, the peasants did not have the capital to buy the land even when it was available for sale. The rate of land purchase increased after 1911, when a special office was established within the Territorial Government of Bosnia and Herzegovina to provide peasants with credits. Peasant land purchasing was interrupted by the First World War. When the war ended in 1918, most land, including that cultivated by my family, was still owned by feudal landlords.

During the First World War (1914-1918), my family zadruga suffered from a shortage of food, largely because the lands could not be cultivated and because of government requisitions of livestock and draft animals. Like other families, it was ordered by the Austro-Hungarian military authorities to move away from the war zone along the Montenegrin frontier into the neighboring hills. The family spent two years in the hills, aided by relatives through marriage, who lived in a nearby village. The purpose of the Austro-Hungarian military decision was to protect the civilian population from enemy gunfire and to prevent possible collaboration between the local population and their Montenegrin Serbian compatriots. Due to need of food and the scarcity of fodder, especially in the winter months, the family was obliged to butcher many of its animals. By the time the war ended, the family's animal herds were reduced to half their pre-war number. They were never restored to their original size.

OUR ZADRUGA IN THE INTERWAR PERIOD

Not a single member of the family lost his life during the First World War. The only visible change in the zadruga was that Uncle Rade replaced his older brother Ivan as the head of the house at the very end of the war. Uncle Rade and Aunt Pava had eleven children. Four died in infancy, and seven survived, five boys and two girls. Uncle Rade cherished power, but Uncle Ivan was happier without it. Uncle Rade, moreover, developed cancer in one of his legs and had the leg amputated below the knee. He could no longer do hard work in the field, but he could manage the household and do lighter chores, such as slaughter animals, plant tobacco and cabbage seedlings, and classify tobacco leaves, from a sitting position.

Uncle Rade was a clever person who had two years of school, and he could read and write. He managed the household autocratically but efficiently. He kept an eye on the squabbling women and children, and maintained domestic tranquillity with an iron fist. Because one of his legs was amputated, he could not chase the children to mete out punishment when they irritated him. However, he had a long memory, patiently waited for a child to stray within his reach, and then struck with his heavy cane.

Another change that affected our zadruga at the end of the war was the arrival of Uncle George and three orphaned children from the United States. I was one of those children, then five years of age, and the oldest of the three. The zadruga was obliged to provide for us. The zadruga family then consisted of twenty-nine members, three married brothers, their wives and children, an unmarried uncle, and the three orphan children.

In 1919 the newly-founded Yugoslav state issued the Agrarian Reform Law, which abolished all survivals of serfdom and established the peasant's legal ownership to the land he tilled. This of itself, however, did not visibly improve the life of the peasantry in Bileća Rudine. Peasant families were large, the yields from starved land low, and the market for livestock bad.

Opportunity for work on the outside was limited. Until the end of the Second World War, the inhabitants of Bileća Rudine continued to engage in a subsistence economy based on primitive agriculture and animal breeding.

The most important cereals produced were still rye, barley, maize, and wheat, but the harvests were rarely sufficient to satisfy family needs. Only about half of our family's income came from crops. Of the vegetables, only potatoes were grown in quantity. Other important vegetables were cabbage and beets. Each autumn, the family sold a number of sheep and goats to obtain cash with which to buy cereals and such items as salt, sugar, and textiles. The family income was augmented by the sale of a few animal skins, and small quantities of wool, cheese, honey, wax, chickens, eggs, firewood, fruit, and vegetables, especially potatoes, all of which the family itself could have used. My family earned some cash income from tobacco, a rigorously supervised state monopoly, cultivated under contract with the government, which purchased the crop. The family managed to retain a few kilograms of tobacco for its few smokers and sold some of it illegally (*škija*). Most families, including our own, were dependent on some outside income, usually on wages earned by one or more members. Occasionally, the family was obliged to borrow money to buy bread and cereals.

Every summer, in late June, after the sun scorched the vegetation and the water sources were depleted, the family joined a summer pastoral association (*smijes, sumjes*) and sent its stock to the mountains for summer grazing. The seasonal pastoral association was usually, though not necessarily, made up of the same families every summer. Nor did the cooperating families always come from the same village.

Our zadruga was one of the few that had the cabin right, that is, the right to build a cabin on the mountain grazing site, paying a modest fee for this privilege. Since the cabin was ours, our family ordinarily supplied the head of the summer association, and the head's wife usually took charge of the cabin, food, and cheese-making. Other members of the association contributed shepherds or an equivalent in food provisions or services. I was once instructed to help drive the stock to and from the mountains and to care for them while in the mountains. The trek to the mountains lasted three days and two nights, a difficult and exhausting assignment I shall never forget.

The purpose of the summer pastoral association was to fatten the stock, to increase the yield of milk, and to accumulate cheese during the summer months for sale and home consumption. In early autumn, the stock returned from the mountain. After the cheese was divided, the association was disbanded. This practice lasted until after the Second World War, when the various decrees issued by the Communist government and changed economic conditions compelled the peasants to abandon it. Today, only a few families in Bileća Rudine still engage in it.

No one seems to know when and how the mountain grazing sites (*katun*) were acquired. The mountains were either state-owned or belonged to individual feudatories and were under certain conditions assigned to peasant families or villages as their pasture lands. After the delimitation of borders between Austria-Hungary and Montenegro in 1878, our family's grazing site fell to Montenegro, and the Austro-Hungarian government allocated to us a new site, called Stari Katun, on its side of the border in the Zelenogora Mountains.

THE ORGANIZATION AND STRUCTURE
OF ZADRUGA

The zadruga resembled a miniature state in which the sovereign power rested with the members of the family (*čeljad*). The executive power was vested in the head of the house, chosen by older male members of the family. The most desirable head was one respected by his family and the community. Although the eldest male member of the family was usually chosen, often the head was selected for his ability rather than his age. Should a family lack a suitable male to represent it, a woman might either usurp the leadership or be chosen for it by the family. One zadruga family within our clan had a woman as head for nearly twenty years. The head of the family retained his position so long as he managed the family well and enjoyed its confidence.

Normally, the head consulted the older male members of the family on all important questions. His task included resolving disputes among the feuding members of the family and, when called upon, arbitrating disputes among individuals or families outside his own zadruga. The head of the house managed the family's properties and issued work assignments to individual members of the household. In the evening after dinner, the head of our zadruga, Uncle Rade, barked out assignments for the following day. He called each person by name, usually directing two persons to herd the goats and sheep, one to watch over the lambs and kids, one to assume responsibility for the cattle, and when needed, one person to go to the flour mill, and one or two to the market. Several persons were always assigned work in the fields, or to mend fences, repair walls, and build corrals. If the head of the house mismanaged the family possessions, caused embarrassment to the family, or abused his position in any way, the older males in the family could replace him.

The headwoman (*domaćica*), who was ordinarily either the mother of the headman or his wife but could also be another married woman, was in charge of the housework. In our zadruga Aunt Pava, the wife of the head of the house, was the headwoman. She assigned work to other women and supervised them. Some women did kitchen chores and others herded animals, milked them and made cheese, or worked in the fields. The women, however, had their preferences; the headwoman of our zadruga preferred work outside the house. Aunt Andja, on the other hand, took charge of the kitchen and was better at it than the other women.

In the morning the women rose before the men; they started the fire, fetched water, foraged for wood, and washed, mended and made clothes. The daughters-in-law deferred particularly to their father-in-law (*svekar*) and mother-in-law (*svekrva*) and other senior members of the household. In general, the males, including the teen-age boys, received more attention than female children. Of the female children, the oldest was treated the best, for she was "the next to marry" (*na polici*). In general, the married women and the older women were treated better than unmarried and younger women.

Jealousy among the women inspired quarrels inside the zadruga family. A married woman often demonstrated preference for her own immediate family, favoring her own husband and children in an institution which expected equal treatment. Fortunately, in our zadruga relations among the women were on the whole harmonious.

Do not misunderstand the position of the women in the zadruga. In Bileća Rudine's patriarchal society, mothers and sisters were honored and protected. Local proverbs said that "A house does not rest on the land but on a woman," and that "Mending and suffering hold the house together." Insulting a peasant's mother or sister was a serious offense that could lead to bloodshed. A husband would not generally make a major decision affecting his household until he had consulted his wife.

No one in the patriarchal society of Bileća Rudine lived a more miserable life than an old maid. She was abused daily by her brothers' wives and sometimes by the brothers themselves. Like young unmarried maidens, she wore a white kerchief; like them, she obeyed and waited on older members of the family.

When left alone in the family, a woman in Bileća Rudine on occasion chose a life of celibacy. One of my first cousins, Ruša, an unmarried daughter of Uncle Ivan and an old maid, considered it her sacred duty never to abandon the hearth and never to marry. She repudiated the role of a woman in a patriarchal society and took up the role of a man. The records tell us that in earlier periods of history such a woman even wore man's clothing and bore arms like a man. Ruša did not go that far, but she did the work traditionally reserved for men. She plowed the fields, sowed grain, mowed hay, took livestock to the market, and bargained with merchants. She celebrated the family patron saint and other major holidays. She swore like a man.

Ruša's worst critics were her closest relatives, with whom she shared the roof of the former zadruga house. Her male cousins feared that she might marry and that an outsider might inherit her lands. The relatives harassed her and tried to persuade her to sell her property to them.

Everyone in the zadruga family, the old and the young, was expected to work and to do his share. Teen-age boys and girls often did a grown-up's job. Some jobs were traditionally done by men (plowing, mowing hay, threshing, slaughtering animals), others by women (housework, reaping grain, fetching water, gathering firewood), and some by both (harvesting vegetables, going to market, planting crops).

A zadruga was a property-owning corporation. It held in common all zadruga properties, and its members shared many of their personal possessions. Possessions acquired by individual members, usually while they were absent from home, were their own. The modern zadruga law confirmed the right of members of a zadruga to own personal property. My father, a generous contributor to the zadruga during his lifetime, had accumulated personal property (*prćija, peculium*), which after his death went to his direct heirs. Personal possessions were often a cause for breaking up the zadruga, because members of the family who acquire private possessions become less reliant on the communal form of life.

Although all members of the family were equal, in actual practice the younger deferred to the older members. In a zadruga, each person's primary allegiance was to the household and not his own immediate family. Married couples avoided showing excessive affection or favoritism to one another or toward their children in order not to upset internal harmony and violate social democracy. They normally called one another by the first name or by a nickname, that is, in the same way that others in the family called them. In a similar fashion, children addressed their parents by personal names or nicknames.

NAMES AND NICKNAMES

The number of personal names used in Bileća Rudine was limited. Even in a single zadruga, several persons sometimes had the same names, although this did not occur in my zadruga. In our clan, however, several persons did have identical names. To distinguish persons of the same given names, a patronymic was used with the Christian name. Thus, one Mary was identified as "Ivan's Mary" (Marija Ivanova), and another as "Peter's Mary (Marija Petrova). Actually, each person had an individual patronymic, depending on the Christian name of his or her father. The children of Peter took the patronymic Petrov, and the children of Rade took Radov. But patronymics are not hereditary and not as widespread as among the Russians. The name form that was hereditary was the family name, derived from the Christian name of a reputed ancestor of the family.

Persons of the same given name could also be distinguished by the use of nicknames, e.g., Vučinuša, Kaporuša, married women of Vučinić origin, one of Kapor origin. A married woman, for instance, was often called by her maiden name or by the name of her husband (Djokovica—"the one married to Djoko"), or by some other nickname. My Aunt Andja after sixty years of married life was still called "nevjesta" ("the bride"), occasionally "Kaporuša," and hardly ever by her given name, Andja.

Another type of name generally found in fairly primitive societies is the to-name, or surname, from which family names often developed. The to-name was personal, non-hereditary, and usually descriptive of appearance, character, or some other attribute of the bearer, and served to differentiate him from others in the community. In Bileća Rudine, this institution survives in the form of nicknames, which may be flattering or derogatory, contrived in jest, out of affection, or in derision. My clan, for example, was nicknamed "koš" (basket), because an eccentric ancestor was said to have rolled down a hill in a large basket when dared by a group of shepherdesses. Nicknames are often inspired by a physical disability. My one-legged Uncle Rade was called "ćoto," and my Uncle Djoko, who lost a finger, was known as "čopo." One of my relatives was thought by peasants to be unusually intelligent and, therefore, was called "brainy" (*mozgonja*). My father's first cousin, Miško, a tall, well-built man and a kindly soul, sluggish in body and thought, was nicknamed "The Camel" (*deva*), because of a large lump on his neck. Most everyone accepted his nickname without demur, whether it flattered or insulted him.

Individual clan families are also identified by special labels. The Vučinić clan in Orah is comprised of four groups of families, named respectively after an ancestor (*Lučići*), a Turkish feudal landlord (*Ćapinovići*), and a geographic location (*vinogradi, okruglica*). My zadruga was one of the three families identified as *okruglica* (circle), because their homes surrounded a large İllyrian *tumulus.*

KINSHIP

One important reason for the cohesion and stability of the zadruga was the fact that it was organized on the basis of blood kinship. The strong attachment to the zadruga family and kin is reflected in the precise terminology for all degrees of their relationship. In Bileća Rudine, unlike some other parts of Yugoslavia, kinship terms are of Slavic origin. The emphasis on kinship reckoning is on agnatic ties. The relatives are distinguished by male blood (*muška krv*), or thick blood (*debela krv*), and by female blood (*ženska krv*), or thin blood (*tanka krv*).

The kinship terminology distinguishes the father's from the mother's relatives. The distinction is dictated by the rules of patrilocality and patrilineal inheritance.

The local kinship terminology distinguishes between mother's and father's brothers. A distinction is also made between nephews and nieces from the male and the female side. Although the children of brothers and sisters are first cousins and presumably equal in kinship, in actual practice the children of brothers were closer because of the patriarchal character of society and because the children of the brothers lived in the zadruga family and had daily contact, while sister's children lived elsewhere and rarely saw the brother's children. Kinship in the female line does not go beyond the father's or mother's mother. Thus, the third cousins on the mother's side could intermarry, while the cousins of the male line could not intermarry for something like seven generations.

Every zadruga family has many relatives (*svojta*) through marriage who are called "friends" (*prijatelji*). The prestige of the house is judged in terms of how many friends/relatives it has. One hears peasants say how they had recently become relatives (*sprijateljili smo se*) with a particular family. The groom refers to the family into which he married as his *tazbina,* and the bride refers to the family from which she came as her *rodbina* (or *rod*).

Finally, several types of kin are adoptive (spiritual). In this category *kumstvo*, the most common, is still important, though greatly weakened in most families, including my own. *Kumstvo* is an artificial kinship, "kinship in the sight of God." Some writers believe that *kumstvo* has its roots in a practice that predates Christianity, and others that it has its origins in Christian religion, in sponsorship of new members of the Church by old members. Whatever its origins, *kumstvo* has a firm place in Orthodox canon law and theology, and is held in great reverence.

There are two kinds of *kumstvos*: baptismal *kumstvo* (*kršteno kumstvo*), established by the godfather at baptism, and wedding *kumstvo* (*vjenčano kumstvo*), established by the best man at a wedding. Canon law requires a *kum* (witness) at baptism and at marriage. Often the same families provide *kums* for baptismal and marriage purposes. There is a saying that "He who baptizes also marries." Through the act of sponsorship (*kumstvo*), the persons directly participating in the sacraments of baptism or matrimony and their respective families become linked by ties of kinship, and are bound by sacrament to respect this relationship. Social custom spurned marriage between members of families which are in *kumstvo* relationship.

The zadruga family was proud of its *kumstvos*. The more of them it had, the prouder it was. My zadruga family has exchanged *kums* with six families for as many as three and more generations. When the zadrugas broke up, they divided the *kumstvo* among the ensuing nuclear families. A nuclear family chose the one with which it wished to exchange visits on patron saint days and other festivities.

The *kums* were present at one another's homes in time of crisis, death, weddings, and on the patron saint day. In the final years of the nineteenth century, the clans Kureš and Vučinić in the village of Orah entered into *kumstvo* relations in order to assure village harmony. In 1860 the abbot of Dobrićevo persuaded my grandfather and his Andjelić adversary to stop feuding by entering into *kumstvo* relations. The two clans never again feuded. Murderers could be forgiven for their crime if they became *kums* of the families whose kinsman's life they had taken, and often they were persuaded by friends and relatives to enter into such relationship.

In recent years, growing secularism and modernism, coupled with Communist anti-religious legislation, have greatly weakened traditional religious beliefs in Bileća Rudine. The institution of *kumstvo* has lost its erstwhile importance. Yet, the *kumstvo* is still respected by most Serbs, including my family, even though it has lost much of its religious content.

INHERITANCE

Nearly every Christian family in Bileća Rudine has descended from Montenegro, bringing with them customs concerning family affairs, including the question of inheritance. The Ottoman Turks allowed the local customary laws to operate in those spheres of social relations, including the question of inheritance, which Ottoman Islamic law did not reach.

The Austrian Civil Code of 1811, introduced in Bosnia and Herzegovina after the occupation, likewise did not affect the customary law concerning family inheritance, which remained in force in Yugoslavia during the interwar period. It was superseded on April 13, 1955, when the Yugoslav Communist government issued a new inheritance law prohibiting the exclusion of female children.

Thus, until Communist law was enacted, inheritance was patrilineal. No male member of a zadruga could be denied a part of the inherited patrimony, but he could be excluded from sharing in property acquired by the zadruga itself. Only those who worked for or contributed to the zadruga earned the right to share its acquired possessions, but a disobedient son who had been banished or who moved out and took up employment elsewhere would not lose his share of the family's inherited patrimony.

One characteristic of Montenegrin customary law was that it excluded women from inheritance in order to prevent the fragmentation of the peasant's patrimony that would occur if women were to inherit the land. A woman member was assured of a wedding at the zadruga's expense, symbolic dowry (*otpremnina*), and nothing more. The symbolic dowry consisted of such items as handkerchiefs, kerchiefs, blouses, stockings, and soaps. Upon marriage, the woman thereby relinquished whatever claim she might have had to rights or properties of the zadruga. Special regulations concerned the rights to inheritance by widows and orphaned children. In general, even if there was no one of the fourth generation in the male line to inherit the property, it would not go to a woman. The property a woman brought into the zadruga remained her personal possession. Women were discouraged from acquiring personal property. They were obliged to turn over any personal property they acquired to the zadruga in order to avoid a potential source of intrafamily friction. Should a woman have personal property, her husband or her children inherited it after her death.

LIFE INSIDE OUR ZADRUGA

The Zadruga House and Its Furnishings

Our zadruga house, built in the Dinaric style (*polača*), was larger than most others in the village, but nonetheless small. It contained about 1,000 square feet of floor space, divided into the hearth room, a middle room (*tavan*), and a guest room, or simply "the room" (*soba*). Little light entered the house because the windows were few and tiny. At the hearth (*ognjište*), slept Uncle Ivan and Aunt Andja, and two or three children. The hearth room had no chimney and was always full of smoke, especially when the wood was green. Sometimes the smoke was so heavy that those sitting around the fire could hardly see one another. The family spent most of their free time sitting around the fireplace for at least nine months of the year. This was the only warm place in the house.

The hearth was invested with the attributes and powers of the fire which burned there. The notion of the hearth as a magic place in the house could be traced back to the time when it had served as a place of sacrifice and as a religious shrine. Traditionally, the hearth linked the living family with descendants yet unborn. The hearth was a fetish which was approached with reverence and faith for its tutelary powers. Nearly all the major customs and religious ceremonies in the house took place at it. The family met at the hearth to discuss the most important family problems. The part of the building in which the hearth was located was often called the "house" (*kuća*), the terms "house" and "hearth" being frequently used interchangeably, because the hearth was the heart of the house, and because the peasant's dwelling once consisted of a room with a hearth. The importance of the hearth in the peasant family is reflected in sayings, "No one will dare attack me at my hearth," or "I am free at my hearth." After the end of the Second World War, however, the Communist government ordered the peasants to install stoves in place of hearths for reasons of health, sanitation, and economy. Since the oven could not serve as a substitute for the exercise of traditional rites and customs that centered upon the hearth, the disappearance of the hearth brought to an end many customs which it traditionally symbolized.

The middle room had a small hearth with an outlet for smoke. The fire was built rarely. Most of the family slept in this room. Sleeping space was reserved for the senior members of the family, married couples, and their small children. The rest of the floorspace was not assigned, each person trying to occupy the most desirable spot for the night's rest. To sleep with as many as a dozen persons of different age and sex on the floor in a small, crowded room is quite an experience. The guest room had a small heating stove, but the fire was made rarely, usually on festive occasions when guests stayed over night. Uncle Rade, the head of the house, his wife, my Aunt Pava, slept in "the room," which was the only part of the house that was finished. It had a wood ceiling, roughly plastered walls, and three small glass windows with wooden shutters.

The house was poorly furnished. "The room" had a small wooden table with two benches, two or three stools, and a single iron bed, the only bed in the house, which Uncle Rade had commandeered for himself. Someone "liberated" the bed from the military barracks in Bileća after the collapse of Austria-Hungary in 1918. Elsewhere in the house were a few simple stools, two foot-high circular tables (*sinija*), one or two huge wooden boxes, and for storage purposes two large elliptical wicker baskets plastered with cow dung. There were no curtains, draperies or rugs. The bedding was simple and consisted of heavy goat-hair blankets called *guber*. There were no bedsheets and only a couple of crude pillows in the house. One slept on a *guber*, covered himself with another *guber*, and improvised a pillow from his own clothing.

When we were all together, food was generally eaten off the *sinija* in shifts. The spoons were wooden, but there were not enough of them, and at mealtime after each swallow one was obliged to pass the spoon to his neighbor. The house had fewer than half a dozen simple metallic forks, and no table knives at all. We ate from a single large wooden or metallic bowl. This shortage of eating implements and dishes reflects a curious self-effacing attitude. It was certainly no major task to carve additional spoons. Materials were plentiful, and the peasant was skilled in wood-carving. Peasants in Bileća Rudine are talented masons and stonecutters and built beautiful public buildings for wages, but never built comfortable and finished homes for themselves. They are excellent woodcutters, but did not spend their talents on their own furnishings, utensils, and home. Not until the late thirties did the family at long last obtain a sufficient number of wooden and metallic eating implements, a concession to urban influence.

Our zadruga home was disorderly and crowded. The sanitary conditions were appalling. We had no toilets and no washing and bathing facilities. The water in the cistern was polluted, and the dishes were never thoroughly washed. The animals moved in and out of the house, leaving their droppings. Swarms of flies were everywhere. The house was infested with fleas, bedbugs, and lice. The sanitary and hygienic standards in the village have greatly improved since the end of the Second World War.

The Diet

The diet of my zadruga family was simple and monotonous, due more to conservatism and ignorance than to want and poverty. My family and other peasants in Bileća Rudine were traditionalists with regard to food. They clung to simple culinary tastes, detested urban cuisine, and avoided experimentation with food. Milk and dairy products (sour milk, soft and hard cheese) constituted an important part of the peasant's diet. Of great importance for the diet were maize, introduced in the early eighteenth century, and potatoes, which became an important crop in the second half of the nineteenth century. The most common dish was *pura*, an everyday menu of boiled coarsely ground maize flour, with a bit of salt added, normally eaten with freshly boiled milk or sour milk. Occasionally, *pura* was seasoned more lavishly with fat, cream cheese (*kajmak*), and hard cheese. When prepared in this fashion, it was called *cicvara*.

Another frequently served dish was *čorba*, a heavy soup which included potatoes, cereals, fresh and dry beans, pasta, beets, and greens of one kind or another; it was cooked with meat, fresh or smoked. Fresh and smoked meat was eaten once a week, on the average, and it was served in plenitude only on Christmas, the patron saint day, and at weddings. Since the end of the Second World War, however, the peasant's menu has changed dramatically, for at long last much of the urban cuisine has penetrated his kitchen.

Holidays and Festivities

The religious holidays, Christmas, Easter, patron saint, and festivities associated with the rites of passage (weddings, baptismal, funeral), are celebrated by a zadruga in a more impressive way than by a nuclear family, because more persons are involved in the various rites and customs, and more hands are available to help with the preparations required for the event celebrated. The crowd is always present, and only a pretext is needed to animate it. Deaths in a zadruga are likewise greater events than in a nuclear family, because more people come to the funeral, burial, and wake, and more people are left in mourning.

Preparations for Christmas and Easter involved many days of fasting and preparation. In my youth, the rites involving Yule Log day (the cutting, installing, blessing, and burning of the log), Christmas (the three-day celebration), the role of the *polaznik*, the invocation of the peace of God (*mirboẑiti*), the roasting of an animal, Easter (the coloring and cracking of eggs) and the *slava* bread (*kolač, česnica*), and the saint's day (*slava*) feast were still fully practiced.

The *slava* feast is of special importance; it is the culminating point in the rites at which representatives of all families in kinship and close friends are present. The *slava* (ours is St. George) is the feast of a patron saint, not of an individual, but of a family and a clan, or a community and a church. One of its original social functions was no doubt to cement the intra-kinship relations.

The personal religion of members of my family was a mixture of pagan and Christian beliefs and practices. Many of the local religious rites and rituals are of pagan origin and related to family health, livestock breeding, and grain harvests. They derive from many different sources, pagan, Christian, and Moslem, some indigenous and some borrowed from Illyrian, Graeco-Roman, Slavic, and Turkish cultures. Hardly anyone in my family knew anything about the history of Christianity and the Serbian Orthodox Church. The Church represented little more for them than the social functions connected with birth, marriage, death, patron saint's day, and other major holidays, and its position as a pillar of nationalism. Hardly any member of the family went to church more than twice a year, and some may not have entered the church more than half a dozen times in their entire lives. On Christmas and the patron saint day, the head of the household led the prayer, in which he pleaded for peace and divine mercy for those who had died, for a bountiful harvest, and for divine blessing on the living. His prayer was spontaneous and ungrammatical, but sincere.

Since the Second World War, growing urbanization and secularization have stripped most customs of their color and flamboyance. Less time and money are spent on religious celebrations, which are simplified and adapted to modern town life.

THE DECLINE OF ZADRUGA

As a social institution, the zadruga began to break down in the more advanced parts of Yugoslavia in the first half of the nineteenth century. It lasted longer in socially and economically less developed regions, such as Bileća Rudine, where the patriarchal form of existence was strong and the influence of modernism slow in coming. With the Austro-Hungarian occupation, Bileća Rudine was for the first time exposed to modern urbanistic influences. The result was more accelerated social change, slow at first and accelerated by the First World War and by the emergence of the national Yugoslav state. The political and economic conditions in the interwar period contributed considerably to the transformation of Bileća Rudine's patriarchal society.

The new political order also produced a greater degree of social mobility. Two of my cousins who served in the army brought home knowledge of urban civilization. Changes in dress and everyday life style began to take place. The chance of acquiring personal property greatly increased.

As economic and political conditions changed, group living became a burden rather than an advantage. The urge for personal possessions and independence, always existent in the zadruga, grew more pronounced. The advantages of private ownership, improved communications, the growth of a market economy, the introduction of new methods of production, and the changed relationship between the individual and the state militated against zadruga communal family life. The ascendancy of the modern legal system, which stressed individualism, clashed with zadruga law and the notion of family unity. Increasing taxes, paid in money, and the high cost of living often forced the zadrugas into debt.

Gradually, the members of the family began to neglect communal property and to concern themselves more with matters that served their personal gain. The young man increasingly sought freedom from zadruga regimentation and the bossiness of the *domaćin*. Because most zadrugas were no longer able to provide for their increasing needs, more and more members moved to the city in search of employment. Military service exposed young peasants to modern civilization and a better life, and on returning home they found it hard to readjust to zadruga life. Increased opportunities for travel broadened the horizons of peasants long restricted to their own environment; village isolation began to break down. All these developments clashed with the obsolescence of the zadruga.

The Yugoslav state, founded in 1918, provided the people of Bileća Rudine increased opportunity to attend school. All the male children in our zadruga went to school; they walked nine kilometers to school located in Bileća Rudine, where they mingled with their urban counterparts and came to know and appreciate many aspects of urban life. The school became an important instrument of social change. It introduced country pupils to the advantages of urban living, and they began to look down on their primitive village and zadruga existence. In the thirties, an elementary school built at Čepelica, only three miles away, became a local social and cultural center.

Two of my cousins, Obrad and Jefto, the sons of Uncles Ivan and Rade, respectively, were a few of the fortunate peasant children who graduated from the elementary school and then were admitted into the *Donskoi kadetskii korpus Aleksandra III-ago* (The Don Cadet School of Alexander III), founded by the royal government for the Russians who found refuge in Yugoslavia after the Bolshevik advent to power. The *korpus,* an equivalent to a gymnasium, was patterned on the comparable imperial Russian military schools. Instruction was in Russian, but the pupils, that is the cadets, were obliged to study Serbian. My cousins graduated from the eight-year *korpus,* and one of them continued his studies at Belgrade University and ultimately became a prominent agronomist. The other one perished as a resistance fighter during the Second World War.

The zadruga thus lost its *raison d'être.* Once a bastion of patriarchalism, the zadruga had begun to retreat before the challenges of modernity. Where it continued to exist in Bileća Rudine, it survived less because of the need for it than because of strong feeling of family kinship, lingering respect for tradition, primitive fear of losing respect in the community, and sometimes because the family wished to avoid conflict over the division of the patrimony. The life of some zadrugas was extended simply because the family did not wish to lose its substantial prestige in the community by breaking up into nuclear families.

Beside these general reasons for the weakening and dissolution of my zadruga, others were rooted in the family itself. In the early twenties, Uncle Djoko married and moved to Bileća, a small town located about ten kilometers north of Orah, with his wife and the three orphaned children whom he had brought from the United States. There he opened a small grocery store. The two brothers and their families who remained at home made no important decisions affecting the zadruga without counseling with their brother in Bileća; they continued to look upon him as a traveled man and a person of good judgment. From time to time, especially at the height of the harvest season, Uncle Djoko sent his wife and one or two children to the village to help harvest maize and potatoes, and to mow and gather the hay. Whenever he could afford, he sent to the family left at the hearth coffee and sugar, luxuries always in shortage. In turn, he received for his own family in Bileća a certain amount of hay, potatoes, firewood, and cheese.

Initially, the two brothers in Orah did not object to the third brother's moving, because they believed that the latter's commercial activities would benefit the zadruga as a whole. However, the grocery business failed, and the brothers in Orah began to resent their brother in Bileća. They felt that the brother in Bileća did not contribute his share and that he had snubbed them. This soon led to a certain amount of intrafamily bickering.

Still another factor undermined our zadruga harmony. Since Uncles Rade and Djoko had acquired personal properties, they had begun to think that their own immediate families would be better off if separated from the zadruga. Rade's son Maksim engaged in freight transport. He delivered goods by horse and wagon from wholesale firms in Dubrovnik to retailers in Bileća. Unencumbered by zadruga obligations, Uncle Rade and his son felt that they could keep for themselves all the money earned from transporting freight. Djoko, who saved some money as a wage earner in the United States, also came to believe that the zadruga was an economic burden to him. Ivan, the eldest of the three brothers, who depended entirely on the zadruga, favored its retention. He had no personal possessions. Moreover, if the zadruga were to break up, his family would not have been able to provide enough working hands to cultivate the land and to care for the animals.

DISSOLUTION OF MY ZADRUGA

One must distinguish between the natural splitting up of the zadruga into nuclear families, each of which became a nucleus for a new zadruga, and the terminal abolition of zadruga as a form of social existence. The natural breaking up of a zadruga occurred in Bileća Rudine when the third generation of its members reached the time of marriage and began to marry. The individual families stayed together in a zadruga until they married their daughters and sons, for it was easier for a zadruga to absorb the cost of the wedding than for a nuclear family. Sometimes, however, a zadruga split up when the heads of nuclear families decided for economic or personal reasons that they could no longer live together and that their own immediate families would prosper if they lived separately.

The question of breaking up a zadruga is discussed for many days before the final decision is made. In some parts of Bosnia and Herzegovina, tradition required that the zadruga be divided in a certain month and even week and day, but that was not the case in Bileća Rudine. The breaking up of a zadruga in Bileća Rudine customarily came soon after the summer harvest.

Division of the zadruga possessions was usually accomplished with the assistance of "witnesses" or "arbitrators." If the division involved only two brothers, each of them named an "arbitrator," but more "arbitrators" were chosen if there were more than two brothers. Two or more brothers, however, may often select one and the same "arbitrator." It was always difficult to divide the land equitably, because the landed parcels were not of the same value and size, and they were varying distances from home. The zadruga possessions normally consisted of the family house and furnishings, arable and non-arable lands, livestock, farming installations, farming tools, food stores, wool, and the like. If the home was not large enough to provide space for all nuclear families, arrangements were made for construction of additional quarters. At an earlier period, the *uljanik*, where the beehives were kept, was not divided, but was retained by the brother who inherited the hearth. Frequently, a single fruit tree, orchard, or threshing field (*guvno, gumno*) remained a common possession.

Many peasants considered it a disgrace to have the zadruga divided in a court of law. Often, they neither made surveys of their individual properties nor had them entered into the cadastral records after dividing the zadruga. Consequently, the annual taxes remained undivided, and the families of the former zadruga had to make arrangements for payment. The failure to survey and record individual holdings in some instances became a serious problem when the Communists came to power after the Second World War and demanded proof of legal title to land.

In 1925, my uncles decided to split up. Three villagers were asked to serve as witnesses and "arbitrators." The zadruga properties were divided in four parts, among three surviving brothers and the orphaned children of the fourth. The fifth brother who died in America was not married; his share of the family patrimony was divided among the living heirs. By drawing lots, it was decided which brother would choose the first piece of property. Because the properties were of unequal value, bargaining and compromise was necessary. Each brother tried to get the best of everything; success depended on the ability to distinguish a good from a bad piece of land, or to select the best livestock.

One by one, each of the larger parcels was divided among the brothers. The oldest brother proposed how to split the first parcel in the required number of parts, and then the youngest brother was given the first opportunity to choose the part he wanted. Each brother was given an opportunity to suggest how parcels of land should be divided, and an equal opportunity of being first in choosing the parcel of land he wanted. A few parcels (*vrtovi*) of land were so small that they could not be divided. These small properties were distributed in some equitable fashion among the family heirs. Each family received a share of good and poor land, woodland and meadow, barns and other buildings, and farming tools.

Like land, the livestock was also of different value. A fair division of sheep, goats, cattle and draft animals was therefore difficult to achieve. A few extra head of stock often went to brothers with older children, on the assumption that they had contributed more work to the zadruga than the others. The animals belonging to our zadruga, about seventy sheep and goats, ten cattle, four horses, four hogs, and a dozen chickens, were divided between two brothers. Because the third brother, who had moved to Bileća, could not keep livestock in town, he took only two milk goats and received instead an added parcel of land.

The equipment and the farming implements were divided equitably. One brother obtained a cart, another a plow, and the third another item or items of comparable value. Uncle Rade received the *uljanik*, but gave up one of the threshing fields. The grain, cheese, wool, and other provisions were divided by the number of persons in each family. The largest share thus went to the second brother, for his was the largest family. The sole cistern and most of the grazing land and woodlands remained under joint ownership.

Each brother and the heirs of the deceased brother received a part of the zadruga house, a typical dwelling in Rudine. The eldest brother received the room with the hearth. The second brother received the middle room, in which the grain and clothes were stored. The youngest of the three brothers and the orphaned children received "the room." Because the brother in Bileća acquired "the room," the best part of the house, he yielded all the farming tools, sheds, and nearly all of the livestock to the other two brothers. Because the second brother wanted the only wagon, he received two horses and in turn conceded three oxen to his older brother. Thus came the end to our zadruga. A few other zadrugas in Bileća Rudine survived a while longer.

COOPERATION AFTER SEPARATION

One of the most remarkable things is that many of its attributes survived after the zadruga was dissolved. In Bileća Rudine, the nuclear families which emerged from a zadruga remained bound by close kinship ties, and often continued to cooperate in farming, livestock herding, and various other economic and social endeavors. The field work was done under the direction of the former head of the extended family, the participating families dividing the harvest and seed on the basis of the size of their families, and the hay and straw according to the number of animals each owned. This sort of cooperation did not satisfy all, especially since every family paid the same amount of taxes, regardless of its size and the share of the harvest it received.

Post-zadruga cooperation, however, was not always of the same kind. Cooperation among the nuclear families of the dissolved zadruga occasionally occurred because some did not have enough hands to work the land they got, or the zadruga land could not be divided, or a zadruga lacked sufficient land to provide each member family with a living.

After the dissolution of a zadruga, some or all of the separated families continued to live under the same roof of their erstwhile joint home. When my zadruga broke up in 1925, two brothers and their families continued to live in the zadruga house, one of them occupying the hearth quarters of the house and the other the *tavan* quarters. The two residences had their own separate entrances from the outside, but there was no connecting door between them. The *soba* which was allocated to the third brother, who had moved to Bileća, could be entered only through the *tavan*. Since the *soba* was rarely occupied, the brother who obtained the *tavan* took it over.

The brother who had moved out of the zadruga home continued to cooperate with his brothers' families in various ways and made arrangements with them to cultivate his land on a crop-sharing basis. In turn, when his brothers asked for help, he extended it whenever he could. The two brothers in Orah died during the Second World War, but their families continued to occupy the parts of the zadruga house which they had inherited, and for the most part they cooperated in farming and stock breeding.

Except when fraternal relations were strained, the brothers of the erstwhile zadruga who continued to live in the separate parts of the zadruga home frequently celebrated the family's patron saint together. When they eventually stopped this practice, they divided the relatives who were usually represented at the patron saint feasts in such a way that each family received a share of relatives with which it was related through marriage or *kumstvo*.

The length of the post-zadruga cooperation depended on a variety of circumstances. Our families cooperated for about forty years, but the cooperation was not consistent and was accompanied by many crises. Jevto Dedijer recorded families who held some lands in common for as many as nine generations.

When the Trebišnjica river was dammed in 1968, all but three of the fifteen families in the village of Orah were obliged to move out. The former members of my zadruga and others whose homes sank under the Trebišnjica waters grieved over their losses, despite adequate financial compensation for the lost properties. The peasants insisted that the losses of their hearths and family cemetery could not be assuaged with money, but they were forced to submit. My relatives were scattered in many directions, and ties between them had all but disappeared. Once transplanted from their village, they were forced to discard many traditional customs. After moving to town, they soon adopted a new, a more advanced form of social and economic existence. The peasants retain longest the deep-seated habits of mind and some elements of the spiritual culture. They continue to speak nostalgically about the erstwhile zadruga life, remembering the positive and forgetting the negative aspects of that life.

12: THE TOMAŠEVIĆ EXTENDED FAMILY ON THE PENINSULA OF PELJEŠAC

Jozo Tomasevich

This paper concerning the development of the Tomašević *zajednica* on the Peninsula of Pelješac in Dalmatia supplements Philip E. Mosely's classic study, "Adaptation for Survival: The Varžić Zadruga" by presenting the history of other extended families in other areas of Yugoslavia living under different legal and socioeconomic conditions than those of Varžić,[1] Some fifteen years ago during a visit to Pelješac, I discovered in a heavy walnut chest in the attic of my ancestral home a series of original documents from one hundred twenty to one hundred and sixty-five years old. During my latest visit to Košarnido in September 1974 I was given additional family and other documents by distant cousins, Ivan Tomašević, now eighty-one and Branko Tomašević, now fifty-four and a lawyer living in Zagreb. These provide detailed information of a kind rarely available concerning the acquisition of land and division of property of an extended family, in this case the Tomašević *zajednica* in the village of Košarnido. The history of this small section of Yugoslavia, of the land tenure system which prevailed there until the division of the original *zajednica* and afterwards, of its economic life, and of the division illuminate the significance and diversity of this fascinating institution. These documents also provide information concerning the public service of one member of the family Tomašević and the emigration overseas of men from the Tomašević families.

The village of Košarnido is located in the northwestern part of the central plateau of the peninsula of Pelješac in southern Dalmatia. It is about seven miles from the townlet port of Orebić on the open sea side and about three miles from the townlet port of Trpanj on the land side. In my childhood, the village had eleven families. Administratively, with about eighteen other villages, it belonged to the commune of Kuna, which in turn was part of the county of Korčula. The Pelješac peninsula is about forty-five miles long and some three to five miles wide. In 1949, only 11.5 percent of its land was under cultivation. The remainder was forest or grazing land of little real value. In the same year 7,567 people lived on the peninsula.[2]

The chief agricultural product of Pelješac is red table wine. In earlier times olive oil apparently was of considerable significance. The peasants raise a variety of other crops for their own use: grain, potatoes, vegetables, and fruits. Most families raise a few sheep, a pig or two, and some poultry.

Until 1946, the Pelješac peninsula had no roads for vehicular traffic. During the French occupation at the beginning of the nineteenth century, some primitive roads were built, but these could accommodate pack animals only. Immediately after the Second World War, the new government built a dirt road for motor traffic and this is now asphalted. This road and the new Communist regime have been responsible for transforming life on the peninsula during the past thirty years.

After the 1550's, especially during the eighteenth and nineteenth centuries, seafaring was the most important occupation other than farming. Most of the sailing ships were owned by a group of families from Orebić and others by a family from Janjina, a large village about seven miles east of Košarnido.[3] Some ships were owned also by people from other localities, including my great-grandfather Nikola, who with his partners owned the brigantine "S.Niccolò" between 1802 and 1806.[4] The continental blockade produced a severe crisis for the Pelješac shipowners, and a large number of ships were laid up for years or sold. After the end of the Napoleonic era the shipping industry recuperated. During and following the Crimean War it experienced its greatest prosperity. Some of the Orebić families then established shipping and trading businesses in Russia, Italy, and France. In 1865 a portion of the Orebić shipowners established a shipping corporation. Three years later, the shipowners from Pelješac owned sixty-five large sailing ships for transoceanic navigation, with a capacity of over thirty thousand tons and a value of about two million forints (approximately one million dollars).

However, the conservative shipowners failed to shift to steam. Between 1879 and 1885 three Orebić shipping firms, including the corporation, and later also the Janjina firm, were forced into liquidation. In 1907 the last large Pelješac sailing ship was sold.[5] From the beginning of the nineteenth century to the outbreak of the First World War, the Pelješac peninsula produced about a thousand merchant marine captains and about six thousand seamen from a population averaging between seven and eight thousand people.[6]

After the 1850's a great deal of emigration took place from Pelješac to Argentina, Chile, Peru, Australia, and New Zealand, Louisiana, and especially California. When the First World War broke out, the eleven families in the village of Košarnido included two retired merchant marine captains, one bosun and one seaman, two masters and one first officer. One cadet and one seaman were at sea, and one young man was about to graduate from the merchant marine academy. Seven people from the village were living in California, and one had returned from California to the village. No family had more than one adult young man at home.[7]

The families of Košarnido and of three other neighboring villages of approximately the same size shared another interesting feature: each had another farm located on the coast, about three miles south of Orebić. These formed a conglomerate village, Postup, in which the houses and land of all four villages were intermixed. The houses were smaller and less elaborate and the land holdings of Postup were smaller than those on the plateau. Since the differences in climate between the central plateau and the coast allowed for a staggering of farmwork, the families usually lived in Postup when work required and during the August lull, when there were few tasks on the main farm. Postup produces one of the best red wines in all of Yugoslavia, the Postup.

The Republic of Dubrovnik, or Ragusa, bought the peninsula of Pelješac in 1333 from the Serbian Czar Dušan, agreeing to pay a basic price and an annual tribute.[8] Since the Bosnian king also claimed the peninsula, Dubrovnik paid a separate tribute to him. Even so, Dubrovnik was extremely pleased to add this large area to its territory. The peninsula was first divided into twenty-four carats. This division was soon abandoned and the peninsula was then divided into three hundred sections and apportioned to the noble families of Dubrovnik with a very small amount given to selected commoners. Those given land were required to pay taxes, which were used for payment of the annual tributes and for administrative services and defense. Pelješac was administered by officials named by the republic government. As in the republic itself, all offices were of short duration.[9]

When new routes to the East were discovered and the Mediterranean area lost importance, Dubrovnik's political and economic power declined greatly. It plummeted after the catastrophic earthquake of 1667. French troops controlled the area between 1806 and 1814. The republic was abolished in 1808. In 1815 the Congress of Vienna assigned the territory of the republic, together with the rest of Dalmatia, to Austria. After 1867, it was a part of the Austrian half of the Dual Monarchy, and it remained under Austria until 1918.

The land tenure system on the peninsula of Pelješac prior to its purchase in 1333 had been feudal, like that in Serbia. After the purchase by Dubrovnik and apportionment of the land to the noble families, a new system gradually came into being, steadily moving against the interest of those who worked the land. The system was too loose and varied to classify. Some call it feudalist. Others deny that it was feudalist in any sense. Still others describe it as feudalist *sui generis*. The provisions of the contracts regulating the relations between the landlord and those who tilled the soil varied greatly from one area to another, from landlord to landlord, and especially from one period to the next. Three consistent patterns prevailed; there was no freehold on land and to live on the peninsula the tillers had to work the land of a noble, the conditions of the tillers became steadily worse, and the church (Roman Catholic) was not allowed to become a landlord of any consequence.

A contract always regulated the relations between the landlord and the tiller of soil. Besides the farmland, the landlord furnished the tiller a house and garden or permitted him to build a house. The peasant gave the landlord a share of the crop. In exchange for use of the house and garden, he was obligated to render labor services on the personal holdings of the landlord. In the fourteenth century, when the system began, labor service amounted to only a few days annually. By the eighteenth century it had risen to ninety days annually. This was also the norm when the republic was abolished in 1808. Furthermore, the tenant was obliged to make certain gifts to the landlord on specified holidays, usually a loaf of bread, a lamb or a hen. However, the tenant was not legally bound to the landlord's land, as in the regular feudal system, and the landlord had no jurisdiction over him. In fact, the tenant could have, and some did have, contractual relationships with more than one landlord at the same time. These contracts between landlord and tenant ran from three to twenty to five hundred years and even into perpetuity. The peasant was bound to the soil economically, if not legally, and was generally harshly exploited. Thus, materially, if not formally, the land tenure system on Pelješac during the Dubrovnik republic was based on serfdom.

During the seventeenth and eighteenth centuries some of the Pelješac families who had become rich by engaging in shipping and trade freed themselves from serfdom by buying the land their families tilled.[10] However, in 1777 the republic government issued a decree prohibiting the peasants from owning and buying any land on Pelješac.[11] Under the French and then the Austrian rule, the land tenure system on Pelješac evolved into a mixture of freehold and sharecropping in which the tiller retained two-thirds and sometimes even three-fourths of the harvest. After the establishment of Yugoslavia all sharecropping contracts were annulled according to the rule "Land belongs to those who till it." Landlords were supposed to obtain an indemnity in the form of government bonds. However, the final legislation on the agrarian reform in Dalmatia was delayed until October 1930. Processing of indemnity claims was very slow and only a few had been settled when the country was invaded in 1941. So far as I know there are no state farms or collective farms on Pelješac at the present time.

Land ownership among the Dubrovnik nobles on Pelješac and elsewhere in the territory of the tiny state was far more stable than in other parts of the

Balkans where the Ottoman conquest annihilated the local nobility or forced it into Islam or to the west. On the Pelješac peninsula many Dubrovnik noble families who had acquired land in the 1330's still retained most of their holdings in 1808, and Tomašević families bought land from them until the 1860's.[12]

The first historical record of which I have knowledge which mentions the village of Košarnido is the population census made by the Dubrovnik authorities, with the help of the parish priests, in 1673-74, a few years after the great earthquake. This shows only three families in the village, two families Tomašević and one family Radoš, with a total of twenty-one members. Apparently, none of these families was an extended family. In those rural areas of the republic covered by the census, there were 3,964 households, of which 3,742 households had one to eight members, 81 had nine, 75 had ten, and only 62 had more than ten. Thus, three hundred years ago in the rural parts of the republic the extended family was an exception rather than a rule.[13]

Apparently, neither of the two Tomašević families in Košarnido in 1673 was connected to my family. Indeed, throughout the nineteenth century and until the 1920's, the village contained two distinct, unrelated Tomašević stocks. I assume from family tradition that my ancestors arrived sometime during the eighteenth century, coming from the mainland or more probably from the neighboring village of Oskorušno, which the census of 1673 reveals had some Tomašević families.

The documents which I found some fifteen years ago date from the first decade of the nineteenth century and from the 1850's.[14] The earliest, dated July 4, 1809, is a decision of the General Administration of Dubrovnik and Kotor (the French occupation authorities) to allow my great-grandfather Nikola and a man from a neighboring village, Baldo Orhanović, to acquire a bloc of land on Pelješac from a Dubrovnik noble, Ivan Ghetaldi. The other five documents, written half a century later, form a series. The first is a decree of the court in Orebić, dated June 24, 1854, showing how Nikola disposed of his share of property in the communal ownership of the extended family Tomašević in his will. This is followed by an agreement, dated April 30, 1856, among the members of the extended family Tomašević regarding the division. Next comes a document entitled Sentence and Division, which was executed on the basis of the above agreement and is dated October 22, 1856, as well as, of the same date, a document of the court in Orebić conveying copies of the Sentence and Division to the parties concerned. The final document, dated November 22, 1856, is a petition of my grandfather Ivan Tomašević and his married sister, acting through their lawyer Smrkinić in Korčula, charging irregularities and near fraud in the division and asking its annulment. Documents which I obtained from my cousins in September 1974 refer to various land acquisitions and challenges to the land claims of the Tomašević family.

The 1809 document is especially interesting because it shows that my great-grandfather and his partner Orhanović were permitted to buy land even though ownership of land by commoners was prohibited by an old law of the republic which was still formally in effect. The reasons for the permission are specifically stated: some earlier precedents existed, the new (French) government did not prohibit anyone from owning land, no special privileges were recognized, and all citizens were treated equally. The two men bought the land in 1813, the transaction was recorded in the landownership books in Dubrovnik, and the land is still in possession of the Tomašević and Orhanović families. In both families the financial means to purchase this land had come from seafaring.

My great-grandfather Nikola was then or soon became, the head of the Tomašević extended family and remained so until his death on October 6, 1850. He had two brothers: Andrija, who died in 1836 without progeny, and Anton, who was still living in 1856. He had two sons, Ivan and Petar, and a daughter, Ana, who by 1854 was married into the family Bogoević in a neighboring village. In 1856, Anton had four sons living, Ivan, Nikola, Baldo, and Pavo. A fifth son, Andrija, had died.

Between 1813 and 1856 the extended family Tomašević acquired additional land. In partnership with the family Harlović from a neighboring village the Tomašević family purchased a bloc of land in Postup on November 26, 1816 from a Dubrovnik priest, Gašpar Radilović, who had bought it in 1805 from the noble family Gradi. On December 11, 1838 a nephew of my great-grandfather, Ivan Tomašević, bought a bloc of land from the estate of the Dubrovnik noblewoman Ana Menze for 1,655 forints. According to other documents, the families Tomašević and Cibilić (from a neighboring village) bought a bloc of land on November 30, 1853 from the Dubrovnik noble family Sorgo for 8,261.50 forints, the Tomašević's half paid partly by communal and partly by personal funds. Additional small blocs of land were bought in 1816, 1829, and 1830, and on at least four other occasions from commoners in the commune of Kuna. On two occasions in 1827 and 1830 the Tomašević brothers and their partners were hailed to court for alleged unlawful possession of land and unlawful posting of property markers. Unfortunately, I was unable to locate documents containing the court decisions.

These purchases of land and the building of a new house in the 1830's or 1840's indicate that the family prospered as it grew.[15] Another indication of its prosperity is the fact that a nephew of my great-grandfather, Pavo, was sent to the merchant marine academy at Livorno, Tuscany, from which he later graduated and became a merchant marine captain. The cellar of the new house contained a mill for crushing olives and oil presses, a source of income because the equipment was used for olive crops from other families and even other villages. By 1853 one of the nephews of my great-grandfather, Ivan Tomašević, had been either elected or appointed syndic or mayor of the commune of Kuna, and he remained in that position for over twenty years.[16] Throughout these years the offices of the commune were located in the "new house" in Košarnido. Toward the end of his term his nephew Baldo became secretary of the commune. In 1856, the extended family included about twenty-five members, counting the children, who were rather unevenly distributed between the two lineages. One of Nikola's sons, my granduncle Petar, was by that time already settled in California.

The 1854 document shows that the will of my great-grandfather Nikola gave five-twelfths of his share of the communal property to each of his two sons, Ivan in Košarnido and Petar in California, and two-twelfths to his married daughter. The will also obligated the sons to provide the daughter an appropriate dowry.

When great-grandfather Nikola died, the headship of the *zajednica* went jointly to his surviving brother, Anton, and to two of his nephews, Ivan and Nikola. The triple headship is a novelty I have not seen mentioned in literature on the zadruga, although it may have occurred in other cases.

The chief problem in the *zajednica* after the death of my great-grandfather was most probably the imbalance in manpower and earning power of the two lineages. At any rate, agreement was reached on April 30, 1856 to divide the *zajednica*. This document specifies not less than eleven points concerning the wish of all involved for division, selection of two arbiters, and the principles upon which the division was to be made, including rules governing which land possessions were included in the division and which were separate property of individual members. The Sentence and Division document of October 22, 1856 is immensely detailed: it covers fourteen pages of legal-size paper in fine, small handwriting.

The division was made first according to lineage, dividing the communal property into three equal parts: one to the surviving brother Anton, one to the heirs of my great-grandfather Nikola, and one to the heirs of the third brother, Andrija, who had died in 1836. Since Andrija had died without progeny, his brothers' sons, both living and dead, were declared his inheritors. Thus, my part of the family, Ivan and Petar, received only two shares in the property of their late uncle Andrija, while the other part of the family, Anton's, received five shares, one for each of the four living sons and one for Anton's dead son Andrija. In other words, the division was based partly on the principle of lineage and partly on the principles of actual membership of male inheritors. Thus the communal property was theoretically divided into twenty-one parts, of which nine went to my part of the family and twelve to the other. The same formula was applied to the other communally owned assets. Due to the difference in property and the number of family members, my family was thereafter referred to as the small (*mali*) and the other as the big (*veliki*) Tomasević́. The agreement further stipulated that a third arbiter would be selected if disagreement occurred between the arbiters, and that the decision of the arbiters would be final and beyond appeal, except in the case of a breach of juridical procedure.

The arbiters first decided that the land purchase in 1813 was made with communal funds and was therefore subject to division. The land bought in 1838 by Anton's son Ivan, but apparently for the account of his brother Nikola, was deemed a private purchase, not subject to division. The 1853 acquisition which was purchased with both communal and private funds, was divided accordingly. Other land was considered communal property and thus subject to division. The division of 1856 resulted in a nuclear family, my grandfather's and a new *zajednica,* which consisted of a father, two married sons with children and two bachelor sons.

The arbiters then proceeded to divide all the communal property, consisting of arable land, land held by sharecroppers, forest and grazing land, houses, stables, movable possessions, cash, and outstanding claims, as well as outstanding obligations. The cultivated land, amounting to ten or twelve hectares, consisted of 182 separately identified parcels. Most of these were duly divided into three equal parts; two of these went, by lot, to the two families. The third part was divided into two unequal parts, two-sevenths and five-sevenths, and added to the respective thirds. The property was widely scattered because it had been acquired at different times and from different sources. Because of the terrain, the quality of soil often differed greatly within short distances. Naturally, each party to the division wanted its share of the good land and therefore had also to take its share of the poor land. Even some trees were considered special items of division. For example, the branches of a large olive tree which stood near the property line were divided, three to one family and two to the other.

The division of houses was somewhat more difficult. The old house and the detached kitchen with its space for eating and for food storage were assigned to my grandfather, and the new house and another kitchen and storage space to the other family. Wine cellars were located on the ground floor of the houses. On this principle, the olive mill and olive oil press in the new house went to the other family. However, since access to the old house was through the courtyard of the new house, free passage was assured in perpetuity.

The stables were also divided, as were all livestock, pack animals, farm equipment, and all furniture, linen, kitchen utensils, jewelry, and clothing. This was done informally, without written record. Cash holdings of the family were also divided according to the agreed-upon formula, twelve twenty-firsts and nine twenty-firsts.

The arbiters also prepared a List of Debitors (a *Specifica*) who owed money to the *zajednica*. This, prepared in duplicate, was part of the document of division, but I have not found it. The total amount of receivables was 2,011.39 forints.[17] All the communal claims from and debts to third persons were divided by the same formula.

The document also set forth clearly financial matters between the two families and among the various members of the two families. The obligations between the two families had to be settled within fourteen days after the day of the division. One of the nephews of my great-grandfather, Baldo, became a creditor of his brothers for 1,500 forints.

One part of the document of Sentence and Division dealt with a number of items which the arbiters declared not divisible and therefore to be held henceforth as communal property. This included all the land of the original *zajednica* held by the sharecroppers, all the forest and grazing land, of which there were several hundred hectares, certain trees in the immediate vicinity of the houses, a pit for making lime, four water cisterns, a still for making brandy, several types of measuring utensils, a sledgehammer, and a hook for fishing out pails which fell into the cisterns.

Just a month after the execution and recording of the Sentence and Division, on November 22, 1856, my grandfather and his married sister, Ana, filed suit against their relatives and the man who acted with the power of attorney for their brother Petar. They charged that the arbiters, "instead of having acted within the limits imposed upon them [by the Agreement of Division], have pronounced a sentence with division manifestly unjust, not to say fraudulent, and exceeding their powers," and asked that the division be declared null and void. They made several specific charges: (1) the arbiters had not divided all communal property, especially the land held by the sharecroppers and wooded and grazing areas, which could have been easily divided; (2) the houses were not divided by lot, as specified by agreement, but rather at the pleasure of the arbiters, and the new house and other choice appurtenances had gone to the other family; (3) of the movable property, such as furniture, the other side had been given "twenty times more than they"; (4) they were not present when the lots were drawn; (5) the plaintiffs had not agreed that there be no written record of the movable objects involved, and, finally, (6) it was not true, as the Sentence and Division document asserted, that the various members of the other family had acted under oath in making statements regarding property items and claims. Furthermore, the suit added, only one copy of the List of Debitors had been made, and the other side held it.

Alas, the decision of the court on this petition has been lost, and I must rely on my childhood recollections to fill in the gap. The suit apparently had no effect on the principal terms of the division, either with regard to cultivated land or to houses, but certain amendments were made concerning the land held by sharecroppers and forested land, for in my childhood none of the land held by the sharecroppers and only a small part of the forested land was held communally. It is also probable that some rectification was made in the division of movable property.

In any case, the original extended family Tomašević came to an end with this division in 1856. However, some forested lands were held communally with the other Tomaševićs and several other families, but each family knew its share in the communal property. Furthermore, property rights in several land parcels were contested by the Tomašević families among themselves as late as 1908 and were gradually settled by court decisions.

After 1856, Anton's branch of the family continued as a *zajednica,* not only between Anton and his two married sons, but also later between the married sons of these sons. All four of Anton's surviving sons were grown at the time of my great-grandfather's death and were either at home or at sea when the division took place. Ivan and Pavo were married and had sons of their own, while Baldo and Nikola were still bachelors.

In 1855, in conjunction with several partners, Baldo undertook to buy a bloc of land and a wine cellar in the townlet of Kuna from the Dubrovnik noble family Giorgi. However, probably because he heard about great opportunities in California from my granduncle Petar, he emigrated to San Jose, California in the second half of 1858, when he was forty-one years old. His brother Ivan, the mayor, took over his contract for the purchase of land in Kuna. Baldo remained interested in his share of property in Košarnido, however, as well as in collecting his claims from his brothers. Between 1861 and 1874 he sent three different powers of attorney, first to one of his brothers, then to a friend, and then to the other brother, in order to settle his property affairs and claims in the old country. Apart from the share of property left to him by his father, his claims amounted to 3,714.48 forints.[18] He never succeeded in collecting any of the claims, nor did he obtain any money for his share of property. From San Jose he moved to Los Angeles, married for a second time (a Mexican woman thirty years his junior), and apparently had no progeny.

In the following generation his nephew, the son of Captain Pavo and also named Baldo, emigrated to Chile and then to Peru after he was disinherited and thrown out of the house by his father for wanting to marry a girl of whom his father disapproved. The old man later stated in his will, however, that the sons's share of property should be reinstated if he made a substantial financial contribution to the family. This did not occur. I was unable to find out when the two Baldos died, but my granduncle Petar died in an accident in San Jose on October 17, 1894.[19] Whatever land possessions the three men had in Košarnido remained in the hands of their respective immediate relatives.

To accommodate the growing number of people in the new *zajednica*, a third house was built in the same courtyard, completing what was known as the "Tomašević korta" or courtyard.[20] The word *korta* connotes more than just the houses and court; it has a sociological sense as well, meaning the Tomašević families as they lived next to each other before and after the division of the original *zajednica* in 1856. I well remember such questions as, "What is new in the *korta*? " "What does the *korta* think about this or that? " "Is everybody in good health in the *korta*? " Of course, every family in the *korta* knew what was happening in the other families, and there was a great deal of mutual assistance, including lending money without charging interest. The standing of different members of the *korta,* both men and women, was commensurate with their sense of kinship, their good neighborliness, intelligence, achievements, care for the family and farm, egoism or lack of it, and tolerance.

The new Tomašević *zajednica* lasted until 1912, after the 1870's as an extended family of first cousins. It was one of three extended families in our village. The second consisted first of three and later of two brothers and their families, and the third consisted of two married brothers and their families. One of the two extended families divided in 1899 and the other in 1910. All three of these extended families had one common feature: one of the brothers or cousins was a merchant marine captain. One of the families divided a few years before the captain retired and the remaining two a few years after the captains retired and returned home to live as gentlemen farmers.

When the division of 1912 occurred, one of the Tomašević families had two grown sons, Pavo and Luka, both merchant marine captains.[21] Luka, who never married, died in his seventies. Pavo married and had only one son, who became a lawyer and now lives in Zagreb. Pavo died when he was about eighty and his widow, now eighty-one, lives most of the time in a hostel for retired people in Dubrovnik, but by periodic visits to Košarnido still looks after the farm. The only son in the other branch, Ivan, never married. He is eighty-one years old, and the family faces extinction.[22]

Something of the same sort almost befell my family at an earlier date. My grandfather, Ivan, had four sons and two daughters. One son who went to sea decided to remain a bachelor. Another son, my father, went to California in the 1870's. The other two sons died in a scarlet fever epidemic when they were in their twenties. My father therefore was given the sobriquet, "Nado," or "Hope" of the family, because continuation of the family in Košarnido depended on him. He fulfilled that hope by returning to Košarnido in 1894 and marrying the daughter of his first cousin.

My parents had four sons, all of whom married. One, who was trained to be a merchant marine captain, jumped ship in western Australia, later settled in Auckland, New Zealand, and is childless. The other three have in all five daughters and three sons. My father's farm was divided in 1938. My brother in New Zealand and I assigned our shares to our two brothers, so that each one had half. My elder brother died a few years ago and his only son manages a vacation hostel belonging to a Belgrade bank in Orebić but remains a part-time farmer. He has one son and one daughter. The only son of my younger brother is now working as a mechanic in Zagreb.

The decline in the fortunes of the "Korta Tomašević" began during the First World War, then inflation wiped out considerable savings these families had accumulated, as well as claims in the form of outstanding loans and Austrian war bonds. The war and the political changes which ensued also caused severe dislocation and long depression in shipping which greatly reduced employment opportunities. A third factor was the decline in the peninsula's population, as young people looked for employment in the urban sector of the economy.

Conditions of life on Pelješac have greatly changed during the last half century, especially since the Second World War. Thus, in September 1974, twenty of the forty families in Košarnido and the neighboring three villages had passenger cars and most have modern household appliances. The families no longer process their own grapes and store wine in the cellar as of old, but they have a cooperative cellar with professional technicians in a neighboring village and sell part of the wine under a trade mark. Finally, Postup is beginning to engage in the tourist trade. The standard of living of those who have remained on Pelješac has greatly improved during the past two decades. However, the once proud and prosperous "Korta Tomašević" at Košarnido has almost completely disappeared as a kinship and close neighborhood group. To borrow a leitmotif from the man we honor with this volume, the "Korta Tomašević" failed to adapt for survival.

NOTES

1. It is impossible to describe the legal differences between the *zajednica* in Dalmatia during the nineteenth century and the zadruga in other parts of present-day Yugoslavia. In Dalmatia civil law issues, including the *zajednica,* were regulated by the Austrian Civil Code of 1811, which was based on Roman Law. In other areas the zadruga was regulated by common law or other civil codes or by special laws, as in the case of the Croato-Slavonian Military Frontier and later in Croatia-Slavonia.
2. Population on the peninsula of Pelješac has shown a marked decline in recent decades. According to the census of January 1921 its population then amounted to 11,203 people. See Nikola Z. Bjelovučić, *Poluostrvo Rat (Pelješac)* (Peninsula Rat [Pelješac]), in Serbian Royal Academy, *Srpski etnografski zbornik* (Belgrade), XXIII (1922), 177-178.

3. The most complete study of the history of shipping based on the peninsula of Pelješac is Stjepan Vekarić, *Pelješki jedrenjaci* [Sailing ships of Pelješac] (Split, 1960). In addition to ships operating under the Dubrovnik and later the Austrian flag, Pelješac sailing ships operated under Russian, British, and Tuscan flags.

4. I have a copy of the contract between the two principal partners, my great-grandfather Nikola and Nikola Bogoević, on the purchase of the brigantine, dated March 23, 1802. See also Vekarić, p. 270.

5. Vekarić, pp. 63-68, 103-104. The first steamship was acquired by an Orebić family in 1888. Some other families also bought steamships and administered their business from Orebić, but these operations were on a very limited scale. At the same time some merchant marine captains from Pelješac became partners in shipping firms operating from Trieste. See Vinko Foretić, "Through the Past of the Peninsula of Pelješac," in Justin V. Velnić, ed., *Spomenica Gospe Andjela u Orebićima 1470-1970* [The jubilee book of Our Lady of the Angels in Orebić, 1470-1970] (Omiš, 1970), pp. 313-314.

6. Nikola Z. Bjelovučić, *Povijest poluotoka Rata (Pelješca)* [A history of the peninsula of Pelješac] (Split, 1921), pp. 171-174. The estimate of the average population is my own.

7. Bjelovučić reported (*Poluostrvo Rat*, p. 178) that about 1,300 persons born on Pelješac were living in overseas countries in 1921.

8. For the successive steps in the territorial expansion of the patrician republic of Dubrovnik, see Francis W. Carter, *Dubrovnik (Ragusa): A Classic City State* (London and New York, 1972), pp. 124-128.

9. Dragan Roller, *Agrarno-proizvodni odnosi na području Dubrovačke republike od XIII. do XV. stoljeća* [Agricultural-production conditions in the Republic of Dubrovnik from the thirteenth to the fifteenth century] (Zagreb, 1955), pp. 173-224. See also Foretić, *loc. cit.*, pp. 259-264. 271-275, 287-288.

10. Roller, pp. 218-224; Foretić, *loc. cit.*, pp. 273-275, 303.

11. Historical Archives, Dubrovnik, *Liber Croccus*, II, fo. 40-41.

12. Josip Lučić, *Prošlost dubrovačke Astareje* [The past of Dubrovnik's Astarea] (Dubrovnik, 1970), pp. 51-53, mentions the noble families of Ghetaldi, Menze, and Sorgo as landowners in the rural parts of the Dubrovnik republic before Pelješac was bought by the republic.

13. Zdravko Šundrica, "The Population Census of the Dubrovnik Republic of 1673/74," *Arhivski vjesnik* (Zagreb), II (1959), pp. 419-447, 454.

14. These documents are in Italian, which remained the official language under French and Austrian rule in all Dalmatia. Serbo-Croatian was introduced as an official language in the administration and courts in Dalmatia only in April 1909. See Vjekoslav Maštović, *Razvoj sudstva u Dalmaciji u XIX. stoljeću* [Development of the judicature in Dalmatia in the nineteenth century] (Zagreb, 1959), pp. 79-90. However, Serbo-Croatian must have been used earlier since I have several court documents from the 1890's and early 1900's in Serbo-Croatian. Half a dozen letters written by three members of the Tomašević family from the sea and from California between 1840 and 1876 to their relatives in Košarnido are in Italian.

15. The old house is 12.45 meters long and 6.70 meters wide. The adjoining new house is 13.20 meters long and 7.50 meters wide. Both are stone structures with walls 45 centimeters thick. Each house has four bedrooms on the main floor and a hall in the middle.

16. Copies of commune documents which I obtained in September 1974 include affidavits, reports on taxable heads in the commune, annual crop reports, decisions on the establishment of an elementary school with a list of boys subject to compulsory education (including the names of both my father and his older brother), expenditure reports, public announcements, and the like.

17. Money was apparently loaned by the Tomašević *zajednica* as such and by its members as individuals. Thus, according to a contract dated June 21, 1851 between Ivan Tomašević (the later mayor) and Mato Ilias from the neighboring village of Podobuče, the latter's personal note for 262 forints was transformed into a mortgage loan, repayable in six years at an interest of five percent per annum.

18. I have two of these powers of attorney with notarized signatures confirmed by the Austro-Hungarian Consulate in San Francisco. Baldo's claims against his brothers were specified in great detail in a letter of his representative, Mato Harlović, to his brother Ivan, dated May 3, 1873.

19. As many another immigrant into California in the 1850's, Petar apparently first tried gold prospecting. According to information from Adam S. Eterovich, a specialist on immigration of South Slavs into the western United States, we find him in the gold producing counties of California under a somewhat changed name of Pedro Tomaso (from Austria). In the late 1850's he settled in San Jose. At one time he was a fruit merchant. Later he kept a restaurant in San Jose. In his last years he worked at odd jobs, mostly for a compatriot from Pelješac who owned a winery in San Jose. While working at that job, he had his accident and met his death. (*San Jose Daily Mercury*, October 18, 1894).

20. The third house, on the base of a smaller existing building, evidently was built soon after the division, since the Division and Sentence document assigned to the new *zajednica* all of the already assembled building material intended for it. In the 1880's and early 1890's, both families built new houses in Postup.

21. Pavo had some brief encounters with California while still a young cadet. His ship once took a cargo of redwood from Eureka in northern California to Liverpool. On another trip he was shanghaied in San Francisco and taken to a Far Eastern port.

22. One of Ivan's four sisters, Ana, emigrated in 1912 to California, where she later married but had no children.

13: "THE DEMOCRATIC SPIRIT" OF THE POLJICA COMMUNE

Ante Kadić

That all may live!

My family lived for generations in the little village of Krug on the southern slopes of mount Mosor in the Jesenice parish in maritime Poljica in Dalmatia. I spent the first ten years of my life in Krug, before I was sent to secondary school in Split, about the time the mercantile enterprises of my father and uncles led my family to move to Mali Rat on the coast. However, I returned often to my native village, where three of my brothers still live, and I remain attached to the hearth of my ancestors and to my fellow-villagers. I describe here the communal life which I remember and which has quietly disappeared within my own lifetime, as well as the views of Russian and other scholars on the social organization of the Poljica Republic in the fifteenth century. This community, safely sheltered from the realities of Balkan warfare and tyranny, was such an attractive society then that some scholars see it as an ideal Slavic commune and others even mistakenly consider it the source or model of St. Thomas More's *Utopia*.

INTERPRETATIONS OF THE POLJICA STATUTE

The two most important socio-legal documents from early Croatian history are the Vinodol Law and the Poljica Statute. The Vinodol Law of 1288 was basically imposed by the feudal prince upon his subjects, while the Poljica Statute of 1440 contains both a collection of customs which prevailed in the ancient tribal community and new decrees reached by agreement between the nobles and commoners.

The Poljica Statute was written in Bosnian script (bosančica), an alphabet which was dominant for a long time in Poljica and other regions of Dalmatia, and in a mixture of ča-kavian and što-kavian dialect. It has been published several times, first by Matija Mesić, then by Vatroslav Jagić, Mate Tentor, and

201

Stipe Kaštelan, and finally by Zvonimir Junković, who translated it into contemporary Croatian.[1] It has also been translated into Russian and German,[2] and it has attracted an abundant literature.[3] I shall mention in particular the work of Russian scholars, because they have written more than others about the internal order of Poljica, though they sometimes stretch certain Statute articles in order to fit their theories.

As soon as the Poljica Statute was first published by Mesić in 1859,[4] scholars were surprised by the similarity of the terms the Croats used in Dalmatia to those in Russian Law (*Russkaia Pravda*). They were especially interested in the word *vrv* (Russian *verv*), which Fedor Leontovich first interpreted in 1867, as a family commune (*semeinaia obshtina*).[5] Leontovich sought to construct a general outline of the social structure of the ancient Slavs.[6] He devoted special attention to communal ownership of the land, to assemblies, and to election of the Prince. Concerning the folk of Poljica, he wrote that "they, as the ancient Slavs, did not submit to one ruler, but from the beginning lived under a government they chose." Further, he affirmed that "Poljica, until the most recent times, was ruled by the principles of the old Slavic zadruga, without the slightest sign of distinction between the people and their prince. In Poljica, the community with its assembly and elders (the Prince was one of them) was the main legislative factor." Leontovich embellished this idyllic tableau of the old Poljica commune even more when he wrote that "the Poljica folk, in the course of long centuries, lived so intimately within the framework of their zadruga, with its interest and needs ... that their life was merged with these customs; so little was innovated by additional rules that there was no sign of change in the social life of Poljica in the centuries which followed the epoch of the Statute."[7]

This interpretation of Leontovich reflected the spirit of the Slavophile outlook, and he saw the incarnation of justice and democratic organization among the old Slavs in the Statute. The Soviet academician Boris D. Grekov in his book on Poljica in 1951 sharply criticized Leontovich's views. Grekov correctly affirmed that Poljica was not an ideal community, but he also exaggerated when he sought proof in the Statute that a feudal relationship existed between the lords and the commoners in the fifteenth century in both Poljica and Vinodol.

Grekov proved that Leontovich incorrectly interpreted even the first article of the Statute: "The first law of Poljica is to elect a prince from the lords, who is loyal to the lord and acceptable to the people. . . ." Leontovich read the first part, "to elect a prince from the lords," that is, from the Split aristocracy, to mean "elect the lord prince." He interpreted the second part "loyal to the lord," that is, to the Venetian Doge, as "faithful to God," and he concluded that "the office of the great prince in Poljica has long meant someone who was elected by his people."[8] Grekov especially attacked

Leontovich for finding communal life (zadruga) where, Grekov asserted, it no longer existed. "In Poljica from the fifteenth to the seventeenth century, we undoubtedly have feudal society, and that no longer in its early phase. . . . In the feudal order there can be no equality."[9] Grekov's entire book was an attack upon Leontovich's views, so naturally he viewed the Poljica commune differently: "The Poljica commune (*selo-obshtina*) is a quite complex and diversified organization: here are both remains of the past which live only in memory, which are manifestly dying, which sometimes are already dead, and new rules with perspectives for the future. Before us we see, without a doubt, the evolution of the clan system, which had already gone quite far."[10]

Grekov's books about the socio-legal order of coastal Croatia in the Middle Ages, his 1948 book about the Vinodol Law, and his volume about Poljica were attacked strongly by numerous Croatian and other experts. Marko Kostrenčić and Miho Barada showed that Grekov was unfamiliar with "the basic features of Croatian history"[11] and that his work about Vinodol was therefore mistaken. Zvonimir Junković and Juraj Marušić emphasized Grekov's ignorance of and therefore his misunderstanding of specific Poljica conditions.[12] Junković wrote that Grekov "did not bother to give a faithful translation, but gave a free commentary, which served as evidence for conclusions he had drawn in his study. Unfortunately, very often even this commentary is not in harmony with the principles which the Poljica lawgiver sought to express."[13]

THE POLJICA COMMUNE AND MORE'S *UTOPIA*

Many other Russian historians, legal scholars, and ethnologists have written about the medieval social organization of Croatia, always with some reference to Poljica. Moreover, academician Mikhail P. Alekseev in 1960 drew most attention to it in his study of the Slavic sources of Thomas More's *Utopia*, in which he expressed the opinion that Poljica with its Statute was one of the models upon which More constructed his conception of the Utopian land.[14]

Alekseev, who accepted Grekov's criticism of Leontovich, nevertheless was closer to Leontovich than to Grekov in his interpretation of Poljica law and custom. Alekseev also believed that the spirit of democratic social organization once dominant among all Slavs was preserved in Poljica "up to the modern age," especially in the election of the great prince, the commander, the procurators, and the county attorney. He believed that More could have been referring to these functions when he wrote of the election of the ruler, tranibors, and phylarchs, and of the way in which people's assemblies were held.[15] Alekseev not only saw a similarity between More's work and the institutions of Poljica, but he even formulated a hypothesis concerning the way in which More, who had never visited Poljica and was not acquainted with its patriarchal setting through his reading, nevertheless could have learned about the residents of those inaccessible hills.

Sebastian Giustiniani, the Venetian envoy to London from January 1515 to October 1519, was a friend of More's. More wrote in a letter to Erasmus in September 1516 that he liked Giustiniani, because he was an honest man and well versed in worldly affairs. [16] The envoy wrote to the Venetian government in February 1518 that More was intelligent and virtuous, and that he was most devoted to him among all Englishmen. [17] Since "they became friends a year before the publication of *Utopia* in 1516," Alekseev thought it probable that Giustiniani told More about his experience in Poljica before his arrival in England.

In 1512 Giustiniani was named the Venetian governor-general in Dalmatia. Those were troubled times, because the plebeians on the island of Hvar, under the leadership of Matija Ivanić, were in rebellion against the nobles. The governor pressed the men of Poljica into service to help crush the popular uprising. Ivanić meanwhile asked the Venetians to guarantee to him the same privileges as they did to the prince of Poljica. Perhaps this prompted Giustiniani to become acquainted with his allies from Poljica.

Alekseev also referred to More's Utopian alphabet, comparing it to Glagolitic, the script which Poljica priests used in the Mass. Though these two alphabets have some similarity, at a first glance the Utopian alphabet seems clearly different from Glagolitic.

Alekseev remarked that it was not necessary that all his arguments be equally convincing and that every detail of Poljica's traditional law match More's Utopian system. Alekseev did conclude that More found a model for his Utopia among contemporary Adriatic Slavs, no doubt because his friend Giustiniani told him something about the patriarchal Poljica community and touched the writer's imagination when he was creating his vision of Utopia. Alekseev did not deny that other sources, such as Tacitus' description of the Germans or the reports of Amerigo Vespucci concerning the native tribes of Brazil, also influenced More, but he assigned the greatest influence to Poljica. [18]

This suggested relationship between More and the Poljica community through Giustiniani does not appear convincing. Giustiniani had spent only a few months in Dalmatia, in a punitive expedition, and he behaved undiplomatically and cruelly. He was mainly responsible that the pending agreement between the Hvar aristocrats and plebeians was not realized. The commoners wrote to Venice that they were displeased with the haughtiness of the *providore,* and for a time he fell into disfavor. [19] He was named unexpectedly as envoy to England, when Donato, previously appointed, suddenly fell ill. [20]

Giustiniani had no special relationship with the Poljica people. They were obliged, by the agreement of 1444, to fight for Venice without pay in the region between the rivers Cetina and Krka, but they had the right to pay and plunder when they were called into the army beyond this area.[21] When they were ready, in Bol on the island of Brač, to launch the attack against the plebeians on Hvar, a disagreement rose between him and the Poljica soldiers and he angrily discharged them.[22]

The Venetian was obviously on the side of the privileged class, so he could not have been enthralled by the free Poljica republic. Had Giustiniani had even a little understanding of social justice, he would have succeeded in his mission.

Furthermore, and this is most important, More had written the second half of *Utopia* before 1515 or while he resided in Flanders between May and December of that year as a member of the diplomatic delegation. It is hardly likely that information from Giustiniani, who arrived in January 1515, could have made a weighty impression on More.[23] It is more likely that his biographers are correct in concluding that the second volume of *Utopia* was written after many years of reading and reflection and was not affected by a sudden injection of new information.

I should like now to examine the basic ideas of More's *Utopia* to see if anything in the Poljica Statute suggests a particular similarity between the order in Poljica and that of Utopia.

It is clear that the Utopians differ radically from the English of More's time, but many opposing interpretations have appeared concerning More's goals when he was writing *Utopia*. Some Marxist theoreticians, from Karl Kautsky through Volgin, who is much quoted by Alekseev, see in More a critic of early capitalism and a prophet of modern socialism or communism; others, such as O'Sullivan and Surtz, consider *Utopia* mainly a religious and philosophical book. A third group, which includes Chambers and Bevington, esteem especially its literary and ironical value. Finally, Ames and others maintain that More was attacking decadent feudalism, not capitalism, which at that time was just beginning to develop.[24]

More surely was well acquainted with the vestiges of English feudal society, but he also saw the consequences of capitalism, which already in its early phase was driving the peasants from their land, forcing them to fight wars, and making them invalids or poverty-stricken vagrants, tramps, and bandits, treated harshly by the authorities. In short, More was keenly aware of cruel English reality. He had also read widely among ancient writers, beginning with Aristotle, Plato, and St. Augustine, and including all those who concerned themselves with government and social order. He was heavily influenced by his teacher and friend, Erasmus, who dedicated to him his *Praise of Folly*, which bitterly ridiculed the rulers of Church and State.

At the end of the first book of *Utopia*, which described the pitiful conditions of the poor, More attacked the principle of private property. Though he was influenced by the Bible, Aristotle, and Erasmus, he was more systematic and categorical than his predecessors. More agreed with Plato, who "refused to make laws for those who rejected that legislation which gave to all an equal share in all goods (*ex aequo omnes omnia partirentur commoda*)." He maintained that where private property exists and "all men measure all things by cash values, there it is scarcely possible to have justice or prosperity."[25] After he had emphasized that rich people are usually dishonest and worthless, while the poor are modest and useful to society, More declared that, "unless private property is utterly abolished (*nisi sublata prorsus proprietate*), no just and even distribution of goods can be made."[26] Though he allowed that it is possible to pass laws to restrict the power of rulers and the size of large estates, still he concluded that these measures would be only temporary, because "there is no hope of a cure and a return to a healthy condition so long as each individual is master of his own property (*dum sua cuique sunt propria*)."[27]

Since the Utopians have no private ownership, communal life is therefore possible among them. However, the basic features of More's Utopian commune are more similar to a communistic bureaucratic *kolkhoz* than to a patriarchal Slavic zadruga. Every city, More wrote, has its own assigned land; the citizens do not desire to extend their territory, because they consider themselves more the cultivators than the masters of land. In the fields, at suitable distances, are located houses supplied with agricultural implements. In them reside citizens who come in shifts. Every village commune (*familia rustica*) has at least forty members, men and women. At the head of the commune are the host and hostess, serious and experienced people. Thirty such communes have a headman (*phylarch*). Twenty members of each commune return to the city after they have completed two years in the village. As substitutes for them, an equal number comes from the city; they are taught by those who have been there a year and who therefore are expert in farming.[28]

Although there are superficial similarities between *Utopia* and the social organization of Poljica, the Utopian government differs in essence from the Poljica reality. In Poljica, until the Austrian rule came in 1815, a sharp division existed between the nobles (*didići, vlastela*) and the commoners (*kmetići, vlašići*). The prestige of the upper class was so great that some tenaciously tried to prove their descent from either Bosnian (*didići*) or Hungarian (*vlastela*) lords.[29] Though the entire Poljica community discussed some important questions at meetings, the nobles alone made many decisions. All significant positions of public service were in the hands of the noblemen. In just a few villages, Srinjine, Podstrana, Jesenice, and Duće, the village chiefs (commoners) managed current affairs independently of the nobles and participated with them in the election of the highest Poljica officials.[30]

Justice was not equal for everyone in the Poljica Statute. For the same violations, commoners were more severely punished than nobles. If a laborer cursed his landlord, his tongue was cut out, and if he dared to raise a hand against him, his right one was chopped off. Marušić therefore correctly states: "Such a condition was very far from being idyllic."[31]

At the time of the writing of the Statute, Poljica was not a pure feudal society. Yet, it was not without a strong admixture of feudal elements.[32] Thus, one finds two kinds of ownership, common and private. Though communal property was more widespread and extended to the whole tribe or all relatives at the beginning, later it was confined only to some relatives.[33] This is obvious from those articles of the Statute which discuss joint property (*plemenšćina*).

In article 49a, the Statute declared that "he who possesses the old patrimony, which was passed on to him by his ancestors, must cultivate it, enjoy it, and live from it. It is not honorable to disperse it except in case of great need; everyone should pass it on as it came to him." Thus, one could dispose of the estate inherited from ancestors, but only if one was in great need. Furthermore, one was able to divide the ancestral estate (*plemenšćina*) not only among distant relatives, but also between brothers. Thus, the Statute stipulated at the end of the very significant article 33 that "Until brothers or other parties divide the estate, everything is common to them, both good and bad, benefits and damages, and debts which they owe or are owed to them; all this is common to them until they divide. And when they divide, then each one is on his own." The definition of the Poljica zadruga (or *plemenšćina*) is given with this paragraph about "division": As long as they live together, everything is common to the members of the zadruga; in real estate, no one possesses anything of his own. This same paragraph revealed the difference between the Poljica joint family and *Utopia,* because the Statute allows those who are related or who until that moment shared everything to divide up and start to cultivate their own possessions.[34]

Thus, private ownership existed in Poljica. It often consisted of tiny fields (*poljica*). It gradually squeezed out communal property, which in later centuries was limited to pastures and woods. It is understandable that some had more land than others and that some had no land at all. The majority of laborers (*kmetići*) were forced to cultivate the land of the nobles or the land-owning commoners (*pučani*); unto the landlord, they had to render a certain percentage of the crop. *Vlašići* were hired as shepherds on the upper slopes of mount Mosor.[35]

Poljica was not a community like the one in the Acts of the Apostles (4:32) or in *Utopia,* where everything was held in common. The people of

Poljica were neither religious zealots nor More's Utopians, but humans of flesh and blood who believed that they could call something their own and pass it on to their offspring. The feeling for private ownership was so strong that neighbors had to take care that no chicken, pig, or other animal might cross the fence and cause even the smallest damage to a garden or vineyard. Many ordinances of the Statute were concerned with such minor issues. Thus, articles 53 and 54 noted that "the chicken in the vineyard pays with its head; it could be killed and eaten. And when it scratches around someone else's house, it is permitted to kill it. . . . When chickens damage a garden or vineyard, then the land-owner, after he announces it, may kill and eat one of them. If a rooster is among them, he may then kill another chicken, but never the rooster."

Thus, it seems clear that Poljica could not have been a model for *Utopia*. However, it is also evident that Poljica possessed greater freedom and democracy than did other Dalmatian communities. While the Venetians elsewhere were rulers, in Poljica they were satisfied with annual tribute and a certain political authority which was not clearly defined. They left the old privileges of Poljica intact. According to the first decree of the Statute, the Venetian Doge had the right to approve or reject the election of the Prince, but the nobles of Poljica strove to limit Venetian interference in that basic manifestation of their independence. Though at the start they took (*vazimali*) the prince from the Split aristocrats, later he was elected only from among the Poljica noblemen. [36] The little peasant princes, who were elected by their parishes on St. George's Day, took part in this election.

Everyone participated in the assemblies in which war and peace were decided and in which relations with other countries or essential questions were discussed. Articles 23-25 several times contained the same formula: "All men of Poljica concluded unanimously and ordered to all nobles, laborers and shepherds. . . . All the noblemen and the entire community of Poljica decided when they were together in assembly. . ."

One can rightly affirm that there was no class conflict in Poljica. The fact that the inhabitants of Poljica were surrounded by powerful enemies, the Turks and Venetians, forced them to close ranks to preserve their more or less independent status. Further, although at the beginning the lords stressed their noble origin, they gradually became assimilated to the masses. One must remember that the people of Poljica were by and large uneducated, and there was no difference between the upper class and the lower strata in their houses, dress, behavior, or mentality. I still remember a story I heard in childhood. A neighbor asked where our village headman (*knez, glavar*) was, and his kin answered: "There he is, in the shed, patching mocassins."

It was possible in Poljica for a farm-laborer to free himself from his landlord. This is foreseen in article 89, which begins: "When a laborer intends to leave a landlord . . ." and ends with the meaningful declaration: "If he can, a man is free to run from evil."[37]

The Statute decreed that a free laborer could increase his holdings upon division of the village pasture or wood. This anti-feudal article 59 thus specified: "When it happens that a village wants to divide the wood or pasture, that is when they cannot or will not graze it or hold it in common; if the land of a laborer borders on the communal area, he participates in the division in the same way as the others." This law is extremely important because it emphasizes the philosophy typical of the "democratic spirit" of Poljica, namely, that "all men may live, because nothing exists that does not change." This means that the Statute admitted that the justice of life is stronger than written laws, which must adapt to the times.[38]

In the Poljica peasant community, where there were no slaves, the poor associated into the "poor men's council," which came united to general assemblies and was able to counterbalance the influence of the rich.[39]

Therefore, Poljica was not a Utopian paradise, because the feudal system and private property both gradually penetrated it. However, the configuration of that hilly region, facing the permanent danger of losing the freedom and the land which its peasants enjoyed, helped make Poljica into a sort of fortress, whose citizens were conscious that their republic with its Statute was their best defender. During the feudal and subsequent capitalist era, they were proud to be the privileged inhabitants of an isolated and barely accessible commune.

COMMUNAL LIFE IN POLJICA BEFORE
THE SECOND WORLD WAR

Marshall Marmont, who destroyed the independence of Poljica in 1807, described in his *Mémoires* the hills of Poljica and its independent residents: "The Principality of Poljica is located in beautiful, high valleys; there are no passable roads, thus it is easy to defend. The isolation of this region, coupled with the desire of the men of Poljica to submit to no one, is beyond a doubt the reason why the Venetians allowed them special privileges: they paid no taxes, they were their own masters, they named their own leaders, and among them were neither soldiers nor seamen. When Frenchmen wanted to remove these privileges, they rebelled. Looking at that land, we come to the conclusion that their administration was good: there is nothing more carefully cultivated than their fields, nothing more charming than their villages."[40]

Although the French annulled the Poljica Republic, and the way of life was much changed under subsequent Austrian rule, 1815-1918, the people of

Poljica still continued to live quite isolated on the slopes of mount Mosor. These highlands, which made possible the creation of their independent republic and were for centuries a mighty bastion against the Turkish conqueror, helped also to preserve the clan spirit of their inhabitants until the interwar period.

A highway was built along the seashore in 1856, and somewhat later steamboats began to transport passengers from Split to Omiš. Only rarely, however, did a man go from Jesenice and Duće to Split or down to the sea for recreation. When a factory opened in Dugi Rat in 1911, the poorer peasants sought work, not to become permanent workers, but to obtain money to buy some land, fix the house, or pay off debts. I remember how quickly they returned home in the evening, as if being driven, as if they felt insecure away from home and its hearth.

I have examined carefully two studies of the population of each Poljica parish. They contain the family names at the beginning of the eighteenth and again at the end of the nineteenth century. In each case I found mentioned only those families familiar to me from childhood.[41]

As in the rest of Poljica, our village was a closed society. Everyone was an old settler, Croatian and Catholic. The village contained not a single member of another faith or nationality. It was said (or rather whispered) that some in the old times had come from Bosnia as Moslems but had long ago become completely assimilated. They too kissed the altar and lit candles before the saints.[42]

Local people usually married within their own parish. If someone were to bring a bride from over the hill, from central Poljica, less than an hour's walk, this caused a sensation. The women felt that they must know the parents of the newlyweds, what their property was, whether there was any black mark upon their name, from what disease the members of the household usually died, in short, answers to all the questions which village women would raise when they met other village women in the church. Villagers did not usually marry close relatives; in such cases, special permission was required from the Pope. Still, we were all somehow related! When I strolled through neighboring Jesenice, Zeljeviće, Duće, and Tugare, I always met someone who called me "cousin." I had to stop while they filled me with food and drink, but also pumped information concerning whom my aunts were to marry. They were amazed that our family was satisfied with their choice, when they could have picked better ones than a Zemunik or a Brničević. Then their commentary followed: "Till now your aunts have been served, but from now on they will do the serving; that is, little one, from a horse onto a donkey."

As in other villages, there was a great difference in ours between rich and poor peasants. Some lived in hovels of rough stones, through which the wind whistled, while others resided in lovely buildings with tile roofs and slept in real beds. Some families lived in abundance, while others even in the fall lacked food and drink.[43] Only those who owned large vineyards, olive groves, and cherry orchards were considered true landowners. Some entered into business, selling wine and cherries, while others opened taverns in Trieste and Rijeka. Still others sold meat, flour, cloth, salt, coffee, and other household necessities.

Some peasants owned no land, and worked the land of the rich, to whom in the fall they rendered a fifth or a sixth of their crop. Others worked as hired laborers in the vineyards; the owner fed them. If they came from afar, he gave them a nook for sleeping. When the work was done, he paid them off. Sometimes this labor was done even by well-off peasants who needed some ready cash to buy a cow or horse, or to enlarge their holdings.

Wealthier houses had servants and maids, either lads from upper Poljica who wanted to learn how to manage estates efficiently or girls who came for a few years to earn a little before marriage. Some, usually bachelors, stayed their whole lives with their masters, and the members of the family honored and cared for them as if they were their kin. If the master of the house died and the rest of the family was too young or were all females, the servant often directed the family's affairs temporarily.

Even though our clan had a few houses and each family lived in its own, we still ate in the same kitchen and kept wine and oil in the same basement. Unless sick, no one ate by himself. All important decisions were made around the hearth. First, the children were driven off to bed. Then the family elders sat on the benches around the fire, while the women watched from the corners to see that wine pitchers were filled and that the fire remained burning.

My grandfather's house, which was considered communal, and in which we all gathered for ceremonial occasions, for Christmas and Easter dinner, receiving guests, weddings, christenings, house blessings, and funerals, was built of large stones and had a metal-edged impenetrable door, with a gun port nearby. It was our "mother-house" (*matica*), a remainder from the Turkish times. In the middle of our court was a tower (*kula*) several stories tall, by then completely abandoned. There were no more Turks, so it was not necessary to watch from the highest floor to see if they were coming.

All villagers with our family name lived near our house. There was not a single man with our last name in any other place; all of us gathered around the tower like chicks around a hen. When anyone in Poljica, from Dolac down to Podstrana, uttered our name, he knew that meant the clan which lived in the middle of Krug, neither at the top nor bottom of the village, but just a little above the church. That we were all of the same tribe was also evidenced by the kitchen, which consisted of two hearths; distant relatives, who had in common with us our great-great-grandfather, did their cooking in its second part.

Communal consciousness had been so deeply implanted that when a villager moved to the seashore, he went to a spot where some of his people already resided and built his house nearby. He could have built it in a better location, but he did not wish to be separated from his flesh and blood. Even though they no longer had a communal kitchen, the longing for the clan or the fear of flying too far from the nest remained, because they believed that in hard times and at old age woe befell the loner.

Sons from the big families with little land began to emigrate to the United States in the 1880's, always with the hope of returning. There they married immigrant girls .from their parish or sent word to maidens back home to follow them. On holidays, they gathered around a roasted lamb and told tales about the old country. They were proud of their villages and made the past of Poljica seem more beautiful than it really was.

Poljica was not a paradise on earth. It had many barren areas, and rain in the summer was awaited like manna from heaven. Central and lower Poljica had more fertile land than upper Poljica.[44] In the higher areas, the villagers concentrated more on sheep herding than down below, but even in the lowland sheep and goats grazed in communal pastures. However, the villagers in the lowlands concentrated upon cultivating the land. The field meant to them as much as the house; they usually spent the whole day there. One was ashamed when he found himself obliged to sell a piece of a vineyard. On their deathbeds, some boasted, "Though I have not gained anything, at least I have not dissipated ancestral patrimony." They cared for their estate as the apple of their eye. They inspected their meadows and looked at the grapes as a mother does at her child. The gardens had delicious fruit and vegetables. On the terraces and in windows, women placed flowerpots. Though sources of water were rare and the people usually drank from rainwater cisterns and village wells, they were very clean. When the word *Poljičanin* (man from Poljica) was uttered, it rang with pride. It meant a well-shaped and industrious man, someone with deep roots, closely bound to his family and people.

Poljica was in my youth in transition from a patriarchal to that tourist and workers' society now totally dominant. In the past, the air was perfumed in Mali Rat by huge wine barrels, from which wine was drawn into casks and shipped to Trieste. Now it is a crowded settlement. Above it lie abandoned vineyards. Krug has become a ruin, a place for a picnic on Sundays, there to sit beneath an oak tree and spin tales about the good old days, when the prince ruled and all was strictly regulated by the "honorable" Poljica Statute.

NOTES

1. Frane Brničević, Drago Ivanišević, and Jure Kaštelan, eds., *Poljički Zbornik* [A miscellany about Poljica](Zagreb, 1968), I, 32-103.
2. Boris D. Grekov, *Politsa. Opyt izucheniia obshchestvennikh otnoshenii v Politse XV-XVII vv.* [A study of social conditions in Poljica in the fifteenth through seventeenth centuries] (Moscow, 1951), pp. 211-307; Grekov, *Die altkroatische Republik Poljica* (Berlin, 1961), pp. 183-279; Tomo Matić, "Statut der Poljica," *Wissenschaftliche Mitteilungen aus Bosnien und der Herzegowina* (Vienna), XII (1912), 329-396.
3. Frane Brničević, "Gradja za bibliografiju Poljica" [Material for the bibliography on Poljica], *Poljički Zbornik*, I, 267-286.
4. Matija Mesić, "Poljički Statut" [The Statute of Poljica], *Arkiv za povjesnicu jugoslavensku* (Zagreb), V (1859), 225-318.
5. Fedor I. Leontovich, "O znachenii vervi po Russkoi pravde i Politskomu statutu" [The meaning of *vrv* in Russian justice and the statute of Poljica], *Zhurnal ministerstva narodnogo prosveshcheniia* (1867); Ivan Božić, "Vrv u Poljičkom Statutu" [*Vrv* in the Statute of Poljica], *Zbornik Filozofskog Fakulteta u Beogradu* IV (1956), 89-112.
6. Fedor I. Leontovich, *Drevnee horvato-dalmatskoe zakonodatel'stvo* [Old Croato-Dalmatian Legislation] (Odessa, 1868).
7. Ibid., pp. 75-76; Mikhail P. Alekseev, "Slavianskie istochniki Utopii Tomasa Mora" [The Slavic sources of Thomas More's *Utopia*], in *Iz istorii angliiskoi literaturi* [From history of English literature] (Moscow-Leningrad, 1960), pp. 112-114.
8. Grekov, *Politsa*, p. 126.
9. Ibid., p. 181.
10. Ibid., p. 87.
11. Miho Barada, *Hrvatski vlasteoski feudalizam* [Croatian feudalism] (Zagreb, 1952), p. 10; Marko Kostrenčić, "Vinodolski Zakon" [The Statute of Vinodol], *Historijski Zbornik* II (1949), 151.
12. Juraj Marušić, "O agrarno-pravnim pitanjima i društvenom uredjenju Poljica" [About agrarian-legal questions and the social structure of Poljica], *Poljički Zbornik* I, 181-182.
13. Zvonimir Junković, "Bilješke uz tekst i prijevod Poljičkog Statuta" [Remarks on my translation of the Statute of Poljica], *Poljički Zbornik* I, 106.
14. Alekseev, "Slavianskie istochniki," pp. 40-134.
15. Ibid., p. 113.
16. "Plane delectat me; videtui enim honestissimus et rerum humanarum peritissimus ac iam divinarum cognitioni deditissimus," in P. S. Allen, ed., *Opus epistolarum Des. Erasmi Roterodami* (London, 1910), II, 339. R. W. Chambers, *Thomas More* (London, 1935), p. 171.
17. Sebastian Giustinian, *Four Years at the Court of Henry VIII*. R. Brown, ed. (London, 1854), II, 162.
18. Alekseev, "Slavianskie istochniki," pp. 115-116.
19. Jaroslav Šidak, *Enciklopedija Jugoslavije* (Zagreb, 1960), IV, 402-403; Grga Novak, *Prošlost Dalmacije* [The Dalmatian Past] (Zagreb, 1944), I, 210; *Historija Naroda Jugoslavije* [History of the Yugoslav nations] (Zagreb, 1953-1959), II, 270.

20. Brown, "The Giustinian Family," introduction to Sebastian Giustinian, *Four Years at the Court of Henry VIII*, I, 25-26.

21. Marko Šunjić, *Dalmacija u XV stoljeću* [Dalmatia in the fifteenth century] (Sarajevo, 1967), pp.67-68.

22. Brown, "The Giustinian Family," I, 25-26.

23. "Sebastian Giustinian . . . was known to More by the time that the manuscript of *Utopia* was dispatched to Erasmus." (St. Thomas More, *Complete Works*, IV: *Utopia*, ed. Edward Surtz and John Hexter (New Haven, 1963-1973), clxxii. F. M. Nichols, commenting on More's letter of September 3, 1516, wrote that Giustinian "only lately made his acquaintance" (*The Epistles of Erasmus* [London, 1904], II, 381). The manuscript of *Utopia* was sent to Erasmus with this epistle.

24. See Ligeia Galagher, *More's Utopia and Its Critics* (Chicago, 1964).

25. St. Thomas More, *Utopia*, ed. Surtz (New Haven, 1964); More, *Complete Works*, IV, 103-105.

26. More, *Utopia*, p. 53; *Complete Works*, IV, 104-105.

27. More, *Utopia*, p. 54; *Complete Works*, IV, 104-105.

28. More, *Utopia*, pp. 61-62; *Complete Works*, IV, 113-115.

29. Stipe Kaštelan, *Povjesni ulomci iz bivše slobodne općine-republike Poljica* [Historical fragments from a former independent commune, Poljica] (Split, 1940), p. 47; Ferdo Čulinović, *Državnopravna historija jugoslavenskih naroda* [Legal history of Yugoslav nations] (Zagreb, 1961), p. 182.

30. Čulinović, *Državnopravna historija*, p. 182.

31. Marušić, "O agrarno-pravnim pitanjima i društvenom uredjenju Poljica," p. 183.

32. Čulinović, *Državnopravna historija*, p. 192.

33. Ibid., p. 181.

34. Marko Kostrenčić, "Poljički Statut" [The Poljica Statute], *Enciklopedija Jugoslavije* (Zagreb, 1965), VI, 534.

35. *Vlasi* are not mentioned in later documents. (See Čulinović, *Državnopravna historija*, p. 184).

36. Kostrenčić, "Poljica," *Enciklopedija Jugoslavije*, VI, 533.

37. Marušić, "O agarno-pravnim pitanjima i društvenom uredenju Poljica," pp. 183-184.

38. Ibid., p. 186.

39. Ibid., p. 193.

40. "Rien de plus soigné que leur culture, rien de plus joli que leur villages" (Marshall A. F. Marmont, *Mémoires* [Paris, 1857], II, 49).

41. Frano Ivanišević, *Poljica: Zbornik za narodni život i običaje južnih Slavena* [Poljica: collection on life and customs of the South Slavs] (Zagreb, 1904), IX, 224-226; Benedikta Zelić-Bučan, "Obiteljska prezimena u Poljicima 1725. godine" [Family names in Poljica in the year 1725], *Poljički Zbornik*, I, 231-236.

42. Ivanišević, "Poljica," IX, 285-288.

43. Ibid., IX, 263-278.

44. Ivo Rubić, "Poljica. Geografska Studija" [Poljica. A geographic study], *Poljički Zbornik*, I, 25-26.

14: TIME AND FORM: CONTEMPORARY MACEDONIAN HOUSEHOLDS AND THE ZADRUGA CONTROVERSY

David B. Rheubottom

The large Balkan household, or zadruga, has disappeared from the country-side, except for occasional well-preserved specimens in some out of the way corner. However, the memory of the zadruga, or the myth of the zadruga, is still alive among the peasants, supported by the authority of history lessons learned in school, and it survives in a scholarly debate on the causes of its decline and fall.

Much of this debate seems confused and pointless, the proponents arguing from first principles and dealing with such slippery entities as national character. The writings of Professor Philip Mosely on the zadruga are an obvious exception, for Mosely combined detailed first-hand knowledge of life in peasant households with careful discussion of the historical issues. As Edward Evans-Pritchard and Marc Bloch noted, his writings show how an intimate acquaintance with the lives and thoughts of contemporary peasants can shed light on the lives of their ancestors.[1] A combination of anthropology and history underlies the genius of Mosely's writings on the zadruga. In this paper, I will follow Mosely's example to see how the study of some contemporary Balkan households can help to assess some recent theories propounded on the decline of the zadruga.

The zadruga is generally understood to be a very large household, sometimes containing up to one hundred members. In Mosely's classic definition, it is

> a household composed of two or more biological or small families. . . owning its means of production communally, producing and consuming the means of its livelihood jointly, and regulating the control of its property, labor, and livelihood communally.[2]

Note that the zadruga has three distinguishing features: it has a sizeable membership, it combines two or more families, and it has a special form of organization marked by the terms "communal" and "joint." Thus, when

215

scholars speculate on the dissolution of the zadruga, they have tried to explain why zadrugas divided, why the resultant units did not reach the same size as the parent unit, and why they did not preserve the "communal" form of organization.

Let us begin with this last question. Maitland once said that "collectively" was "the smudgiest word in the English language. . . ." The words "communally" and "joint" might easily vie for second place. Whatever these terms may mean, recent studies indicate that contemporary rural households are probably no less communal or joint in production, consumption, and property control than the classical zadruga. The ownership question is complicated. However, if I can anticipate some conclusions reached in the following pages, I think we can safely assume that contemporary households closely approximate the "communal" type of organization. Therefore, if we eliminate the question of organization, the dissolution of the zadruga becomes a question of change in size.[3] Why did the zadruga divide, and why did the new groups not grow to the size of their parents?

Most arguments about change in size have the same logical form. In the first part, they provide a conjectural description of the zadruga. In the second part, they describe the households after the zadruga had broken down. In the last part, they identify the changes that took place which might account for the transition.

First, the description of the classical zadruga. Upon marriage, each man brings his bride home to live in his father's household. This same pattern is then repeated generation after generation. If the group does not divide and if the fates of demography are kind, the household will grow and flourish. After a few generations, a household may contain third, fourth, or even more distant cousins. Under these conditions, we can expect some very sizeable units. Students of the zadruga have tended to concentrate on these.

Some zadrugas are truly phenomenal in size. The Varžić zadruga studied by Mosely is tiny by comparison. In 1938, it had only twenty-six members.[4] Compare this with a household visited by Louis Adamic in 1932. Located near the city Skoplje, it contained sixty-eight members. He says:

> We met about forty of the members, including the head of the family, a patriarch of seventy. . . . The enormous household . . . was all but self-sufficient economically. . . . Six women and girls . . . did nothing but cook and bake. Eight other females only spun, weaved, sewed, and embroidered. Five men and boys attended to all the sheep, goats, buffaloes, cattle, and horses. One man was the family shoemaker. And so on.[5]

Apparently, this was not the upper limit in size that a household could reach.

While the gargantuan units have drawn the most attention, recent studies are beginning to demonstrate what has been suspected for a long time. At all periods, including the height of the classical zadruga, most households were relatively small. E. A. Hammel has painstakingly reconstituted household composition in a group of shepherding households near Belgrade. These data drawn from Ottoman censuses in the first third of the sixteenth century indicate that mean household size was about nine members.[6] They are consistent in size with the households of the nineteenth century.[7] These special studies, restricted in time and place, add weight to Mosely's and Tomasevich's judgment that the classical zadruga was always small.[8] Large units may have been the ideal, but they were also the exception.

When we speak of the zadruga, therefore, we mean a household that probably had between six and twelve members, fathers and sons, brothers, occasionally uncles and nephews, and rarely cousins.[9] Under special circumstances, a unit might grow to exceptional size due to demographic peculiarities, as when one man has four or five sons, or if some special circumstances restrained a group from dividing. Most households never reached that, but routinely divided sometime after the father and head of the household died.

Now we come to the second part of the zadruga argument, that which describes households after the zadruga has disappeared from the scene. As before, young men bring their brides home to live in their fathers' homes, but division is much more likely now, often immediately after the death of the father. As a result of this earlier division, the population has more small households and very few large ones. If we compare these contemporary households with the reconstructed picture of the zadruga, the major difference is that present households divide earlier. Today, brothers live together only until their father's death. In the past, they might have remained united for some additional time.

The last part of the argument identifies the factors which might account for the change. Generally, two types of explanation are offered. The first holds that peasant attitudes have changed and that ". . . the zadruga, like the native costume, is discarded merely because it is 'old-fashioned.' "[10] Emigration, education, military experience, and the introduction of "western" ideas are all seen contributing to attitude change. Perhaps peasant attitudes have changed. However, I have found that the zadruga is extolled by peasants for its numerous virtues. They claim life was easier in the zadruga, work was better organized, substantial economies of scale existed, a wider variety of goods were produced, and security was provided against the hazards of illness and death. I find this argument unconvincing.

A second type of explanation, one not incompatible with the first, states (in effect) that leaving the household is easier or more desirable under conditions of change. The corollary to this is that members would have left the classical zadruga but were constrained from doing so. An example of this second type of argument is the contention that the Ottoman Turks collected tax on the basis of households. If the population is confined to a small number of households, so the argument goes, they would pay less tax than if they were living in more numerous dwellings. When the Turks left and the tax system changed, the incentive for living in large households disappeared.

These explanations raise a number of problems, particularly because they are difficult to test. First, our knowledge of the classical zadruga is limited. Many studies of the zadruga are accounts of recent households presumed to maintain zadruga size and operation. Furthermore, this evidence pertains to only the largest households of the recent past. We cannot be certain that the pattern of life described applies to the smaller households of the more distant past. Second, we now possess several excellent studies of household size and composition for the more remote periods. These studies enable us to determine whether changes in household size and composition have occurred, but they are too few in number to permit us to identify the agents of change and to assess their influence.

There is an alternative strategy, the one which I shall adopt. I will examine the pattern of growth and decline in a number of contemporary households. The shape of these units accords very well with the shape of households in the more distant past, in the period of the zadruga. Seeing why some households continue to grow and develop as others split and wither may enable us to assess the agents of change. Armed with this information, we may then make some analyses of the past which may help guide the more detailed historical inquiries.

First, I briefly describe Skopska Crna Gora, the region where my study was conducted. I then examine those jural and economic aspects of peasant households which affect the unit's growth and development, a type of analysis known as the developmental cycle in domestic groups.[11] Each domestic unit has a regular cycle of development. Household members age, accept new social responsibilities, occupy new social positions, and also relinquish or change old ones. This pattern of development is fairly constant from one household to the next. So too are the principles of social organization which underly and explain the pattern of development. However, this does not mean that different households will look alike at the same point in time. Neither does it imply that households, as units, go through the same developmental sequence.

In this type of analysis, I intend to isolate and describe the principles which give rise to the developmental cycle within the domestic group. These principles in their various combinations and permutations generate the various "forms" which we see when we study the size and composition of rural households. To use Fortes' suggestive phrase, these forms are the "crystallization" of various organizational principles.[12] Therefore, I seek the principles which generate the household forms I studied in 1966-67 and in 1970.

In a final section, I shall put the principles into "reverse," as it were, to see if I can generate the form of the classical zadruga.

The region of Skopska Crna Gora lies immediately to the north of Skoplje. the capital city of Yugoslav Macedonia. When one leaves the old Turkish quarter of Skoplje and travels north, the road winds through rolling countryside. Those fields closest to Skoplje are generally planted in cereal grains and are significantly larger than those located near the villages. Beyond the grain fields are plots devoted to vineyards and melons, and close to the villages are small garden plots irrigated with water from mountain streams. The distance from Skoplje to the edge of the mountains is about twenty kilometers. Skoplje's Black Mountain (Skopska Crna Gora) appears as a semi-circle of sharply rising hills and mountains which separate this region from Serbia and Kosovo-Metohija further to the north, and from the Kumanovo plain to the east. Most of the eleven nucleated villages in the region cling to the base of this arc of mountains, and their fields are in the shape of a wedge with its point at Skoplje. In the hills beyond the villages are scattered vineyards, and clan-owned flour mills line the mountain streams. Further on are pastures and mountain forests.

The people of this region are known to others as Crna Gorans. In Skoplje, the Crna Gorans are seen as prototypical country bumpkins, and their exploits in town are the basis of many city jokes. The feeling is reciprocated by villagers, particularly of an older generation, who look upon city dwellers as morally depraved. Amongst themselves, affiliations of nationality and village come to the forefront. A Serb from the village of Banjane does not believe he has anything in common with a Macedonian from Ljubanci. The Serb claims to speak Serbian, and the Macedonian speaks Macedonian, although to an outsider they share a common dialect.

In 1961 there were almost 9,000 people living in these eleven villages. Their most important crops are cereals: wheat, corn, oats. Loaves of dark bread are the basis of the peasant diet and a working adult may consume as much as one or two kilograms of bread per day. This diet of bread is complemented by other dishes which add variety to the meal. Beans, tomatoes, peppers, grapes, melons, and other produce are grown for this purpose. In addition to these crops and the activities they require, some Crna Goran households also keep sheep, tend large vineyards, or work outside for wages. Every village is within walking distance of Skoplje's markets and regular bus service now reaches most villages. And yet, given their spectacular vantage point in relation to the city, most Crna Gorans are uninterested in city affairs and show only slight interest in Skoplje as a market for their crops.

The households of Skopska Crna Gora can be quite large. I took a random sample of fifty-four households in the village of Kučeviste, one of the Serbian villages,[13] the largest in the region, with about 280 households. At the time I surveyed these households in 1967, the largest unit had twenty members, another had nineteen, and several had sixteen. If one must make a judgment on size alone, one could conclude that some of these households approximate the zadruga. But there is additional evidence. Twenty-eight households contain two or more nuclear families. Multiple nuclear families are among the criteria Mosely lists in his definition of the zadruga. Of the remaining households, eleven contained one nuclear family and the survivor, usually an elderly widow or widower, of another. The other fifteen contained only one family, mostly young couples with growing children. But many villagers living in the midst of such large units told me that I had arrived too late: a large household with over forty members had split into four separate units a few years before my arrival. Previous investigators have been told similar stories. Both Petrović and Filipović, who studied the region at the turn of the century and in the 1920's, report that they arrived too late to see really large households.[14] Yet it was not until I began reconstructing the composition of the forty-member household that I began to suspect the accuracy of peasant memories.

During the twenty-year period prior to its breakup, over fifty people were members of this household. However, at no single point in time did the household contain more than twenty-two. There was a steady traffic of people in and out. Births, deaths, and marriages accounted for most of this. Therefore, when villagers recall a very large household of the past, they may have in mind the many people who had been affiliated with the group at one time or another.

In making inquiries, I told peasants that I was particularly interested in large households. Almost everyone mentioned two households as the largest in the village. Estimates of their size ranged from fifteen to thirty members, and most thought they contained about twenty. Their actual membership was fourteen and nineteen, respectively. Yet no one pointed to the largest unit in the sample, and villagers were surprised to learn that it housed twenty souls. For villagers as well as anthropologists, reliable data are at a premium. Most of them, and of us, make use of what is readily available, hearsay. If my experience is typical, peasant accounts of the size and composition of other households, past and present, should be treated with great caution.

Villagers refer to a household as a *kuća*, the same word that they use for "dwelling." Many dwellings contain several distinct households, but the context usually indicates which meaning is intended. The word "zadruga" is known to Crna Gorans as a term for the large traditional household, but it is never used in this way in normal conversation. If a Crna Goran is pressed to distinguish a very large household from a smaller one, he uses the word "*čeljad*" for the larger unit. In size and composition, therefore, many of these households resemble the zadruga. But what can we say about the criteria of consumption and ownership?

Each household has a single leader, and the unit is known by his name. He is usually the eldest male. This leader, or *domaćin*, represents the household to the outside. He alone can make binding commitments on behalf of the entire group. The *domaćin*, for example, not the father of the bride or groom, makes wedding arrangements and presides at festivities. The *domaćin* determines who will go to market or represent the household at a wedding.

The *domaćin* also represents the group in dealing with its individual members. For example, he keeps the common purse. Shoes, taxes, wedding expenses, and cigarettes, indeed almost all expenditures come out of this common fund, which the *domaćin* supervises. Similarly, all household income and products come under his control. If a young man works in the city and commutes, his wages are not personal income, but are placed in the common coffer. The group views the wage earner as a representative of the common economic enterprise.

While the *domaćin* enjoys considerable authority, its exercise is hedged by many customs. Older children, for example, are entitled to better and more fashionable clothing, and younger ones must be content with hand-me-downs and poorer quality. The *domaćin* cannot play favorites. Peasants say that older children should have better clothing because they are more widely known in the community. They are, in a phrase, walking showcases of household prestige, and all members have an interest in insuring that they are outfitted in proper style.

To the outside world, the household is seen as a single entity, and the *domaćin* is spokesman, treasurer, purchasing agent, and coordinator of activities. He embodies in his person the unity of the household. Internally, only one person has the authority to coordinate the group's internal affairs.

When someone joins a household, the unit acquires rights over his time and labor. He can fashion his own routine and pursue his private interests only during certain customary "free" intervals, which fall generally in the evening hours or on religious holidays. If he should earn some money during these periods, it is his to spend.

We should not conclude that the peasant is a slave to the household and its routines. On most occasions, he follows customary patterns without direction. Everyone knows what is to be done, how urgent it is, and how much labor will be required. There is give-and-take in the system, and no one feels bound by iron rules. The rights of the household become evident when conflict occurs, as when several members want to attend a wedding but the current workload can permit only one to go. Even here, patterns of procedure and rotation are followed, and everyone gets a turn. But the principle which underlies the obligations of membership is clear. As villagers say, a person who is supported by the household must work for the household.

Let us now return to Mosely's definition of the zadruga and see how it accords with the Crna Goran materials. Paraphrasing Mosely, I think we can conclude that Crna Goran households produce the means of their livelihood jointly, and they regulate (through the agency of the *domaćin*) the control of their labor and livelihood communally. But what can we say about the other parts of the zadruga definition: joint consumption, communal ownership of the means of production, and communal control of property? Let us consider consumption first.

A common purse and a common kitchen are apt symbols of joint consumption. Each household has a single kitchen where all the meals are prepared and consumed. If the anthropologist could count the number of kitchens in a locality, he would have a reasonable estimate of the number of households. The correspondence is not perfect, because a household in the process of dividing may have separate kitchens, or at the very least the opposing factions will prepare separate meals. The appearance of separate cooking arrangements is a clear sign that relations are badly strained and division is imminent. However, at most times the basic equation holds: one kitchen equals one household.

Clear principles govern the distribution of consumable items. In the long run, no single individual is favored over another. Household unity depends upon strict adherence to these principles, and a good *domaćin* should follow them faithfully. Thus, most wool is knitted or woven into sweaters, socks, heavy yard goods for clothing, and blankets. The wool is divided so that each member of the household receives the same amount. Each married woman then takes the allotment owed to her family and decides how it will be used. If one of the maidens in the house is working on her dowry, she receives a special allotment, but everyone understands that in due course every maiden will receive a comparable amount.

Further examples of the distribution of consumable items could be given. I have already discussed how children's clothing needs are determined. But whatever the item or the circumstance, the principle remains the same, equitable distribution among household members. The distribution of a particular item might favor older household members over children, or males over females, but the total effect is that no particular individual should receive favored treatment and that over the long run all individuals should be treated alike. It is reasonable to conclude that Crna Goran households jointly produce their means of livelihood, and jointly consume it.

When we turn from consumption to ownership and control of property, we confront some complex issues. Let us begin with a backward glance and recall that peasants say that anyone who is supported by the household has an obligation to work. They also say that anyone who works is entitled to support. This explains why the household as a unit helps a maiden to acquire a dowry. It also explains why the household meets the wedding expenses of its members. When a wedding is held and guests bring gifts, villagers insist that those gifts belong to the entire household, not just to the bride and groom, because all household members helped to meet the wedding expenses. The gifts are eventually divided among all the members who were working adults at the time they were acquired. If a member had been away at school or was in the army, he would not receive a share.

Property acquired from household labor or household resources belongs to the household. We might say, following Mosely, that this is communal ownership. A plot of purchased land belongs to all working members. Similarly, the crops and all foodstuffs belong to the unit and are divided on a per capita basis. From this description, it might appear that almost all objects of property would be household property, or at least the amalgamation of shares of what had once been household property. But this is not the case. To understand why, we need to see how rights to property are transmitted from generation to generation.

Ordinarily, a man's estate is divided equally, *per stirpes,* among his sons. Thus, if a man has two sons, A and B, each receives one-half of his estate. If A in turn should have two sons, and if B should have only one, A's sons will each receive one-quarter of the original estate and B's son will inherit the remaining one-half. This principle of division is followed, even though A and B may have kept their father's estate undivided during their own lifetime.

A man may not claim a share of his father's estate while the latter is still living. Sometimes an aged or infirm Crna Goran father may divide his estate, but village sentiment holds that such "anticipatory inheritance" is very unwise. Crna Gorans say that a son who acquires his inheritance will not respect his father, and the old man is likely to be left with no sons to care for him. The relationship between many fathers and sons is marked by suspicion and hostility. Several popular folktales have patricide or paternal tyranny as their theme, and contemporary incidents of violence keep the folktales timely. Most Crna Gorans believe that disinheritance is the only device that can keep father and son together in the same household. If a man leaves his father's household, he is very likely to be disinherited. Brothers sometimes attempt to provoke one another into leaving so that one will be disinherited. As we might expect, this lends a strong air of distrust to relations between brothers and helps set the stage for their eventual division.

Because of the distrust among household members and the importance of property in buttressing social relations, Crna Gorans naturally make an explicit connection between inheritance and support. A person who lives and cares for a man has a right to inherit his estate. Lack of support deprives one of that right. A son is the preferred heir, but he will not inherit unless he continues to live with his father and takes care of him until his death.

Daughters do not inherit, since they go off to live in their husband's households. As villagers say, they have no "need" to inherit any of the father's estate. In the cases of inheritance I examined, no woman with living brothers at home inherited any of her father's estate. However, sometimes a man has no sons. In this case, he may try to entice a daughter and son-in-law to live with him and evenutally to inherit. In the cases I studied, the father of the daughter always had a much larger estate than the father of the son-in-law. If a man has no children, or if he has been unable to keep them at home, he may try to find an impoverished family to look after him and eventually to inherit. For our purposes, we need only keep in mind that inheritance is firmly tied to support. While ties of kinship provide a kind of "queuing order," as it were, to the position of heir and successor, kinship ties carry no guarantee of inheritance.

Under Crna Goran customary law, a widow may not alienate her husband's estate except to provide for direct maintenance of his heirs. The widow has a right to support, but she cannot prevent her husband's heirs from dividing the estate.

We can now return to our theme of ownership in the household. As we have seen, acquired property belongs to all working members and is parceled out to those who have claims when the household is divided. When members die, it is acquired by their heirs. Acquired property, therefore, is continually being converted into personal property. Most of the productive assets used by a household are owned by a single individual, the *domaćin*. Other members tend to be his dependents, heirs, and their dependents. But it is not quite accurate to say that most property is private property. Crna Gorans do not see it that way.

Household members speak of the land, livestock, and buildings as "our property." They say that it would be wrong for the *domaćin* to sell it or give it away without the consent of the other members. If there is a sharp difference of opinion on whether to sell or not, the *domaćin's* faction can always win, but household members tend to see such action as an abuse of the *domaćin's* authority as household agent, not as his legitimate right as owner. I find it significant that the *domaćins* talk about property as if they were temporary trustees of an enterprise. Their task, as they phrase it, is carefully to husband that estate and add to it. From this brief sketch, we can see that many subtle issues are bound up in "ownership." For the purposes of our analysis, we can conclude that Crna Goran households approximate the zadruga pattern of "communal ownership," provided, of course, that we keep in mind just what that term represents in the present case.

After considering production, consumption, and ownership, I think it is clear that Crna Goran households, at least the larger ones with two or more nuclear families, closely follow Mosely's definition of the zadruga. Other households appear to be zadrugas in decline or households in the process of becoming zadrugas. If this much can be accepted, then we must ask why households divide, and when they divide to help understand the dissolution of the zadruga in other regions and times.

Fissiparous tendencies are strong in Crna Goran households. All working members contribute their labor to the common welfare, and each family receives according to the number of its members. These same principles generate strong pressures towards household division, if one of the component families contributes more labor, or receives more of the household's assets. The family of an elder brother is frequently larger than the others, since siblings marry according to birth order. The younger brother with a smaller family is likely to feel victimized, since he and his wife provide as much labor as his elder brother, but their smaller family receives less of the wool, new clothing, and spending money. There are many sources of inequality.

The central importance of the *domaćin* in domestic affairs also generates pressure toward division. The *domaćin* has wide-ranging authority on behalf of the household. One of the consequences of his authority is the relative impotency of other members in making decisions, especially since the *domaćin's* decisions have profound implications for their own future well-being. A man can fully carry out his obligations as husband, father, and citizen only when he establishes his own household and becomes *domaćin*. While some men enjoy their lack of responsibility, others regret it and eagerly anticipate the day when they will be *domaćin* in charge of their own affairs. Inequality of treatment and lack of responsibility work hand-in-hand with suspicion and distrust in leading towards household division. Thus, Crna Gorans rightly are insistent that only disinheritance keeps father and son together.

When division occurs, it is most likely between full brothers whose father, the former *domaćin*, has recently died. Only a few men are willing to leave their father's household in his lifetime and strike out on their own. They take almost nothing from their paternal home to establish homes of their own, and they are almost certain to face disinheritance upon his death. It is not surprising that these men have found secure wage-paying jobs in the nearby city of Skoplje before dividing. Their households depend upon wages for livelihood. These men remain in the village, because of the economics of having a village home and garden. It is particularly striking that their natal homes are very poor, even by village standards. While I have no direct evidence, it is reasonable to assume that they divided from their natal home because their inheritable share was poor compensation for remaining under their father's control.

In households with larger landholdings, the threat of disinheritance has some potency. Most men find it in their interest to remain in their father's household until his death. If there are several heirs, division can be expected shortly after the death. When the old *domaćin* dies, the co-heirs become co-holders of the estate, and none can disinherit the others. But only one of them, usually the eldest, becomes the new *domaćin*. This produces an unstable situation. If the new *domaćin* is autocratic and unfair, his co-holders and brothers can demand division and establish their own households. While this decision results in independence for the brothers, it usually represents a marked loss of prestige and of significant economic advantages as well for the *domaćin*. These economic advantages stem from the larger labor pool, certain economies of scale, and division of labor. Why, then, does not the new *domaćin* make every effort to insure that his brothers and co-holders remain satisfied?

There are several answers. Even if the *domaćin* is scrupulously honest and even-handed, he is the decision-maker and his brothers are not. As the head of a large household, he is a respected and honored member of the community, while his brothers are treated as jural minors. The *domaćin* also knows that he has no effective sanction against division, which brothers can demand at any time. He also knows that he can depend only on his own heirs, his sons, to care for him when he is old. They are the only ones whom he can disinherit. But unless he actively works to their advantage, they are likely to leave him. The *domaćin*, therefore, is stretched between the interests of his co-holders and the interests of his heirs. Previous incidents, the heady power of the *domaćinship*, and the constant complaints of his wife and children usually drive the *domaćin* into favoring his own family.

A few households maintain unity for long periods after the original *domaćin* dies. How do we account for the continuing cooperation between the co-holders? Since these households hold part of the key to the zadruga puzzle, let us examine them closely.

In comparison to the other households I studied, these units had relatively little land. In absolute terms, their landholdings might be quite sizable, but they were meager in terms of the number of people who depended on them. Their per capita landholdings place them in about the same position as many of the marginal households in the village. This seems puzzling. Recall that it was in these poorer households that we discovered sons separating from their fathers and being disinherited. Why are land-poor sons willing to risk disinheritance, while full brothers remain united?

First we note that these undivided, full-brother households are large. The brothers are often young men with growing families. Only rarely does one encounter a unit where the brothers have grandchildren, but we find a large number of working members even in such households. They include the brothers and their wives, often their mother, and several youths and maidens who are full members of the household work force. When major agricultural tasks are undertaken, these units can muster a sizable work force. With half a dozen workers, they can reap a wheat field in an afternoon or hoe a vineyard in a day or two. Peasants are quick to point out the advantages of this kind of work force, increased efficiency, security against the hazards of illness and weather, and more pleasurable working conditions.

These advantages are real, and they can be important, but they do not account for continuing unity. Such advantages can be enjoyed only during periods of intensive activity, particularly during harvest time. During the bulk of the agricultural season, this kind of work force is not efficient. The additional units of labor do not yield comparable units of productivity. By and large, a sizable labor force is not beneficial if the labor is devoted to the usual round of agricultural tasks. Significantly, the large households do not use their labor in this fashion.

Rather than add labor to agricultural tasks already well staffed, these households "invest" their surplus labor in highly profitable supplemental activities, large-scale viticulture, shepherding, and wage labor. These activities share three characteristics: they are in addition to the usual round of agricultural tasks; they require large amounts of labor, primarily the labor of males; and they are profitable. Consider shepherding. A herd of about sixty sheep will provide a large household with all its wool, cheese, and mutton, and the household can still sell cheese, milk, lambs, and the older ewes. The amount of income from the herd is equivalent to the wages of a village school teacher. In order to keep sheep, the household must contain at least three adult males, one to be the shepherd, another to undertake normal male agricultural tasks, and the third to make trips between the mountain sheepfold, village, and city market. Large-scale viticulture and wage labor yield comparable returns, and they, too, require the labor of males.

In short, the households that remain undivided have marginal landholdings and large numbers of workers, and participate in one or more of the supplemental activities. The high standard of living which they enjoy explains their unity. If they divided, none of the new households would have the labor needed to continue the supplemental activities, and their level of economic well-being would drop drastically. Together, they flourish; divided, they would suffer.

If I were to continue the analysis, it would be appropriate to offer some predictions on how these households could be expected to fare in the future. But I intend to put the process in reverse, to ask what form the classical zadruga might have taken and to see what conditions permitted, or facilitated, the growth and unity of really large households.

In the past, cases of separation between father and son must have been rare. For example, in the sample I studied, division between brothers may occur anytime, and in general division seems as likely in one year as in the next. However, we find that all the instances of father-son separation are associated with periods of great opportunity. We have few cases for statistical testing, but most occur around 1954 and 1963, periods of great economic opportunity. In 1953, the program of collectivization in agriculture was radically changed, and peasants were permitted to leave the collectives and to take the land and equipment they had brought with them. At the same time, industry was undergoing rapid expansion. In similar fashion, the great Skoplje earthquake of 1963 and the monumental reconstruction which followed was a period of great opportunity. Yugoslav and foreign funds poured into Skoplje, and numerous village men found employment in construction and transport. Therefore, cases of father-son separation appear to occur in extraordinary times when opportunities outside the village clearly outweigh the "costs" of leaving and the "benefits" of staying behind.

There were fewer employment opportunities in the past. Employers required the approval of the household head before hiring one of its members. Depending upon the household head's instructions, wages might be remitted directly to the household, not to the employee. There were other ways of leaving, of course. Some men might use military service as a means of escape, and others may have simply wandered away from the village to seek their fortune. But when a man left, so far as we can tell, he went by himself. All things considered, it seems that father-son separation was extremely rare in the past.

It is somewhat more difficult to assess the likelihood of division between brothers or, as our sources remind us, between cousins. Once again, I believe such cases of division were relatively rare. Consider the following.

According to elderly villagers, less land was under cultivation in the past. Distant fields near Skoplje were not worked, because troop movements in and around the Skoplje garrison made cultivation hazardous. Distant fields are larger than fields near the village. Apparently, they have not had time to fragment with successive divisions. Further, distant fields do not contain vineyards, and they are not bordered by fruit-bearing trees, which are signs of long-term cultivation.

If less land were under cultivation in the past, fewer people were also dependent upon the crops. While reliable evidence is difficult to obtain, it seems certain that villages were considerably smaller in the past. Maps and direct observation indicate many fewer dwellings, and, given the census returns of the past fifty years or so, fewer villagers as well. Judging from the size of older houses, I believe that individual households had many more members, although each household probably had periods of full occupancy and periods with many vacancies.

But this raises a problem. If we assume that the range of per capita landholdings was about the same in the past as now, then how were those households able to maintain themselves? Without wages, how did households with low per capita landholdings survive? The standard of living was perhaps lower. I suspect the reverse.

The answer, I think, is found in those supplemental activities mentioned earlier. We observed that large contemporary households allocate extra labor to profitable, labor-intensive activities, such as viticulture and shepherding. It appears that the variety and intensity of these supplemental activities were even greater in the past. The mountains behind the villages contain numerous abandoned sheepfolds and pastures. Villagers say that every household kept sheep, and the shepherding enterprise was more efficient. A good shepherd can manage a herd of sixty sheep with only occasional losses to wolves and the dangerous terrain. Two shepherds, one leading and the other following the herd, could herd over two hundred sheep. In addition, households of the past apparently maintained herds of goats, swine, and cattle. Each of these herding activities requires men to look after the herd. If several herds were kept by a single household, as elderly informants insist, each household would require considerable labor resources. These labor resources and the variety of productive activities which they permit account for the well-being of traditional households. To put it in a formula, a sizable membership permits an extensive division of labor which, in turn, yields an adequate standard of living.

Furthermore, in frontier areas of substantial forests and only a few remote towns, the zadruga could be largely self-supporting. Only a sizable unit could have a well-developed division of labor. We should note that only a sizable unit might also offer some security against the hazards of sudden and frequent deaths. Few peasants could expect to live a long life and to see themselves surrounded by a circle of children and grandchildren. Many would die at an early age, leaving behind a young spouse and small children. A large household could provide for them. Some other peasants might live to a ripe old age, only to see their descendents die before them. A large household would provide care and support for these elderly people.

If my argument is correct, we are now in a position to understand why the traditional zadruga was less prone to division than contemporary households. Simply stated, a small unit which split off from the zadruga would not have been viable. Only the largest households could divide and still survive.

I began my remarks by talking about the zadruga controversy. Our examination of division in contemporary households suggests that the zadruga problem has been misstated. As it is ordinarily posed, the question asks: What changes in the external social and cultural environment led to altered domestic relations, such that peasants were no longer willing to live together in large households? The evidence from Skopska Crna Gora suggests that peasants were never ecstatic about communal living and that the fundamental tensions and conflicts which I observed in domestic life were probably always present. The change is that peasants no longer need to cling together in large groups to survive as an economic unit.

In this paper, I have tried to show how intimate acquaintance with the lives and thoughts of contemporary peasants can shed light on the lives of their ancestors. The work of Philip Mosely contains the suggestion that this is one way in which social anthropology can contribute to historical understanding. But it would be unwise to boast. While the anthropologist can witness much, his acquaintance is generally limited to a period of months. The anthropologist derives his models of society from these observations but, as Trevor-Roper suggests, "the test of the model is the way it works, as the test of the car is the way it runs." The running of the anthropological model is history.

NOTES

1. Edward E. Evans-Pritchard, *Anthropology and History* (Manchester, England, 1961), pp. 12-14; Marc Bloch, *The Historian's Craft* (New York, 1963), pp. 43-47.

2. Philip E. Mosely, "The Peasant Family: The Zadruga, or Communal Joint-Family in the Balkans, and Its Recent Evolution," in Caroline F. Ware, ed., *The Cultural Approach to History* (New York, 1940), p. 95.

3. Joel M. Halpern, *A Serbian Village* (New York, 1958), pp. 134-150; Lorraine Baric, "New Economic Opportunities in Rural Yugoslavia," in Raymond Firth, ed., *Themes in Economic Anthropology* (London, 1967), pp. 256-257.

4. Philip E. Mosely, "Adaptation for Survival: The Varžić Zadruga," *The Slavonic and East European Review* XXI (American Series II) (1943), 148.

5. Louis Adamic, *The Native's Return* (New York, 1934), p. 215.

6. Eugene A. Hammel, "The Zadruga as Process," in Peter Laslett and Richard Wall, eds., *Household and Family in Past Time* (Cambridge, 1972), p. 362.

7. Joel M. Halpern and David Anderson, "The Zadruga, a Century of Change," *Anthropologica* N. S. XII (1970), 83-97.

8. Mosely, "The Peasant Family," p. 106; Jozo Tomasevich, *Peasants, Politics and Economic Change in Yugoslavia* (Stanford, 1955), p. 179.

9. Hammel, "The Zadruga as Process," p. 366.

10. Mosely, "The Peasant Family," p. 107.

11. Jack Goody, ed., *The Developmental Cycle in Domestic Groups* (Cambridge, 1958).

12. Meyer Fortes, "Introduction," in Goody, *The Developmental Cycle in Domestic Groups,* pp. 1-14.

13. A detailed examination of this sample is contained in David B. Rheubottom, "Strategy and Timing in the Division of Macedonian Domestic Groups," forthcoming in Anthony T. Carter and David B. Rheubottom, eds., *Decisions and Constraints: Analysis of the Developmental Cycle in Domestic Groups* (London: Athlone Press).

14. Atanasije Petrović, "Narodni život i običaji u Skopskoj Crnoj Gori" [Folk life and customs in Skopska Crna Gora], *Srpski Etnografski Zbornik* I (1907), 335-528; Milenko S. Filipović, "Zadruga Spasića u Bulačanima kod Skopje" [The Spasić zadruga in Bulačani near Skoplje]. *Glasnik Skopskog Naučnog Društva* VII-VIII (1929-30), 369-379.

15: THE CULTURAL ECOLOGY OF ALBANIAN EXTENDED FAMILY HOUSEHOLDS IN YUGOSLAV MACEDONIA

C. J. Grossmith

The Albanians who are the subject of this paper live on the lower slopes of the mountains between Skoplje and Tetovo, ten miles west of the city of Skoplje. They are patriarchal, patrilineal, generally patrilocal, and Moslem. The twenty-five villages in the area form a more or less endogamous group.

The history of Macedonia has been a harsh one, and this area is no exception. Following five hundred years of feudalism under Ottoman rule, the area in 1913 became a part of Serbia. Bulgaria occupied it from 1916 until 1919, when the Serbs returned. From 1941 until 1944, when Tito's Yugoslavia was established, the Germans and the Bulgarians occupied Skoplje. Under Bulgarian occupation, the villagers were very badly exploited and lived in conditions of extreme poverty.

Since World War II, Macedonia has made enormous strides, but the Albanian villages are only just beginning to reap some of the benefits of modern industrial society. Solid modern brick and cement block houses are now being built near the main Skoplje road. They provide a vivid contrast with the old Turkish-style houses of wood and mud bricks, clustered round the mosque in the upper part of the village. This change has occurred very recently and reflects new opportunities for employment outside the village.

In the past, village houses were grouped together in *mohullas* or neighborhoods. Each *mohulla* represented a *fis* or patrilineal descent group, some of whom can trace their origin back to Albania. Today the *fis* are scattered, and their function has diminished, since they are no longer corporate land-holding groups. *Fis* still serve as exogamous units and provide economic and moral support for marriage, circumcision, and other major financial and economic needs among their member households. Male and female members of households belonging to the same *fis* mix and talk freely, in sharp contrast to household members of different *fis* who are neither related by marriage nor proximity. Women in such households are mutually secluded, and men will visit such a household only on invitation or important business. Not a single woman in the village has employment outside her household.

Many households have left the village for Turkey or migrated to Skoplje. A number of households have moved in from surrounding villages, because the village I have studied is an administrative center for the area. It contains a school for pupils up to the eighth class, an outpatient clinic, and the headquarters of the agricultural cooperative. The villagers share the overall demographic characteristics of the Albanian minority in Macedonia, who, according to the 1971 census, have a birth rate of 39.5 per 1,000 population, compared with 18.1 per 1,000 population among Slavic Macedonians.

THE EXTENDED FAMILY HOUSEHOLD

In their recent monograph,[1] the Halperns have provided an example of a large extended family zadruga in Serbia in 1905. The household of Svetozar Stojanović is reproduced here with ages. Such zadrugas can no longer be found in Serbia or elsewhere in Yugoslavia, except among Albanians, who live mainly in Kosovo, Macedonia, and Montenegro.

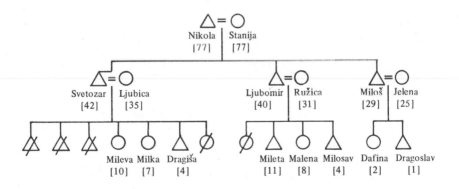

The following diagram outlines an Albanian household in 1973 in an Albanian village ten miles from Skoplje and 150 miles south of the Halperns' village.

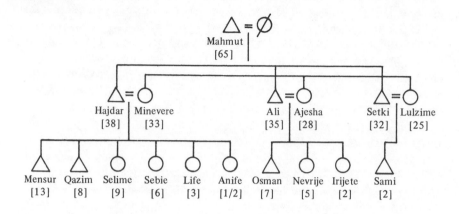

In 1973, the seventeen members of this household lived in a four-room house with a kitchen and a store room. Mahmut had a room to himself, and each of the sons had one room, in which he slept with his wife and children. The family planned in 1974 to build three smaller houses in a common compound on one of their pieces of land, so that each son would have a house of his own. The whole household eats communally. The three houses will be used only for sleeping, and the family will continue to eat together. The household provides an example of three brothers who are married to three sisters from a nearby village. One-fifth of all village households contain two or more brothers married to women who are sisters.

The Mahmut household has eighty-five *shenik* of land, registered in Mahmut's name. A *shenik* equals five hundred square meters. Mahmut inherited forty-eight *shenik* from his father, and the household bought thirty-seven *shenik* between 1943 and 1972. After the First World War, one *shenik* of land cost ten kilos of wheat. The price of one *shenik* today is about nine hundred dollars.

The work patterns of Mahmut's sons and grandsons are as follows. Mahmut's three sons, Hajdar, Ali, and Setki, began grazing the household sheep when they were six or seven years old. At the age of eleven, Hajder and Setki began to work the land with their father, continuing until age nineteen, when they went into the army for two years. From the age of ten to twelve,

Ali attended a school six miles from the village. He then returned to work the land until he was nineteen, when he too went into the army. On returning from army service, all three brothers continued to work the land. Three years ago, Hajdar became a private house builder. Ali obtained a job as clerk in the village school three years after returning from the army, and still holds this position. Setki continues to work the land with his father and the occasional assistance of Hajdar. Last year, Setki took an adult evening course at the village school to complete the eighth grade. This will give him a better chance to obtain state employment in Skoplje, where he is currently registered at the employment bureau. Hajdar's sons, Mensur and Qazim, began going to school at age seven. The household no longer possesses any sheep, but Mensur grazes the draft oxen during vacations. Ali's son Osman will enter school this year.

When on private contract, Hajdar earns 6,000 new dinars ($400) a month; village construction work pays well. Ali, as a state employee, receives 1,200 new dinars ($80) a month. The household land produces 4,000 kilograms of wheat flour a year. This feeds the seventeen members of the household. In addition, the household produces all its own fruit and vegetables and collects ten liters of milk a day from its two cows. Last year, it received 14,000 new dinars from the sale of the grape harvest. A conservative estimate of the household's monthly income over and above the food consumed would be $550. Last year, they bought a second-hand Fiat for $600.

In order to put the Mahmut household in perspective, the table illustrates the frequency of different household types in the village by numbers of members. I have selected seven household types. The table shows that one-third of the village population lives in households containing two or more married brothers and their families, with or without their parents. About forty percent of the village population lives in households containing ten or more members.

HOUSEHOLD TYPES

Type 1 Nuclear Household.
Type 2 Husband and/or wife, and married son with or without children.
Type 3 Husband and/or wife, and two married sons with or without children.
Type 4 Husband and/or wife, and three married sons with or without children.
Type 5 Two-generation household, with two married brothers and children.
Type 6 Two-generation household, with three married brothers and children.
Type 7 Three-generation household, with two married brothers in oldest generation.

TABLE OF HOUSEHOLD TYPE BY NUMBER OF HOUSEHOLD MEMBERS

Number of Household Members

Type	Total	1	2	3	4	5	6	7	8	9	10	11	12	13	14	15	16	17	18	19	20	20+
1	61	2	6	8	4	9	10	10	7	1	3	1										
2	25			3	2	2	2	5	2	2	4	1	1	1								
3	12								2	3	1	3	1	1					1			
4	3														1	1				1		
5	5					1	1						1		1			1				
6	1																					1
7	3							1		1											1	
Total	110	2	6	11	6	12	13	16	11	7	8	5	3	2	2	1		1	1	1	1	1

ACCUMULATION OF WEALTH

Within the Albanian extended family household, two kinds of wealth can be accumulated, material and non-material. Material wealth consists of land and income, and the latter may be described as the potential and actual contributions of household members to the prosperity of the house and the honor which they are able to accumulate.

Land is accumulated by inheritance and purchase. Inheritance involves equal division of a father's land holdings among his sons. Division may occur before or after the father's death. Daughters, although entitled by Yugoslav law to share in their father's property, in fact receive nothing. If division occurs while the father is still alive, it is ordinarily not formally registered with the taxation authorities. In this way, sons employed by the state do not declare their possession of land and therefore are entitled to child benefits. If a couple has no son, occasionally a son-in-law will come to live with them and work their land, later passing it on to his children. Such a situation occurs only if the son-in-law's father has another son to inherit his land. Alternatively, a couple without a son may sell their land and live with one of their daughters. The cash from the sale of their land may be given to the son-in-law for buying more land. A few cases of both these situations have occurred in the village I have studied.

Opportunities for buying land occur when someone leaves the village. During the last fifty years, several emigrations have occurred. After the First World War, village land became very cheap when large numbers of Turks returning to Turkey sold their land in Tetovo and Gostivar to Albanians from mountain villages nearby. A number of families from the village studied moved into the Tetovo District, buying better land and selling their village land. During the 1950's, another emigration to Turkey occurred because of the pressures on Moslems to conform to certain state regulations, such as sending daughters to school. A father who violated this law was sent to prison. More recently, about twenty households migrated to Skoplje because of favorable opportunities for employment. Occasionally, families left the village because of a *bela* or quarrel.

When a man decides to leave the village, he first offers to sell his land to members of his own *fis*, then to his *miks* (affines), then to those who have land bordering on the land he wants to sell. Then, if he has been unable to sell it, anyone can purchase it.

Since the last war, agricultural stock has been considerably reduced in size in Yugoslavia. After the First World War, many families had large flocks of sheep and goats. Goats have now been banned by law, because of the destruction they cause to the crops and vegetation on the mountainside. Flocks of sheep have also been considerably reduced. Most households are content to have a donkey, a cow, a pair of draft oxen, and perhaps a few sheep.

Today four different kinds of economic opportunity are open to male household members: work on the land, state employment, private enterprise, and migrant labor abroad. If a household has land, a member in state employment, and a member either in private enterprise or in migrant labor in Germany, it will prosper. Work on the land meets all the household's food requirements, and may in addition bring in large amounts of seasonal capital through the sale of grapes and other produce. State employment provides a low but regular income, and migrant labor abroad provides relatively large amounts of capital, which are used for buying land, building houses, arranging marriages, and buying modern luxury items, such as cars, television sets, and refrigerators.

HOUSEHOLD WORK PATTERNS

When an extended family household divides into separate nuclear families, the major economic change which occurs is that each nuclear family produces and consumes products separately from separate areas of land. This represents the basic criterion in defining a household. The saying "Who will give you bread this evening if you don't work today? " serves to emphasize the dependence of household members on their own domestic and agricultural labor.

The majority of village households still maintain many characteristics of a traditional peasant economy. The only regularly purchased domestic supplies are rice, cooking oil, matches, sugar, salt, tea, coffee, detergent, and soap. Some families grow their own sunflowers, which they have made into cooking oil in a Skoplje factory. Many families still cook on wood fires from wood gathered on privately-owned village woodland. Bread, leavened and unleavened, is baked every day from home-grown wheat and forms the staple diet. It is eaten with home-grown fruit and vegetables, eggs, domestic milk products, and vegetable conserves. Water is drawn by hand from the household or neighborhood well. Many families grow their own tobacco, and the brooms used to sweep the house and court yard are also grown on household land. Old men can still be seen wearing clothes made at home from material woven on domestic looms, and everyone possesses thick white woolen home-knitted socks from domestic sheep.

All household members from six years of age are expected to help with household work. A member who does not do his share is known as *çelepurxhi,* someone who waits for everything to be handed to him. Villagers say, "Some people live by buying everything, but we work in the fields to have something in addition."

Male members who work the land have their hardest period between May and September. During that time, the corn fields are plowed and planted. The grape vines are tied and sprayed, the meadows scythed, and the grass made into haystacks to dry. The vegetable gardens and melon patches are dug and planted, manured, and then hoed. From time to time, men go up the mountain to cut wood and graze cattle, or else to transport bags of wheat on the backs of their donkeys to the water mill in the next village. In July and August, the wheat and rye are harvested. Until two years ago, harvesting was done entirely with sickles, and threshing was done separately in the yard by a horse trampling the ears of wheat as it walked slowly round a central pole. This method is still used among village households. Now, in addition, the village has the use of a combine which threshes as it harvests. In upland fields, harvesting is done by hand, though often threshed by machine later.

During July, which is the hottest month, the kitchen gardens and cornfields have to be irrigated with water from the mountain streams which flow through the villages. By September, after the corn and beans are harvested, the agricultural work slacks off and people await Ramazan, which for the past ten years has fallen in autumn and winter.

Men who are in state employment, unless they have a job in the village, take the five o'clock bus to Skoplje every morning for work at six. They remain until three in the afternoon, when they catch the bus back to the village, arriving at three-thirty or four o'clock. If there is work to be done in the fields, they then join their brothers and fathers on the land until five or six in the evening.

Men who have retired from state jobs and are too old for heavy work on the land still contribute in numerous ways to the household. They take the oxen out to graze, or watch and feed the poultry. Some work at hand crafts, such as basket-making, or take dried corn off the cob for seed. From time to time, they may visit *fis* or *affines* to arrange some household business. In short, there are always jobs for everyone, according to his abilities.

In the extended family which contains two married brothers, the *kunata* or sisters-in-law are responsible for most of the housework. The mother-in-law directs their work and watches the children. Usually, one sister-in-law will sweep the house and yard, draw water, prepare food, and bake bread, while the other washes the children and the clothing for the whole household, milks the cows, makes the milk into yogurt, and churns it into curds and whey. Each week, the sisters-in-law change jobs. In addition, during the months from May to September, the sisters-in-law may go into the fields to work with the men, dig the vegetable garden, hoe the corn, collect fruit, harvest the wheat with a hand sickle, and pick beans. In winter, when work is lighter, they embroider handkerchiefs or head scarfs for themselves or a future bride, knit woollen sweaters for their husbands, or weave aprons on the loom. This work pattern is followed whether the sister-in-law is healthy, sick, or pregnant. During pregnancy, she works in the fields with the men until the ninth month. She usually labors in the fields when her children are old enough to be left but too small to work, and when there is an insufficiency of adult males.

When children have reached the age of five or six, they are expected to fetch and carry round the house, take trays of food to the kitchen, pour water for other household members to wash their hands, sweep the floor after meals, draw water from the well, fetch ash trays for guests, and take messages to other houses. After heavy rain, they collect sand from the bed of the village stream for use as building material. They watch the poultry, and carry the midday meal to the fields for their father or uncles working there. They also go to the cooperative store to buy cigarettes, bottles of fruit juice, and other items required suddenly when relatives arrive.

THE ROLE OF HONOR

The Albanian household is entwined in a network of relations essential to its preservation. It forms part of a patrilineal descent group and is also linked with a series of other households through marriage. In addition, it is linked with neighboring households, which, although related neither lineally nor affinally, occupy a somewhat similar status. Women of neighboring households talk to their male neighbors. Such households visit each other often and cooperate in the day-to-day round of agricultural and domestic work. In addition, the household is linked with the rest of the village households by language, religion, ethnic and village identity, common way of life, contact on ceremonial occasions, and, often, male members at work in Skoplje.

Within such a complex network of relationships, self-respect or honor is an essential ingredient of the Albanian household. A household can accumulate honor in a number of ways. Working for the household is one way, and keeping the rules is another. In a patriarchal society, one set of rules involves showing respect to one's elders and therefore, by extension, to the household. Honor also involves keeping the rules of Islam. Daughters and wives are secluded from all males who do not belong to the household *fis*, and the fast of Ramazan must be kept. A son must be circumcized and sons and daughters married in the proper manner. In the case of a son's marriage, bride wealth consisting of as much as two thousand dollars worth of Turkish gold lira and clothing must be sent to the bride's family as the daughter's personal property and insurance.

If a household has an honorable reputation as well as wealth, its sons and daughters can obtain wives and husbands easily. The families with whom their marriages are arranged become *mik* (affines) to the household, and such households then enter into a relationship of cooperation and support. Thus, a *mik* who is a builder will construct a house for half the price a non-related builder will ask. Relationships of reciprocal assistance develop with *mik* households which assist in the exchange of domestic produce and help with the agricultural work.

When either honor or wealth are in short supply, brides are obtained by the use of additional strategies. In 12.3 percent of village households, the husband had obtained a wife by exchanging a sister. In twenty percent of the households, a wife was forced to fetch her younger sister for her husband's younger brother. On occasion, sums of money have been paid directly to the bride's father, and a few families have obtained Slavic Moslem women from Bosnia.

When a man obtains a bride, he has an opportunity to have sons who will enrich the house, support him, and provide him with leisure in old age. Meanwhile, his bride will carry out the arduous domestic work essential to maintenance of the household.

The activities of the Albanian household are clearly directed towards the prosperity of a group of resident male agnates. Women serve as an important means towards this prosperity, but their benefit from it is incidental.

WOMEN AS A DIVISIVE ELEMENT

Women are often the divisive element in extended households. They lose much of their identity with their own *fis* when they move into their husband's house, and they are also strangers there. A young bride before going to her husband's house swallows a bead which she later collects from her stool and takes to the *hoxha*, or Moslem priest, who recites over it. This bead is always kept on the bride's person as protection from *seire* (witchcraft) of members of her husband's *fis*. Fear of witchcraft is only one sign of the tension which exists between women and their in-laws.

An extended family depends for its existence on subjugation of individual interests and loyalties to the common cause of the house. However, women often feel no particular loyalty to their husband's *fis* or extended family. Their loyalty crystallizes and develops with the development of their immediate nuclear families. Albanian women want children as quickly as comfortably possible. Many mention three years as the maximum period they prefer between deliveries. This enables them to recover from the previous birth, wean the child, teach it to feed itself, take it out of swaddling, and dispense with the laundry involved. After this, they are ready to deliver the next child. The sooner they can produce a son, the sooner they can ensure their relationship with their husband and therefore their status in his house.

Until a son is born, they are on trial. If they are unable to produce a son within a few years, they may be divorced. In any case, they must expect constant tension in the household from their husband and in-laws. The sooner they have a son, the sooner he will grow up, marry, and enable them to hand over a large part of the domestic work to his bride.

The birth of a daughter has initial advantages, because she will soon be able to provide help around the house. However, from puberty until she is married, she is a constant worry to her mother, who must protect her from contact with non-related males and ensure she marries in the proper manner, not by running away with someone. After a daughter has been married, she is of no further direct economic benefit to her household.

For a woman, one son is not enough because an extended household needs to exploit three of the four economic possibilities for male employment if it is to prosper. Two or three sons will not only enrich the house, but will act as a safeguard if one of the sons should die or enter into the non-Moslem, alien world of the city. Finally, several sons will provide the economic base which will enable a woman to bring about a division in the extended family, if intra-household relations are strained.

In extended households which have two or more married brothers, relationships between the sister-in-law and the mother-in-law are most conducive to conflict. Sisters-in-law tend to favor their own husbands and children in their daily work. As a result, constant accusations arise that the other sister-in-law is not doing her share, and mutual distrust develops. One sister-in-law will use the ethic of household equality to spite the other: "After my son was born, she got jealous, and didn't allow me to give the boy milk. We often quarrelled when I fed him biscuits, milk, or eggs. She did not have a son and therefore did not want me to feed him with those things." Mothers-in-law often resent the threat posed to their nuclear family relationships by the arrival of a daughter-in-law. One daughter-in-law said of her mother-in-law, "She thinks she has been left without a son, and says, 'I had one and I got left without him. My daughter-in-law took him for herself.' "

Such patterns of conflict, not unique among Albanians, acquire a special significance in the Albanian extended family, where household organization is geared to the preservation of a group of resident male agnates, and female members are constantly at odds with the system.

Extended family households of fifteen or more members still exist among Moslem Albanians in Yugoslavia. These households are independent economic units and rely upon the subjugation of individual interests for the prosperity of the house. Household economies are ecologically generalized in that household members exploit several kinds of economic resource. If one resource fails, several alternatives are available. Better state employment opportunities and migrant labor abroad have increased these alternatives recently. In order to function as an economic unit, the household must maintain a network of reciprocal relations with other families. Keeping such relations in good repair provides the household honor, and thereby enables it to obtain women to produce sons and replenish the household manpower. Honor and adherence to religious beliefs have very similar functions.

Women act as a divisive element in the extended family because their loyalties center around their immediate nuclear families. Both male and female household members want several sons, but not for the same reasons. For male members, sons help replenish the work force and provide security in old age. For females, sons provide security of status in the husband's household and help create circumstances which enable a woman's nuclear family to separate from the extended family.

As long as an Albanian is group-oriented, rather than individually oriented, that is to say, as long as his household's prosperity comes before his own, Albanians will maintain a high birthrate in order to provide household manpower in both rural and urban areas.

In their relations with non-Moslem nationalities in Macedonia, Albanians still seek the maintenance of cultural separateness and distance. Integration will be a slow and painful process. In the long run, household authority among Albanians may diminish as education and employment levels among males increase. The creation of culturally acceptable possibilities for the extra-household employment of Albanian females in the near future would probably produce an immediate decline in the birthrate, particularly if emphasis were placed upon skills currently possessed by Albanian females, such as handicrafts. These do not require high educational qualifications, but would permit Albanian women to participate in extra-household activities. This would make them wage earners, and increase the number of people with whom they are in regular contact. Studies of many different parts of the world have shown that employment among women helps produce a sharp decline in the birthrate. However, opposition to such a change lies deep in the roots of the Albanian interpretation of Islam.

NOTES

1. Joel M. Halpern and Barbara K. Kalpern, *A Serbian Village in Historical Perspective* (New York, 1972), p. 36.

16: THE LAST BIG ZADRUGAS:
ALBANIAN EXTENDED FAMILIES
IN THE KOSOVO REGION
Vera St. Erlich

The extended family in rural Yugoslavia, the zadruga, does not belong entirely to the past. Many large zadrugas still exist, preserving their traditional structure and way of life in the south, in Macedonia, and in the region of Kosovo. The largest, which have also best preserved the patriarchal way of life, are those of the Albanian ethnic group. How does this happen?

The Albanians in Yugoslavia are a minority group, speaking a non-Slavic language, and including about three-quarters of a million people. In the Kosovo region, an autonomous administrative unit, they form the majority of the population. They generally live in compact homogeneous settlements, but are sometimes in villages mixed with others. This region borders the state of Albania, and the people are closely related in language and tradition with those across the border. In the Kosovo region, almost the entire Albanian population is Moslem, while many Catholics live in Albania proper.

The Albanians of Kosovo are the most fertile population of Europe, and their natural growth is exceptional. In the 1950's, their birth rate was about forty-six per thousand, more than double that in some other Yugoslav regions. Natural growth was more than twenty-five per thousand, three times that of other regions, and much above the Yugoslav average of ten per thousand. These facts strengthen the zadruga organization considerably.

Although several studies on the zadruga in Kosovo have been completed in recent years, we do not know their precise number. One figure may be indicative: households with over nine members appeared only in four percent of the cases throughout Yugoslavia as a whole, but amounted to nearly twenty-one percent in the Kosovo region. One of my students, Shaban Hysenaj, himself an Albanian, presented the results of the research of Belgrade and Priština scholars as well as his own original research on his native area, Dukadjin. Hysenaj found and described ten big zadrugas, each

244

embracing from thirty-five to one hundred twenty members. The Osmanaj zadruga, with eighty members, the Haruni zadruga with ninety-two members, and the Halil Luma zadruga with one hundred twenty members are among the largest ever studied.

These studies reveal that these large zadrugas possess all the characteristics scholars have found typical for zadrugas in other regions, where they have since disappeared. The hierarchy is sharp, any difference in age producing a difference in status. An older brother has more authority than a younger one; a daughter-in-law introduced into the zadruga earlier has more authority than a late-comer. All men are higher in rank than any woman.

The Senior, usually the oldest man, has a position of command. He is succeeded by the next oldest, but this is not a strict rule, for an active, intelligent man can be elected, even if he is not the oldest. In most cases, the decision concerning succession is settled during the lifetime of the Senior. There are no formal elections and no arguments. The age principle is maintained when possible.

The Senior has a younger assistant, who is more mobile than the older man and frequently deals with "foreign affairs." For the work of the women, the *Batchitsa,* usually the Senior's wife, is responsible. She divides the daily work among the women, and is in charge of the kitchen and of milk and milk products, the most important food next to bread. She selects the women who work in rotation kneading bread, the heaviest manual work, for three consecutive days.

One of the highest responsibilities of the elders is arranging the marriage of the zadruga's boys and girls, of finding good houses for the girls and fine brides, who will fit in the zadruga establishment, for the boys. Very little initiative or activity on the part of the young people is involved in choosing a spouse, nor do they ordinarily resist or oppose. The chronological sequence of the marriages is strictly maintained, for it would be a disgrace to marry off a younger member before an older one. Exceptions are sometimes made with orphans, in order to show the zadruga has great care for them.

The cooperative principle is strict with regard to property. Everything is zadruga property, including cattle, tools, and kitchen utensils. Private property consists exclusively of clothes and bedding, items brought to the zadruga as the trousseau of the daughters-in-law. These items are kept in the sleeping rooms of the married couple.

Anything earned by zadruga members outside their home, such as from artisan work for other peasants, is handed over to the Senior. Indeed, migrant workers, zadruga members working in Western Europe, send most of their wages to him. I know of a case of a "Gastarbeiter," a laborer in Vienna, who won the big lottery prize there. When he was asked by news reporters what he would do with such riches, he answered: "I am sending it to our Senior. He will know how to deal with it." Women's handicrafts do constitute exceptions, for women are allowed to keep the money earned that way.

Cooking and eating in common is considered the principal characteristic of zadruga life. The food is cooked in one kettle on one fireplace or baked on one oven. The men sit separately, at the low round tables, as do the women and also the children. In many houses, the women eat in the women's room, where the cooking is also done.

Clothes and food are produced at home. The zadruga purchases only salt, sugar, matches, coffee, rice, oil for the lamps, and cotton for clothes, precisely those articles which were purchased before the Second World War by zadrugas throughout Yugoslavia, except for cotton, because only flax and wool, which were produced on the zadruga, were used then.

The attitude towards the zadruga remains the same in Kosovo as a generation earlier everywhere. The same words which I heard then are still used: "It would be a disgrace to part from a living father. It would be a shame to leave uncles and homestead." All speak in this manner, although thousands of young men from these zadrugas go to Western Germany for years in order to earn money.

PECULIARITIES OF THE ALBANIAN ZADRUGA

The Albanian zadruga shares most characteristics with the classical form, but also has some specific features of its own. First of all, life in the Albanian zadruga is shaped by Islam. Women are segregated in their living and cooking room, where they also work on handicrafts and entertain guests. They sleep with their husbands and their children in rather small rooms, a separate room for each conjugal family. Rooms for older boys and others for older girls are common for the Albanian zadruga.

Other Yugoslav regions with a Moslem population had only a few zadrugas before the war, and they were generally small. I believed then that Islam did not favor the zadruga. However, the Albanians have shown that Islam and zadrugas are compatible, perhaps because the houses in the Kosovo region are much larger than elsewhere and the members therefore do not live in close proximity. The Albanian zadrugas have much bigger buildings than zadrugas in other parts of Yugoslavia, where even prosperous zadrugas had very plain houses, with small cabins sometimes for single couples.

Many Albanian zadrugas have large houses which are as high as towers called *kula*, built often with two or three floors for warfare and resistance. One very large room is a guest hall, where the Senior sits near the open fireplace and the other men sit around in precise sequence. The guests sleep here, usually with some young men who serve them. The sleeping rooms for the couples are in lower buildings next to the *kula*. The large houses often have small windows and loopholes for guns, as the house might have to resist attackers seeking vengeance or loot.

In Albania proper, tribal organization is prevalent. The *fis* (tribe) live in geographical proximity, often in valleys separated from each other by forbidding rocky mountains. The tribes are divided into clans or brotherhoods. In the Kosovo region, however, the Albanians are immigrants, and their tribes are dispersed over different villages. Therefore, they do not enjoy the security of having the tribe and clan at hand in moments of danger, and the zadruga assumes some of the functions of the larger social unit. The *kulas* are like fortresses, often with as many as twenty "guns," that is, grown-up men ready to fight.

The strength of the tribal organization is shown by the strict exogamy rules: girls have to marry into other tribes. This system is different from that of Montenegro, the other part of Yugoslavia where tribal organization was also prevalent. There, only members of the clan (*bratstvo*), the subdivision of the tribe stemming from one ancestor, were considered blood relations. Therefore, marriage within the clan was excluded, but not inside the tribe. With Albanians, exogamy is extended also to the tribe.

Another characteristic of the Albanian zadruga is the bride price, which is obligatory. The groom's family gives a considerable sum of money to the bride's family when the couple are engaged. While the bride price is also customary in the Christian villages of Kosovo, as well as in Macedonia, it was never an absolute rule, and it has now been abandoned to a great extent. With the Albanians, the custom remains alive, and precise regulations have been established. The money has to be used exclusively for the bride's trousseau and for wedding expenses.

Wool, cotton, linen, and silk are purchased with this money, and the girl uses the materials for preparing her trousseau, frequently with artistic embroidery. She will use this all her life. Moreover, at the wedding she will give many items to her in-laws and the wedding guests. The relatively high bride price which is customary forces small familes to sacrifice, and young men may work for years to collect it. However, the Albanians resolutely deny that they purchase their wives, and they become exasperated when the bride price is interpreted as purchase.

Pecuniary considerations are involved in such customs, as they are with the custom of giving dowry. In one zadruga, two women became widows. Both remarried within the zadruga, one marrying the brother of her husband and the other an uncle. When people asked surprised questions, one zadruga member answered that it would be better that they remained in the zadruga because so much had been spent for these wives.

Islam is not the only factor which connects Albanian culture with the Middle East; the importance of bread as the main food represents the same connection. Great quantities of bread are kneaded and baked each day from wheat and corn. Milk and milk products are the main sources of protein, with beans next. Meat is eaten on special occasions. Very little alcohol is consumed, especially by the older men, who follow meticulously the Koran's prohibitions. Coffee is made all day for the grown-ups and especially for guests. It is frequently prepared by the Senior himself during entertainment of his guest. It means a major expense in cash.

One of the striking features of Albanian domestic life is the proverbial hospitality and the loving care and devotion shown guests and visitors, including casual ones. Each person who approaches the house is accepted as an honored guest without being questioned concerning his identity or his interests. There were thirty-four guests in one day in one zadruga, and all remained for the night. The Senior is always surrounded by visitors, sitting around him near the fireside and called "friends," which has the double meaning of cronies and in-laws. Most visitors are fathers and brothers of the zadruga's daughters-in-law. Honoring guests is a holy duty. If someone enters the house, he stands under the zadruga's protection, and the zadruga will never surrender him to enemies pursuing him for revenge in blood feuds. These customs of hospitality rooted in the tribal sphere color all zadruga life.

IMPERIAL HERITAGE

The historical role of the Albanians inside the Ottoman Empire may help explain the survival of the zadruga among them. Their high position in the past may also explain in part the strength and vigor of their general conservativism. For centuries, Montenegrin and Albanian tribes lived as neighbors with similar social organizations, but with entirely different attitudes toward the Ottoman Empire. The Montenegrins were the eternal foes of the empire and gained independence early, while the Albanians supported Turkish power. Although they too were freedom-loving tribal men, they were devoted to the Empire. The orthodox Slavs in the Balkans were for many generations rebels against the Empire, while the Albanians fought them incessantly for centuries as the sworn enemies of these "rebels."

The national pride of the Albanians strengthens old customs and unwritten laws. Their ties with Islam and the old Ottoman tradition are closely related to their opposition to any innovation, including schools. The great majority of Albanian peasants remain illiterate, due partly to the lack of schools in this area but also due to their animosity towards schooling. Many have become "secondary illiterates" that is, they have forgotten completely what they had learned in school. They also have had no reading material in their own language, and lack reading habits. The backwardness of the entire economy in this region is the sad inheritance of the Ottoman Empire.

THE TRIBAL COMPONENT

The tradition of tribes living free in the mountains near the Adriatic coast from Roman and Illyrian times is a decisive factor in the social organization of the Albanians of Kosovo, although Oriental elements are strong in family relations. Yet the family too is affected by the tribal custom of the blood feud. As with the Montenegrin tribes, the blood feud was unwritten law. Each member of the household and of the clan was obliged to revenge a killed "brother." If not able to reach the killer, he had to kill another man of the family or clan who "owed blood." Frequently, twenty and more killings followed a quarrel among shepherds about a source of water for sheep. In Montenegro, this custom has disappeared nearly completely during this century, but it remains very much alive with the Albanians of the Kosovo region.

Although these customs have long been prosecuted by law as crimes, they still persist in the Kosovo region. It is hard to estimate how many blood feuds still survive, because everything in connection with these feuds is handled secretively and hidden from the authorities. Some observers estimate that about two thousand men are virtually prisoners in their houses, since they are threatened with death as soon as they appear in the open. They "owe blood" mostly because of old feuds in which they personally were not involved. The custom of blood feud strengthens the tendency to remain in great households, in zadrugas, because zadrugas alone are able to feed and defend men in danger. The commitment of every man adds a compulsive quality to the whole social structure.

The power of resistance to innovation in any form is immense. When I carried out surveys in different parts of Yugoslavia on the eve of the Second World War, I wrote on Albanian family relations:

> In Yugoslavia, the Albanians were considered anti-national and an 'undesirable element' because of their political role in the past. As producers of tobacco, they suffered much under the policy of state monopolies, the agrarian reform, and bureaucratic hostility. Yet although they had fallen from a high position to a rather low one, the effects on family life were hardly noticeable. The subjective reactions to the objective pressures were surprisingly weak. People of this area did not appear pauperized or declassed. Alcoholism and prostitution, squandering of property, or crime did not occur. Patriarchal dignity and responsibility remained. Concentrated pressure could not bend or break them. Many of the poorest boys and men left their native villages in search of labor in distant cities without straying from the path of patriarchal honor and tradition, and the women who were left behind behaved in like manner.

After the war, they showed resistance again to other pressures, to pressures this time against zadruga life. Government agrarian policy sought to include ever more land and people in the socialist sector of the economy, inducing peasants to abandon individual farming. Zadrugas were considered a part of the private sector, and therefore their taxes were as high as they were for rich peasants. Property over a certain size was nationalized, and large sections were taken away from individual peasants and zadrugas. Most peasants could easily determine that taxes would be considerably smaller and that much land would be available after division of a large zadruga. But still they divided their land only rarely.

Government policy produced rapid urbanization in most parts of the country, and its significance cannot be overestimated. The strength of the pressure is reflected in many figures. Thus, before the war, Yugoslavia's peasant population amounted to more than eighty percent of the total, the highest percentage in Europe. In 1973, that figure was about thirty-five percent. It dropped to less than half in a single generation. Rapid urbanization in Yugoslavia is guided by government policy, which considers speedy industrialization a first priority. The persistence of the Albanian zadruga again shows the strength of this institution.

The attitude of individuals towards their traditional customs also reveals unbroken loyalty. Young Albanians on military service in different Yugoslav garrisons are often exposed to sharp criticism because of their customs, especially the bride price. However, they rarely criticize this custom or indeed reject any Albanian customs. Albanian students in high schools or universities also remain surprisingly loyal to old Albanian ways.

Still more impressive is their resistance to the attraction of pecuniary gain and temptation. A considerable number of Albanian teachers and employees now work in different cities far away from their native zadruga. Many still consider themselves members of the zadruga, sending the greater parts of their salaries "home" and receiving products in return. Many Albanian villagers become bakers and confectioners throughout Yugoslavia, earning relatively high sums. However, they too remain zadruga members in the economic sense, as well as in their emotional dependence. The workers in western Europe, mostly in Germany, are extreme examples of unsevered family and zadruga ties.

The inner strength is also evident in the zadruga's economic progress. Many zadrugas grow not only in membership, but also in the volume of goods and production. Several have begun truck farming, and transport green peppers, tomatoes, and melons to markets in distant cities. Some zadrugas purchase additional land. Under postwar laws, individual peasants holding land often had to give up their plots, as the government sought to enlarge the collective agricultural sector. Great areas of land were taken away from some zadrugas. Yet the same zadrugas now purchase land with their savings; such transactions are permitted by more liberal laws. Some zadrugas have succeeded in overcoming serious difficulties and impediments in enlarging their estates.

It is also remarkable that Albanian zadrugas do not dissolve into "nuclear families," but into smaller zadrugas. These new zadrugas are growing rapidly because of the high birth rate. Many parents have ten or more children, and ever more remain alive. Brothers seldom part in quarrels and hostility. There are fewer fights and trials than in most other parts of the country.

Thus, the stable patriarchal order, which was still entirely intact when the first blows came, has shown extraordinary staying power. Family relationships remain also completely uninfluenced by the money economy, although many men have left the zadruga to earn money. In spite of all adversities, family living in the Kosovo region has remained almost completely in its original patriarchal form.

FORECAST

It is always easier to diagnose than to estimate. In the case of the Albanian zadruga, forecasting is even more difficult than usual. Will they disappear as zadrugas have in the other Yugoslav regions, or will they remain?

No doubt, there are cracks and fissures in the walls. School education no doubt has an effect, Educated youths are beginning to reject the rules of the blood feud. Pupils and students acquire aspirations for professional work, dream of university studies, and sometimes come into conflict with their elders. Many elders oppose schooling, feeling that in school "the belief in God will be destroyed as well as the authority of the older ones and the old customs." On the other hand, many young men are struggling for schooling for themselves, for their younger brothers, and even for their sisters. In one case, a father took a gifted boy out of school after his brother, the boy's uncle, threatened to leave the zadruga if the youth continued his education. Some years later, this boy succeeded with ingenuity and sacrifices to send his younger brother to school. When their uncle again warned that he would depart, the zadruga was divided in two.

Another sign of change can be found in the religious sphere. The young men returning from work in Germany, permanently or on leave, seem alienated, although not completely, from Islam. They neglect such religious customs as bowing in prayer. They do not rebel openly, but they do abandon some traditions. Yet, the same youth are still very close to zadruga life, as they give abundant financial assistance and contribute to its progress.

The symptoms of change are not such that we can foresee mortal sickness of the zadruga. The zadruga may still survive in Kosovo, at least for one or two generations, perhaps for much longer, because of the special traditions and situation of the Albanians there.

17: THE ZADRUGA COMMUNITY: A PHASE IN THE EVOLUTION OF PROPERTY AND FAMILY IN AN AGRARIAN MILIEU

Emile Sicard

The title of this paper fits very well within the framework of multi-disciplinary and inter-disciplinary studies which are more and more respectable and fashionable today. It centers on the zadruga, which many scholars of Slavic studies would probably call Serbian or South Slavic and would consider a basically localized phenomenon. I am a specialist in Slavic studies and a member of Institut des Etudes Slaves of the University of Paris. I did, indeed, for a time follow the lead of my teachers in considering the zadruga a phenomenon confined to the Slavic peoples, especially the South Slavs, and one which was on the verge of disappearing in the 1930's. But this title applies more than to the Slavic peasant family alone, for the joint family is not unique to the Slavic peoples. In fact, throughout my career, first as a specialist of comparative literature and then as a sociologist, I have sought to discover the characteristics which define the zadruga among other peoples in what we call today "developing countries," at the level of the Balkans of the 1930's, although the terms "developing," "under-developed," "deferred development," and others of that kind had not yet been applied to those social realities. Thus, today's sociologist must become a historian before attempting to discuss questions of economics, political economics, and politics. Our science is thus a highly complex one. Professor Philip E. Mosely's treatment of complex questions in diverse fields made him a precursor of multi-disciplinary studies.

The subject of this paper can be summarized, in effect, by the following question: is the zadruga, as has long been thought, a characteristically Serbian or South Slavic organization, or perhaps even Slavic, or must that domestico-economic group be considered a phase in the general evolution of every global society? I can treat this dilemma freely because I have changed

Translated by Virginia Coulon.

my position several times in the forty-five years I have devoted to research on this and closely related subjects.[1] I confess this with neither pride nor shame, but in the spirit of intellectual honesty. Indeed, this essay in a sense is a history of my research on this question or on the development of the objective and internal conditions about which my positions have varied in important proportions.

A few historical remarks better than any reasoning process indicate the limits given by early scholars to the ethno-geographic area of the zadruga. The diameter of the zadruga area was taken by those first researchers from a dictionary, the famous *Lexicon serbico-germanico-latinum* of Vuk Stefanović Karadžić, who included the term zadruga in his work and called it definitively and categorically a *more serbico,*[2] by implication exclusively Serbian. It is also important to note that the term zadruga is not found among the dialects in usage in Serbia, and that the term is a learned expression, or one used by scholars, at least according to Valtazar Bogišić.[3]

In reviewing my own research on the question, after almost fifty years, I know that Bogišić found himself confronted, as I did, with an almost incalculable number of dialect forms, all somewhat different, which expressed the same social reality, except for a few non-structural details.[4] The multiplicity of terms co-existing in the same cultural region seems important in the light of the large number of terms from different languages that I have inventoried and which all designate the same phenomenon. This multiplicity is important when one also considers the linguistic situation in Serbia at the end of the nineteenth century. The great diversity in dialects matched the great diversity in regions, sub-regions, and micro-regions which were forming a political entity which had yet to appear on the international scene as a state. Against a backdrop of linguistic unity, each region had its own quite specific dialect forms.

It is not my aim to enter a discussion of linguistics. We are confronted with such a great number of terms coming from many countries, all with the same meaning, that I need only point out the multiplicity of terms designating the same social reality. The peasant zadruga is certainly a social reality, but one centered essentially upon domestic[5] and economic[6] elements. I therefore reject the term "family" as too general and too varied in interpretation and would ask that zadruga be considered from the outset as a domestico-economic group,[7] wherever this "thing" may be found. It must be repeated that the zadruga should be seen from a dual perspective which goes much further than the conceptual content of the term "family," whatever the qualifier one could wish to add and which in any case would provide a bad translation of the conceptual content of the expressions used to designate this "domestico-economic group." As Bogišić showed, the limits established by Karadžić in his expression *more serbico* are no longer valid, and the phenomenon cannot be applied only to the Slavs but to all peoples living in every region where this social fact exists.[9] On the other hand, in the nineteenth century it was "necessary" to single out the Slavic character of this phenomenon, when governments were preoccupied with such things as "the Balkan Question" and nation-building, based on "the right of peoples to free determination." This could be seen wherever native and popular dialects manifested themselves, more often than not in the form of dictionaries comparable to that of Karadžić or of the famous almanacs edited by intellectuals who fostered nationalistic sentiment, either by themselves or through "learned societies" such as the *Matice*.

However, these "domestico-economic groups" existed outside of Serbia and Croatia in Bulgaria, Hungary, Albania, and Romania, and in the Macedonian parts of Bulgaria, Serbia, and Greece. Differing expressions refer to the same identical fact, but all of the general zadruga type. Here I must undertake a minimum of linguistic analysis to help localize the zones of the zadruga and to reveal the contents of the concept in the various forms in which it appears in those regions.

It is impossible within the framework of this paper to list all the terms or expressions which designate the "domestico-economic" group called the zadruga. I will limit myself to examination of the conceptual content of a few, first to the forms in which *drug, skup, kuća*, a few others play a role. *Drug* ("the other" but also "the companion" and "the comrade") gives us, aside from zadruga, the forms *družina* or *društvo* used in the north-west of Yugoslavia today, as well as *skupština* for the few cases of communal organization of the domestico-economic type found in Slovenia in the thirties. The expressions used to designate the domestico-economic group in Serbia or in Macedonia during the same period are formed around *kuća* and its derivations: *neodeljena kuća, zadružna kuća, kućna zajednica* or, for the Macedonian zone, *velika kuća* or *bogata kuća*. What are the comparable expressions in use in Bulgaria today? We can find an even greater number proportionally: *kup, kupčina,* and *družina* to the north of Sofia, and *zadružna kušta* or *bratska opčina* to the south. In the rest of the country, however, the expressions *golema kušta* and *golema čeljad* are in general usage or were so in the 1930's and 1940's. This last term, *čeljad,* brings us to a zone of extensive Slavic influence, Hungary. The term *nagycsalád* represents in part the Magyar rendition of the Slavic *čeljad,* which means "family" and to which the Magyar form, *nagy,* meaning "big," has been added. This is the same process as for *golema čeljad* in Bulgaria or for the *velika kuća* to the north of Skoplje.[10]

The linguistic designation of a social phenomenon is only part of our analysis. The same social reality known as zadruga has different terms when the domestico-economic group is constructed vertically only, with descendants and several degrees of ascendants and without any collateral line (though possibly with some verticality), including both several generations and several collaterals. In the first case, the domestic group is called *inokosna kuća*, which means "the house of a single lineage" in Serbo-Croatian. In the second case, it is the domestico-economic group under study, the zadruga, a name once a learned expression which has now passed into everyday language with one of a number of distinctly regional names or terms. Thus, in the work by Bogišić, one can find the expression *inokosna* defining one of the forms of the peasant family among the Serbs and the Croats, the other form being, *par excellence,* the zadruga.[11] A much more interesting element can be found by extending our vistas to Russia at the end of the nineteenth century and the beginning of the twentieth. Two expressions were used there to designate the two domestico-economic realities, one constructed vertically and the other essentially horizontally, though often horizontally and vertically. The first appears in the terms *malaia familiia* or *otečevskaia,* corresponding to the *inokoština*[12], while the second takes one of the following forms, *rodovaia familiia* or *bolshaia familiia.*[13]

This dualism in terms is all the more important because it is found in other regions and in other languages where the domestico-economic group exists. The communal family organizations in certain Arab zones of North Africa have two words: *akhkham,* which seems to be the "extended family;" and *takhkhamt,* the house of a single couple. Numerous dialectal forms exist in Berber to designate one or another of the phratries which are known generally as *Kharouba.* Other cases in which linguistics can help us reveal the dualism in designation, a dualism which would be of little significant interest where different terms refer to the same thing. A family group in Burundi is based upon a racial distinction, called *ubwoko,* which is neither patriarchal nor couple-oriented but communal in nature. It takes the name *umuriango,* when, for example, one speaks about the community of authority. To remain in Black Africa, and the *umuriango* of the Burundi is only one example in a thousand existing in this part of the continent, a recent study[14] illustrated that the *gida* compares indeed with the zadruga, with an important qualification: the expression *mutanen gida* refers to "the people of the compound," a case to which I will return when I speak about the community of life or authority.

But the phonetic and linguistic argument must be extended even more, and in some ways turned around, to consider the peasant zone of Iran, in which only one term designates the "family" but also means "extended family." For if one and only one substantive exists which really does represent the big family, the enlarged family, the extended family, the domestico-economic group, in fact, we could generalize about the existence of the domestico-economic group outside Slavic or Slavicized zones.

To go even further in the search for the domestic community, or more precisely the domestico-economic community, one could speak about a case found in the early years of the twentieth century in the mountainous region of Auvergne in France, the Quittard-Pinon community, or even of the valleys of the Pyrenees, where domestico-economic groups quite comparable to the zadruga exist even today. After glancing at these special cases, it is necessary to proceed to an interpretation of the fundamental elements of the zadruga or of one or another of the forms of the domestic groups which, if not identical, are at least comparable to it.

There are four fundamental elements of this type of group: the community of blood of the male members; the community of life and labor; the community of property; and the community of authority. For this last element, most scholars who have studied the zadruga have refused to see more than the rule in its absolute form, such as exists in the *Srpsko Zadružno Pravo*, the *Hrvatsko Zadružno Pravo,* or the *Crnogorsko Zadružno Pravo,* without taking into account the sociological reality which is often quite different from the legal reality.[15]

Community of blood of the male members? It is certainly true in most cases, but in addition to the case where pure chance brings a man with no blood ties into the community, the written law does provide that a man with no blood ties can join the community in two situations. Economic motivation, however, does play a role, and I have long thought it necessary to call the zadruga a "domestico-economic group." A man can, in fact, join the community, quite normally, without creating any problems and without drawing the least bit of criticism from his new peer group, where the zadruga lacks a sufficient number of hands to till the communally-held lands and where a man marries one of the daughters of the community. This is the specific case of the son-in-law, a case observed a relatively large number of times. The second case is that of the servant who has been in the service of the same zadruga for such a long time that he sees the possibility of becoming a zadrugar, or member of the zadruga, with all the rights attached to this title. In fact, the other male members come to consider him as a full member, and then proceed to give him the title of zadrugar. This is done in the name of the work to be accomplished, the economic element, and he joins the community for a basic economic reason. Domestic reasons are, at the most, exterior to the question. The advantage of the *zet*, the brother-in-law for some and son-in-law for others, is that he is a member of the family, by marriage at least, whereas the farm worker who is promoted zadrugar after a certain number of years of labor shares no basic family or domestic element.

Another case, the *pobratimstvo*, which symbolizes the synthesis of both the domestic and the economic elements, is even more frequent than the two just mentioned.[16] The *pobratim*, this is, the blood brother, is generally a masculine phenomenon, and no female form of *pobratimstvo* exists in any dialect. However, the community of blood in the *pobratimstvo* is simply symbolic. This symbol assumes considerable importance among the South Slavs, as well as among Slavs in general, but one must not consider this form of brotherhood as only symbolic, without the least biological justification. In contrast, among the domestico-economic groups of Africa, Latin America, or Asia, one can find similar forms of brotherhood by adoption, expressed by a variety of names. The situation is a little different in that all the male and female members of the group, collectively, and not any separate member, are considered brothers (or sisters) of the one who joins the community in this way. One can see how relative is the rule about the community of blood as it is applied concretely. However, it is evident, if only by the presence of the exceptions to this symbolic rule, that the community of blood is indeed one of the constituent elements of the zadruga.

The community of life and labor is just as essential a factor as the community of blood. "Life" refers mainly to meals and rest-time. "Meals" means, first, communal cooking arrangements under the direction of the *domaćica,* with the help of the daughters and the daughters-in-law of the community. It is nonetheless true that some external division concerning the phenomenon of the meal can occur when the community reaches a certain size. This division is physical in nature and is motivated by the necessities of the task. This does not mean that there is any structural modification, even if there is also some division concerning rest-time. But it is a division within the same enclosure. It has too often been thought that separation in the organization of the meal or of rest-time was the sign of a disintegrating community. In general, earlier scholars either observed the community only once or merely consulted the legal documents without studying court-suits entered by a member when a division of the zadruga occurred. It is important to understand that meals and rest must be taken in a given spatial entity, that of the commonly-held property. Neither multiple houses nor separation for meals (a separation which is less clear than separation for rest) constitutes disintegrating elements for the community. One must note that these communities are continually evolving, and that in time of war or revolution, for example, the community may be made up momentarily of an elderly man and a group of women and children, without any other adult males. To affirm at that moment, as has often been done, that the community is in a state of disintegration is to see only part of the facts. In my opinion, one must visit the communities in question several times in the same ten-year period and measure not only the degree of disintegration but also of reconstruction to avoid erroneous conclusions which might result from a single visit.

One can find the idea of the enclosure not only in the forms of communal organization in the Slavic countries or those that have been Slavicized, but also in Africa, where we have already seen the expression, *mutanen gida,* "the people of the compound." This is far from the promiscuous situation which some thought existed in communal living arrangements in a primitive era. On the contrary, we are discussing a total experience which is expressed at each evolutionary phase through the structural conditions which characterize the domestico-economic group.

The conditions of life and labor when taken as a whole bring forth certain consequences, for the zadruga as well as for the other communities of this same type all over the world, a minimum of specialization and role-division, although the possibility remains open for anyone to undertake any task. Role division? A certain number of roles are basically masculine. The group of men and "future men" have various special activities reserved to them according to their different stages of manhood, from pre-puberty to adulthood. Moreover, although the men of a particular generation may collectively participate in the tasks of tilling and sowing, each one may have his own minor specialty, such as the man obliged to work alone in the mountains, although his zadruga was in the plains, and who became a cheese-making specialist.

Specialization among the women? In addition to the biological specialization of procreation, women also have the special role of child-raising[17] and of upholding community traditions. Specialization by age? Elderly men are sometimes reduced to accomplishing the tasks of women or adolescents, except, of course, in the case of the head of the zadruga, who can, nevertheless, be helped by specialists. Special tasks which fall to the leader include not only arranging the marriages of the daughters of the community but a more precise role which he is called upon to fulfill more frequently, that of organizing the relationships of the community with all outsiders, from a neighboring community to civil or religious authorities. This is such an important role that around 1930 this man was introduced to visitors as the "Minister of Foreign Affairs."

The community of property also includes a certain number of characteristics valid not only for the zadruga but for any similar form of the domestico-economic group everywhere. The idea of private property is so infrequently invoked that I do not believe that I ever heard expressions, such as "my house," or "my field," during my field work. The landed property of the community and its livestock do indeed represent the economic system which ensures the community's survival. When there is no legally-motivated division, a member's share is defined in an extremely interesting way: each one is entitled to an "ideal share." It is difficult to define this share precisely. It could conceivably take on some concrete form, but that would be contrary to the communal spirit of this domestico-economic group. The interpretation of the share in vague terms is necessary to prevent the landed property of the zadruga's taking on the form of an association, as we know it, of parcels and plots of land held at one time or another by individuals participating in the association.

One must emphasize that the "ideal" share of each one varies continually according to two natural elements, births and deaths, which control the number of members entering and leaving the community, and an additional element, the member who leaves the zadruga voluntarily. The departure of a member can take place in either of two ways. He who leaves with the consent of the zadruga's *savet,* or council, can theoretically retain the "ideal share" he had before leaving to become a *pečalbar.*[18] He can return when he pleases, especially if he has sent his earnings, or at least a part of them, home to the community. However, if a member of a zadruga or a similar group leaves against the advice not only of the older and wiser members of the council, but also of all the others in the zadruga, he is divested of all ownership and of any possibility of communicating with the zadruga. It would be an exaggeration to say that he is excluded, because such persons on occasion have been welcomed, years later, into their original community, even though they had been considered not the black sheep of the family, but as someone who had broken all ties with the group.

In discussing the community of property, it would be incorrect not to specify that the expression covers only landed property, livestock and buildings. Thus, women do have individual possessions. In the good-sized communities which continue to observe traditions faithfully, a woman owns her loom. Her jewels belong to her, as do certain articles of clothing. This one may consider very little, but it is more than the man, who has no possessions of his own, strictly speaking, aside from his "ideal share." To put it more clearly and scientifically, the community's land, buildings, and livestock are looked upon as indivisible, in the sense that the Romans gave to the expression *indivisio.*

This idea takes us beyond the problem of property in the domestic or domestico-economic community in the Slavic countries. It is conceivable, for example, that a very appreciable proportion of the land, buildings, and livestock in North Africa, perhaps even as much as half, is still today ruled by the concept of indivision. This is one of the most solid of the community's rules, remaining intact even after the community of blood and the community of life and labor disappear, so long as it remains within the framework of a communal form of authority.

To continue with the community of property, one must note a small exception to the rule, which holds not only for the *bolshaia familiia* but for the farm zadruga as well, when it comprises a large number of households. A tendency to disintegration appears in both cases, but it is never entirely complete: each nuclear family, the couple and its children, quite often may have its own plot of land on community property, thus allowing it either to give the produce from this land to the woman in charge of the larger household and of the organization of community meals or, on the contrary, to consume it among themselves within the smaller family circle.

On the whole, the interpretations of earlier scholars, Slavs and non-Slavs alike, have been most unfortunate when they consider community of authority. It has been repeated too often that the community leader has absolute power over the property as well as the men. Classifying the zadruga under the ambiguous category of "patriarchial family" is only a further step, and some scholars have made that error, a grave error, first, because of the existence of the *savet,* and second, because of the distinction between administrative power and the power of disposal.

Every zadruga has a *savet,*[19] a council, not only a consulting body, but a deliberating and perhaps decision-making body. The council is made up not only of the old men of the community but of the men who are in full adulthood; some domestico-economic groups of the zadruga type even admit young unmarried men past adolescence. The *savet* governs the community much more than their elected leader, for governing consists essentially in the power to dispose of the landed property and goods of the community in whatever way one sees fit.

Some explanation about the name and the exact role of the leader of the community is necessary. One sometimes encounters the term *gazda,* meaning "owner," but the more common term among the South Slavs, as well as among Slavicized peoples, is *domaćin,* "head of the domus." The *domaćin,* in reality, holds administrative powers, within the limits already defined. The *domaćin* does indeed organize, regulate, and order the distribution of work among the different male and female members of the community, although the details of the women's work is handled by the *domaćica.* One can therefore say that the head of the community has full authority on an administrative level. However, with regard to disposing of community property he, by himself, has practically no authority. Thus, my interpretation is quite different from that of my predecessors.

Moreover, if the term "elected" has a far too political meaning for the *domaćin,* one can say, at least, that he is chosen by his peers. On what basis? It has been repeated too often that age constitutes the basis for selection, that the *domaćin* is necessarily the oldest man of the domestico-economic group, and this is the sole criteria for designating the leader. If this interpretation is true in most cases where the community has an elder, which is but one phase in the development of a zadruga, an entirely different criterion comes into play in a community which has lost its elder and where a number of brothers and possibly sons and nephews live. The criterion in this case is essentially the competence the individual is thought or hoped to have, whether he is the oldest living member or one of the younger brothers. In a domestico-economic group of the zadruga type, I have seen a primary school teacher or a priest a *domaćin* in either the same village as his community or even in a village located quite distant. These are unusual examples, but they do exist. Moreover, even when the oldest member is chosen as *domaćin,* it is not because of his age but rather because his age is the sign of his greater experience. Experience and the qualities one has acquired over a lifetime are more important in the choice of a *gazda* or a *domaćin* than the color of one's hair.

One last argument supports the specific and non-patriarchal nature of the zadruga and its leader. In certain cases, the *domaćin* can be replaced: for mismanagement of community property, harmful influence on the inter-personal relationships of the community, or the decline of his intellectual capacities. At such times, the *savet* can exert pressure on him to step down, while continuing to grant him the respect due his age and the services he has rendered.

This interpretation takes us far from the habitual conceptions of authority concerning the zadruga and other similar forms of the domestico-economic group. However, I do not mean the *gazda* or *domaćin* has no authority or that it can not take on quasi-dictatorial proportions in situations where the *savet* relinquishes some of its power. It is obvious that individual personalities, the location of the group in question, the age of the members of the *savet,* and the way it was formed are all subjective but real conditions which can influence the degree, the manner, and the form by which authority is expressed. Some *domaćin* do hardly more than obey the *savet*. Others consider the *savet* an external element whose authority has absolutely no influence. The leader of a community in Montenegro, for example, has or believes he has much more authority than the *domaćin* of the Croats. It is interesting to note that in certain zones of Croatia a woman may play this role.

However, it is the fourth element, the community of authority, which requires an analysis such as the one I have just suggested, but this authority can display various degrees of severity or laxity, depending on the different regions of Yugoslavia, Bulgaria, or Slovakia. The same is true of the authority of the head of the family, defined in its widest sense, outside of Europe, as in Black or North Africa. The differences are ones of degree, not of nature. One must look at structures as they are rather than at theoretical criteria, so long as these criteria do not contradict the general definition.

Many questions still need to be answered about the domestico-economic group in either its Slavic, African, or Amer-Indian forms. Among them is that of the existence of domestic communities in an urban milieu which have no relationship with agriculture. Thus, certain upper-middle class family groups in Bordeaux in the south-west of France are composed of several households which maintain a single budget for such basic necessities as coal, fuel, salt, and cooking fats. In this, the family has simply incorporated itself, in the strictly legal sense of the term, and only members of the family are admitted into the corporation. This means sociologically that domestic cohesion weakens, for the individual households live apart, although perhaps on the same property, and that economic cohesion has on the contrary grown even stronger through legal means. The concept of *indivisio* has been used in these regions to further the development of a capitalism which from the outside has all the appearances of a strictly upper-class phenomenon. One must point out here, too, the extremely slow transition from the domestico-economic community to the nuclear family, which could better be called the post-industrial family ("famille de type industrielle") and defined as the couple which becomes a couple again, outside the original milieu, after reproduction and child-rearing. We can see how dangerous it is to speak of the constituent parts of the domestico-economic community in terms of the couple and therefore of the nuclear family.

I believe one problem of a methodological nature is at the root of most errors of interpretation concerning the existence or the non-existence, the survival or the death, of the domestico-economic group. Something remains hidden, unconsciously hidden, in the personalities of men and women who live together in a group. Thus, when I questioned them, they seemed to think I was seeking too complicated a thought process for a phenomenon that they were living through, day-to-day. Consequently, they tended to generalize. To summarize one of Durkheim's ideas, one knows very well that to live through something is not necessarily to know it.

Other difficulties that one encounters in investigating domestico-economic groups concern members who have been to school or have learned about a way of life external to the group. Such people are always bothered, if not ashamed, that they live in this way and that they are therefore "behind times." This tendency is even greater among intellectuals of developing countries. They are so imbued with the idea of progress that their shame at being a product of a pre-industrialized family, of a domestico-economic group, makes them deny the fact before their very eyes: the existence of the domestico-economic group. These intellectuals not only claim but fully believe that the domestico-economic group is dead, long dead, and their behavior is completely consistent with this claim.

Allow me as a conclusion to relate a true anecdote of an eminent professor I met in the thirties who lived in a country not yet called "developing." He said I had "arrived" fifty years too late to find the zadruga, although only a few months before my visit he, himself, being of peasant stock, had been a member of a zadruga. Similarly, a Hungarian school teacher who was knowledgeable about the way of life in his village categorically denied the existence of the *nagycsalád*. Upon seeing the lay-out of a particular house, I insisted on entering. There I found three brothers, old enough to have grandchildren, and their families all busy at cleaning and sorting grapes. When confronted with the concrete, material existence of the domestico-economic group, my young Hungarian informant persisted in maintaining a negative reaction, as always for reasons of so-called progress. The same reaction can be found in Africa, concerning the *harouba*. Wherever I went during my field-work on the domestico-economic group or the so-called "extended family," I found that the natives were convinced of the superior life styles of the developed countries and that they denied the existence of their domestico-economic group.

One of the most basic problems concerning the domestico-economic group centers on the question whether the zadruga, among other groups, continues to exist today, in the strictest sense of the term, in South Slavic countries. To answer that, let me briefly indicate two cases. In 1972, Professor Blaga Petrovska observed a certain number of *seljačke zadruge* in the purest tradition in Macedonia. Although the number of members was not large, the structures had been preserved perfectly. In 1972, I accompanied my eminent colleague, Professor Petrovska, around Macedonia and noted a certain number of these domestico-economic communities. Then, in the company of Academician Radomir Lukić, I made a genealogical survey of domestico-economic groups of the zadruga type in Serbia. Contrary to what has been announced for more than a century, it is clear that the zadruga has not yet died out.

Finally, can the existence of domestico-economic groups like the zadruga facilitate the transition to an agrarian-based form of socialism, or is it but an added hindrance? I will answer in the following way: in general, it was thought that the zadruga had first to be destroyed before agrarian property could be restructured along socialist lines. In my opinion, it would have been better to take into consideration the absence of private property within the framework of the domestico-economic group and then to extend the limits of the peasant zadruga to that of kolkhoz. This is what I attempted to demonstrate in my short study, "De la Communauté domestique dite de 'Zadruga' à la coopérative kolkhozienne."[20] Such an approach would appear more logical than trying to eliminate a phenomenon which cannot be eliminated, as demonstrated by the fact that it has remained unchanged over such a long period of time.

NOTES

1. My principal work on the subject was my doctoral thesis ("doctorat d'Etat"), defended in 1943: *La Zadruga sud-slave dans l'évolution du groupe domestique* (Paris, 1943), 711 pp., which was awarded the Halphen Prize by the Académie Française in 1944. This work was completed by another, complementary thesis, *La Zadruga dans la littérature serbe, 1850-1912* (Paris, 1943), 205 pp., which won the same award in 1944. My first investigations on the Balkans date from 1932 and continued from 1935 to 1941, when I was Professor at the Institut des Etudes Français of the University of Belgrade. A few results were published at that time in the journal, *Arhiv za*

pravne i društvene nauke XXXII (Belgrade, 1936), under the title "Osnovni elementi jugoslavenske porodične zadruge" [The fundamental elements of the Yugoslavian zadruga]. After that date, I had stays of varying lengths in Yugoslavia in 1945, 1946, 1955, and 1972, during which I kept touch with the zadruga and its changing meanings and with the agrarian question in general.

2. V. S. Karadžić, his dictionary, and his anthology of Serbian poetry must be seen within a historical context, particularly that of the Serbian peoples. He was born in 1787 and died in 1864. Serbia gained independence a few years later. Karadžić belongs to the preparatory phase of independence, the politico-intellectual phase known as "the Eastern Question." This period was characterized by a renewed interest in language and by a certain number of literary works, mostly ethnographic, which are meaningful in the literary history of a people in search of their independence.

3. "Vuk Karadžić was truly in error when, in a dictionary devoted exclusively to a popular, living language, he inserted the word, zadruga, giving as meaning 'several families forming one household,'" Valtazar Bogišić wrote in his study, "De la forme dite *Inokosna* de la famille rurale chez les Serbes et les Croates," *Revue de droit international et de législation comparée* XVI (1884).

4. One must emphasize that none of the terms in usage in the micro-regions under examination contradicts the fundamental conditions necessary for the existence of a zadruga, that is, community of blood of the male members, community of life and labor, community of property, and community of authority, to which we will return in the course of this study.

5. In the sense of "that which concerns the house," the classical definition in French, and which can be found in Serbo-Croatian with *kuća* or its various dialectical forms. This would take us much further than the regions of Serbia or even Croatia, however, for this idea of "house," of the *kuća* (meaning the house, itself, and the people in it), is one of the fundamental structural elements of the social reality under examination. The idea of indivision can also be found among the South Slavs, with their *neodeljena kuća*, as well as among the Slavs of Central Europe, with the *rodinný nedil* of the Czechs. This is the foundation of the social reality in question: the human elements represent the "house" and nothing more, and they are indivisible, inseparable, cannot be portioned out.

6. One forgets too often that the zadruga, in its pure form at least, is an economic unit of production, distribution, and consumption.

7. I must insist on the need to use this expression and to exclude a term such as "family," even when accompanied by a qualifier of any sort, such as "extended family," which is obviously ambiguous. I would suggest this emphasis all the more strongly because the conclusions of this article tend to generalize about the possible universal application of this social reality.

8. The meaning here is that of Durkheim, who spoke about the need to "consider social facts as things" [*Régles de méthode sociologique* (Paris, 1895)]. The formula "consider . . . as things" suggests a non-materialist interpretation of social reality and affirms once again the need for finding ways of treating social reality comparable to those used in classical scientific experimentation, as in physics.

9. Bogišić devoted himself in numerous articles to the study of the zadruga. A quasi-exhaustive list of his works can be found in the

aforementioned work, *La Zadruga sud-slave dans l'évolution du groupe domestique,* in particular in the bibliography, pp. 659-688. The text mentioned here is Bogišić's "De la forme d'étude *Inokosna* de la famille rurale chez les Serbes et les Croates."

10. It is not possible here to analyze either the Slavic terms or the Slavic derivations. For this linguistic or lexical interpretation, see my *Zadruga sud-slave dans l'évolution du groupe domestique,* particularly Chapter I of Part I: "Le terme 'Zadruga' et les divers vocables," 47-54, and all of Part IV: "Les Comparaisons," pp. 413-546.

11. See, for example, my study, "De la Communauté dite de 'Zadruga' à la coopérative kolkhozienne," *Revue d'économie politique* LXIII (1953), 84-103.

12. On a linguistic level, note the use of the substantive, *inokoština,* representing something that exists, that is real, which changes into an adjective, *inokosna,* used to modify a word only. Thus, in one case it is *inokoština,* and in the other, *inokosna kuća.*

13. *Rodovaia* is the family of the lineage, the "extended family," the *bolshaia familiia. Malaia familiia* or *otechevskaia* is the "nuclear family," the family of the father or, one could say, the family where there is only one father, as in *inokoština.*

14. See C. Raynaut, *Structures normatives et relations électives. Etude d'une Communauté villageoise haoussa* (Paris, 1972).

15. Serbian Law of the zadruga, Croatian Law of the zadruga, Montenegrin Law of the zadruga: legal documents which go back to the beginning of the century or the end of the last century and which are no more than the written transcription of customary law in its previous oral form. In these same three laws, one can find mention of the *pobratim* and of the *zet,* the farm worker, which most occidental scholars before me refused to see, because they were influenced by the Roman Law, which is the basis of their legal outlook.

16. *Pobratimstvo:* brotherhood by adoption, in which one sucks the blood of the other. Blood brothers share a symbolic biological aspect.

17. I was one of the first, if not the first, to use this term when speaking about the role not only of the mother but of all the women in the community, first in handling the problems of life in general and next, in looking after the physical well-being of the children, up to the time the boys are admitted into the men's group, which occurs in late adolescence. It is in the men's group that boys are really educated to be men, to be *zadrugari,* citizens.

18. In its general sense, the *pečalbar* is a worker, mainly a farm worker, who leaves his home and thus his community to go to work elsewhere.

19. The term *savet* in Serbo-Croatian is very easily related to soviet. In any case, it concerns a council whose members are elected and which holds some, though, not all, power.

20. *Revue d'économie politique* LXIII (1953), 84-103. See also, "Traces, persistences et résurgences de la tradition dans lés sociétés 'en voie de dévelopment,' essai de calcul du changement en fonction des générations," in Georges Balandier, ed., *Sociologie des mutations* (Paris, 1969), pp. 380-407; "Les Persistences, communautaires," *Archives Internationales de Sociologie de la Coopération* III, No. 5 (1959), 73-120.

Appendix

ZADRUGA (KUĆNA ZADRUGA)

Milenko S. Filipović

Zadruga (household commune) is a term for a particular institution of communal life, wider than a biological family. The institution was very common until recently in Croatia, Bosnia and Herzegovina, Serbia, Montenegro, and Macedonia. The zadruga union consists of a number of families (at least two) whose members live and work communally according to the principle of division of labor, communally distribute the means of production which belong to the union, and communally consume the fruits of their own labor. The families which make up the zadruga usually are related; they have common ancestors, but kinship is not an obligatory condition for a zadruga. The small family, the biological or nuclear family, sometimes called a solitary family (*inokoština*), is in contrast to the zadruga. At no time and in no location were all the households in a particular village or region zadrugas, even though every small family represented a potential zadruga and maintained basically the same relations as within a zadruga. With the disappearance of the zadruga as an institution, the modern type of nuclear family is spreading to the village.

TERMINOLOGY

Even though the zadruga was a well-known institution in most of Yugoslavia until the last few years, and even though it has existed in Yugoslavia since ancient times, the peasants do not have a common term for this institution.

From *Enciklopedija Jugoslavije* [Yugoslav encyclopedia] (Zagreb), VIII (1971), 573-576. Translated by Richard March. Dr. Filipović was a Professor on the Philosophical Faculty at the University of Sarajevo, a member of the Academy of Sciences and Director of the Institute of Balkan Studies, both at Sarajevo.

The term "zadruga," as adopted in science and literature, is new. Vuk Karadžić was the first to use it with this meaning in his dictionary, in 1818. Through the influence of schools, literature, and legal documents, the term has become widely known and used. Otherwise, in place of the term zadruga, the people most commonly use the terms *kuća* (house) and *čeljad* (band or lot), which could also mean an ordinary family. In the General Law Code for Montenegro in 1888, Valtazar Bogišić used the term *kuća* to mean zadruga. The Law Code of Czar Dušan in 1349 used the word *kuća* with the same meaning. Other terms which have a wide distribution are *zajednica* (known everywhere); *skupčina* (Croatia); *tajfa* (Turkish—group or company), a term used especially in Macedonia; *familiia, golema familiia, golema kuća, na edno mesto* (Macedonia), *društvo* (Vojvodina), and *glota* (Banat and East Serbia). In the former Military Frontier region, where German was the official language, the laws and regulations call the zadruga *Hauskommunion*. In the Banat, the term *komunija* is still heard in reference to the zadruga. All members of a particular zadruga collectively make up the *kuća* or *čeljad*; for example, *Čurkovska kuća* refers to them all. The people are part of the *društvo* or *glota*, and the elder will usually refer to his co-habitants as his *čeljad, narod, roblje,* or *državina*.

SCHOLARSHIP AND THE ZADRUGA

Though the South Slav zadruga is occasionally mentioned in written sources as early as the twelfth century, scholarly interest in this institution did not appear until the late eighteenth century. In 1776, Ivan Lovrić described the zadruga in Dalmatia, and in 1783, M. Piler and L. Mitterpacher did the same for the zadruga in Slavonia. Great interest did not appear until the second half of the nineteenth century. At that time, zadruga institutions had already disappeared among the other peoples of Central and Western Europe, convincing many scholars that the zadruga of the Slavs, especially that of the Croats and Serbs, is a kind of particular distinction of their own. In connection with this, theories rose concerning the Slavic origin of the zadruga. Today, all scholars agree that the zadruga is a form of family life not unique to the South Slavic or Slavic peoples. Such institutions existed or exist among many ancient and contemporary peoples. Even the Germanic peoples were familiar with the institution in ancient times. Outside of Europe, zadruga life survives among the various peoples of the Caucausus, in India, in western, eastern and northeastern Africa, and even among the Indians of North America. The zadruga exists not only among peoples with a patriarchal order, but in matriarchal societies as well.

THE ZADRUGA AMONG THE
YUGOSLAV PEOPLES

The oldest written information concerning the Croatian zadruga dates from 1177 and 1197. According to data in the documents of Serbian rulers of the thirteenth and fourteenth centuries, zadrugas were common among the Serbian villagers and Vlach herders. The ruling class and lawgivers of that time were not favorably disposed toward the zadruga. One can judge, therefore, that the institution had existed earlier than this period, and that it is older than its first mention in written sources. The zadruga is constantly mentioned in the early Middle Ages, and later as well, in the regions under the Venetians, Austrians, and Hungarians (except Slovenia), and in the lands which fell to the Turks. The zadruga proved a powerful means of protection and subsistence to the South Slavs while they were under the Turks, and the Austrian court used the zadruga as a source of military manpower and economic resource. Laws and statutes obligated the residents of the Military Frontier to live in household zadrugas until 1871. In the period from the coming of the Turks until the second half of the nineteenth century, the attitudes of the rulers toward the zadruga changed. The Croatian Christian lords and the Turkish landlords, who all demanded annuities from their serfs (called *čivčija* or *kmetovi*), opposed the division of zadrugas among their peasants and prevented it. However, the sources tell us but little about what sort of zadrugas existed in those days. The records of private legal matters from the Croatian littoral, the neighborhood of Dubrovnik, and Boka Kotorska after the fifteenth century often mention proprietors, neighbors, buyers and sellers, together with their sons, brothers, and grandsons. Similarly, the tenants or tillers of a plot often appear not as individuals but as a group of people, including fathers, brothers, and sons.

THE FOUNDATION OF THE ZADRUGA
AS AN INSTITUTION

Early writers stress kinship as the basis upon which a zadruga rested and as the tie which bound zadruga members together. The male zadruga members were indeed related in the male line, that is, they had the same father, grandfather, or great-grandfather. In addition, women entered the household through marriage. In more recent times, the influence of written laws has caused this concept to penetrate deeply among the peasants. Thus, according to the Serbian Civil Law Code of 1844, kinship was an obligatory condition for recognition of a zadruga. However, according to folk understanding, and according to certain laws, members can enter a zadruga through adoption, and zadrugas can include widows who returned to their original home, with or without their children, and some relatives on the female side, such as an uncle or aunt who entered the zadruga along with their sisters. The *domazet* (son-in-law who takes up residence at the bride's home) appears as an extremely rare member of a zadruga. In that respect, the zadruga of recent times significantly differs from the Serbian zadruga of the Middle Ages, when sons-in-law and sisters-in-law were often mentioned as members of a household. A zadruga whose members all derive from a common ancestor could grow to such an extent that certain members would be such distant kin that they could intermarry, even according to canon law. However, this was never practiced among the Orthodox Slavs. In fact, not even members of zadrugas composed of various unrelated families enter into marriage bonds within the zadruga. On the other hand, in large zadrugas of Catholics or Moslems, marriages were sometimes performed between men and women of the same zadruga.

Nevertheless, kinship is not an obligatory condition for a zadruga. Zadrugas of non-kin who could, when they combined, initiate fictive kinship and blood-brotherhood were relatively common, but even that was not obligatory. In Serbia, where the law of 1844 established kinship as a condition for a zadruga, various families who were banded in a zadruga initiated a formal "brotherhood," or blood-brotherhood. In the former Military Frontier, the government by force of law created zadrugas from non-related nuclear families. In so far as those who were combining did not otherwise stipulate, property relations and inheritance were regulated by customary law in the same way as if the founders of the zadruga were brothers.

Ordinarily, all members of a zadruga live in one place, in the same house, or gather around one house and hearth, though individual families can have separate cabins or bungalows for sleeping. The interests of the zadruga often require that individual members or families spend a large part of the year far from home (this is ordinarily the case with zadrugas whose members are herders, carters, or migrant laborers), cultivating a section of the zadruga holdings, tending live-stock in the mountains, or fulfilling some other duty, but always remaining connected to those at home. Zadrugas exist in which the members lived permanently divided in two or three places, even with individual families hundreds of miles apart; these are termed *razdvojica* or *nadvojica,* a divided zadruga. Even in these cases, communal life prevails, because groups are usually sent away from the main house in shifts. They do not work for themselves but for the commune, economic activity is always conducted communally, there is only one authoritative elder (termed *starešina*), and each member retains all his rights in every section of the zadruga. This type of zadruga is connected to a herding economy in some cases, and to migration and re-settlement in others. It is widespread in Dalmatia, Bosnia and Herzegovina, and Serbia.

There is no zadruga without collective property. However, land and immovable property are not an obligatory condition for existence of a zadruga. In both the Middle Ages and in modern times, in both lands under the Turks and others, there were zadrugas which did not own their land, but cultivated the holdings of others as serfs or as ordinary tenants. This type of zadruga in our more recent history especially developed among livestock herding groups, who either did not have any land of their own, or had very little. Even if the zadruga is not the outright owner of the land it cultivates, the land is still cultivated communally, just as their other means of production, livestock, and agricultural equipment, are utilized communally. Since the equipment in earlier times consisted of but a few simple tools, not the quantity of the collective property but rather the means of distributing it was significant; all means of production were communally distributed by the *kuća*. The most essential characteristic of the zadruga is communal production based upon the principle of division of labor. This can be seen in certain recent developments. For example, in the vicinity of Niš, Herzegovina, Boka Kotorska, Montenegro, Old Serbia, and the vicinity of Skoplje, zadruga members have divided their houses and moveable property, but all of the new households continue to cultivate their real estate communally. This was especially common in Osat in Bosnia and in the region of Valjevo in Serbia. As early as the Middle Ages, this kind of life style existed in order to avoid the tax and other obligations required in individual households.

In addition to collective property, there has always been individual property in zadrugas. The clothes, jewelry, and linen of individual members and families are their personal property without regard to their origin, that is, even if they were obtained at zadruga expense. However, an individual member's personal property, especially that of certain women or of certain whole families, can include land, livestock, and money, resources which are in essence only collective property. This is the so-called *osobina, osobac, osebunjak,* or *prćija,* which derives from earnings outside the zadruga, from gifts, from inheritance outside the zadruga, etc. *Osobina* appears with the penetration of the monetary economy into the village and zadruga, bringing with it new principles concerning inheritance. It is the surest measure for determining the condition of a particular zadruga and the condition of that institution in a certain region, because *osobina,* since it is in opposition to the basis of communal life, ultimately leads to division of a zadruga and is a sign of the disappearance of the zadruga as an institution.

A second sign is the appearance of separate sleeping quarters for individual families, the so-called *vajat* in Srijem and Šumadija, *kiljer, kućar* or *komora* in

Slavonia, *koliba* or *zgrada* in Bosnia, *trem* in Kosovo, *ižina* or *košara* in the southern Morava valley, and *tronj* in the surroundings of Skoplje. Such buildings usually lack a hearth, and are considered ordinary moveable property, the personal property of an individual member or family in the zadruga. They are the external sign of a change which took place in the internal order of the zadruga, namely of the differentiation and partial separation of the small family as a component part of the zadruga.

The appearance and persistence of the zadruga as an institution originated in connection with livestock herding. However, the zadruga did not exist only among herders, but also among groups whose main occupation was agriculture, both in the Middle Ages and in more recent times. There have been zadrugas whose economy was primarily based upon a craft, in which the members were stone masons, brick layers or tailors, or based on trading, fishing or even plundering, as for example in Ceklin, Montenegro. Among the majority of Yugoslav peoples, living from only one kind of economic activity has been rare. Rather, a single household engaged in different forms of activity at the same time, in order for its own production to satisfy all its needs as a self-sufficient peasant household. It is just this complexity which has especially contributed to the persistence of zadrugas. While certain members busied themselves with tending livestock in the mountains, others cultivated land in the village. If there were still more members, they were otherwise gainfully employed. Thus, it was not the type of economy which was a condition of the founding and maintenance of a zadruga, but rather (along with other factors) the way the work was done. During the era of subsistence economy, only households with a relatively large number of members could maintain themselves successfully, because they were able to carry out the necessary division of labor, and because only such families were able to overcome the difficulties caused by their meager and undeveloped agricultural equipment. For example, only such a family could use the wooden plow, which would require several yokes of oxen to pull and a number of people to guide it, while the benefit resulting from such cultivation would be relatively insignificant. J. Cvijić has attempted to link the zadruga causally to the type of settlement pattern and topography. However, the zadruga of mountain and dispersed settlements (Herzegovina, Stari Vlah, and so on) is the same as in lowland and concentrated settlements (Macedonia, Vojvodina, Slavonia).

The frequency and size of the zadruga in a particular region, its internal organization, and its survival as an institution are decisively influenced by social factors. In the aforementioned economic environment, large zadrugas were the result of social pressure. Feudalism in the Middle Ages, the later Turkish era, and also the imposed heavy obligations on the peasantry in Croatia and Slavonia until 1848 provoked resistance which led to the formation of large zadrugas. As soon as this pressure was removed in Croatia in 1848, the division of zadrugas immediately began. This happened in the same way in Bosnia with the abolition of feudal relations in 1919. In the former Military Frontier, zadruga life was obligatory. As soon as the Frontier was abolished in 1881, the falling apart of zadrugas immediately began. The dependence of the zadruga upon certain social factors can be seen in its relations to the brotherhood (*bratstvo*) and tribe (*pleme*). Where there were brotherhoods and tribes, as for example in Montenegro, the zadrugas were neither numerous nor large, because there was no need for them, since brotherhoods and tribes carried out certain of the zadruga functions, such as holding communal property (pastures, forests, fisheries) and providing common defense. On the other hand, the technical and cultural backwardness, and especially insecurity in regions of lawlessness and danger to person and property, resulted in the development of large zadrugas (for example in Macedonia and Old Serbia in the nineteenth and early twentieth centuries). It is obvious that neither feudalism nor the tax system was entirely responsible for the creation of the zadruga, but they influenced its appearance, development, and internal order in some regions.

The changes in the social and economic conditions of life and the introduction of improved implements and working procedures changed the basis upon which zadrugas and the institution as a whole rested. Along with the monetary economy, money and the *osobina* have entered the zadruga, as more individuals labor and earn outside of the zadruga. Their needs become more varied, and the zadruga can no longer satisfy them with its own production but must go to the market. Also, more sophisticated tools and implements are introduced into the zadruga. When these changes take place, it is no longer possible for even the nearest of kin to remain together in a zadruga. Thus, it is completely natural that the zadruga disappeared first among migrant laborers, and that the process of the disappearance of the zadruga in villages first caught hold in northern and western regions and gradually penetrated into the mountainous south.

PRESENT STATE

In Slovenia, the zadruga disappeared long ago. In Croatia and Slavonia, it has been in rapid decline since the mid-nineteenth century, while its disappearance in Serbia and Bosnia is presently in full swing. No large research projects have been undertaken or published in the years since the Liberation. It seems that great social changes delivered the last and strongest blow to the household zadruga. In the surroundings of Bosanski Šamac, where zadrugas were still relatively common before World War II, in fourteen Serbian villages only 1.3 percent of the households in 1951 represented true zadrugas

(zadrugas with brothers). If households are considered in which a father is in union with his married sons, then in all only four percent of the households lived in zadruga relations. The situation is similar in the Takovski district of Serbia, where in 1953 approximately one to two percent of the households still represent zadrugas. In the small region of Lepenici in central Bosnia, there were in all 714 households in 1958; true (fraternal) zadrugas represented only 3.2 percent: among the Orthodox Serbs 6.4 percent, among the Catholic Croatians only 1.3 percent, and among Moslems 5.1 percent. In Vojvodina, zadrugas are so rare that it can be said that they no longer exist. They are still surviving only in Kosovo and Macedonia.

THE ZADRUGA AMONG THE
NATIONAL MINORITIES

It is significant that the zadruga still survives among some nationalities who live in the border areas of Yugoslavia. Most important are the Albanians, among whom the zadruga is common even today. Neither the Albanians nor the Turks have a special term in their languages for zadruga, but rather use expressions which mean "house" or "life in one place." A peculiarity of the Albanians in Metohia and likewise among the Kuči is the existence of zadrugas whose members are divided in faith: some members of the same family are Catholics, and some are Moslems. The zadruga also exists among the Turks in Macedonia, but with a relatively smaller number of members. Among the Vlach herders, or the Tsintsars in Macedonia, zadrugas are common even today.

ZADRUGA ORDER

At no time were the zadrugas of various regions everywhere alike. Moreover, in a relatively small area zadrugas with different internal orders exist. For example, just in the vicinity of Skoplje, among just the Macedonian Slavs, at least two types of zadruga exist. In Skopska Crna Gora, where the residents engage in a good deal of woodworking, including the production and sale of looms, according to custom, there is only one loom in the houses, regardless of the number of women in the house. But in other parts of the Skoplje basin, every woman in the house has her own loom, even though these peasants buy their looms. Furthermore, while the peasants of Skopska Crna Gora all reside in one house, in Blatija every family had its own bungalow (*tronj*). By the number of bungalows in the courtyard, one can immediately determine how many families are in the zadruga. However, the internal order of the zadruga has more or less common outlines. Most important, every zadruga has its single authoritative elder (*starešina, domaćin, gazda, gospodar, stopanin, kesebašija, kutnjik, naprežen,* etc.). A father or grandfather will become this sort of elder in the natural course of the gradual development of a small family into a zadruga. This kind of zadruga is called a "paternal zadruga" (*očinska zadruga*), and the father as elder is truly the authority figure and can distribute the holdings more or less independently. After his death, if the sons, or rather brothers, remain in union, that union or zadruga generally changes in character: it is then a true "fraternal zadruga" (*bratska zadruga*), in which the brothers are co-workers and co-owners. To become the elder of such a zadruga, one may be selected by the father while he is still alive, prepared for the role and recommended, or one may be formally picked as the new elder. He need not always be the eldest; he who is experienced, skillful, just, and tactful at home, and accepted by outsiders is the one selected. If the elder fails to lead the zadruga successfully, he can be replaced. On occasion, brothers have periodically taken turns as elder. In Slavonia, zadruga authority is constituted as a duumvirate. In the zadrugas of Hrvatsko Zagorje of former times, the lord, and later the government, named the elder. The elder can also be a woman.

The true household zadruga is a strictly democratic institution. Authority in it is a duty and not a power, for all power resides in the council of all adult male members. The elder actually carries out the decisions of the council; makes the work schedules; sees in the name of the union that all work is completed on time and that the needs of all the members are provided for; supervises the behavior of his co-residents; represents the household in the village assembly in dealings with the government, when there is a house guest, and so forth; but may not make any major decision or purchase or incur a large debt on his own initiative. The only reward to the head of the household is the respect shown him by his co-residents and neighbors. He has an honored place in his house, in the Dinaric region even a special chair, which he relinquishes only to an honored guest.

Along with the elder is a woman who is considered the authority over the females with regard to women's duties. In this respect, she is advisor to and mediator for the elder. She is concerned with keeping order among the daughters-in-law and with food, directs the production of dairy products, and so on. She is called *stopanica; domaćica, domaćinka, gazdarica, maja.* She may be the wife of the elder, under whose direction the zadruga grew and developed, and after his death, if she remains living, may continue her duties. Otherwise, the house-mistress may be the wife of some member other than the elder. All of the more important matters concerning completed and remaining tasks are decided by the council after supper in informal conversation, and decisions are arrived at by consensus. The power of the council is indeed great; in earlier times, such a council could decide to expel a member who was working against the interests of the zadruga.

The internal relations of the zadruga are especially characterized by the division of labor, based upon different schemes. Most important is division of labor by sex. Men's tasks are caring for livestock and working on the land, and women's tasks are preparing food, caring for children, weaving and making clothes. Women also help in some tasks in the fields, digging, weeding, harvesting, and also work with livestock, milking and making dairy products. Where flax and hemp are cultivated, this is entirely a female task, except for the plowing. The mixing and baking of bread, and preparing meals are performed by women in a weekly order, taking turns. (The woman on duty is known as *redara, reduša, mesarija, kućnica*.) Old women are freed of these duties, as are brides for one year. Men's tasks are scheduled according to daily or seasonal needs: plowing, going to the mill, working with livestock.

In some areas, especially in Macedonia, an annual division of tasks is performed, with one member named to take care of the oxen and plowing, another to tend the sheep, and so on. It is common among stock-herders to send in shifts a family of a few male and female zadruga members to the summer pastures to stay with and tend the herds. (They are known as *stanar* and *stanarica, bač* and *bačica, planinka* or *maja*.) In large zadrugas, individual members may be designated to work at some handicraft, such as tailors, carters, or clerks. Originally, their earnings would belong entirely to the zadruga. In general, care is taken that each contributes according to his abilities; taking this into account, tasks are equally and justly distributed. Thus, every member has an equal right to food and clothing according to his needs and his labor, and has the right to be defended by the zadruga. The aged and invalids enjoy complete security. All zadruga members eat together. Clothing needs are supplied in a slightly different manner. The raw materials which the zadruga produces or buys (wool, cotton, flax, hemp) are divided among the women according to the number of members in their families, and they make the needed clothes for them. For a shepherd or for a girl about to be married, some extra material is provided. Whenever ready-made clothes are purchased or a tailor hired to sew them, the money comes from the communal account.

When the institution of the zadruga is at full strength and represents the normal way of life, individual zadrugas naturally tend to grow and the number of members increases. In the course of that growth, a zadruga will reach the point where it can no longer hold together in one place, but must divide. The maximum size attainable depends upon the times, zadruga holdings, general social conditions, and internal relations in the zadruga. Average zadrugas contain up to twenty members, medium-large have from twenty to thirty, large have from thirty to sixty, and the very large over sixty members. There are known examples with more than eighty members and even exceptionally unusual cases of zadrugas with one hundred. In general, large zadrugas have been rare.

The division of the zadruga, under normal circumstances, is something foreseen and expected by the zadruga itself. In certain regions, such as Bosnia, Herzegovina, and Montenegro, the zadruga builds new houses in advance, because the members know into how many sections it will be divided. In such cases, everything is carried out peacefully, and the divided members continue to live in harmony and to help one another. Where the zadruga institution is troubled and in decline, this is reflected in the life of individual zadrugas. Divisions are usually preceded by squabbles and cannot be carried out by the household members themselves, but require the participation of villager arbitrators (*dobri ljudi*) or government officials.

On the question of division, as with inheritance, the customs of different regions are extremely varied, due to the influence of written laws whose provisions are often in opposition to customary practice. Basically, at the time of division, the inherited property is distinguished from that which the zadruga members acquired. The inherited property (called *stožer, dedina, dedovina, baština, plemenština*) is divided by generation, each family receiving an equal share. That which was acquired by the zadruga is divided in proportion to the number of adult male members. The food which the household has accumulated is divided according to the number of members in the family, but with a smaller portion allotted for nursing infants. Deceased members who died less than a year prior to the time of division receive a share of the food and drink: their portion goes to the household that will provide the commemorative offerings in honor of the deceased. Usually, the now former elder receives a special allotment (for example, a horse and saddle) as a sign of recognition. Cash resources and debts are also divided. If the old parents are alive, they also receive a section which the heirs will later divide; it is more customary, though, that they receive only a field and some stock and reside with one of the heirs, who will be responsible for their funeral and requiem. Their portion (called *ukopnina* or *grobnina*) will thereafter belong to that heir. Many rules, which vary by region, specify items not to be divided but to remain in the old house, such as dough troughs. It is significant that at division the principles of primogeniture and ultimogeniture intertwine. Ordinarily, the eldest carries out the division of the property into portions, and the youngest has the first choice. In many regions, by custom, the youngest remains at the old hearth. Individual items which are not in everyday use, such as the brandy still and the scale, often remain communal property, especially in the southern Morava valley. It is customary that mills and often also wells and fruit trees remain communal, as do forests, certain meadows, and fields. Among the Orthodox in Serbia and Macedonia, the *kumstvo* (godparenthood) of the zadruga is also divided. In earlier times, the new households usually developed into new zadrugas. More recently, where there are still zadrugas, they have become fewer in number. At the same time, the custom of brothers' dividing immediately after their father's death has spread. In northern regions, it is already the custom that a son divides from his father immediately or soon after marriage.

INDEX